COMMUNISM IN INDIA

Communism in India

EVENTS, PROCESSES AND IDEOLOGIES

Bidyut Chakrabarty

OXFORD
UNIVERSITY PRESS

Oxford University Press is a department of the University of Oxford.
It furthers the University's objective of excellence in research, scholarship,
and education by publishing worldwide.

Oxford New York
Auckland Cape Town Dar es Salaam Hong Kong Karachi
Kuala Lumpur Madrid Melbourne Mexico City Nairobi
New Delhi Shanghai Taipei Toronto

With offices in
Argentina Austria Brazil Chile Czech Republic France Greece
Guatemala Hungary Italy Japan Poland Portugal Singapore
South Korea Switzerland Thailand Turkey Ukraine Vietnam

Oxford is a registered trade mark of Oxford University Press
in the UK and certain other countries.

Published in the United States of America by
Oxford University Press
198 Madison Avenue, New York, NY 10016

Library of Congress Cataloging-in-Publication Data
Chakrabarty, Bidyut, 1958–
  Communism in India : events, processes and ideologies / Bidyut Chakrabarty.
    p. cm.
  Includes bibliographical references and index.
  ISBN 978–0–19–997489–4 (hardcover : alk. paper) 1. Communism—India—History.
2. India—Politics and government. I. Title.
  HX393.5.C3398 2014
  320.53'20954—dc23
                            2014003207

9 8 7 6 5 4 3 2 1

Printed in the United States of America on acid-free paper

My mentors, for being so generous

Contents

List of Tables ix
Preface xi
List of Abbreviations xiv

Introduction 1

PART I | PARLIAMENTARY LEFT IN INDIA 13
1. The Parliamentary Left in Tripura: A Creative Blending of Ideology
   and Organization Prevailing over Ethnic Division 19

2. Parliamentary Left in Kerala: A Creative Socio-Political Engineering
   of Governance 32

3. Parliamentary Left in West Bengal: Organizational Hegemony Established
   through an Ideological Churning 71

4. Parliamentary Left in West Bengal: A Nemesis Failing to Rekindle
   the Old Charm in Globalizing India 92

PART II | MAOISM: ARTICULATION OF LEFT-WING EXTREMISM IN INDIA,
WRITTEN WITH RAJAT KUMAR KUJUR 115
5. Genesis of Maoism in India 123

6. The Maoist Blueprint for the Future India 149

7. Maoism: A Utopia or "Jacobean" Reign of Terror? 176

Conclusion 206

Postscript 232

APPENDIX: PARTY CONSTITUTION OF THE COMMUNIST
PARTY OF INDIA (MAOIST) 239
NOTES 257
BIBLIOGRAPHICAL NOTES WITH SELECT BIBLIOGRAPHY 291
INDEX 305

List of Tables

1.1 Governments in Tripura since 1972 26

1.2 Performance of the Contending Parties in Assembly Elections, 1983–2008 27

1.3 The Results of the 2013 State Assembly Election 28

2.1 Numerical Strength of Coalitions in Kerala, 1982–2011 51

2.2 Results of the 2006 Kerala State Assembly Election 54

2.3 Results of the 2010 Local Polls in Kerala 56

2.4 Outcome of 2011 State Assembly Election 58

3.1 The 2006 West Bengal Assembly Results 76

3.2 Share of the Left Front Votes in the Panchayats and Zila Parishads 79

3.3 Economic Conditions of West Bengal 81

3.4 Election Committee for Assembly Segment 87

3.5 Electoral Performance of Trinamul Congress, 2006 89

4.1 Comparing the 2011 and 2006 West Bengal Assembly Results 95

4.2 West Bengal Assembly Election Results 2011, by District 95

4.3 Share (Percentage) of Gram Panchayats, Won by Major Political Parties, 1978–2013 110

5.1 Profile of Naxal/Maoist Violence in the Affected States, by Year, 2008–2012 124

5.2 Left-Wing Activities since 2009 125

5.3 Left-Wing Activities in Bihar 138

6.1 Outcome of Left-Wing Activities 150

Postscript
   Performance of the Parliamentary Left since 1971 234

Preface

THIS BOOK WAS finally completed during the summer break in 2013, though I had been nurturing the idea of writing a full-length monograph on communism in India since my college days at Calcutta Presidency College, which, as an elite institution for higher education, has been a germinating ground for creative politics since its foundation in the early nineteenth century. My idea took concrete shape in a breakfast meeting with Oxford University Press (New York) editor Angela Chnapko in San Diego in late September of 2011 when we met to finalize a book on political thought. Once the meeting was over, I knew that I had a project in hand. After my return to Virginia where I was teaching at the time, I received an email from Angela asking me to write an extended proposal on the topic, which I readily agreed to do given my interest in the project. While preparing the book proposal, I found it very difficult to combine the two forms of communism in India, which are diametrically opposite but share identical ideological legacies. After pondering over it for a week, the problem was sorted out, and the proposal was dashed to Angela to proceed further. The OUP decision to go ahead with the publication of the book was forwarded to me on 4 July 2012 when I was in New York to witness the celebration of US Independence Day along with my family. The book contract was signed on 9 July again in a luncheon meeting with Angela in a restaurant very close to the headquarters of Oxford University Press in New York City. I am thankful to Angela because without her constant persuasion and personal interest in the project, it would not have been possible for me to embark on such an ambitious work. I am grateful to her for being so supportive during the preparation of the manuscript.

I owe a great deal to the participants who listened when I presented some of the draft chapters in seminars/workshops in various campuses in different countries. The project would not have been complete had the activists who are associated with radical politics and the government officials who are responsible for policy framing seeking to halt the progress of the Red Corridor not been generous in sharing their experiences and thoughts. Surender and Sampat deserve special thanks for having given me a chance to witness the socio-political churning in the remote villages in Uttar Pradesh. This experience was an eye-opener for me because it brought me face to face with what is being euphemistically identified as a "silent revolution" at the grassroots. I am particularly thankful to Dr Bob Kolodinsky of James Madison University for having procured articles and other texts for me whenever I asked. The support extended by Saurav Tripathy of Tripura cadre IPS and his office colleague, Sudeep Sen, was very useful in understanding the complex nature of the parliamentary left in Tripura in light of the constant friction between the Bengali (who are mainly migrants) leadership of the parliamentary left and those propped up by the indigenous population. I am also happy to pay a tribute to my mentor at the London School of Economics, Professor Tom Nossiter, in the form of a chapter on Kerala, which Tom always considered as his second home. I wish that he was around to assess whether I possess the intellectual capability of conceptualizing the growing salience of the parliamentary left in Kerala despite being ideologically deviant in the classical Marxist–Leninist sense. By analytically dissecting India's parliamentary left, my book seeks to respond to a question that Tom had raised in his *Marxist Government in India* (London: Pinter Publishers, 1988) on whether there is an "Indian form of communism." It is difficult to provide a conclusive answer to this question though I endeavor in this book to trace out some of the distinctive features of Indian variety of communism that are, despite being "revisionist" in the authentic Marxist–Leninist sense, mostly context driven, whether one talks of the parliamentary left or its bête noire, the Maoists.

In this neo-liberal world of obsession for cash and material goods, academic works are not always appreciated because the financial reward is hardly proportionate to the labor that an author usually applies. There are families that tend to publicly appreciate an academic author since it is politically correct; however, for most, time spent writing academic texts can feel like wasted time. Colleagues and friends are encouraging, though most do not appear very enthusiastic when academic books written by their friends hit the stands. So, an academic is "a very lonely person" and is generally pushed to an unfriendly environment when he or she undertakes an academic work. Nonetheless, this is hardly a deterrent, and authors keep on pursuing their profession despite these circumstances. I did encounter these familiar hurdles, though the task was made easier by the cooperation of my friends and mentors who always stood by me. I am grateful to them for having sustained my zeal to engage in fruitful intellectual challenges in circumstances that are not favorably tilted toward academic creativity. I would not have attempted such an exercise had I not been encouraged by my students in various parts of the world where I have taught. If they find the text provocative and intellectually stimulating, I will have achieved what I am looking for. I am particularly thankful to Dr. Rajat Kujur of Sambalpur University, Orissa (India) who has co-authored part II of this book with me. Without his filed inputs, it would not have been possible to comprehend the complex dynamics of Maoism, which is also a response to the over-zealous endorsement by the Indian state of the neo-liberal economic design for rapid industrial growth at the cost of multitudes. *Communism in India* draws on my earlier works on Indian politics in general and communism in particular. Some of the arguments that I have made here were initiated in books and articles that I have published so far. I am thankful to my friends, colleagues, and publishers who always remain helpful. Last, not the least, my heartfelt gratitude to my mentors in academia who always remain the main pillars behind my every successful endeavor.

Bidyut Chakrabarty
University of Delhi, India
June 2013

List of Abbreviations

AICCCR	All India Coordination Committee of Communist Revolutionaries
AITMC	All India Trinamul Congress
AOBSZC	Andhra–Orissa Border Special Zonal Committee
BJP	Bharatiya Janata Party
CCOMPOSA	Coordination Committee of Maoist Parties of South Asia
CPI	Communist Party of India
CPI (M)	Communist Party of India (Marxist)
CPI (Maoist)	Communist Party of India (Maoist)
CPI (ML)	Communist Party of India (Marxist–Leninist)
CPN (Maoist)	Communist Party of Nepal (Maoist)
CRZ	Compact Revolutionary Zone
CSP	Congress Socialist Party
FDI	foreign direct investment
KMPP	Kisan Mazdoor Praja Party
KSP	Kerala Socialist Party
KTP	Karshaka Thozhilali Party
LDF	Left Democratic Front
MCC	Maoist Communist Centre
MCC–I	Maoist Communist Centre–India
NDA	National Democratic Alliance
NSS	Nair Service Society
PDF	People's Democratic Front
PLGA	People's Liberation Guerrilla Army
PPC	People's Plan Campaign
PSP	Praja Socialist Party
PW	People's War
PWG	People's War Group

RSP	Revolutionary Socialist Party
SAARC	South Asian Association for Regional Cooperation
SEZ	Special Economic Zone
SNDP	Sree Narayana Dharma Paripalana Yogam
SSP	Samyukta Socialist Party
TTAADC	Tripura Tribal Areas Autonomous District Council
UDF	United Democratic Front
UF	United Front
UPA	United Progressive Alliance

COMMUNISM IN INDIA

LEFT-WING EXTREMIST AFFECTED AREAS IN INDIA

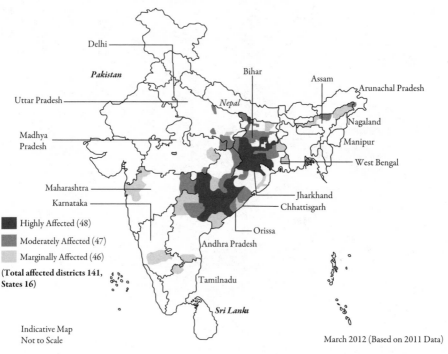

Delhi

Pakistan

Bihar

Assam

Arunachal Pradesh

Uttar Pradesh

Nepal

Nagaland

Madhya
Pradesh

Manipur

West Bengal

Maharashtra

Jharkhand

Karnataka

Chhattisgarh

■ Highly Affected (48)

Orissa

■ Moderately Affected (47)

■ Marginally Affected (46)

Andhra Pradesh

**(Total affected districts 141,
States 16)**

Tamilnadu

Sri Lanka

Indicative Map
Not to Scale

March 2012 (Based on 2011 Data)

Introduction

SET IN MOTION in the 1920s with the formation of the Communist Party of India, the communist movement has manifested differently in different phases of India's recent political history. *Communism in India* is a contextual study of this phenomenon, which was articulated in two diametrically opposite ways. The parliamentary left, by subscribing to social democracy, used the prevalent democratic institutions of governance to create conditions for the fulfillment of the Marxist–Leninist goal of establishing a classless society. Conversely, ultra-left-wing extremism views radical social change in the sense of dramatically altering existing class relations as simply inconceivable under parliamentary democracy, which its followers consider as an elite-driven device for justifying the age-old system of class exploitation but with a different label. Once the system of governance is appropriated by those with vested socio-economic interests, as frequently occurs, democratic institutions, despite being sensitive to the needs of the underprivileged, always reflect class prejudices when attempting to change the prevalent class relations. There are innumerable instances of landed gentry becoming involved in left movements and later in the government "not due to any ideological commitment to the poor, but to re-establish their dominance in the region."[1] Given the diverse nature of communism and its social base, it is useful to focus on the social, economic, and political metamorphosis of a country with a long colonial past that is evident not only in the institutions of power but also in the ideological underpinnings that support liberal democracy of the Westminster type. Even in the changed political environment following the transfer of power in 1947, governance in India was articulated largely in liberal democratic terms whereby dissenting voices were accommodated as long as they did not disrupt the prevalent social, economic, and political order. Also at this time the state's response to dissent became more calibrated than ever, presumably because protest movements, when articulated in a liberal-democratic format, were always considered to be refreshing socio-economic and political inputs from the grassroots, which were also useful in reinventing strategies for effective governance for long-term gain.

By attempting a contextual explanation of the growth of several constituencies of power outside the arena of the state, this introduction draws on the wider social, economic, and political milieu to grasp its importance in shaping and defending a movement that challenges the conventional conceptualization of transformation of grassroots socio-political discontent into effective ideological onslaughts. This is largely an outcome of the deepening of democracy over the years during which "the bulk of . . . the population acquires binding by being involved in struggles against efforts at denying their rightful claims over resources."[2] With their sustained participation in the ongoing democratic struggle, people remain integral to the processes of governance. Furthermore, when India integrated into global capital following the acceptance of neoliberal economic reforms in 1991, the scene became far more complicated. New players have arrived in the economic arena who have no emotional obligation to the indigenous population. In collaboration with the state, which supports the private operators and their local representatives for specific political gains, these investors have been unobstructed in their partisan goal of making profit at any cost. The one exception to this has perhaps been the organized mass confrontations, including those at the behest of the Maoists in India's tribal land. The mass protests against the well-planned efforts by global capital seeking to radically alter the prevalent socio-economic and political texture of the polity are also symptomatic of "the processes of the deepening of democracy" in areas that traditionally remained outside the arena of the organized world of parliamentary and extra-parliamentary politics. Thus it is not strange to find that the issues of gender, ethnicity, or region have become critical constituencies of concern in contemporary politics. Democracy as a culture has brought about revolutionary changes not only in the social constituencies of protest movements but also in our conceptualization that has set in motion fresh debates involving new political actors seeking to articulate their roles differently by imbibing the spirit of the era.

What is striking in contemporary India is the salience of both the contrasting varieties of Marxism–Leninism. On the one hand, those pursuing the constitutional path of parliamentary democracy claim to be Marxist–Leninist notwithstanding the severe Marxist critique of parliament being "a pig sty." On the other hand, those upholding violence as the only means for revolution consider themselves to be true followers of Marxism–Leninism. The latter group sees Marxism–Leninism as having completely lost its revolutionary potential at the hands of the parliamentary left in India. Nonetheless, there is no denying that both versions of Marxism–Leninism seem to have consolidated effective ideological platforms for mobilizing the socio-economically marginalized sections of society. While the parliamentary left remains a strong contender for power in West Bengal, Kerala, and Tripura, the Maoists have also succeeded in mobilizing the indigenous population in several parts of the country. Not only have the parliamentary communists moved away from a revolutionary to a reformist Bernsteinian social democratic orientation, they have also fulfilled their ideological commitment to the preservation of democratic institutions by forging broad social alliances to pursue a well thought out system of wealth distribution that does not alienate the propertied sections of society. With their moderate agrarian policy to accommodate the rural middle class in the power structure, the parliamentary left never became an effective mouthpiece of the poorest of the poor, the landless laborers, and thus failed to mobilize them for their ideological battle. This failure created a natural constituency for the Maoists in rural India, especially in those areas where the incumbent left government agreed to follow a forcible land acquisition policy for private investment even at the cost of displacing the local inhabitants. In the changed environment of globalization, the economic scene has suddenly shifted, and concern for the poorest of the poor seems to have considerably disappeared. There is hardly a difference in the perception between the parliamentary left and other leading bourgeois political parties in this regard: by agreeing to follow a neoliberal path of development, both the left and its bête noire do not appear to be ideologically different at all.

II

The principal argument that the book therefore makes relates to the growing importance of the left parties in India's liberal democratic governance. It is now evident that the parliamentary left parties, instead of emphasizing "class antagonism" as a means for the establishment of an egalitarian society, seem to have confirmed their clear antipathy toward violence by accepting election as a meaningful instrument of socio-economic changes. The parliamentary left appears to have flourished in circumstances in which the state is utilized for facilitating "development with redistribution." Once elected to power, the communist party, as the records show, has thus "transformed from an essentially agitating and confrontational force to an administrative patronage-dispensing institution."[3] Drawing on a social alliance of apparently contradictory class forces, the reformist left parties sustain their viability as a democratically elected government within an economy that is not favorably disposed toward the classical ideological goal of the left. There is no doubt that the political power of the left depends on the degree to which it has consolidated its social base through legal and extra-parliamentary struggles. While the party leadership is a significant determinant of success, its chances are also circumscribed by its organic relationship with the party managers at the grassroots. By a well-knit organizational network (sustained in a Stalinist way), the parliamentary left maintains and retains a support base that crumbles once mass disenchantment leads to the rise and consolidation of parallel power centers capable of challenging those in power. Unlike the parliamentary left that keeps on changing its ideological strategies, Maoism is an ideological continuation of the past, and yet it is also a contextual response to the peculiar Indian reality that differs radically from one place to another. In the past, ultra-left movements seem to have uncritically accepted the "one size fits all" approach by accepting the classical Marxism–Leninism as sacrosanct. Given the obvious socio-economic and cultural diversity of the continental variety, India can never be comprehended in a single axis. By being sensitive to this well-entrenched diversity, Maoism has reinvented Marxism–Leninism in a most creative fashion by rejecting the straight-jacketed Marxist–Leninist formula of socio-economic changes. Even within India, the issues that the Maoists raise differ radically from one state to another. In Andhra Pradesh, Maoism draws, for instance, on anti-feudal sentiments whereas in the tribal belt of Orissa and Chhattisgarh rights over forest produce remain the most effective demand for political mobilization. This context-driven articulation of Maoism is certainly a critical factor in its emergence as perhaps the most effective ideological voice of the downtrodden, notwithstanding the determination of a coercive state to crush the campaign.

III

Communism in India is uniquely textured. By discarding the violent revolutionary method of capturing power, the parliamentary left has, for instance, flourished because of its success in pursuing effective policies of "redistribution" of basic economic resources within the parliamentary form of governance. So, domestic imperatives transformed Indian communism into a movement with legitimacy among the dispossessed sections through the middle classes, not the wretched of the earth, which was always the main constituency of the communist revolutionary movements elsewhere. The middle class has remained at the helm of the affairs. The movement achieved electoral success but "paradoxically failed to advance communism."[4] It is thus argued that the parliamentary communism, despite being a significant political force in contemporary Indian politics, has ceased to be a movement for revolutionary changes in India. There is thus an ideological vacuum that is filled by the Maoists who have successfully mobilized the exploited masses for movements as possibly the only way out of their subhuman existence. Maoism in India has thus provided the dispossessed with a powerful voice to challenge the prevalent class balances that support high economic and income disparity and exploitation of the impoverished. It is also an ideological challenge against "an extremely oppressive social system, where those at the bottom of multiple layers of disadvantage live in condition of extreme disempowerment."[5]

India's development strategy since independence was hardly adequate to eradicate the sources of discontent rooted in massive economic imbalances in most parts of the country. The history of India's political economy since independence in 1947 reveals how policy paralysis retarded India's growth to a considerable extent. By their preference for the state-led planned economic development, the founding fathers championed the role of the state in guiding the economic system "in a desired direction by means of intentionally planned and rationally coordinated state policies" in which inputs from the grassroots were hardly taken into account.[6] Planning thus became a mere bureaucratic function and was "institutionalized . . . as a domain of policymaking outside the normal processes of representative politics."[7] As an integral bureaucratic wing of the state, the planning commission, which was a unconstitutional body, had an unassailable position in the government because of the functions it discharged within the government. It became a "demi-god" that was responsible for disbursing funds for development in accordance with what the principal political functionaries in government felt appropriate for development. It is therefore not surprising that, despite the claim of the planners that they brought about a balanced growth of the country as a whole, India continues to suffer from lopsided growth. With planners as drivers for economic growth, the founding fathers hoped to distribute the fruits of growth equitably, of course, with an emphasis on the eradication of poverty. By adopting the mixed economy strategy, the nationalist elites created space for businesses to participate in this task. It was a creative arrangement that did not, however, yield results to the extent expected because of the stringent application of "the licence-permit-quota-raj"[8] by the Indian state to translate into action the plan-led development strategies. The result was "tragic" because the Indian economy "had grown too slowly to qualify as a capitalist economy . . . [and] by its failure to reduce inequalities had forfeited any claims to being socialist."[9] Explaining the failure of the state-led development paradigm in India, Atul Kohli argues:

> The Achilles heel of Indian political economy is not so much its statist model of development as much as the mismatch between the statist model and the limited capacity of the state to guide social and economic change. . . . [By] trying to reconcile political preferences of both the left and right in the context of a fragmented state, [the Indian policymakers] failed both at radical redistribution and at ruthless capitalism-led economic growth.[10]

The enthusiasm for the role that the public sector would play in achieving balanced economic growth was short lived. Except for financial enterprises in banking, insurance, and petroleum-producing enterprises, none of the public sector units became viable.[11] This created a paradoxical situation. While "socialist rhetoric" was useful for building and sustaining "a stable political base" for the ruling authority, the failure of the state to effectively pursue the pro-poor developmental strategies and policies eroded the base that was built out of mass euphoria over the acceptance of the socialistic pattern of society. As a result, not only were businesses alienated because of the state's insistence on socialistic policies, but the poor also felt cheated since the attack on poverty was largely confined to slogans. This perhaps explains why "the state-led economic growth or political efforts at redistributions and poverty alleviation" did not succeed to the extent that they did in Korea, where the state pushed (rather ruthlessly) capitalist growth, or in China, which followed state-directed radical poverty alleviation programs.[12] Nonetheless, the Nehruvian socialist pattern of society cannot be so easily dispensed with for historical reasons; globalization without shackles may not be an appropriate strategy for economic development in a poor country like India because in its present form, argues Joseph Stiglitz, it seems like "a pact with the devil." A few people may have become wealthier, but, for most of the people, closer integration into the global economy "has brought greater volatility and insecurity, and more inequality."[13] Economic liberalization is thus a double-edged sword that, while improving the lives of some Indians, has also left millions more untouched. Hence it has been rightly pointed out that the essence of economic liberalization in India can be captured in the Buddhist proverb "The key to the gate of heaven is also the key that could open the gate to hell." Indeed, danger and opportunity are so intricately intermingled in economic reforms that "the journey to the promised land of [economic prosperity] could easily turn into a hellish nightmare of poverty and widening inequality for the majority."[14] It is therefore not surprising that economic reforms, instead of contributing to a balanced economic growth, have caused mass resentment among the dispossessed who are effectively exploited by radical groups for their own gain. In other words, the impact of neoliberal economic reforms is paradoxical. On the one hand, the opening up of foreign markets has generated skilled employment and enormous wealth, shared fairly widely among the benefited section of the population. On the other hand, foreign operators who have been allowed to extract mineral resources from various parts of the country will deprive many people of their principal source of livelihood and their land-connected social identity. The wealth accrued from mining goes to the mine owners and the political class that works in connivance with them. Those losing out are the villagers beneath whose land lie the precious minerals. As a result, they will be "rendered homeless and assetless, and left to cope with the degradation of the ecosystem that will be the inevitable consequence of open-cast mining."[15] What is at stake here is neither development nor industrialization but the issues of justice and democracy because "in the name of development and industrialization, the common resources of the country are being handed over to private corporations by displacing those who have inhabited that land for centuries."[16]

The phase that began with the official acceptance of economic liberalization is different from what had gone on before on various counts. Besides the obvious drawbacks of market-driven development plans, this phase also included mass mobilization regarding numerous "new macro issues," particularly the environment and displacement of people due to indiscriminate industrialization. The indigenous population seems to have been hard hit, and it is therefore not surprising that Maoism has struck an emotional chord with the tribal population in areas where forest land is being taken away for industrial purposes at the cost of the habitat. By challenging the land grabbing by the industrial houses and the government, the Maoists in these areas have become the "true savior" of the tribal population. In fact, this is a major factor explaining the growing consolidation of Maoism in a large number of constituent Indian states. Besides attacking feudal forces, the Maoist radicals have also championed the cause of the indigenous population who lost their land due to reckless mining operations at the behest of the state.

The increasing importance of Maoism and the parliamentary left is an outcome of the steady democratization of the political processes with the participation of the masses not only during elections but also in the interim period. In other words, sustained participation of the people in the democratic processes has created a process that has gone beyond mere voting by empowering the people in a manner that has radically changed the contours of Indian politics. The process is getting translated as rage and revolt, making India "a country of a million little mutinies."[17] But these mutinies have created tangible space for democratic aspiration to flourish. They also make the state available for those who were previously peripheral to any political transactions. The process is significant for another related reason, namely, that the democratic empowerment of the lower strata of society and formerly excluded groups has led to an articulation of voices that had remained "feeble" in the past. Since these groups interpreted their disadvantage and lack of dignity in caste terms, "social antagonism and competition for state benefits expressed themselves increasingly in the form of intense caste rivalries."[18] Thus the growing importance of caste in contemporary Indian politics is essentially a modern phenomenon and not a mere continuation of the past. This is theoretically puzzling since caste-specific action in India, articulated in modern political vocabulary, cannot be comprehended within the available liberal democratic discourses unless one is drawn to the empirical context that radically differs from the typical liberal society in the West. In the changed socio-economic context, caste has gained salience because of its "'encashability in politics' [which] is now dominated by the numerically stronger lower and middle castes [and] the upper castes are now facing a very real reverse discrimination."[19] Thus democratization seems to have set in motion a process whereby peripheral sections of society who were previously delinked from the political processes because of well-entrenched caste prejudices have become politically significant due to their sheer demographic prevalence in socially segregated India. This may sound paradoxical since democratization, as an empowering process, has made the numerically stronger sections aware of their importance in contemporary politics without undermining the caste identity that brings people together irrespective of class differences. In this sense, democratization seems to have legitimized the caste system by reaffirming its role in cementing a bond among various social groups whose members, despite being differently placed in class terms, are drawn to each other because of their inherent affiliations.

Politicization and democratization seem to be dialectically interlinked. As a result, the outcome of this intermingling may not be predictable. In a typical Western liberal context, deepening of democracy invariably leads to consolidation of liberal values. In the Indian context, democratization is translated in the greater involvement of people not as individuals, which is the staple of liberal discourse, but as communities or groups. Similarly, a large section of women is being drawn to the political processes not as women per se or individuals but as members of a community holding a sectoral identity. Community identity thus becomes a critical governing force. It is not therefore surprising that the so-called peripheral groups continue to maintain the social identities (caste, religion, or sect) to which they belong while getting involved in the political processes, despite the fact that the political goals of various social groups remain more or less identical. Nonetheless, steady democratization has contributed to the articulation of a political voice, until now unheard of, which is reflective of radical changes in the texture of politics. By helping to articulate the political voice of the marginalized, democracy in India has led to "a loosening of social strictures" and empowered the peripherals to be confident of their ability to improve the socio-economic conditions in which they are placed.[20] This is a significant political process resulting in what is euphemistically characterized as a "silent revolution" through a meaningful transfer of power from the upper caste elites to various subaltern groups within the democratic framework of public governance.[21] Rajni Kothari captures this change by saying that "a new democratic process" seems to have begun "at a time when the old democracy is failing to deliver the goods [leading to] a new revolution representing new social churnings that are already under way . . . in the electoral and party processes, as also within the deeper arenas of the non-party political processes."[22] It is true that democracy in India has given voice to the peripherals. What is ironic is its failure to create an adequate space in which "a sense of public purpose can be articulated." Hence, citizens are "left with a profound sense of disenchantment." A pattern seems to have developed where "individuals and groups expend inordinate energy to colonize or capture government institutions in seeking to promote their interests over others; there is much activity in politics, but little of it is directed to public purposes that all can share."[23] In theoretical terms, the process can be said to have led to what Anne Philips calls "the politics of presence,"[24] which is articulated as responses of the "dispossessed or disinherited" to social exclusion, nurtured by age-old socio-economic imbalances. What is critical here is "the presence of a voice," powerful indeed on occasions, testifying to the resentment of "the marginalized" seeking to redress their genuine grievances within the democratic space available. In this sense, the politics of presence can metaphorically be described as "nurseries" of "the politics of violence" if the former is found to be inadequate in addressing meaningfully "the well-entrenched social exclusion" on ethnic, racial, religious, or gender considerations.[25] This is a major paradox in Indian democracy that, while it certainly gave voice to the masses, failed to make the vox populi or the voice of the people meaningful in governance. It is thus being increasingly felt that "representative democracy . . . has failed and has become more oppressive and serves the interest of the market and acts as a collaborator of global market-capitalists."[26] Nonetheless, the state no longer remains "an external entity" to the people presumably as "a result of the deepening reach of the developmental state under conditions of electoral democracy."[27] The increasing democratization (whether through electoral politics or otherwise) resulting in the participation of the socio-economically peripheral sections in the political processes therefore seems to have articulated alternative discourses by challenging the state-sponsored market-centric neoliberal policies.

The introduction of market-driven economic reforms in 1991 in India was ostensibly due to a fiscal crisis that the Indian state had overcome with financial support from the

World Bank and International Monetary Fund. However, the reforms hardly brought benefits to the marginalized. Furthermore, the opening of the economy also legitimized the operation of the private players in the domestic economy, and, as a facilitating measure, Special Economic Zones (SEZ) were created by forceful acquisition of prime agricultural land for industrial purposes, which rendered the land-dependent population jobless and homeless. The SEZs are those special-earmarked territories that are duty-free and tax-free enclaves that are considered "privileged territories" for trade operations and tariffs. Their ostensible purpose is to attract large volumes of investment by providing "world-class infrastructural facilities, a favorable taxation regime, and incentives for sectoral clustering."[28] SEZs offered the neoliberal state a means to accomplish its ideological goals, and it was a policy decision supportive of private investment for rapid economic development facilitated by the state. True to its newly acquired neoliberal role, the state was not hesitant to undertake even coercive measures to forcibly acquire land for these private operators because they felt that opposition to the SEZ policy threatened "to sabotage the dream of a more prosperous, efficient and powerful India."[29] This led to mass consternation especially in the tribal districts of Chhattisgarh, Orissa, Jharkhand, and Andhra Pradesh, which the left-wing extremists exploited to build a stable social base in opposition to the displacement and dispossession of the indigenous population. At the heart of the protests were "the perceived abuses of the Land Acquisition Act."[30] To the affected population, the SEZ policy was not for economic growth but a means for fulfilling the partisan aims of the global capital that had devastated India's rural economy in league with the state. A party document underlines the adverse human consequence of SEZ:

> Today the reactionary ruling classes of the country are bent upon transforming vast tracts of fertile agricultural land into neo-colonial enclaves even if it means enacting blood-baths all over the country. . . . The CPI (Maoist) calls upon the oppressed masses, particularly the peasantry, to transform every SEZ into a battle zone, to kick out the real outsiders—the rapacious MNCs, comprador big business houses, their (boot lickers) and the land mafia—who are snatching away their lands and all means of livelihood and colonizing the country.[31]

As a result, the state that zealously pursued the path of reforms seems to have lost its credibility with those involved in the "everyday struggle" for mere survival. The period since the late 1980s has thus seen growing resistance to such policies by the dispossessed groups in different parts of the country. The Red Corridor is also described as "the mineral corridor," given the rich reserve of minerals in this large tract of tribe-inhabited areas. The Maoists aim to resist "the handover of mineral wealth of India to multinationals and foreign capitalists"[32] by transforming the area into a war zone. This is a different kind of war being waged in parts of India where people "are fighting in their own territory to save their land, forest, water, minerals from being grabbed and they are convinced that they have an alternate vision, not just for themselves, the Adivasis, but for Indian people as a whole."[33] In such volatile circumstances, the installation of the SEZs seems to have provoked new issues and resistance movements even in areas which were, until then, free from Maoist radical politics. It is therefore not just coincidental, as will be shown in chapter 4, that localities rose in rebellion against the ruling parliamentary left in West Bengal when the incumbent Left Front forcibly took over land from the farmers in Nandigram and Singur for an automobile factory. The forcible land acquisition led to the fusion of diverse strands of discontent into a powerful political movement. Maoists were reported to have participated in the movement against forcible land acquisition, which was basically a spontaneous mass outburst in opposition to the policy of dispossession. Even without being ideologically compatible, several bourgeois political outfits joined the resistance movement against land acquisition. This suggests, perhaps, the building of a powerful critique through pertinent questions regarding the applicability of neoliberal economic reforms in India where the proportion of people living below the poverty line is staggeringly high. So, SEZs are not merely an articulation of a specific form of economic development, but they are also ideological tools to pursue an alternative path of development. In this path the stakeholders are informed but not at all consulted, while the state seeks to integrate India with global capitalism through neoliberal economic reforms.

IV

This book provides a synthesized account of the rise, consolidation, and the changing nature of communism in India by focusing on its two different faces, which have identical Marxist–Leninist ideological goals. While the parliamentary left gave up militancy and decided to build mass support around reformist social democratic and regional nationalist themes, its bête noire, the Maoists, continue to pursue violent revolutionary means in their endeavor to achieve an exploitation-free and classless society in India. This is broadly the story that will be told in seven chapters. Before presenting the narrative, a note of caution is in order. In the book, the terms Naxalite and Maoist are used interchangeably, as is usually the case in the government reports and other nonofficial accounts. However, there are differences if one is sensitive to the historical roots of these two ideologically complementary socio-economic and political movements, notwithstanding their similar intellectual legacies. While the Naxalbari movement, organized in the 1960s, consolidated the ultra-left wing extremists, it gradually dissipated. Still, it continued to remain ideologically inspiring to new groups of activists subscribing to Marxism–Leninism and Maoism. There were various left radical organizations that built solid social bases in different Indian states. Since 2004, with the coming together of these groups under the Communist Party of India (Maoist), left-wing extremism not only became a powerful ideological force but also a strong political platform to pursue the Marxist–Leninist and

Maoist socio-economic design of human emancipation. Despite having identical intellectual lineage, the erstwhile Naxalbari movement and contemporary Maoism are different, as will be shown in chapter 5, presumably because of the contextual variations in which they had their organic roots. For the Maoists, state enthusiasm for neoliberal economic reforms unfolds newer contradictions that the Naxalites did not confront. The Naxalbari movement was primarily an anti-feudal crusade while its contemporary counterpart, Maoism, is a challenge to the global corporate magnates and their local allies, besides being an ideologically charged endeavor against well-entrenched feudal socioeconomic values and their political mentors.

The story of communism in India also reveals that, despite maintaining a universal ideological perception, Marxism–Leninism is articulated differently in different parts of the globe presumably because of the different nature and texture of human exploitation in specific socio-economic contexts. Besides its class dynamics, exploitation in India has multiple axes around caste, religion, ethnicity, and regions. In fact, it would not be an exaggeration to suggest that class identity is enmeshed in one's caste, religious, ethnic, and regional location. Thus, to comprehend the contextual roots of Indian communism and the factors contributing to its sustenance and expansion, one needs to be sensitive to the wider socio-economic and political environment not only to grasp the phenomenon but also to conceptualize its peculiar texture in a post-colonial context.

To provide an analytical narrative, the book is divided into two parts. Part I deals with the parliamentary left by reference to its contextual socio-cultural and political roots in Tripura, Kerala, and West Bengal, respectively, and Part II is devoted to left-wing extremism, christened as Maoism in India, that has flourished as a powerful ideological tool at the hands of the impoverished against the exploitation of human beings by human beings. In this first part, there are four chapters, each focusing on the distinctive experience of the parliamentary left in Tripura, Kerala, and West Bengal. Chapters 1 and 2 focus on the specific nature of the parliamentary left in Tripura and Kerala, and chapters 3 and 4 discuss how it has evolved, consolidated, and finally declined as a significant political force in West Bengal over a period of more than three decades. The story of the left consolidation and its gradual decimation in West Bengal, one of the major left bastions in India, also reveals the evident weaknesses of social democracy as an ideology, especially in a transitional society like India where primordial values of caste, clan, and ethnicity seem to have been critical in one's political choice. Whereas the parliamentary left is confined to three Indian states, its counterpart, left-wing extremism, is reportedly expanding its sphere of influence every day. Part II thus concentrates on Maoism, the Indian variety of left-wing extremism. Based on a historical-sociological understanding of the phenomenon, chapter 5 provides an account of its growth and consolidation in various parts of India essentially as a Marxist–Leninist political platform seeking to radically alter India's semi-colonial and semi-feudal political authority supportive of vested socio-economic interests. Chapter 6 is an elaboration of the Maoist blueprint for future India as well as an ideology-driven contextual critique of neoliberal political economy. Not only is this chapter illustrative of the distinctive Maoist approach to contemporary India's socio-economic reality, it also seeks to articulate a persuasive methodological alternative for understanding a transitional society in a non-Western context. The final chapter is a stock-taking exercise. By assessing Maoism as an ideological assault on the Indian state, chapter 7 seeks to intervene in the wider debate regarding its nature: given the growing number of violent attacks in the recent past on the symbols of institutionalized political authorities in various parts of the country, resulting in the brutal killing of innocent people, can Maoism be recognized as a rightful step toward a rightful cause? The question is difficult and does not have a clear-cut answer, but it is indicative of a quest for an alternative ideological path based on a creative blending of Marxism–Leninism with Mao Tse-Tung's socio-political ideas.

In light of a detailed discussion of communism in India in its two manifestations, the book makes two arguments. First, by ideologically pursuing the social democratic line of thinking, more or less in a typical Bernsteinian way, India's parliamentary left is an innovative socio-political design that flourished in specific socio-economic and political circumstances. That it remains confined to West Bengal, Tripura, and Kerala just confirms the validity of a contextual explanation of its consolidation anywhere else other than these three states. The second argument is linked with the growing popularity of Maoism as a pro-people ideology, especially among the vulnerable sections in the face of ruthless repression by the state. Concomitant to this is a complementary argument that despite having engaged with the masses at the grassroots in their struggle for existence, the hegemony of the Stalinist-feudal mindset in the Maoist organization seems to have degraded its ideological salience even to the extent of considerably eroding its base. Nonetheless, on the basis of an overall assessment of two versions of communism in India, Maoism is an ideology-driven political challenge seeking to build an innovative theoretical critique of the neoliberal avalanche that appears to have crippled the parliamentary left. Instead of creatively reassessing the role of global capital in the changed milieu, the parliamentary left exposed its ideological bankruptcy by agreeing to steer the economy in accordance with its dictation, and this is where the debate starts.

PART I

Parliamentary Left in India

⌒──

THE PARLIAMENTARY LEFT in India is a revisionist socio-economic and political design conceived in a post-colonial situation. Uniquely textured, it is also an ideological response to the claim that without revolutionary violence, social change, in its essence, can never be accomplished. Rooted in the Marxist–Leninist understanding of the stages of the growth of human civilization, the parliamentary method is perhaps the most effective strategy in a liberal-democratic polity to create circumstances for radical social changes. By agreeing to align the institutional facilities in accordance with the ideological priorities, the left has not only reinvented classical Marxism–Leninism in a liberal democratic context, but it has also brought to light the relative utility of social democratic methods, especially when revolution to bring about a classless society is a remote and unrealistic possibility. There is no doubt that parliamentary democratic means are perhaps the most effective in a transitional society that is not yet ready for radical social transformation in the classical Marxist–Leninist sense because democracy "is a condition of socialism to a much greater degree than is assumed, i.e., it is not only the means but also the substance."[1] For the left clinging to the parliamentary-democratic line of thinking, democracy represents "an absence of class government, as the indication of a social condition where political privilege belongs to no one class as opposed to the whole community."[2] Given the effective role in addressing the genuine socio-economic problems of the aggrieved section of the masses, the constitutional legislation is always considered to be "stronger than the revolution scheme where prejudice and limited horizon of the great mass of the people appear as hindrances to social progress, and it offers greater advantages where it is a question of the creation of permanent economic arrangements capable of lasting; in other words, it is best adapted to positive social-political work."[3]

In this context, the role of the parliamentary left is most critical in organizing the underprivileged "to fight for all reforms in the state which are adapted to raise [the deprived] and to transform the state in the direction of democracy."[4] Thus, reform is a predominant means of meaningful social change in a milieu where the revolution in the classical Marxist–Leninist sense seems to be a distant possibility. The parliamentary left is thus a powerful conceptualization within the classical Marxist–Leninist paradigm showing how the prevalent system of governance can be directed to achieve revolutionary socio-economic and political transformation without disturbing existing class relations. This is what perhaps explains the growing ascendancy of social democracy as an ideological path even in countries where the situation is propitious to pursue a radical means for revolutionary aims. Genuine parliamentary institutions are effective in radically altering the prevalent socio-economic texture through reforms.[5]

The parliamentary left is a powerful institutional force in Indian politics. Even before it became an important constituent of a national coalition (2004–2008), the Communist Party of India (Marxist) (CPI [M])-led Left Front was critically important in the three Indian states of Kerala, West Bengal, and Tripura. Though the Communist Party was founded in the 1920s, it was not until the late 1930s that it had become a significant political force, succeeding in building a stable social base among the peasants and workers through its leadership of peasant movements and trade unions. With the election of two of its members to the Bengal Legislative Assembly in 1946, the Communist Party began a long journey of its parliamentary career in an Indian state that would become its bastion in the days to come. Jyoti Basu,[6] who was trained as a barrister in England and had a long involvement with the All India Railwaymen's Federation, rose to prominence after being elected from the Railways constituency. Christened as "the star performer of the left,"[7] Basu remained an important ideologue supporting the social democratic line of thinking that loomed large in post-independent India. From 1952, the party acquired "a parliamentary forum of consequences as the leading opposition party in West Bengal."[8] The transformation was not free from friction: a section within the party accused the party high command of "chauvinism," saying that "the revisionist clique has given up the path of international proletarianism and taken to blind nationalism and betrayal of the revolutionary masses and working class."[9] Not only was the parliamentary left subject to severe criticisms, its top leaders were hounded by the radical section in Calcutta while they sought to persuade their opponents to accept social democratic means of mass awakening.[10] Interestingly, the majority of the left-wing radicals in Bengal accepted the parliamentary method notwithstanding their active participation in the Tebhaga movement in 1946–1947,[11] a left-wing extremist agrarian movement following more or less the classical Marxist–Leninist path of revolutionary transformation. West

Bengal readily accepted the communists, presumably because of their sustained pro-people activities at the grassroots. These activities paid off once the communists approached voters for their support in elections. At the same time, in the Telangana region in Andhra Pradesh, where the parliamentary path had not developed organic roots, the radical section within the Communist Party launched an agrarian struggle against the Nizam-supported local feudal landlords. As history shows, left-wing extremism developed as a powerful ideological challenge involving the people at the grassroots level. Maoism, the twenty-first-century manifestation of left-wing extremism, is undoubtedly a critical political force in Andhra Pradesh, where the parliamentary left never became a significant political force.

For the communists, the parliamentary path was the best strategic means to chart out a pro-people course of action, which the bourgeois forces were simply incapable of pursuing. With the acceptance of a social democratic line of thinking, the party thus announced in its program:

> The Party will utilize all the opportunities that present themselves of bringing into existence government pledged to carry out a modest programme of giving immediate relief to the people. The formation of such governments will give great fillip to the revolutionary movement of the working people and thus help the process of building the democratic front. It however, would not solve the economic and political problems of the nation in any fundamental manner. The Party therefore will continue utilizing all opportunities for forming such governments of a transitional character which give immediate relief to the people and strengthening the mass movement.[12]

The above party resolution is illustrative of the argument that the parliamentary path is an appropriate transitional means to get the best and maximum benefit for the people, even within the bourgeois system of governance. In a typical Bernsteinian way, the party also reiterates the importance of creating a democratic front involving the underprivileged for the final assault on the class-divided social system. Despite being transitional, the governments, formed by the parliamentary left, are likely to reshape the available structure of authority by making people integral to its articulation and functioning.

With a definite ideological mandate, the parliamentary left formed governments in West Bengal, Kerala, and Tripura. By adopting revolutionary agrarian and pro-worker reforms, the parliamentary communists were also able to create stable social bases in these three Indian states. Except in Kerala, where the left was voted out of power at regular intervals, the parliamentary left continued in power in West Bengal until 2011. Tripura is the only Indian state where the left has been in power without interruption since 1993. Besides having adopted far-reaching agrarian reforms, what accounts for the continuity of the Left Fronts in West Bengal and Tripura was certainly the absence of a viable opposition. In the 2011 West Bengal assembly election, the parliamentary left lost miserably to a united opposition, led by a local political outfit, Trinamul Congress. The opposition halted what would have been the eighth successive left victory. The left maintains its citadel only in the northeastern province of Tripura, where it has been voted back to power five times in a row since 1993. There is hardly an opposition to challenge the cadre-based constituents of the front here. The only respectable political outfit that could have been an effective opposition is the Congress Party, which is in shambles due to internal factional divisions. Similarly, the failure of the tribal organizations to remain united gives an obvious advantage to the Left Front, which has a stable social base in both rural and urban Tripura.

The onset of globalization seems to have created new circumstances for the parliamentary left to negotiate. In fact, by welcoming private investment for rapid industrialization in the left-ruled West Bengal, the parliamentary left seems to have taken the wind out of their own sail. Their policy of forcible land acquisition from the reluctant farmers in Nandigram and Singur created a base for the opposition. As chapter 4 shows, the policy of ruthless land takeover for private investors has been a failure on the part of the leadership among the people at the grassroots. Despite its support for external investment, the parliamentary left did not waver in its staunch opposition to the United States' uniform backing of capitalistic-imperialist ideological design, as was clearly articulated in the context of the 2006 Indo–US nuclear deal that was formally ratified as the 123 Agreement in 2007. In the left's perception, the Indo–US nuclear deal had nothing to do with India's energy situation; it was, instead, a cover for an Indo–US strategic alliance that would subject India to US hegemony in foreign relations. To be ideologically justified, the left thus seemed to have put "disproportionate emphasis on the political dimensions of the nuclear deal [and] . . . focused greater attention on the deal as the litmus test of national sovereignty than on the disarmament agenda and the government overstated energy claims."[13] Parting ways with the national ruling alliance in 2008, the left set in motion an argument challenging the involvement of perhaps the most despised state power championing unbridled capitalism in the twenty-first century in India's domestic economic policy. Such an ideology-driven stance vis-à-vis the Indo–US nuclear deal did not pay any dividend to the left in the 2009 national election. The left's numerical strength in parliament was reduced drastically both in West Bengal and Kerala; the parliamentary left lost miserably in the former, where it failed to resolve the contradiction emanating from its invitation to the private investors at the cost of local farmers who were opposed to the forcible land acquisition for industrial growth. As discussed in chapter 4, it simply escaped the notice of the complacent left in West Bengal when its support base, both in urban and rural areas, showed visible cracks, especially in the aftermath of the implementation of the land acquisition bill. The well-organized party that had sustained the left in power for decades remained a mute observer in the face of an avalanche of mass grievances that the incumbent Left Front failed to withstand because it lacked the ideological creativity to reinvent social democracy in the changed environment of globalization. What the parliamentary left had learned in West Bengal by paying a heavy price seemed to have given clear ideological directions to its counterparts in Kerala and Tripura: while the parliamentary left in Kerala that lost power in 2011 to the Congress-led United Democratic Front never approved of forcible land acquisition for private industrial houses, the incumbent Left Front in Tripura did not find, as its 2013 election manifesto clearly articulates, any merit in antagonizing the farmers by snatching their land away for "partisan motives."[14]

As is evident, the trajectory of the parliamentary left in India does not seem to have followed a pattern. Despite being broadly committed to social democratic goals, the left parties devised different strategies in different contexts. Undoubtedly, radical land reforms made the parliamentary left invincible in West Bengal, Kerala, and Tripura. It is also true that the left's failure to protect the farmers' interests in the context of forcible land acquisition in West Bengal severely dented a social base that had remained stable until the 2006 assembly election, when the CPI (M)-led front obtained an enviable two-thirds of the assembly seats. The aim of Part I is to delineate the growth and evolution of the parliamentary left both in the overall Indian historical perspective and in the specific context of each state in which it became a serious political force. By dwelling on the specific stories of the parliamentary left in West Bengal, Kerala, and Tripura, this part will also focus on its distinctive context-dependent nature, demonstrating perhaps the peculiar texture of state-specific socio-economic realities in which ideologies other than social democracy do not appear to be acceptable.

1

The Parliamentary Left in Tripura: A Creative Blending of Ideology and Organization Prevailing over Ethnic Division

WITH ITS RETURN to power following its victory in the 2013 state assembly election, the parliamentary left, led by the Communist Party of India (Marxist; CPI [M]), has created history in Indian communism especially in light of its defeat in West Bengal and Kerala despite being organizationally stronger and ideologically invincible in the immediate past. Until 1977, the state was governed by the Indian National Congress, which was replaced by the left parties in 1978. After ruling the state until 1988, it lost power to a coalition of Congress and its post-election partner, Tripura Upajati Juba Samiti. In turn, Tripura Upajati Juba Samiti was completely decimated by the Left Front in 1993. Since then, the parliamentary left has remained in power. In 2008, the left parties won forty-nine of sixty assembly elections and their leading constituent, CPI (M), won forty-six seats. This trend went undisturbed in the state assembly election held in March 2013. The parliamentary left added three seats to its 2008 tally of forty-nine and registered a 1 percent increase over its 51 percent share of votes in 2008. This is significant because neither the Congress nor its allies have succeeded in denting the parliamentary left's well-nurtured social base, even though it is socio-culturally diverse due to a peculiar demographic composition of the state. The principal aim of this chapter is to comprehend the evolution of the parliamentary left in Tripura with reference to its socio-economic roots. In view of its peculiar demographic composition and its geographic location as a state adjacent to Bangladesh, Tripura communism is an interesting narrative in the evolution of the left in India. The left in India does not conform to its classical articulation elsewhere, presumably because of India's societal pluralism.

EVOLUTION OF COMMUNISM

Originally known as Twipra, which in the local parlance means "land beside water," Tripura, like other northeastern Indian states, is an agrarian state. More than half of the population draws its sustenance from agriculture and allied activities. However, due to hilly terrain and forest cover, only 27 percent of the land is available for cultivation. Given the overwhelming importance of agriculture, the parliamentary left, like its counterpart in West Bengal and Kerala, focused primarily on agrarian issues and devolution of power at the grassroots through a rejuvenated panchayati raj form of governance. What appears to have been difficult for the left was developing an ideological platform that accommodated the region's ethno-culturally diverse social groups. Besides Bengali, the dominant ethnic groups include Manipuri, Tripuris, Jamtia, Reang, Noatia, Koloi, Chakma, Garo, Mizo, Mogh, Munda, and Santhal, among others. Bengalis are the largest of the ethnic groups, and, for a variety of historico-political reasons, Bengali culture seems to have prevailed over other indigenous cultures. This fact remains a constant source of irritation to the local tribal people. As an inevitable fallout of the 1947 partition Tripura became a natural shelter for the Bengalis and other Hindus from the adjacent east Bengal, which merged with Pakistan. This influx changed the demographic composition of this previously princely state, fueling fierce ethnic conflict between the migrants and the indigenous tribal population. This had a visible impact on Tripura's political arithmetic given that the tribals were reduced to a minority, and the settler Bengalis, by being demographically preponderant, became most critical with the introduction of the first-past-the-poll system of election in India.[1] This obvious demographic shift did not receive adequate attention even from the parliamentary left. This was evident when former left leader, Biren Dutta of CPI (M), pleaded with the top leadership to make the former king of Tripura, Dasarath Deb (who had already joined the party) the chief minister of the state after the left trounced the ruling Congress coalition. Dutta's plea was never conceded presumably due to the hegemonic influence of the Bengali contingent in the party leadership, and Nripen Chakrabarty was chosen instead. This was "a big mistake," lamented Dutta, who felt that "tribal extremism would never have taken off had Deb been made the chief minister and we would have been able to spread the communist movement to other tribal-dominated states in north-east India";[2] by preferring Nripen Chakrabarty, who was always described by tribal extremists as "the refugee chief minister,"[3] the parliamentary left lost an opportunity to reinvent Marxism for the socio-economically peripheral local tribals. Hence, it has been argued that partitioning transformed Tripura's political texture. With their attraction to left ideology, the displaced Bengalis contributed, on the one hand, to the rise and consolidation of the parliamentary left. On the other hand, the parliamentary left was responsible for the crystallization of ethnic rivalry for its failure to conclusively address the grievances of the deprived ethnic groups against the relatively organized Bengalis.[4] To the tribals, the situation could hardly be reversed, given the endless influx from east

Bengal; besides their demographic preponderance, their hegemonic presence in bureaucracy also added to the tribals' feelings of being "marginalized" in their own land. This
feeling became "real" with the ruthless crushing by the central police forces of the tribal
organization, known as Upajati Gana Mukti Parishad (All Tribal Liberation Front) and
the thriving Bengali-dominated communist movement.[5] The Bengali domination was a
constant source of irritation to the indigenous population. This was evident in various
pamphlets that were circulated to mobilize movements against the Bengali hegemony.
The tribals had reasons to feel aggrieved because "the cultivable land which once the
Tripuris prepared by cutting and clearing jungles is no longer in their possession. Land,
trade, and commerce—everything is now owned and controlled by [the refugee Benga-
lis]. The Tripuris have no place in government jobs either. They are now foreigners in
their own land."[6] Although the communists initially managed to control the "ethnic
groundswell," the success was short lived, as the tribals formed their own political outfits to pursue their ideological goals. In 1967, Tripura Upajati Juba Samity was constituted since the Bengali-dominated Communist Party never took up the tribal cause in
a meaningful way; the second group, Sengkrak (clenched fist), a tribal militant outfit,
was also the outcome of the communist indifference to the tribals' genuine
socio-economic grievances. With the formation of these anti-communist outfits, a
trend seemed to have begun in Tripura that radically changed the state's political chem-
istry. In this changed environment, the Tripura National Volunteers and National Liberation Front of Tripura appeared in 1978 and 1989, respectively, with far more militant
strategies to ensure that the tribals got what they deserved in democratic India.[7] The
communists, instead of trying to regain the tribals' confidence by being sensitive to their
claims and grievances, devoted their energies to winning over the demographically preponderant Bengalis—a tactic that they considered to be most critical in electoral politics. This was indeed a reflection of the communists' ideological bankruptcy. They failed
to conceptualize their socio-economic mission in the broader Marxist framework of
human salvation. Hence, it is argued that "if partition gave the communists a great
chance to build a political base by utilizing the nationality question, it also created an
arena for bitter ethnic conflict which subsequently reduced their base."[8]

SOCIO-ECONOMIC CIRCUMSTANCES

Besides a serious cultural threat to the distinctly tribal way of life, the Tripura story also
narrates the hapless socio-economic conditions of the local habitat that occurred due to
the forcible takeover of the land to accommodate the refugees following the partition of
India in 1947. A contemporary study confirms that more than 40 percent of tribal land
was taken away by the government for refugee rehabilitation. The obvious impact of the
refugee influx in Tripura was "the opening of the state's forest interiors for the settlement
of refugees." For their survival, these immigrants began capturing the available *jhumland*

in the hills, which the tribals traditionally owned under the community customary law. This led to "a large scale alienation of tribal lands to the immigrant Bengali peasants and a growing incidence of indebtedness among the tribes."[9] Through these measures, "the state," it is argued, "fulfilled its moral duty of rehabilitating the refugees, but in so doing, it ignored the interests of the tribes."[10] The tribals appeared to have been deceived because of their ignorance of the colonial law, which derecognized land ownership without formal registration. Being illiterate, most of them did not realize the consequences of such an enactment until land was taken away. In a similar vein, the tribal land was indiscriminately acquired for developmental projects such as the Dumbur dam, which was built for production of electricity, and other infrastructural facilities. Legally speaking, the tribals did not have a right over the land that was taken away because it was not registered to them; however, in reality, they were the real owners given the recognition of their customary rights over generations. Nonetheless, the outcome led to a massive displacement of the natural habitat once the government-sponsored developmental projects took off. In his study of displacement due to the construction of the dam, Subir Bhaumik notes, "8000 to 9000 families (40–50,000 people) were made to lose their only source of survival for the benefit of the already socio-economically advantageous section of society."[11] The forcible land acquisition triggered protest movements that the government squelched by being as coercive as possible. It can thus be argued that insurgency in Tripura was clearly rooted in agrarian discontent, which, if addressed meaningfully then, could have charted the course of history differently. However, in the name of development, the government kept acquiring tribal land without learning a lesson from history. As the contemporary evidence suggests, a large tract of land that was used for building infrastructure in the state during the last six decades actually belonged to the tribals; the government, by being insensitive to their claim, generally remained "an outsider" and was hardly "an instrument for change as far as tribals are concerned."[12] Unlike their counterparts elsewhere in India, the tribals in Tripura drew their sustenance primarily from the land, which belonged to them so long as the community-based customary laws were recognized. Because they unknowingly failed to register the land, they lost their only source of survival and their social identity, which was associated with the land and other customary markers. By derecognizing community ownership of the land, not only did the present legal system take away land from the tribals, it also delegitimized their distinct socio-economic identity in the wider world in two specific ways. First, by not allowing a monopoly of resources, the customary laws ensured equal distribution of the available resources to take care of everybody's needs, and, second, tribals believed that because the resources that they used had been handed over to them by past generations, they had an equal responsibility to protect and renew resources for posterity. So their attachment to the land is not merely for their sustenance but also for a socio-economic cause that they represent as an ethnic group. Politics in Tripura is complex because of the distinct significance of land among the tribals and their well-defined and clearly land-linked identity, which is inconceivable if understood conventionally. Thus, the intermittent militancy that is evident in Tripura may be linked with the failure of the state to take care of tribal frustration in a meaningful manner.

STEPS TOWARD FULFILLING THE IDEOLOGY-DRIVEN SOCIO-ECONOMIC GOALS

One of the earliest significant economic steps that the parliamentary left adopted to lift them out of endemic poverty and indebtedness was the introduction of plantation crops to the tribals, especially the large-scale cultivation of rubber. The tribal rubber cultivators, comprising a mix of poor *jhumias* (slash-and-burn cultivators) and a tiny section of tribal government employees, teachers, and petty traders, have now emerged "as a powerful social block in Tripura's tribal society." They are increasingly getting involved in rubber plantation because of (i) the immediate financial return of their endeavor and (ii) the sustained commercial viability of rubber in the international market, which ensures a regular source of income and thus a livelihood. Rubber cultivation, an analyst comments, "has not only drawn the tribals away from the slash-burn-cultivation (*jhum*) but also from insurgency and the process has turned the tiny state into India's second largest producer of natural rubber."[13] Besides building confidence among those involved, rubber cultivation was socio-economically rejuvenating, making the tribals stakeholders and taking the steam out of the militant outfits.

The other important step that the parliament seriously pursued was the implementation of the principle of democratic decentralization in governance. The first significant effort in this direction was certainly the adoption of the panchayati raj governance in rural Tripura; the other equally important move was the formation of the Tripura Tribal Areas Autonomus District Council (TTAADC). Formed in 1982 and recognized constitutionally with the adoption of the Forty-Ninth Amendment in 1985 to the Constitution of India, this legally backed formal institution of governance was an endeavor to bring the tribals into administration at the grassroots level. The principal objective behind the setting up of the council was to empower the indigenous people to govern themselves and to entrust the tribals with the task of protecting and preserving their distinctive culture and traditions without interference from outside. This is a rare example in which the communists sought to address the nationality question within the available parliamentary means. Although the council is part of overall governance, it is independent in matters relating to tribal well-being. Institutionally, it was an innovative design that took serious steps to integrate the alienated tribals into mainstream politics; it has thus significant conceptual value in Marxist understanding of the nationality question, which the communists until then had not addressed, fearing Bengali backlash and a serious dent in the organization. "A product of the joint struggle of tribal and non-tribal democratic movements to protect the identity and rights of tribals, . . . the TTAADC is an example of the practical relevance of regional autonomy within linguistic States."[14] It was not therefore an exaggeration to suggest that the council "is a sign that the communist movement has increasingly recognized tribal nationalism as a distinct [socio-political] force in the state not merely a second-order derivation of capitalism reducible in the last analysis to the economic distortions of true class consciousness."[15] CPI (M), the ruling party, endorsed several resolutions that showed that it was serious in meaningfully addressing the genuine socio-economic grievances of the tribes. These resolutions laid out clear directions to the party cadres: by insisting that "the struggle for the conservation of tribal rights is a struggle for the whole party,"[16] the leadership left no doubts about its priority. The result was obvious; unlike other northeastern states where militancy of the sons of the soil continued to be threatening, Tripura remained relatively free from militant attacks on civilians or institutions of governance. It is thus fair to argue that TTAADC took, to a significant extent, the steam out of the militant outfits that had thrived on the relative neglect of the Bengali-dominated CPI (M) political authority in the state. The militant claim no longer held water because of the guaranteed legal authority of the council to champion tribal rights, language, culture, and autonomy. Despite the formation of the council, it has not yet been possible to install elected bodies within the council's jurisdiction although "the enthusiastic and large scale participation, in the face of extremist violence, of the people of TTAADC territory in the [recent] elections to the TTAADC stands testimony to the faith that the people have in the institution."[17] A contemporary report confirms that in the 526 village development committee elections in 2006 voter turnout was more than 85 percent in twenty-five of the forty blocks: the lowest was 77 percent, and the highest was 92 percent.[18] The trend remains unchanged even today.

While TTAADC seems to have taken critical action to draw the tribals away from militancy, the meaningful adoption of panchayati raj governance contributed to strengthening left rule in Tripura. Besides devolving power to the elected local bodies in rural areas, which became mandatory with the 1992 Seventy-Third Amendment to the Constitution of India, the parliamentary left took complementary administrative steps to make the *panchayati* governance an effective set of governmental institutions at the grassroots. There were two important interventions that dramatically changed the complexion of rural local government: first, in 1998, the CPI (M) government in Tripura reconstituted its planning board to bring about inclusive development in the state through a new scheme called the Peoples' Plan. The main objective of the Peoples' Plan was to devolve power meaningfully "in order to enhance peoples' participation and to orient the work of the government departments in the direction of enabling and facilitation, with a strategic focus on improving productivity and enhancing output, especially in the primary sector."[19] The second significant effort in this direction was the conceptualization of Gramoday (self-sufficient villages). Departing from the earlier top-down planning approach, the left government introduced a new scheme of decentralized planning that actively involved the people in devising what was most appropriate for their localities. Launched in 1999–2000, the main objective of Gramoday was to ensure the role of the villagers as the main stakeholders in planning and other programs for development. Under this scheme, the village makes the initial plans, which are then vetted by government officials at the block, district, and finally state levels. This is advantageous to the villagers in two ways: not only does Gramoday enable the people at the grassroots level to suggest area-specific developmental plans and programs, it also provides adequate inputs to the higher-level decision-makers on the deficit of specific resources constraining the implementation of what is decided. Similar to Gramoday, the left political authority also instituted Nagaroday (self-sufficient towns) in the capital city of Agartala and other satellite towns in the state. Described as "a program of resource-based participatory planning" Nagaroday is an institutionalized mechanism "to ensure direct participation of people in the process of planning and implementation with a view to provide [*sic*] better civic amenities and facilities to people living in urban areas and for improving the quality of life, environment and economic condition."[20]

OUTCOMES OF REDEMPTIVE MEASURES

Two important points come out of the preceding discussion. First, unlike its counterparts in West Bengal and Kerala, the parliamentary left in Tripura strengthened its social base by meaningfully implementing pro-people social democratic welfare schemes for the people irrespective of creed, clan, or color. Second, true to its electoral pledge to the voters—and unlike its colleagues in the two other formerly left-ruled states—the ruling CPI (M) did not hesitate to sternly control efforts to appropriate the party machinery for partisan goals. Whether in rural Tripura or in the towns, the party is usually governed by its ideological goal of inclusive development. This is evident in the outcome of the *panchayat* polls and election to TTAADC. People are not only zealous in taking part in the election, they also willingly participate in the planning for allocation of resources for particular projects that they feel will add to their well-being. Even in regard to the number of women involved in local government, the scene does not seem as gloomy as elsewhere in India. A contemporary report shows that one-third of the total elected representatives in *panchayat* institutions are women.[21] On the whole, the electorate seems convinced that there is little discrepancy between the ideological goal that the parliamentary left seeks to achieve and its fulfillment when in governance. As history shows, the decline of militancy is largely attributed to adoption of effective socio-economic and cultural policies that neutralize the militant outfits by making the alienated tribals integral to the endeavor of inclusive development. Unlike other northeastern states plagued by almost uncontrollable militant insurgency, Tripura is perhaps the only northeastern Indian state in which tribal participation in institutionalized governance (like the TTAADC) is not only remarkable but also pertinent in its identification of the factors for tribal alienation in the context of the failure of the development paradigm pursued in India since independence in 1947.

The left juggernaut seems unstoppable given the successive electoral victory of the parliamentary left since 1993. As Table 1.1 confirms, besides two terms of five years each, the parliamentary left has remained in power in Tripura since its inception as a constituent Indian state in 1972:

TABLE 1.1

Governments in Tripura since 1972

Duration of the Government	Political Parties/Alliance
1972–1977	Indian National Congress (41/60)
1977–1983	Left Front (54/60)
1983–1988	Left Front (39/60)
1988–1993	Indian National Congress and Tripura Upajati Juba Samiti (31/60)
1993–1998	Left Front (44/60)
1998–2003	Left Front (41/60)
2003–2008	Left Front (41/60)
2008–2013	Left Front (49/60)
2013	Left Front (50/60)

Note: Figures in parentheses show the number of seats won by the ruling coalition against the total number of seats in the Legislative Assembly.

Sources: For statistical input of elections until 2003, Government of Tripura, *Tripura Human Development Report* (Agartala: Government of Tripura, 2003), 117; for poll outcomes for 2008 and 2013 elections, *Frontline* 30, no. 5 (9–22 March 2013): 1–2.

Table 1.1 reveals that not only has the Left Front increased its tally over its 2008 numerical strength, it has also enhanced its share of votes from 51 percent to 52 percent, which is a significant increase in a northeastern state not entirely free from insurgency. The result is identical in the case of the Lok Sabha poll since in the 1996 national poll the Left Front had won both the parliamentary seats from the state. While the electorate almost rejected the parliamentary left in Kerala and West Bengal, in Tripura, there was hardly a crack in its social base: the left held its bastion by winning two parliament seats in the five successive Lok Sabha polls since 1996. The fact that almost two in every three votes in the 2009 Lok Sabha poll went to CPI (M) is a testimony to its immense popularity as a party. The party is maintained with an effective organizational network in the state. The social profile of its supporters, as one study reveals, has two interesting features: on the one hand, the overwhelming support for the parliamentary left conceals "a crucial social cleavage in Tripura resulting in occasional skirmishes between the indigenous communists and Bengali migrants"; on the other hand its failure to attract Muslim and non-Tripuri Scheduled Tribes is perhaps indicative of the left's inability to address their socio-economic and political grievances effectively.[22] Nonetheless, the CPI (M)-led Left Front has not only consistently captured more seats than its bête noire, the Congress and its partners, but it has also sustained its social base to the extent of holding power without interruption.

TABLE 1.2

Performance of the Contending Parties in Assembly
Elections, 1983–2008

Year	Left Front[a]	Congress
1983	39 (49.96%)	12 (30.51%)
1988	28 (45.82%)	25 (37.33%)
1993	47 (48.51%)	10 (32.73%)
1998	41 (49.08%)	13 (33.96%)
2003	41 (50.90%)	13 (32.84%)
2008	49 (49.49%)	10 (36.38%)

[a] The partners of the Left Front are the Communist Party of India (Marxist),
Communist Party of India, Revolutionary Socialist Party, and All India
Forward Bloc.

Note: Figures in parentheses show the share of total votes.

Sources: Prepared from the data, available from the Election Commission,
Government of India, New Delhi.

One exception occurred in 1988, when the Congress formed the government in alliance
with its post-election ally, Tripura Upajati Samiti, which had seven seats in the assembly.
Table 1.2 is illustrative here.

As is evident in Table 1.2, in an assembly of sixty seats, the Left Front has always won
more seats than the Congress; it has also consistently won more of the vote share since
the 1983 assembly election. It is also clear that, other than in the 1988 election, none of the
ethnic parties seems to have had any impact on the poll outcome; in the last election, held
in 2013, these parties have failed to register victory even in one of the sixty constituencies,
as Table 1.3 confirms.

The convincing victory of the left in the 2013 assembly elections was the outcome of
sustained effort by the government and the left parties in building bridges between the
two conflicting ethnic groups, namely the Bengali migrants and the indigenous Tripuris,
especially the tribal population, which accounts for 31 percent of the total population of
the state. This is the ruling Left Front's fifth consecutive win, since the 1993 assembly election, out of a total of seven electoral victories since the formation of Tripura as constituent state of federal India in 1972. Besides the government-sponsored efforts for inclusive
development, supported by the party organization, one of the political instruments that
neutralized much of the tribal anger is surely the TTAADC, an institutionalized administrative forum where tribals themselves set in motion various developmental schemes
and programs focusing primarily on their genuine socio-economic needs. The left's efforts in bringing about peace and stability, argues a commentator, "have not only paved
the way for smooth economic development but also created an environment of trust

TABLE 1.3

The Results of the 2013 State Assembly Election

Conglomeration/Parties	Seats Won	Vote Share (in % points)	Vote Swing since 2008 (in % points)
Left Front	50	52.3	+0.9
CPI (M)	49	48.1	+0.1
Communist Party of India	00	1.6	+0.1
All India Forward Bloc	00	0.7	+0.5
Revolutionary Socialist Party	00	1.9	+0.3
Front, Led by Indian National Congress	10	44.1	+1.4
Indian National Congress	10	36.5	+0.2
Indigenous Nationalist Party of Twipra	00	7.6	+1.2
Bharatiya Janata Party	00	1.5	+0.05
Nationalist Congress Party	00	0.03	−0.07
Janata Dal (United)	00	0.02	−0.04

Source: Prepared from the detailed constituency-level results, made available by the Election Commission of India, *Economic and Political Weekly*, 15 June 2013: 79.

between the tribals and the Bengalis."[23] This is not a simple achievement in the context of the ethnic rivalries of the terribly devastated northeast India. The parliamentary left succeeded in containing the insurgents by following, according to a commentator, a "three-pronged approach": first, following a political approach, the efforts to create ethnic bitterness and, consequently, rivalry are scuttled by exposing the hollow argument in its favor; second, coercive forces are used efficiently to contain the militants; and, finally, TTAADC is created as an autonomous institutional forum for the tribals to address meaningfully their genuine socio-economic and political grievances.[24] It has thus been argued that "the politics of basic needs and of peace" seem to have played a critical role in the consecutive electoral victories of the parliamentary left. Unlike other parts of India, the scope of the federal government–sponsored Public Distribution System is utilized to ensure the supply of essential items besides those meant for mere survival. Bread alone is not enough for human dignity; education is also a critical resource for meaningful human development. Hence the state supplies electric bulbs to households at a subsidized rate through the Public Distribution System to support learning at home, which is also monitored by village-level workers. This is not a foolproof system. Nonetheless, it has set in motion a new process in rural areas whereby the importance of education is internalized by the people at the grassroots. This is evident in the 2011 Census of India, which revealed that there has been an increase of literacy in the state by almost 20 percent since the last census: now, the overall literacy rate in the state is 88 percent, with 92 percent literacy among males; female literacy is 83 percent.[25] While there has been a growth of almost 20 percent in Tripura, the report card of the parliamentary left in West Bengal is not so encouraging. As per the census of 2011, West Bengal had a literacy rate of 77 percent, which is slightly better than its earlier record of 69 percent in 2001.[26] Tripura is not far behind Kerala, the other Indian state where the parliamentary left has a strong base: in comparison with Kerala's literacy rate of 95 percent (94 percent for males and 88 percent for females), Tripura's 88 percent literacy rate is definitely impressive. How was it possible? Much of what has been achieved is largely due to the effective implementation of the government-sponsored Nine Point Program which is drawn on the United Nations Development Programme of Millennium Development Goals.[27] The program began in 2003 with the specific objective of improving human development, particularly focusing on universalizing school education and improving school environment, reducing child mortality and improving maternal health, and the environment for better living.[28] Despite occasional hiccups, the Nine Point Program, besides providing actual help to those in rural Tripura, seems to have created an environment for change in which *panchayats* play critical roles in executing and monitoring specific projects that are undertaken to fulfill their ideological goal.

It is true that meaningful developmental steps brought about radical changes in the tribals' attitude toward the state; they no longer consider the state "a predator." The role of the security forces cannot be wished away because it was believed that insurgency needed to be tackled both by coercion and persuasion, which was addressed most effectively by the state police. It was a deliberate decision to complement the developmental project with a stern government policy toward the insurgents, which immediately yielded results. Furthermore, what strengthened the zeal to fight militancy was also the image of the state political leadership, which was generally free from corruption and other vices, usually connected with politics in India. B. L. Vohra, the retired Tripura police chief, while reminiscing, makes this clearly evident:

> Tripura is considered the least corrupt state in the country as the top political leadership including the chief minister, who is a CPM [*sic*] leader, is honest. So much so that even today he deposits his government salary into the party funds from where he gets a meager allowance to run his kitchen. This political leadership also had the political will to take on the insurgents and then quickly implement development schemes in areas freed from insurgency. This only proves that if the top political leadership is honest personally and has the political will to take on the insurgents and support its officers who, considered inefficient elsewhere in tackling insurgency, can deliver.[29]

An effective coordination between government initiative and stern police action resulted in a situation in which the insurgency lost much of its appeal to the tribals, who were persuaded neither by anti-Bengali sentiments nor by an appeal couched in terms of governmental indifference to the sons of the soil. Unlike in Kerala and West Bengal, the Tripura parliamentary left thus creatively applied the conventional social democratic socio-economic designs for inclusive development. Here, along with the government machinery, the role of the party organization acting as a vanguard in the precise Leninist sense remains most critical. In other words, sustained organizational activities by the left among the tribals created an environment in which the militant outfits, which failed to provide a meaningful alternative, considerably lost their credibility. The continuity of the parliamentary left, in power since 1993, is indicative of its success in swaying the majority in Tripura in its favor. It has done this through effective policies for the tribals who, instead of nurturing divisive sentiments, appear to have been integrated with the developmental plans and programs seeking to make Tripura an inclusive state.

CONCLUDING OBSERVATIONS

A perusal of the record of the parliamentary left in Tripura confirms how an effective implementation of social democratic ideological programs has enabled the left to remain in power without interruption for more than two decades. The overwhelming electoral victory of the left since 1977—except in 1988 when the Congress captured power—is illustrative of its ideological popularity and the effective role of a cadre-based, well-entrenched organization in sustaining the left hegemony in governance. Tripura, which was a strife-torn state in the recent past, may not have been industrially advanced, but it has achieved remarkable progress in the area of human development by judiciously utilizing the state machinery and the resources that are available. With CPI (M) winning a majority in every assembly and Lok Sabha elections since 1993, there is no doubt that the parliamentary left has succeeded in retaining its base there, unlike in either West Bengal or Kerala although "the larger context of disappointments and emerging insurgency could result in major challenges to it in the days to come."[30] Like its West Bengal counterpart, the parliamentary left in Tripura maintains a hegemonic presence in the state since the opposition is in disarray; as in Kerala, the CPI (M)-led government continues "to rely on the mobilization of society to achieve its goals although it did not, so far, face the same electoral pressure as in Kerala."[31] The parliamentary left experiment in Tripura is a creative blending of two complementary inputs from its counterparts in West Bengal and Kerala: while the continued left rule in West Bengal has shown how useful a strong organization is in making the party hegemonic, the Kerala instance provides the parliamentary left with a persuasive logic to draw on mass support for sustaining an organization, however strong it is, with clear organic roots among the people.

There is a significant point that needs to be taken into account while explaining the invincible position of the parliamentary left in Tripura, namely, the weak opposition. What still ensures the left electoral supremacy in this tiny state in India's northeast is the failure of the opposition to stand united against the organized parliamentary communists. Besides factional feuds among the contending leaders within the state-level Congress Party, what seems to have plagued its chance is also distrust among the leaders. This distrust was evident just before the 2013 state assembly elections, when a large number of second-rung leaders resigned due to their serious differences with the state leadership over the nominations of candidates for the election. This adversely affected the election campaign: not only did the Congress have less time to campaign as it was busy sorting out internal squabbles, the Party was also handicapped because of a lack of able and dynamic leadership to take on the parliamentary left with an alternative ideological position on crucial issues in state politics. This is a serious weakness that needs to be addressed to chart out a possible course of future action. It is therefore not an exaggeration when a Congress activist laments, "[In] Tripura, the Congress does not have a leader who has the ability to take on the entrenched domination of the Left. Time and again, whoever was entrusted with the party's leadership in the state came up against stiff opposition from rival factions, had to face fierce infighting, and could not expect endorsement from the central leadership."[32] Despite obvious constraints within the organization due to internal feuds, the Congress Party maintains a solid support base. In the 2008 assembly election, the Congress won ten seats with a share of 38 percent of the total votes; in the 2013 assembly poll, besides retaining its tally of ten seats, it also increased its vote share to 45 percent. There are therefore reasons to believe that the parliamentary left is not as invincible as projected, given the increasing vote share of its bête-noire, the Congress Party, since the last election in 2008. In the light of the West Bengal 2011 assembly election, when the parliamentary left lost power to the Trinamul Congress-led united anti-left opposition after an uninterrupted thirty-four-year rule, one cannot rule out the eventual decimation of the left in Tripura. This may be the case unless the poll debacle of the left in West Bengal prepares them to address creatively the emerging issues of globalization within the social democratic ideological format.

2

Parliamentary Left in Kerala: A Creative Socio-Political Engineering of Governance[1]

THE HISTORY OF the parliamentary left in Kerala can be traced back to 1957 when this southwestern state of India became the first—and, until 1977, the only—Indian state to elect a communist government. Besides the tiny Italian principality of San Marino, it was the first instance of a democratically elected communist government in the world. Guided by the charismatic E. M. S. Namboodiripad,[2] the Communist Party of India (CPI) secured 38 percent of total popular votes and one seat less than an overall majority in the assembly. With significant success in electoral democracy, Kerala is usually referred to as having charted a new course in the revolutionary communist movement by articulating the new communist strategies of "peaceful transition" and "the parliamentary road to socialism."[3] Congress leadership at the federal level, including Jawaharlal Nehru, did not rule out the possibility of working with the Communist Ministry in Kerala in the pursuit of socialist objectives, provided it was "genuine about functioning within the terms of the constitution."[4] The apparent positive tilt however did not last long, and Nehru, peeved by "the growing lawlessness in the state" and especially increasing incidences of political murder, declared presidential rule in the state after dismissing the elected communist government in 1959. It was "a bad precedent" in a democracy, as Nehru himself admitted;[5] nonetheless, he was persuaded to take the administrative action because the Kerala government betrayed "the basic spirit of democracy," which was not merely "voting, elections or a political form of government" but was "a manner of thinking, a manner of action, a manner of behaviour to your neighbour, to your adversary and opponents."[6] Though short-lived, the communist rule in Kerala projected an alternative form of governance that could be utilized for radical socio-economic changes within liberal democracy. So, with the formation of Namboodiripad's ministry in 1957, the parliamentary left was no longer a conceptual category but became a form of governance with its theoretical roots in Edward Bernstein's conceptualization of Marxism–Leninism-driven social democracy. Even within a very limited period, the government-initiated radical land reforms and efforts at stopping the church-driven education at the primary and secondary school levels made the left government very popular, which undoubtedly laid a solid social base for the parliamentary left that uninterruptedly continued in power as a significant partner in government in Kerala until 1979.

Confirming that the parliamentary left in India is a context-driven social democratic articulation of popular governance, the Kerala experiment is also unique in at least two ways. First, it reflects a continuity of a specific kind of politics that the Congress Socialist Party (CSP) had begun during the nationalist phase, which, in a very critical sense, contributed to the growth and consolidation of pro-people radical ideologies in the state. Unlike its counterpart in West Bengal, where the CPI was always independent of the Congress Party, the CPI in Kerala not only "grew out of the anti-colonial movement in the region . . . [it was also] a direct outgrowth of the left-wing faction, the CSP, of the mainstream Congress Party."[7] Second, the Kerala experiment led to a coalition government comprising parties with more or less identical ideological aims and programs. The trend began even before Kerala became a full-fledged state in India in 1956. For instance, in the state of Travancore-Cochin, which Kerala inherited, the CPI fought elections in 1952 and 1954 in alliance with the Praja Socialist Party (PSP) and the Kerala Socialist Party (KSP). In both these elections, the CPI-led coalition won, defeating the Congress Party. In its historic 1957 poll victory, the CPI fought on its own, though it had formed a coalition government with five party-supported independents. This became a trend also for those opposed to the parliamentary left. In 1960, the major noncommunist parties, the Congress, PSP, and the Muslim League, backed by the church, formed a pre-poll alliance to defeat the left. The coalition ministry under the leadership of Pattom A. Thanu Pilai of the PSP came to power. Reflective of Kerala's societal pluralism, a coalition provides perhaps the only effective form of governance to accommodate contrasting, if not conflicting, socio-economic interests. This is evident in Kerala's political history since it became one of India's constituent states in 1956. A coalition is thus not merely a political mechanism but is also an acceptable design of governance by which political parties with reasonably compatible socio-political goals come together for a common mission.

Unlike its counterpart in West Bengal and Tripura, the parliamentary left in Kerala has taken a different trajectory in its attempts to articulate its distinctive Marxist–Leninist ideological preferences in an innovative way in a liberal democracy. It was firmly believed by those at the forefront of such a creative ideological exercise that social democracy was perhaps the most effective political design to provide "immediate relief" to the people. In a pattern bearing strong resemblances with European social democracies, Kerala, in contrast with other states in federal India, stands out by following the procedural, effective, and substantive dimensions of democracy. By focusing on the evolution of the parliamentary left in Kerala in recent years, this chapter, while laying out the political texture of the state, seeks to understand the processes that are at work in the electoral victory of the communist coalition at regular intervals. Because the history of parliamentary communism can be traced back to the period immediately after decolonization of India in 1947 even when the State of Kerala was nonexistent, it is important to briefly deal with that period in which the CPI and its ideologically sympathetic partners flourished as important political forces in the state.

ELECTORAL POLITICS IN MALABAR: 1947–1957

When India became independent and Britain transferred power to the interim government, Malabar became part of the Indian Union. The communists organized an armed rebellion while the Congress and Socialists became part of the nation building process. There was little possibility for the Muslim League in Malabar to claim annexation with Pakistan. The ultra-loyalists and the rich were able to migrate to Pakistan, though the number of such migrants was very few. Malabar engaged in electoral politics under the constitution of India starting with the very first general election of 1951–1952. In October 1951, a special committee of the CPI adopted the party program and statement of policy and decided to fight the democratic elections.

The first general election, held in independent India in 1951–1952, was a spectacular victory for the non-Congress parties mainly in the contest for assembly seats in the state of Madras. The Congress won only 4 out of 30 seats. The alliance of CPI and the Kisan Mazdoor Praja Party (KMPP),[8] founded by a group of ex-Congress socialists, won 15 seats, and the Muslim League and Socialist Party won the remainder of the seats. In Travancore-Cochin, the Andhra districts of Madras, and the state of Hyderabad, West Bengal, and Tripura, communists defeated the Congress in a large number of seats. According to Namboodripad, for a party that had been politically isolated from the anti-imperialist masses during the Quit India struggle and whose organization was weakened and divided after the second party congress, this was indeed a worthy achievement.[9] The Muslim League, which was not part of the left alliance, was against the Congress in Madras although with its success in persuading the communal Muslims in Malabar, the League caused a dent in the left social base even though the national Muslims stood with the left against the Congress.[10]

In Madras the governor invited the Congress, the single largest party in the assembly, to form a government. The Congress was able to manage the majority with the support of independents. C. Rajagopalachari became the first chief minister of Madras. Later when Rajagopalachari resigned, the Congress was able to secure the support from KMPP leader T. Prakasham (the leader of allied left opposition) and the Muslim League in the midterm election after the division of Andhra from Madras. The KMPP leaders in Malabar (e.g., K. Kelappan) also switched over to the Congress. The remaining members of the Socialist Party and the KMPP formed a new party called the Praja Socialist Party. In 1953 the CPI fought alone in the elections to the Malabar District Board. It won the elections, and the party held the post of president of the board. It was the first administrative position held by the party through democratic election.

ELECTORAL POLITICS IN TRAVANCORE-COCHIN: 1948–1957

In Travancore, Pattom Thanu Pillai from the Congress became the first chief minister of the responsible government formed in 1948 following the first general election in the princely state based on adult suffrage. Among the total 120 seats, the Congress won 97, Travancore Tamil Congress won 14, the Muslim League won 8, and independents won 1. The CPI fielded candidates in 17 seats and the KSP had candidates in eight constituencies, but all of them failed. The elected body was recognized by the king of Travancore as the first legislative assembly. The communists were engaged in the armed rebellion of Telangana model in several parts of Travancore. The struggles in Punnapra and Vayalar became the most memorable events in the history of communist struggles in South Kerala.

Internal differences and power struggles among the party leaders in Travancore led the Congress ministry headed by Pattom Thanu Pillai to collapse within a year, and T. K. Narayana Pillai succeeded Pillai to the post. The government continued in power when the federal government decided to merge Cochin with Travancore on July 1, 1949. The ministry accommodated Congress leaders from Cochin. But power struggles based on the regional identity of leaders from the two princely states affected the smooth performance of the ministry. In the first general election of 1951–1952 in Travancore-Cochin, the CPI formed an alliance with the Revolutionary Socialist Party (RSP) and the KSP against the Congress, but this alliance was not acceptable to the three main, crucial communities of the Ezhavas, Nairs, and Christians; its alleged prejudices against the Tamils in south Malabar also alienated a significant demographic minority. Despite having failed to win a majority of seats in the state assembly of Travancore-Cochin, the Congress was invited to form the government since it was the single largest political party in the assembly. The divisions between the Congress and its partner, the Travancore Tamil Nadu Congress, led to the resignation of the minority ministry in 1953. In the second assembly election in 1954 in Travancore-Cochin the left front (CPI, KSP, and RSP) made a pact with the PSP against the Congress. The Travancore Tamil Nadu Congress also helped to weaken the Congress. The Catholic Church opposed the left alliance in both 1952 and 1954 elections. The attempt to form a PSP–Left Front government was thwarted by an offer from the Congress to support PSP if it would form a single-party government. As a result, the pre-election coalition collapsed and Pattom Thanu Pillai from PSP, which had only 19 seats in the assembly, became the chief minister with Congress support from the outside. The United Front (UF) strategy of the CPI was in accordance with the party line adopted in the Madurai Party Congress in December 1953 endorsing a coalition with progressive political forces for giving "immediate relief to the people."[11] The PSP government resigned after a no-confidence motion was moved by the Travancore Tamil Nadu Congress in the house in 1955 after 11 months in power, which was passed with Congress support. The communists abstained from voting. Following the resignation of Pattom, the Congress formed the government with Panampilly Govinda Menon as the chief minister in March 1955, who also left office in less than a year after apprehending the possibility of a lack of numerical support for approval of the annual budget. While the Congress was facing factionalism on the question of state reorganization of Kerala, the communists made significant headway in this regard. Despite the efforts of the left parties to avoid presidential rule because of a series of dramatic events, including the disappearance of one member of the legislative assembly from the RSP immediately before the voting was to begin, the no-confidence vote carried and, with the resignation of the ministry, president's rule was promulgated in November 1956.[12]

Even though the CPI had a substantial number of seats in the assembly since the 1951–1952 election, there was no indication of the consolidation of a durable left alternative in the making. Left politics in the south was fragmented between three or four political parties. The available data show that the CPI had a consistent and larger share of support than the others and that it had been emerging as a powerful political force with a solid social base since the early 1950s. The fierce opposition between the socialists and communists led to the weakening of left politics more gravely in southern Kerala than in Malabar. This brief sketch of Kerala's past political history shows two specific trends that appear to have significantly influenced the left's political make-up and its bête noire, the Congress and its alliance partners. First, in choosing electoral partners, the parties acted with strategic calculation—even to the extent of diluting their respective ideological predispositions—which was critically important. Second, besides being ideologically flexible, both the dominant political parties, the CPI and the Congress, couched their electoral appeal in caste/communal language, presumably to consolidate their respective support bases. It is therefore not surprising that this is clearly visible in contemporary political coalitions in Kerala—for both the Communist Party of India (Marxist; CPI [M])-led Left Democratic Front (LDF) and the Congress-driven United Democratic Front (UDF): alliances are chosen not on the basis of ideological compatibility but on the basis of a strategic calculation to secure votes.

ELECTORAL POLITICS AFTER THE FORMATION OF KERALA STATE

The boundary of present Kerala was drawn by slightly modifying the previous political map of Travancore-Cochin and Malabar. The Malayalam-speaking area of South Canara was added to Malabar, and Tamil-speaking Kanyakumari was separated from Travancore-Cochin. Even though language was the factor that united the south and north, the collusion of political cultures and practices that prevailed in these two regions in the post-state reorganization phase produced the most unexpected political result. In the first assembly election following the state reorganization, the Congress, CPI, and RSP contested alone. The PSP had an alliance with the Muslim League. The CPI was striving hard to form a united left front against the Congress. Victor M. Fic rightly points out that, even though it did not get any formal approval from other left political parties such as the RSP and the PSP, it might have raised sympathy among their supporters in favor of the CPI.[13] In addition, the communists also propagated and outlined in their election campaign and other related documents that the CPI was going to implement the economic policies of the Congress Party, which were constantly delayed by the Congress.[14]

The main electoral slogan of the CPI focused on establishing unity among the left parties and all progressive individuals to secure a stable and democratic government against the Congress. But the PSP and RSP, with their supposed mass support to fight the Congress, were reluctant to form an alliance with the communists.[15] For its part, the CPI also did not appear to be willing to establish a pre-election coalition with any other party. Even though the PSP and other socialists were vocally in favor of democratic centralism, due to the reluctance of the leaders to sacrifice individual authority in the party, the principles were hardly followed in letter and spirit. In view of the organizational weakness of other contenders for political power, the CPI gained strength due to its leaders' strict adherence to democratic centralism despite serious differences among them on various other social and political issues. In fact, the CPI was organizationally stronger than other left political parties in the state. With its appreciation of "transitional collaboration with other parties without impairing the organizational autonomy of the communist parties,"[16] the parliamentary left thus created circumstances for its electoral victory at regular intervals. While attributing the popularity of the parliamentary left as an electable formation in Kerala to its successful adaptation to the changed environment, Fic thus argued:

> The operations of the communist government, taken in their totality, amounted to a unique case of systematic adaptation, conversion and exploitation of the institutions of parliamentary democracy for the purpose of its transformation into a special form of the dictatorship of the proletariat, a people's regime. The transformation was conceived as a peaceful process.[17]

After the communists secured state power, they began implementing some of the radical land reform measures, including a fixed land ceiling, which the Congress shelved for its obvious ideological impact on those representing the landed interests within the government and party. The communists were also under pressure to fulfill the expectations of the people who always remained peripheral in governance. During the previous CPI-led agitations, the CPI had made a series of political and economic promises to the exploited peasantry and the working class. The party had mobilized a large number of militant leaders at the local level who were both ideologically and emotionally attracted to the party and its revolutionary path. But the CPI had to satisfy their demands within the limitations of the constitutional democracy. The friction between the constitution and the communists was linked with the fact that the constitution of India was not adequate to establish an egalitarian society in the near future. On each and every occasion, the CPI had to strike a balance between fulfilling the constitutional obligations and ideological commitment to class struggle and dictatorship of the proletariat, with a varying chance of success and failure. Once in government, it was a tightrope walk for the party, which was caught between constitutional democracy and the achievement of a classless society following the fundamental principles of classical Marxism–Leninism, especially in the light of demands of the militant cadres who agreed to sacrifice everything for revolution.

If the party was ready to enter into completely class-based politics in Kerala, the CPI government had to address the worries of the lower and middle caste organizations, led mainly by the Ezhavas, which supplied a majority of its cadres.[18] A crisis seemed to have occurred when the Administrative Reforms Commission, appointed by the CPI government, suggested reserving public jobs for the economically backward sections within the caste reservation. Leaders of Ezhava community reminded the party leadership in public speeches about the sacrifice that the community made for the victory of peasant struggles. Radical leaders like Balaram[19] and Namboodiripad argued that the CPI was uniting lower castes and lower classes together for a common struggle for an egalitarian society,[20] though the experience of CPI government had shown that the caste–class relationship in Kerala was more of a challenge than an opportunity for a class-based political approach of the communists. Scholars of Kerala such as Nossiter and Fic, while seeking to understand the caste/religious composition of the party's leadership and its cadres, seemed to have overemphasized the political significance of such social identities in Kerala politics. Both of them confirm that the CPI in Kerala was predominantly an upper caste Hindu organization, which is not at all exaggerated given the fact that majority of the top left leaders belonged to upper castes.[21]

Among the contributions of the first communist government, the most notable are those related to land reform and education and pro-labor police administration. An anti-eviction ordinance was issued to stop evictions as the preliminary step for proper implementation of land reform. In the education sector the government introduced a bill to regulate the private education institutions, mainly run by the caste/community organizations including a sizeable number of schools under the minority (Christian Church) management. Two important communities, the Nairs and the Christians, rallied against the communist government. In the past, it was also the case that while the Nair Service Society (NSS) was willing to support the left parties and PSP in return for representation of their leaders in the cabinet, the Church was the strongest enemy of the left parties. The bill to stop eviction and to end landlordism had mixed responses from the Nairs, though its leadership was quite convinced about the negative impact that the bill would have on the already declining feudal Nair families.

Educational reforms were criticized as a violation of minority rights by the Church, and the school textbook revisions were interpreted as violation of faith and moral standards of students by the government under the control of the atheists. The managers of private schools, representing powerful community organizations such as the Christian denominations, the Muslim Educational Society, the NSS, and the Sree Narayana Dharma Paripalana Yogam (SNDP), protested against the education reforms. Besides the problems emanating from these radical legislations, the government was also criticized for destroying the efficient management of the institutions. Such a criticism came mainly from the opposition parties and was also widely circulated through the powerful vernacular media. The party cells formed in every government department were considered to be bypassing the bureaucracy in the government, which was also accused of interfering in the judiciary when it decided to withdraw police cases registered under previous governments against the party cadres. The government declaration that there would be no police intervention in the labor disputes also attracted criticism. The earnest appeal to settle the disputes through mediation by the labor department was undoubtedly welcome by the workers, though business groups and factory and plantation owners were frightened because of the shifting of balance in favor of the workers against capital.[22] In the trade union sector the left trade unions run by the other left parties and the Congress were wary of the rising dominance of the All India Trade Union Congress. The one industry–one union principle—that the CPI upheld to prevent splits among the working class—was conceived by their left rivals as a step to establish the All India Trade Union Congress as the only all-India working class organization. Therefore, the forces against the communist government of 1957 were not only from the caste communal organizations and the Congress but also from the trade unions affiliated with other left parties. The government was criticized for adopting more repressive measures against its political rivals. It caused damage to the progressive police reforms initiated by the party, which included the policy of no police intervention in labor disputes. The involvement of the party's local offices in police administration also led to numerous petty struggles between its leaders and rival parties in villages and towns. After finishing the first year of government, the party was facing stiff opposition from a combined force of the Congress, other left political parties, and all the organizations of major castes/communities, including Christians, Ezhavas, Nairs, and Muslims. The left parties such as the PSP and the RSP also joined the statewide agitation known as the liberation struggle against the government. The situation provoked the prime minister, Jawaharlal Nehru, to make a trip to Kerala to verify the situation following the reports that U. N. Dhebar, the president of the Kerala Pradesh Congress Committee, sent to him elaborating the instances of government breakdown in the state. However, the Kerala Pradesh Congress Committee was not united in its agitation against the CPI government. The leaders of Travancore and Cochin were more interested in helping the caste/community organizations to expel the government when compared with the leaders of Malabar who were, though disappointed by the rule of communists, not entirely in favor of joining hands with reactionary forces to pull down the government, which was implementing certain legislative reforms supported by the Congress at the national level. Finally, on July 31, 1959, the central government dismissed the twenty-seven-month-old CPI government based on the report from the governor regarding the breakdown of law and order. Although the Namboodiripad government survived for only two years, the parliamentary left set into motion a series of social democratic reforms that would alter Kerala's agrarian structure in the days to come. It also set "a standard for state intervention and social welfare from which no subsequent government has strayed."[23] Not only did the parliamentary left articulate governance in a new fashion through the 1957 experiment, it also contributed to the unfolding of a new phase of history in a liberal democracy drawing on the Westminster form of governance.

Following the president's rule, a mid-term election was held to the state assembly on 1 February 1960. With the support of all the caste/community organizations and churches, the Congress, PSP, and Muslim League formed an alliance against the CPI. The RSP and KSP decided to fight the election without joining the anti-communist alliance. People seemed to have taken participation in voting far more seriously, as was evident in the gradual increase of voters in just three years: while in the 1957 poll, 67 percent of the total voters took part in the election, in 1980 there was an increase of 13 percent, which was illustrative of how serious the voters were in exercising their democratic rights. It was also a testimony to the fact that the conservative sections of the population increasingly realized the importance of voting after the victory of communists in 1957. Anti-communist votes from the Christian and Muslim communities as well as from the Nairs of the Hindu community became the most decisive bloc of voters responsible for defeating the parliamentary left. However, the CPI won the largest share of votes, indicating its rising popularity after the communists adopted the parliamentary path. But this alone would not be sufficient, as the party failed to get a majority of seats. One of the factors for the defeat was surely the CPI decision to contest alone in all the constituencies while the Congress fought in alliance with partners. So the electoral success of the Congress can easily be attributed to an effective calculation that paid off in the context of the first-past-the-poll system of election in which a person with the maximum number of votes gets elected irrespective of whether he or she has a majority. Formed in February 1960, the newly elected government comprising the Congress and PSP was the first coalition government after Kerala was formed as one of the constituent Indian states. The Muslim League, which had joined the alliance before the election, was denied ministerial birth due to its support of sectarian ideology and due to the opposition of the Congress High Command, which led the League to threaten to quit the coalition. To avoid further escalation of bitterness, the League was accommodated with the offer of the post of speaker in the assembly. For the first time in the history of Kerala, the Muslim League had a political position after the election. To provide stability to the coalition, Pattom Thanu Pillai of the PSP was accepted as the chief minister and R. Shankar from the Congress was made the deputy chief minister.

From the very beginning, the new coalition government faced difficulties because of the strained relations between the Congress and PSP, which was, it was alleged, usually bypassed while making major policy decisions. After the death of incumbent speaker, Seethi Sahib, the Congress did not want a Muslim League candidate to become speaker. Muslim League member C. H. Muhammad Koya had to resign from the League to become the speaker. There were also numerous power struggles between the PSP chief minister and the Congress deputy chief minister. Governor V. V. Giri played the role of a mediator, but the solution that the governor suggested did not work well. The internal struggles within the ruling coalition almost reached a stage of no return just before the 1962 Lok Sabha poll. Koya resigned from the post of speaker and decided to leave the Congress–PSP alliance. A new organization named the All India Muslim League was formed as a result of division within the Muslim League over supporting the Congress. The PSP was also divided over the same issue. In the Lok Sabha election, though the Congress–PSP coalition secured six seats, the CPI, which made an electoral alliance with the RSP, had won six seats with a share of 47 percent of total votes cast. The CPI, RSP, and the independents that supported them shared more than 50 percent of total votes. Soon after the Lok Sabha election R. Shankar from the Congress became the chief minister of the state once the former chief minister, Pattom, was appointed the governor of Punjab. The PSP ministers resigned from the government soon after the party decided to leave the coalition with the Congress, though the PSP and Muslim League did not support the CPI when a no-confidence motion was initiated by the CPI against the Shankar ministry.

The period of 1960–1964 was important for the party system in Kerala when the two bigger parties, the CPI and Congress, besides the PSP and Muslim League, faced organizational splits. The 1962 Indo-China war created a serious ideological crisis within the CPI. Within 10 days of the start of the war, the CPI condemned China as an aggressor while the leftists within the party questioned the leadership for having supported the government decision to wage the war, which was "based on a clear mis-calculation of the Chinese attitude towards India."[24] The right and left wings within the party had serious differences of opinion and failed to remain united even on some major domestic issues, including whether to support the Jawaharlal Nehru–led Congress government at the center.[25] E. M. S. Namboodiripad and A. K. Gopalan were with the left of the CPI, while Achutha Menon, T. V. Thomas, and M. N. Govindan Nair were the prominent leaders of the official CPI in Kerala. The parting of ways came in 1964 when the left wing of the party held a parallel congress in Bombay and formed a new communist party, known as Communist Party of India (Marxist) (CPI [M]). After the split there were local conflicts between the rival factions for the seizure of feeder organizations and party offices. By the time of separation of the party into two organizational units, the CPI had a larger share of the leaders of the united CPI, but the CPI (M) had taken away the major chunk of the party cadres. The CPI (M) attracted the majority of young leaders while the CPI retained those belonging to the 35 to 55 age group.[26] The CPI (M) was recognized as an independent political party by the Election Commission of India a few days before the election to the Kerala Legislative Assembly. From the writings published after the split by the party leaders, it was clear that the split was final and in no way could it be rescinded. Nonetheless, the CPI was reportedly keen to bring back "the disgruntled comrades,"[27] while, for the CPI (M), the split was a historical necessity, and there was hardly a space for coming together given the ideological irreconcilability between the two wings of the former CPI, especially in regard to the tactical line that a true communist party should adopt in a parliamentary democracy. For the CPI (M) ideologues, by uncritically toeing the Congress line of thinking—whether in regard to the Indo-China war or other domestic issues—the CPI lost its independence and thus had become "an appendage to the Congress Party."[28]

Here an assessment of the tactical line adopted by the communists would be highly relevant. They entered into parliamentary politics with an aim of bringing about a structural and institutional change in accordance with their ideology, which was interpreted by the academic commentators as a peaceful transition to communism.[29] In the 1940s and 1950s there were debates in CPI (M) about armed rebellion and participation in democratic politics to mobilize the masses and to transform the society. It was abandoned after the failure of the Telangana agitations; the party decided to contest elections and became a mass revolutionary party aiming at the establishment of a peasant–proletariat state. It was thus announced that "we, the communists must contest parliamentary elections—we must contest any type of elections that can argue for the rights of the people, that can bring together large masses. We have to be there where the masses are; we have to be there where people want us to be."[30]

The split of 1964 was definitely a split over the strategy of the communists in a parliamentary democracy and about the choice of political allies. The inner-party debates regarding the optimal strategy in property distribution led to the next split in the CPI (M) in 1969 leading to the formation of a far more militant CPI (Marxist–Leninist).[31] The much younger cadres and leaders of certain provinces raised doubt about the suitability of a parliamentary path to realize land distribution. This second split following the Naxalbari revolt shall be viewed as a split over whether parliamentary means were appropriate to realize the ideological goals of the communists. All these splits occurring since 1964 made it impossible for the communists of Kerala to form a single-party government. This was in addition to the differences already in existence between communists and socialist parties in Kerala. The present divisions in Kerala's social left are in one way or the other reflective of the debates involving the political left, though a significant number of the social left are seemingly against the mainstream left political parties today in view of their reluctance to lead progressive social movements for lack of adequate political dividends.

There are stories in Kerala about the neutralization of several dedicated party cadres who had to withdraw from the active political life after the split in the parent organization. The split in the CPI seemed to have weakened the parliamentary left immediately, though they gained their lost political strength presumably because of the backing of a solid organization. Here CPI (M) reaped the maximum benefit because the majority of the cadres associated with the former CPI joined the CPI (M) while the CPI had retained most of the top leaders. The split had debilitated Kerala's parliamentary left for obvious reasons; those critical of social democracy as an ideology for survival gradually dissociated from the communist movement since it amounted to, they apprehended, "a complete surrender to the revisionist forces [which would] cause irreparable damage to the mass movement for genuine socio-economic and political changes."[32] What was most damaging to the Kerala communists affiliated with both the CPI and the CPI (M) was also the alleged involvement of the top communist leadership in a factional fight for partisan gains at the cost of the party.

ELECTIONS AFTER THE SPLITS: 1965 AND 1967

Just before the 1965 assembly election most of the CPI (M) leaders were arrested under the defense of India rules. Despite the limitation of a newly formed party with a new symbol given very late by the Election Commission and even though a large number of leaders were in jail at the time of election, the results of the assembly election were very impressive for the CPI (M), which secured forty seats compared to the poor performance of CPI, which won only three seats. The CPI formed an alliance with the RSP and had seat-adjustment with the Congress in certain assembly constituencies. The Congress Party won thirty-six seats, and its poll partners, the Kerala Congress and the Muslim League, won twenty-three and six assembly seats, respectively. The election proved the strength of the CPI (M) over the CPI in terms of support from the cadres. This election did not seem to be exactly an ideological battle between the left and the opposition; it was instead a fight to establish one's political hegemony over the rivals by hook or crook. As Nossiter argues, "The CPI (M) . . . did fight the reactionary and communal forces as represented by the League and Kerala Congress, but was [also] prepared to make arrangements to support 'independents' [with pronounced] communal character if that would avoid a Congress victory."[33] While assessing the social base of the communist parties, it is evident that the CPI drew mainly on the middle peasantry, while the CPI (M) claimed support of the lower peasantry and peasant workers, mainly landless agricultural laborers. Here what is important is the fact that the divisions in the political organization of the communists had given a new class polarization within the lower class, which was already divided mainly between communists and socialists, besides those belonging to other non-left political outfits engaged in mass movements on various pressing socio-economic issues. The most interesting fact of the election result was that among the total CPI (M) candidates elected to the assembly, twenty-nine were in jails under Defence of India Rules since the 1962 Indo-China war. The election produced the first hung assembly in the state, wherein none of the three major parties—the CPI (M), the Congress, and the Kerala Congress—was willing to form a government through coalition. There was thus no option but to apply Article 356 of the Constitution of India to promulgate presidential rule in Kerala until 1967 when the state assembly election was held in tandem with the election for Lok Sabha.

One of the most important developments during this period was the articulation of class division especially among the Christians who, being staunchly anti-communist, always remained with the Congress Party to pursue their ideological goals. It was thus not surprising that major churches in Kerala were generally opposed to the parliamentary left. Instead of being an appendage to the Congress, the church leaders preferred to act independently by forming political parties to fulfill their distinctive social, economic, and political needs. One of the significant developments in this regard was the formation of the Karshaka Thozhilali Party (KTP) in 1965 by Father Vadakkan, who was earlier an active leader of the "liberation struggle"[34] against the CPI government. Opposed to the Congress and the Kerala Congress, the KTP opened a new ideological front since neither the Congress nor the parliamentary left was sensitive to their special needs as a minority.[35] Even though Vadakkan supported the CPI (M) when it joined him in his struggle against the eviction of the Christians in southern Kerala, the communists did not get substantial political support from the traditional laity, clergy, and affluent sections of this community. The vote share of the Muslim League also did not indicate any change in the 1965 election when compared with previous elections. A small faction of Muslims joined the CPI primarily because of its anti-communal stance in the past; nonetheless, Muslims as a community never aligned with the parliamentary left presumably because of its failure to conclusively address the communal issue especially in a context of their rising economic importance due to their access to petro dollars. Like Christians, Muslims too preferred not to play second fiddle in politics, and hence they threw their weight for the parties willing to fight for their cause. The fact that Muslims regularly swung their support for parties other than the Muslim League also confirms that the exclusive communal issue never appeared to be as significant in Muslims' political choice as is usually anticipated.

The UF in 1967

In accordance with a strategy of a national coalition to defeat the Congress, the CPI and the CPI (M) formed the United Front (UF) in Kerala just before the 1967 election with the RSP, KSP, Muslim League, KTP, and Samyukta Socialist Party (SSP) as partners. Under the UF banner, in the 140-member assembly, the CPI (M) contested sixty-one seats; the CPI, twenty-four seats; the SSP, twenty-three seats; the League, fifteen seats; and other minor parties, ten seats. The food crisis following the 1965 Indo-Pak war, conditions of state economy, the step-motherly treatment of the Congress government in Delhi to Kerala, unemployment, and the growing center-state conflict united the partners of the UF against the Congress, which was identified as "the fifth column in Kerala."[36] The Congress got only nine seats in the assembly compared to its tally of thirty-six in the 1957 election. But, the share of votes secured by the Congress had shown a marginal increase, which was not at all satisfactory given the fact that the party had contested every assembly seat. The only consolation for the party leadership was the fact that the splinter Kerala Congress failed to make a dent in the traditional Congress's social base. Although the UF government succeeded in binding anti-Congress political forces together, it was unable to address the points of divergence between the two wings of parliamentary communism, namely the CPI and the CPI (M). When the other minor parties also joined the competition for dominance, the failure of the front was imminent. Within two years of UF rule, the SSP, CPI, and Muslim League formed a mini-front within the ruling group. The split within the SSP led to the formation of the Kerala SSP under the leadership of P. K. Kunju and P. R. Kurup. The leading UF partner, the CPI (M), was reluctant to expel these two leaders from the government despite the insistence of the SSP's national board. The split in the SSP further contributed to a new group called the Indian Socialist Party in Kerala. Besides these splits among the UF partners, the main leader of the front, the CPI (M), also faced internal skirmishes from the ultra-leftists who were inspired by the Naxalbari struggles. Five of the CPI (M) members of the legislative assembly faced disciplinary action from the party. Ministers and their parties were accused of maladministration and corruption inside the assembly several times by their own political allies. The CPI and the CPI (M) differed on the suggestion of forming an independent authority to investigate corruption charges. The coalition politics thus caused irreparable damage to the parliamentary left and especially the head of the government, E. M. S. Namboodripad.[37] Pointing out the failure of the UF government to take care of the Muslims' demand for a separate Malappuram district for the Muslim-preponderant areas of southern Malabar and a university in Calicut, the Muslim League also parted company with the CPI (M)-led coalition in 1969.[38] In view of the lack of required numerical strength on the floor of the assembly, there was no option for the government but to step down, which was what had happened in 1969.

CPI-CONGRESS ALLIANCE: 1969–1979

Following the internal division in the UF and resignation of Namboodiripad, a Mini Front ministry was sworn in with Achutha Menon from the CPI as its chief minister. It was supported by the Congress from outside. The collapse of the UF in Kerala and Indira Gandhi's decision to split the Congress Party happened more or less simultaneously. The Congress and CPI alliance proved useful for the declining CPI and the fractured Congress which, to persuade voters to vote for the alliance, utilized Indira Gandhi's image as one who was more committed to socialist goals than her rivals in the old Congress Party. The Congress–CPI alliance that ruled Kerala for next ten years was making new alignments not only in the party system but also in the public opinion. This alliance had caused serious dents in the left social base in two specific ways. First, it led to the formation of an ephemeral but politically important opinion among many in the left-leaning middle-class public that a combination of left and right political strategies was needed to ensure inclusive development in Kerala. At the outset, the alliance raised hopes because it sought to build a forum of like-minded people by bringing together those who were considered "less militant" in the former CPI and the members of the Congress Party who held a slightly more radical ideological position as compared with the rest. However, it perfectly synthesized the political logic of a middle-class mind. Second, it drove the ultra-left elements away from the party because they now realized that the parliamentary path meant compromise and that it was thus not aligned with the fundamental ideological values of Marxism–Leninism and not an adequate path for mass mobilization for a specific political goal. They were able to mobilize a number of young leftists from colleges and universities to organize the landless peasants for a militant struggle. The alliance was thus said to have created circumstances in which the left lost its credibility to a significant extent.

The Mini Front sought reelection in 1970 with the support of the Congress unit that was loyal to Indira Gandhi. During this phase the Congress was also slowly recovering from organizational splits. In the 1970 election, three coalitions were formed by a total of twenty-two political parties, probably the highest number of parties contesting elections ever in Kerala. The Mini-Front was led by the CPI, the RSP, the Muslim League, and the PSP, backed by the Indira faction of the Congress. The CPI (M) formed the People's Democratic Front (PDF), which included the KSP, the SSP, the Indian Socialist Party, and the KTP. The Democratic Front comprised the Organisational Congress, the Kerala Congress, Jan Sangh Party, and Swatantra Party. The Indira Congress emerged as the biggest group in the assembly by winning thirty-two seats in the assembly. The People's Democratic Front secured only forty-one seats, with CPI (M) winning in twenty-eight assembly constituencies. The Democratic Front won fifteen seats. The CPI had sixteen seats, and its leader Achutha Menon became the chief minister of the Mini Front. The Congress was rejuvenated after the election and gained considerably from the active and nonconservative Youth Congress leaders as its candidates. The infusion of new blood into the Congress that rallied behind Indira Gandhi was the reason that a large number of youth in Kerala preferred the Congress over the CPI (M) in the election. As a result, the advantage that the CPI (M) and other left political organizations had in the public domain seemed to have considerably waned during this decade when the alliance managed to administer the state by effectively negotiating the differences among the coalition partners without jeopardizing the stability of the government.

After the Mini Front–Congress alliance repeated the electoral victory in the 1971 Lok Sabha election in Kerala, the Congress decided to join the Achutha Menon ministry. Though the CPI did not accept the demand of the Congress for the post of deputy chief minister, the presence of K. Karunakaran as home minister in the newly constituted cabinet gave the impression that the Congress, despite being in the backseat, was actually running the administration. The government benefitted from the combined effects of the clean image of its CPI chief minister, its energetic Youth Congress, the growing populism of Indira Gandhi, and the shrewdness of the Congress under the leadership of K. Karunakaran. In the meantime an internal feud erupted within the Congress between Karunakaran and his followers and Youth Congress leaders M. A. John, Vayalar Ravi, A. K. Antony, and V. M. Sudheeran, which caused irreparable damage to the Congress Party and the alliance ministry. Nevertheless, the alliance remained the longest serving government in Kerala and continued until 1977 because it received an extra two years due to the 1975–1977 national emergency when no elections were held and incumbent state governments were given an automatic extension beyond their normal duration of five years.

Despite the efforts of the CPI (M) to intensify struggles against the government, it was not able to defeat the ruling front after the election in 1977. Interestingly, the Youth Congress was mobilizing the people against its own government. The Congress was able to win the election after the 1975–1977 emergency only in Kerala and in no other states in India. This victory was probably due to the rising support for the Congress among middle-class voters who seemed to have been happy with the CPI–Congress alliance, which reportedly served them better than previous governments.[39] The 1970s also witnessed ideological fissures within the left. The CPI (M) lost its iconic image that it had previously enjoyed among leftists when numerous revolutionary and voluntary groups were formed in Kerala, which undoubtedly had an impact on the CPI (M)'s organization at the grassroots. The CPI also experienced occasional hiccups within its organization due to increasing discontent among the activists who felt cheated for being not adequately rewarded for their hard work for the party. The parties failed to register new members as zeal for membership for a party seemed to have waned considerably, which automatically enhanced the importance of uncommitted voters, who reportedly became significant in the elections that followed.

The positive vote for a Congress–CPI alliance that ruled Kerala during the emergency is a puzzle for political commentators. According to Nossiter, the middle classes, in particular, were delighted at the prospect of a respite from agitation and political struggles between parties for power, which many believed to be the bane of Kerala's existence.[40] The ruling alliance became invincible presumably because it had generally adopted populist steps that made people happier and had avoided those that were likely to be harmful to the government's popularity; this explains why the alliance did not pursue the stringent family planning measures, given the apprehension that it would alienate the Muslims, even though it was a policy that the Congress Party had executed forcefully throughout the country. The stories about the police atrocities against political rivals and ultra-left-wing extremists were not allowed to appear in the public domain presumably due to the media-friendly attitude of the government. The state government was able to ensure discipline among the trade unionized government offices, which created a support base among "common people" who felt relieved with the government decision to oppose strikes on flimsy grounds and thus ensured uninterrupted delivery of basic services such as electricity, water, and other basic amenities for human existence. Some voters also found that the new Youth Congress leaders might be an alternative to the corrupt/communal Congress leaders and the "aggressive" CPI (M) leaders in parliamentary politics.[41] In the 1977 election the CPI (M) formed an alliance with RSP (National), the KSP, the Janata Party, the Muslim League, and a faction of the Kerala Congress led by

Balakrishna Pillai. The National Democratic Party formed by the NSS joined the CPI–Congress alliance. The ruling front captured 111 of 140 seats and 53 percent of total votes in 1977.

K. Karunakaran was sworn in as the chief minister of the new government. Achutha Menon had already announced his retirement from politics. The CPI became a minor ally in the front. Within weeks after the formation of the ministry, a case related to the death of an engineering college student, Rajan, while in police custody when Karunakaran was the home minister during the emergency led to a controversy that adversely affected the incumbent government. The chief minister was charged not only with dereliction of duty but also with having a political vendetta against the opposition. The Youth Congress also took a position against the chief minister, and he was forced to resign. Following this, A. K. Antony became the chief minister from the Congress. Here a group war started in the Congress that continued even until very recently between the Antony-led and Karunakaran-led factions within the party. After the emergency, the split within the Congress at the national level progressed so that Antony and other leaders of the Youth Congress in Kerala switched over to the organizational Congress against Indira Gandhi, and Karunakaran remained with the Indira Gandhi–led Congress. Antony resigned as chief minister in 1978 after his protest against Indira Gandhi's by-election. Later he and his followers shifted their allegiance from the Congress to join another Congress outfit, led by D. Devaraj Urs of Karnataka. P. K. Vasudevan Nair from CPI became the chief minister but resigned from the post following his party's decision to join hands with CPI (M); he later formed the LDF in 1979 in collaboration with splinter left groups without party affiliations. C. H. Mohammed Koya from the Muslim League became the chief minister but resigned within a few months. After a brief spell of presidential rule, the next election to the Kerala assembly was held in January 1980.

EMERGENCE OF THE SOCIAL LEFT

It is true that those opposed to the parliamentary left have a reasonably stable social base, which is reflected in the voting pattern. The above overview of Kerala's recent political history reveals that, unlike its counterparts in West Bengal and Tripura, the Kerala parliamentary communists were forced to creatively chart out distinctive political courses to combat the so-called right wingers to carry forward their ideological mission. What is most striking in this politically conscious state in the southern tip of India is a specific kind of socio-political culture favoring debates, arguments, and counter-arguments even among those who are not formally associated with any political party. One can call them integral to civil society for want of a better expression. In Kerala, they are known as "the social left" who, by being engaged with contemporary issues of social relevance, tend to raise their voices even to the extent of annoying those in power. The decade of the 1970s is considered by many vernacular scholars as the turbulent but golden era of Kerala society due to the vibrant culture of public debates and social movements inspired by ideas with different ideological preferences. This was a period of various possibilities, and those participating in such an endeavor were engaged in a serious search for a better ideological alternative even if that involved any sacrifice. The vernacular Malayalam literature in this period provided a platform for radical individualism and anarchy of a post-modern type when compared with the "art for society" approach of the modern literature. In fact, the ultra-left wingers, the Naxalites, in Kerala were not only inspired by these powerful vernacular cultural critiques but were also reported to have joined hands with those involved in charting out the course of Kerala's left politics in a different fashion.[42]

The analysis of the cultural milieu of Kerala during 1970s shows that it gave birth to a wide variety of leaders of the contemporary social left in Kerala. Most of them were baptized politically by the left through their participation in activities involving workers or peasants. The left party leaders also failed to attract many of these leftist intellectuals to their programs. Therefore, the party, to create new leadership, had camped out on university campuses to attract students who were "intellectually receptive and politically challenging."[43] Here one sees the origin of the problem cited by Nossiter: the political left in Kerala is facing a shortage of intellectual and ideologically trained leadership compared to those best brains who were attracted to the CSP and later to the CPI in the pre-independence period and those who led the struggles that deeply entrenched the party in the public mind. He further argues,

> On the one hand in the early days the communists recruited more than their share of the outstanding talent of the time, whether the formally educated Basu and Menon, gold medallist from Madras, or the autodidact, Namboodiripad. On the other hand, student politics, even in the communist SFI and AISF, is a career which leaves little time for study and does not necessarily attract those at the top of their batch. Observers close to the Kerala Assembly certainly drew a sharp contrast between the communist MLAs of the late 1950s and early 1960s, more than a match for their Congress opponents in parliamentary warfare, and their 1980s successors.[44]

The current critics of CPI (M) from the social left were born and raised in Kerala in the 1970s, which ensured the disintegration of the political left in Kerala, and they became the so-called true left voice in Kerala politics today. In politics there was a left party in the government and another one in the opposition. But there were many in the social left who did not align with any of the left political parties—CPI, CPI (M), or with the socialists. Given the organizational strength of the political left and its capability to maintain power through alliances with the non-left forces, the social left never did become a serious political force in the state; their influence remained confined largely to the urban middle class. As a result, the political left was always strong because of its continued presence in the organized domain of politics either as a part of the ruling party or the opposition. By being entirely dissociated with the institutionalized left in Kerala, the social left, despite not being a serious political force in the state, appeared to have created a specific space in the public domain that always remained a critical source of public engagement with issues of social, economic, and political significance.

The political left failed to represent the social left in Kerala because the ideological debates inside the political left failed to address genuine socio-economic issues confronting the masses. The bifurcation of the social left and the political left led to empowering the political moderates first and finally the political right. The compromising political left in Kerala soon became the victims of criticism from the social left. Such a contingency started with the inadequate response from the political left to questions raised by the social left on various issues affecting the daily existence of the marginalized in both rural and urban Kerala. The divergence between the social left and political left was aggravated because many of the social left became theoretical critics of Marxism based on theories of the new left and new social identity movements. In their critique, these new movements did not take class as an adequate conceptual category to understand Kerala's socio-economic texture given the critical importance of caste, religion, and gender in its articulation. The seeds of destruction of the legitimacy of the political left as the representative of the social left started in the 1970s though it was politically crucial at the beginning of 1990 when it came out rather strongly against the dominant political party, the CPI (M). What is interesting to note is the continuity of the political left in power since 1982 despite the hard-hitting critique of the social left, which did not appear to have affected the electability of the parliamentary left in the state.

BIPOLAR COALITIONS: LDF AND UDF

In the 1980 election, the CPI (M)-led LDF secured 93 out of 140 seats, but the government led by E. K. Nayanar collapsed in October 1981. The controversy began with the inclusion in the coalition of two major factions of the Kerala Congress, led by K. R. Mani and Balakrishna Pillai, respectively, who were opposed strongly by the parliamentary left comprising the CPI (M), the CPI, and the RSP for being political right-wingers. The LDF had no argument to counter the charge that it was not exactly "leftist" given the presence of the representative of the Kerala Congress in the ministry. The Congress (Urs) faction, led by A. K. Anthony, also joined the LDF. While the LDF had rightist allies, the UDF had the support of certain socialist groupings. Nonetheless, on the basis of study of the nature of the parties that joined these two fronts, one can safely make the point that the parties that supported the UDF were reportedly far more communal and caste-ist in their ideological preferences than their bête noire, the LDF.

The UDF government, which was formed after the 1982 state assembly election, was supported by the Congress (Urs), the Kerala Congress, and the Muslim League. Also, the two caste-based political parties, the Nationalist Democratic Party of the NSS and the Socialist Revolutionary Party of the Ezhava organizations, joined the UDF. Being ideologically flexible, the parliamentary left also justified political alliances on the basis of what is politically expedient at a particular point in time: winning power appeared to be the main concern regardless of ideological considerations, which provoked a commentator to argue that the parliamentary left had entered a phase of political adaptation against confrontation that they held so dear so far.[45] A perusal of Kerala's electoral history shows that power shifts between these two conglomerations of parties, which are not ideologically compatible but agreed to form a coalition on the basis of certain common minimum programs. What began in 1982 seems to have become a permanent feature in Kerala as Table 2.1 shows.

As Table 2.1 demonstrates, since 1982 neither of the coalitions managed to hold power in two successive assembly elections. In keeping with a pattern of defeating incumbent parties, which has long been the norm in Kerala, the ruling conglomeration of parties is always replaced by the opposition. There is thus a clear contrast between the Kerala experiment and that of West Bengal and Tripura, where the parliamentary left continued to remain in power without interruption for decades, perhaps due to the absence of an organized opposition. The change of government at regular intervals also confirms the fact that the outcome of the state assembly election is largely decided on the basis of voters' assessment of the quality of the administration that the government provides during its reign. The shift of power also provides evidence that a cadre-based organization is not always adequate to ensure victory in the election. The fact that the CPI (M)-led LDF failed to regain power after one term in governance also shows that the voters' choice is governed not by ideological preferences but by the government's capacity to deliver services

TABLE 2.1

Numerical Strength of Coalitions in Kerala, 1982–2011

Year	UDF	LDF	Others	Government (majority)
1982	77 (46.2%)	63 (44.3%)	–	UDF (by 14 seats)
1987	61 (42.4%)	78 (46.1%)	1	LDF (by 16 seats)
1991	90 (49.3%)	48 (42.4%)	2	UDF (by 40 seats)
1996	59 (44.4%)	80 (42.8%)	1	LDF (by 20 seats)
2001	99 (49.1%)	40 (44.2%)	1	UDF (by 59 seats)
2006	42 (42.6%)	98 (49.1%)	–	LDF (by 56 seats)
2011	72 (46.3%)	68 (45.2%)	–	UDF (by 4 seats)

Notes: Figures in parentheses show the share of popular votes. UDF = United Democratic Front. LDF = Left Democratic Front.

Source: Prepared from data available from the Election Commission of India.

to the people at large. There is a pattern in the change of government: the UDF and the LDF capture power interchangeably, and one conglomeration comes immediately after the other, as the outcomes of elections since 1982 reveal. What it also demonstrates is the overwhelming importance of major political parties—the Congress or the CPI (M)—in the formation of a coalition government with alliance partners who remain critical so long as one of the leading partners is willing to accept them as constituents; otherwise, they simply do not have political importance. This is also replicated at the federal level where the regional political parties become important once either of the pan-Indian parties—the Indian National Congress and the Bharatiya Janata Party—agree to unite with them to form a coalition.[46]

What is most striking is the fact that the parliamentary left does not seem to be ideologically rigid in choosing its partners in a coalition: the partners come together on the basis of some common minimum programs for welfare, regardless of religion, ethnicity, and socio-economic location. This is evident in the acceptance by the left of the Janata Dal (Secular) and the National Congress Party, which are not at all drawn from Marxism–Leninism, as a constituent of the LDF despite the fact that these political parties have supported the Congress-led United Progressive Alliance at the federal level since 1999. So, Kerala's coalition experiment is a pragmatic solution to governance in the context of new socio-political circumstances in which no single party, regardless of its organizational strength or ideological appeal, is capable of winning a majority in the assembly election. Nonetheless, the left in Kerala increased its share of popular votes consistently until the 2006 election when it obtained more than 49 percent of total votes polled, but it never became a dominant political force as was the case in West Bengal and Tripura. One of the reasons for its growing popularity was surely the adoption of meaningful pro-people programs: for instance, in 1987, the parliamentary left collaborated with Kerala Shastra Sahitya Parishad (a literary organization) to conduct the "total literacy campaign" and during 1997–2001, the left collaborated with several grassroots socio-political outfits and faith-driven organizations to implement the People's Plan Campaign (PPC) through the newly constituted Local Self Government Institutions, which was specifically conceived as "a vehicle for deepening democracy"[47] toward "taking the State . . . toward building genuine and sustainable institutions of local self-government to a higher level infused with principles of sustainable progress towards genuine autonomy."[48] As a set of far-reaching institutional reforms, the campaign evolved from a comprehensive critique of "the inefficacies of top–down, insulated, command-and-control bureaucracies and of the myriad problems, both practical and normative, of the local participation deficit."[49] The PPC became an empowering mechanism by making the very nature and institutions of the state itself "an object of contestation with the goal of deepening and widening democracy, [creating a legitimate space for] ordinary citizens who have never been afforded an opportunity to effectively engage the state outside of campaign-oriented social movements to now routinely deliberate and cooperate with elected representatives and local officials in deciding how to spend large sums of money."[50] With the involvement of the

Kerala Shastra Sahitya Parishad, which played a key role in the Total Literacy Campaign, the PPC campaign seems to have articulated a new paradigm for participatory planning "by stimulating a public discourse on development [seeking to] redefine the processes of decentralization which is possible due to the high literacy and also high levels of awareness."[51] Despite their role in involving stakeholders at the grassroots in local planning, it is also alleged that PPCs gradually became a mechanism for the "decentralization of corruption"[52] and the breeding ground for "fractious politics."[53] While the charge of corruption may not have substance, that the PPCs failed to realize their full potential due to factional feuding is not entirely unfounded for two important reasons. First, the panchayat system of which PPCs are a part is controlled by the LDF, which is led by a centralized party—the CPI (M); to expand their sphere of influence at the grassroots, the leaders at the level of decision-making tend to be partisan toward those village panchayats, which are tilted in their favor, or the group that they represent. Second, given the lack of constitutional sanction, the PPCs never have the substantial authority to execute the plans that they prepare without the support of the finance ministry in the state government. Notwithstanding the inherent structural problems, the PPCs since their inception gradually became part of Kerala's rural governance by involving stakeholders at the grassroots not only in the processes of planning but also in its execution, especially following the adoption of the Seventy-Third Constitutional Amendment Act (1992), which gave substantial authority to the institutions of panchayat governance. In the consolidation of the left base in the state, the role of the PPCs remains very critical. Besides the PPCs, which naturally helped the left to strengthen the base, the parliamentary communists, to reach out to the people with different political predilections, also undertook various steps to recruit members to local parish committees, temple trusts, and Islamic mosque committees. So, it was an all-out campaign to expand its social base regardless of ideological considerations, which was evident in the 2006 election results.

Table 2.2 shows that the LDF registered a record win in 2006 through its mass campaign involving people from various strata and underplaying, if not disregarding, ideological compatibility. One of the initial sources of discontent of some of the secular partners such as the Janata Dal (Secular), the Kerala Environment Congress, and the Konattumatam Chidrmbara Subrahmanaia was the inclusion of the Indian National League in the coalition given its fundamentalist Islamic character. Besides internal squabbles, the incumbent government began losing its support following its failure to fulfill the promises that it had made in its election pledge. The crack in the coalition was visible though there was no immediate threat to its continuity since the major left parties, the CPI (M), the CPI, and the RSP, had adequate numerical strength to provide the LDF with a majority in the assembly. Nonetheless, in the 2009 parliament election, the left had a setback: against eighteen of twenty Lok Sabha seats in the 2004 national election, the LDF had won only four seats with a loss of more than 4 percent of total votes. The poll debacle is attributed to (i) the failure of the LDF government to fulfill its election pledge and (ii) the incompatibility of coalition partners due to ideological differences

TABLE 2.2

Results of the 2006 Kerala State Assembly Election

Left Democratic Front (98 Seats/49.0% Popular Votes)	Number of Seats	United Democratic Front (42 seats/42.7% Popular Votes)	Number of Seats
CPI (M)	61 (30.5%)	Indian National Congress	24 (24/2%)
CPI	17 (9.1%)	KSMUL	07 (7.3%)
NCP	01 (0.64%)	DICK	01 (4.27%)
JD (S)	05 (2.4%)	KCM	07 (3.3%)
RSP	03 (1.4%)	JPSS	01 (1.51%)
INL	01 ((0.90%)	KEC (B)	01 (0.62%)
KEC	04 (1.75%)	Independent	01 (0.76%)
KCS	01 (0.30%)		
Congress (S)	01 (0.47%)		
Independent	01 (2.1%)		

Notes: Figures in parentheses show the share of total popular votes. Constituents of the LDF: NCP = National Congress Party. JD (S) = Janata Dal (Secular). INL = Indian National League. KEC = Kerala Environment Congress. KCS = Konattumatam Chidrmbara Subrahmanaia. Congress (S) = Congress (Socialist). Constituents of the UDF: KSMUL = Kerala State Muslim League. DICK = Democratic Indira Congress (Karunakaran). KCM = Kerala Congress (Mani). JPSS = Janadhipathiya Samrekshna Samiti. KEC (B) = Kerala Congress (Balakrishna Pillai).

Source: Prepared on the basis of data made available by the Election Commission of India.

and factional feuding within the leading constituent of the LDF, the CPI (M). Unable to create jobs since the LDF had adopted few meaningful steps to develop industries, the government did not have a strong argument to counter when the opposition pointed out its glaring failure in realizing Kerala's industrial potentials. Simultaneously with its failure to articulate an effective industrial policy, the government was also criticized for its neglect of the agriculture and the traditional sectors, such as coir, handloom, fishery, and village-based handicraft industries. In fact, the LDF was charged with continuing with the policies of the UDF, which was held responsible for the lack of development in Kerala by the parliamentary left when in opposition.

Besides the general discontent of the majority of the voters, two issues seemed to have acted critically in the erosion of the LDF support base. First, those supporting the enlightened left felt cheated when the LDF's leading partner, the CPI (M), was reportedly hobnobbing with Abdul Nasser Madhani of the People's Democratic Party, which was primarily "an Islamic fundamentalist organization."[54] Madhani was arrested in 1998 in connection the Coimbatore bomb blast, which was reportedly Muslim revenge against the Hindu-triggered communal violence of the past; though he was acquitted of all the charges, he was reported to have built his social base generally by appealing to the sectarian Islamic identity. To consolidate its Muslim support base, the left underplayed Madhani's tilt toward Islamic fundamentalism, but the majority of left voters were not persuaded to forgive his role in the 1998 blast. Furthermore, even after Madhani's inclusion in the coalition, the LDF made little inroad among the Muslims, as the 2006 Lok Sabha poll shows that as many as 68 percent of the Muslims voted for the UDF.[55] The other serious issue that fractured the parliamentary left to a significant extent was the charges of corruption against the CPI (M) state secretary, Pinarayi Vijayan, in the SNC-Lavalin power project case. Despite clear proof of his involvement in the scam, Vijayan escaped serious scrutiny by any of the state investigative agencies since the party, which he led, never allowed such an investigation. Coalition partners were unhappy and had to swallow their criticism due to the numerical strength of the CPI (M), the CPI, and the RSP, which was sufficient to run the government even without the other constituents of the LDF. So, the parliamentary left lost its grip over the masses to a significant extent in the 2009 national poll largely due "to internal squabbles, inability to project its governance record due to never-ending controversies within the leadership and non-implementation of promises, made in the 2006 assembly elections."[56]

Within a year, in 2010, when election to the panchayat was held in Kerala, the results were identical: the parliamentary left failed and its bête noire, the UDF, captured a majority of seats in the civic bodies in ten out of fourteen Kerala districts. Despite being in power for almost for four years, the LDF seemed to have ignored mass discontent over its failure to implement the promises that were made in the 2006 election. There were many welfare measures that the government, led by V. S. Achuthanandan, had adopted though their implementation was far from satisfactory. What might have alienated a large number of Christian voters was the LDF campaign against the interference of the church in politics, which provoked a counter movement in which the UDF activists in the localities participated to reap the benefit from the discontent of a significant section of "disgruntled Christian voters."[57]

The 2010 local election was a break with the past in two major ways. First, this was an election in which the voter turnout was as high as 75 percent throughout the state. Second, the election campaign revealed an ideological battle between the two conglomerations of parties for political space in rural areas: the LDF sought to mobilize voters on the basis of what the incumbent government accomplished for the benefit of the downtrodden and marginalized while the UDF consolidated its base by puncturing "the tall claims" of the ruling coalition. Despite having initiated some remarkable pro-people programs (e.g., rice at a cheaper rate; the EMS housing scheme for providing cheap dwelling units for the poor, among others), the LDF seemed to have lost its momentum significantly due to the bitter rivalry between the chief minister, V. S. Achuthanandan, and the party general secretary Pinarayi Vijayan. The 2010 verdict clearly shows that, for the first time, the UDF gained ground at the grassroots, which thus far had remained with the parliamentary left. The growing popularity of the Congress Party and its UDF partners, which was evident in the 2009 Lok Sabha poll, was visible, and the UDF decimated the left in the entire

TABLE 2.3

Results of the 2010 Local Polls in Kerala

District	Total Votes Polled	% Votes for UDF	% Votes for LDF	% Votes for BJP	% Votes for Others
Thiruvananthapuram	16,82,099	42.3	42.8	7.9	6.89
Kollam	14,34,817	43.6	47.9	4.7	3.7
Pathanamthitta	6,78,132	46.1	40.5	8.3	5.1
Alappuzha	12,58,095	44.8	45.4	5.4	4.3
Kottayam	11,26,151	49.9	38.6	4.4	7.1
Idukki	6,43,231	53.1	40.1	3.0	3.6
Ernakulam	18,42,321	44.3	40.9	4.4	5.6
Thrissur	17,98,343	45.6	42.3	7.0	5.0
Palakkad	15,54,728	43.9	44.5	6.3	5.3
Malappuram	20,79,413	53.3	33.5	5.2	7.8
Kozhikode	17,34,212	45.1	43.2	7.0	4.2
Wayanad	4,34,912	49.5	40.2	5.5	4.7
Kannur	13,78,964	38.8	52.5	5.2	2.5
Kasargod	6,80,949	40.7	38.1	15.5	4.6
Total	**1,83,26,367**	**46.1 (84,47,977)***	**42.4 (77,63,495)***	**6.3 (11,47,297)***	**5.3 (9,67,598)***

Notes: Geographically, these fourteen revenue districts are divided into (i) South (Thiruvananthapuram, Kollam, Pathanamthitta, Alappuzha, and Kottayam), (ii) Central (Idukki, Ernakulam, Thrissur, and Palakkad), and (iii) North (Malappuram, Kozhikode, Wayanad, Kannur, and Kasargod). Figures in parentheses indicate the total number of votes polled for the parties in the fray. UDF = United Democratic Front. LDF = Left Democratic Front. BJP = Bharatiya Janata Party.

Source: Adapted from the table provided in M. R. Biju, "Local Body Polls in Kerala: UDF Smashes LDF Fortress," *Mainstream* 48, no. 48 (20 November 2010): 7.

central Travancore and the majority of districts in southern Kerala, which were considered to be the left bastions in the past, as Table 2.3 shows.

The LDF was a clear loser in the overall poll outcome except in four districts (Kollam, Alappuzha, Palakkad, and Kannur) whereas the UDF was ahead of its bête noire in a majority of the districts. In comparison with its performance in the 2005 local polls, the LDF lost almost 4 percent of popular votes while the UDF enhanced its share of total votes by more than 6 percent since the last local election. The reasons for the LDF poll debacle are not difficult to find given the fact that the party was plagued by a severe internal feud between the government and the CPI (M) leadership, which explains the failure of the LDF to undertake a united campaign showcasing the achievements of the government in rural areas. Furthermore, anti-incumbency sentiment also acted against the current LDF government for obvious reasons, which were never meaningfully addressed by the party cadres. As a result, the welfare schemes that the Achuthanandan government undertook did not receive adequate attention during the campaign. The convincing UDF victory in central districts also reveals that the CPI (M) planned campaign against the church for its hegemonic influence among ordinary Christians was counterproductive. It did not help the LDF to create a solid vote bank among the majority community; instead, it consolidated the LDF's anti-Christian image, which resulted in a massive transfer of Christian votes to the opposition. What was striking in this local poll was the consolidation of communal votes: if the Christians felt cheated by the government, so were the Muslims, especially those in the north of Kerala who came together under major political outfits (the Muslim League, the Indian National League, the People's Democratic Party, among others) with a clear appeal to sectarian identity. Besides organizational weaknesses due to the internecine factional feud within the CPI (M), the alienation of a large chunk of voters from two major social segments, Christians and Muslims, created a void in its social base that the LDF leadership failed to address meaningfully. The result was obvious, and the incumbent LDF was almost trounced in a state where the voters preferred the left less than four years earlier.

THE 2011 ASSEMBLY ELECTION

In both the 2009 Lok Sabha poll and 2010 local polls, the LDF failed to regain its lost social base in Kerala; its decline was steady. The UDF victory in the majority of the local bodies in the last local poll took the wind out of the left's sails by capturing a majority of the gram panchayats. However, within a gap of six months, the UDF lost its momentum with a victory by a very narrow margin of only four seats in the assembly: while the UDF had won seventy-two seats, its rival LDF's seat tally was sixty-eight. The LDF's remarkable recovery in the last assembly election also confirms that the parliamentary left continues to remain an effective political force along with its like-minded partners in the coalition.

The final outcome of the election followed a pattern of change of government every five years. The incumbent government lost power to the opposition with a margin of victory that is the smallest in Kerala's recent political history. Despite factional squabbles, the CPI (M) emerged as the single largest party in the assembly. Table 2.4 provides the detailed results.

TABLE 2.4

Outcome of 2011 State Assembly Election

Name of the Coalition/Party	Seats Won	Share of Votes (in percentages)	Vote Swing since 2006 Assembly Elections (in % points)
Left Democratic Front	**68**	**44.9**	**−3.7**
Communist Party of India	13	8.7	+0.6
Communist Party of India (Marxist)	45	28.1	−2.3
Nationalist Congress Party	2	1.2	+0.6
Janata Dal (Secular)	4	1.5	−0.9
Revolutionary Socialist Party	2	1.3	−0.1
Kerala Congress Party (Anti-Merger)	−	0.5	+0.5
Indian National League	−	0.2	−0.6
Left Democratic Front–Supported Independents	2	3.2	+1.1
United Democratic Front	**72**	**45.8**	**+3.2**
Indian National Congress	38	26.4	+2.3
Muslim League Kerala State Committee	20	7.9	+0.6
Kerala Congress (Mani)	9	4.9	+1.7
Socialist Janata Democratic	2	1.6	+1.6
Communist Marxist Party	−	0.6	−0.2
Janadhipathiya Samrakshana Samithy	−	1.3	−0.2
Kerala Congress (Bal Murlikrishna)	1	0.7	+0.1
Kerala Congress (Jacob)	1	0.9	+0.9
Kerala Revolutionary Socialist Party (Baby John)	1	0.4	+4.0
United Democratic Front–Supported independents	−	0.1	+0.2

Source: Fourteenth Assembly Elections in Kerala, *Economic and Political Weekly*, 18 June 2011: 135.

In light of the massive seat loss in the 2010 panchayat polls, the performance of the parliamentary left was very impressive in terms of winning seats in the assembly election, though there was an almost 4 percent swing of votes away from the LDF. As a poll survey indicates, neither of the conglomeration of parties witnessed a major shift in its social base: the UDF enjoyed a big lead among Christians and Muslims (constituting 45 percent of the total population) whereas the LDF made up the loss by securing a lead among the Ezhavas (who are Dalits), the rest of the other backward classes, and the scheduled castes. Despite having a solid base among the Ezhavas, the parliamentary left was also charged with its failure to politically involve the Dalit women who are part of "most of the visible forms of public action (such as mass demonstration, strike sit-ins). . . . They remained invisible in both the discourses and the organizational structure of leftist politics at all levels."[58] Nonetheless, a pattern appears to have emerged: the LDF continued to hold its support among the poorer and less educated while the UDF held a lead among the wealthier and more educated.[59] What accounted for massive Christian support for the UDF was "the pronouncement emanating from the religious leadership in its favor."[60] Muslims were alienated because the previous LDF government "adopted a simplistic rationalist approach . . . incognisant of the specific religious atmosphere in those communities."[61] This was certainly a strategic limitation for a party that, by seeking to understand the question of the minority in the classical Marxist class formula, failed to gauge the contextual appeal of Islam in Muslims' identity formation. Hence, there were hardly serious endeavors to ideologically counter clearly religious appeals for political mobilization. The other significant factor that helped the LDF to regain support was certainly the dynamic leadership and clean image of V. S. Achuthanandan, the chief minister of the incumbent government. In the midst of unearthing several scams involving the political bigwigs regardless of party affiliations, Achuthanandan was a great resource for the party that was significantly crippled due to internal squabbles involving the top leadership. Nonetheless, the relatively clean administrative record of the Achuthanandan-led LDF ministry appeared to have consolidated the left base. The numerous scams in which the Congress and its allies, both at the federal and state levels, embroiled themselves "turned out to be a shot in the arm of the left."[62] Furthermore, a sex scandal involving Muslim League leader P. K. Kunhalikutty resurfaced, and the jail sentence of a former UDF leader, R. Balakrishna Pillai, on corruption charges eroded the UDF base to a significant extent. The third factor that influenced the outcome when the traditional bases of the respective coalitions remained more or less stable was the increasing number of unaffiliated voters who expressed their choice on the basis of their on-the-spot assessment of the competitive parties participating in the election. As the field survey confirms, the share of voters not committed to any side was as high as 18 percent of total votes, a clear increase of 5 percent if contrasted with the proportion of unaffiliated voters in the 2006 assembly election.[63] Besides these specific factors that accounted for the left resurgence in the state, by being strongly opposed to the neoliberal development plans and programs, the parliamentary left in Kerala, unlike its West Bengal counterpart, consolidated its pro-people image in pursuance of the Leninist state-led development paradigm. Rather than succumbing to "the fad of privatization, the government turned around loss-making public sector units, started new government ventures to create jobs, revived ailing traditional industries and even took steps to take over a few loss-making private sector companies that had been shut."[64] This was a remarkable ideological stance that halted, to a considerable extent, the left decline in the state. Notwithstanding the internal squabbles over various other issues, the party and the government held identical views in this regard, contrary to what had happened in West Bengal where, as chapter 4 will show, the Left Front equivocally supported the neoliberal design of economic development by providing enormous concessions to private capital to solicit investments. Here perhaps lies the reason why it was not a cakewalk for the UDF, which apparently swayed the public opinion in its favor, as the results of the 2009 Lok Sabha poll and 2010 local elections confirm. By pursuing a well-thought-out pre-election campaign plan highlighting its achievements within the constraints of liberal democracy and by devising context-specific and cadre-driven election strategies, the parliamentary left in Kerala not only sustained but also expanded its traditional social base, as the poll outcome clearly shows.

CHANGING TEXTURE OF THE PARLIAMENTARY LEFT

Kerala is probably the only state where communities are highly compartmentalized largely because of the distinctive socio-economic and political processes associated with their formation. Broadly speaking, there are four distinct communities—Syrian Christians, Muslims, Nairs, and Ezhavas—which are separate from each other though there are distinct socio-economic differentiations within each community.[65] Closely linked with the formation of these distinct communal identities were radical social reform movements within all the major communities. These movements included the weakening of the caste-driven hierarchy and prejudiced social practices seeking to permanently segregate those identified as "untouchables"; the breakdown of matrilineal joint family (*taravad*), especially associated with the Nairs; the spread of nationalist and egalitarian ideas since the 1920s; and the spread of class-based trade union and peasant movements.[66]

The ideological texture of the parliamentary left had undergone dramatic changes. Throughout the 1950s and 1960s ideology was identified as an effective instrument for mass mobilization for a socialist revolution. But from the 1980s, the left political parties had almost become accustomed to parliamentary methods of political struggle for inclusive growth and radical socio-economic transformation. There were forceful debates among the parliamentary left on issues of contemporary relevance though neither the CPI nor the CPI (M) or any other political outfit clinging to parliamentary communism avoided major hiccups in their organization by managing differences of opinions within agreeable limits. Since 1980 two major partners of left politics, the CPI (M) and the CPI, have thus not faced any major organizational split. There were instances of disciplinary actions against certain popular leaders from the CPI (M), such as M. V. Raghavan and K. R. Gouri. But the separate political parties, the Communist Marxist Party and the Janathipathiya Samrakshana Samithy (Association for Defense of Democracy), which they formed after being ousted from the party in 1994, hardly became a major force to threaten their parent organization.

Left politics in Kerala since the 1980s provides us with a different picture, which provides striking contrasts with the past. The parliamentary left in Kerala is now represented by the CPI and the CPI (M) along with a handful of socialists belonging to the RSP. Although the CPI remained in power in alliance with the Congress for ten years, it failed to maintain its social base like its counterpart, the CPI (M), which not only sustained but also consolidated its support base both in urban and rural areas. Despite being committed to Marxism–Leninism, the RSP does not appear to be ideologically constrained while choosing its coalition partners: there is thus hardly any ideological incongruity when the RSP agreed to be part of the Congress-led UDF. Since the beginning of the 1980s, by any count, the strongest left political organization in the state is the CPI (M), which is organizationally far better entrenched across the state than either the CPI or the RSP. This explains why this section of the parliamentary left remains a force to reckon with even in contemporary Kerala. On occasions of conflicts between the left parties within the LDF, none of them point out ideological differences as a reason for conflict but rather mere differences in approaching the major issues. This is an interesting strategy that the party has developed to always project the strength of the LDF despite differences among its constituents.

Coalitions in Kerala are no longer governed by ideological differences between the two fronts but rather by strategic calculations for partisan gains. The fight that usually takes place among the partners of the left conglomeration is generally over the allocation of the number of assembly seats before election or over the ministerial berth in the government. Most important, the left–right difference between the two fronts (the LDF and the UDF) is always projected not in terms of ideology but in terms of the policies that they would like to pursue had they been elected to form the government. This is undoubtedly indicative of a transformation of Kerala politics over time. In the social scrutiny of contemporary Kerala politics, ideological differences thus do not seem to matter since the coalition is more of a strategy-based outcome rather than an ideology-driven exercise. This is evident in all the coalition governments that have been constituted since 1960: except for the 1987–1991 LDF rule, these governments enjoyed the backing of supporters representing the interest of Christians, Nairs, Muslims, and Ezhavas, the four major socio-religious groups in Kerala. Since the government has always been a coalition of diverse social interests, the coalition ministry, reflective of such diversities, never failed to include members from each of these communities.[67] Similarly, the creation of the Muslim-majority district of Malappuram in southern Malabar in 1969 when the Marxist-led front ruled the state was meant to address the Muslim grievances, which undoubtedly provided political dividends to the left. So, coalition governments in Kerala truly epitomize not only political pluralism but also cultural diversities that are ingrained in the state's social texture. The willingness to accommodate people with diverse views seems to have consolidated the coalition culture in Kerala. Despite being persuaded by the Marxist class analysis, the parliamentary left never lost sight of Kerala's peculiar communal texture. It is simply impossible to draw an individual out of his or her socio-cultural environment in which he or she is nurtured. Hence the political importance of one's caste or communal identity cannot be rule out; in fact, they are considered critical resources for the parties, as E. M. S. Namboodiripad very strongly emphasized:

> The consciousness of one's caste, sub-caste or religious community is still a strong force exercising its influence on the functioning of even political parties, with no political party being free to dismiss this particular factor in selecting candidates for election, in making appointments to the ministries and so on. The party of the working class with its advanced ideology has also to take account of this factor.[68]

The fundamental point that comes out of the Kerala experiment of coalition is the critical importance of "the politics of accommodation" as a process whereby social fragmentation based on class, religion, or community is "subsumed successfully into transactional politics."[69] This brand of politics has gradually developed organic roots in Kerala because of the prevalence of (i) a distinctive regional identity emphasizing the coexistence of multiple socio-religious identities, (ii) a balance of power among the contending social groups for historical reasons, and (iii) the gradual consolidation of political maturity of mutual respect for political opponents despite being starkly different in class, ethnic, and communal terms.

Despite being drawn on two different ideological predispositions, the UDF and LDF hardly differ from each other at least in policy perspectives: both of these fronts share identical concerns, which perhaps explain the continuity of the same policy regime in Kerala despite changes in government. The clear compatibility of interests between these two fronts, which are just two different labels of governance, is also indicative of the fact that in Kerala the distinction between the left and right seems to have become solely cosmetic and without any substance. Especially in the context of the neoliberal onslaught, the theoretical ideologues of these fronts are persuaded to believe that the neoliberal design will be of no help to the people at large. Unlike its West Bengal counterpart, which enthusiastically endorsed forcible land acquisition for rapid industrialization, the members of the parliamentary left in Kerala did not seem to be as enthusiastic about such a measure as their colleagues elsewhere. Similarly, the Congress and its other UDF partners agreed with the idea but tactfully underplayed its importance in Kerala given the probable mass repercussion against such a policy. As is evident in West Bengal, the failure of the left to gauge the popular mood, which was opposed to forceful land acquisition, caused a disaster for the Left Front in the 2011 election whereas its Kerala counterparts maintained their social base though it lost power to the UDF presumably due to anti-incumbency sentiments. The 2011 election results proved to be one of the closest elections in Kerala's recent political history, with the UDF defeating its arch rival, the LDF, by just four seats.

An analysis of the evolution of the communist party and the parliamentary left in particular reveals that the agency (party) suitably changes its strategy in accordance with inputs from the prevalent socio-economic milieu confirming the contextual roots of radical politics in the state. This is also a theoretical challenge to the effort at providing a uniform conceptual framework to understand the rise and consolidation of the parliamentary left in different parts of India. Undoubtedly, the party is an important instrument to initiate changes at the grassroots in accordance with its ideological predilections, and the parliamentary left played a significant role in creating circumstances demanding radical socio-economic changes at the grassroots. It has thus been argued,

> The policies of the Communist government, combined with the intervention of the Communist Party and mass organizations and the participation of the people, unleashed a process that brought about a shift in the balance of class forces in the state in favour of vast sections of the poor. It is this shift that has eventually enabled Kerala to achieve high levels of social development despite comparatively low levels of material production.[70]

One of the revolutionary steps that the parliamentary left undertook once in power was the 1959 Agrarian Relations Bill, which was later promulgated as an act. Aiming at stopping the eviction of tenants, including the hutment dwellers (*kudikidappukars*)[71] by the landlords, the bill sought to provide tenurial security to all tenants, including the hutment dwellers, *varamdars* (sharecroppers), and even the landless laborers. The bill also provided for the constitution of Land Boards for speedy implementation of these agrarian measures.[72] Once it was made into a law in June 1959, the act not only ended "the economic oppression and the socio-cultural domination of a small minority of the upper castes on the mass of the rural poor, . . . [it also] unleashed a socio-cultural movement . . . against caste domination, outmoded systems of family organization and obscurantist beliefs and practices [defending] the exploitation of the rural masses."[73] Once in power in 1967, seeking to fulfill the electoral pledge, the CPI (M)-led government amended the Kerala Land Reforms Act in 1969, which reconfirmed tenurial rights and the right to purchase land for the hutment dwellers that radically altered the agrarian social complexion because legal rights to this peripheral section not only empowered them but also made them integral to rural society, which so far had ostracized them on the basis of archaic rules defending the system of social prejudices, including untouchability.[74] Furthermore, the speed with which landlordism was abolished in Kerala had no parallel elsewhere in India.[75] The abolition of a rentier class (including absentee landlords) that enjoyed respectability in a caste-ridden society along with giving rights over land to almost 300,000 *kudikidappukars* (hutment dwellers) ushered in a new era of agrarian relations in which social and economic divisions among the rural populace were sought to be reduced.

The legislative measures that the parliamentary left had adopted once in governance were revolutionary since they, along with abolishing feudal landlordism, provided tenurial security to a significant section of those who were associated with land. These were undoubtedly revolutionary steps. By ensuring fixed legal rights to the *kudikidappukars*, the 1969 land legislation brought about radical changes in the rural labor market in which the previous beneficiaries of feudal labor arrangements lost their hegemony. It is debatable whether these measures were revolutionary enough to accomplish the Marxist–Leninist goal. Nonetheless, it can also be said in favor of such earth-shaking legislative measures that they were undoubtedly significant steps toward building an alternative system of production in which relations between the owners of land and those involved in cultivation were sought to be understood differently.

The victories and failures in elections may not always be an appropriate index to understand the strength and weaknesses of left politics in the state. In the context of coalition politics, the election data should not be interpreted as an authoritative source to prove or disprove the real strength of different parties. A large section of people who refrain from active politics have remained very assertive in mobilizing public opinion in the assembly elections since 1987. The popular zeal for voting in elections has not declined despite the campaign that elections may not be an adequate instrument for meaningful socio-economic and political changes. The increasing voter turnout in polls especially since the 1990s has not shown any substantial decline and thus does not confirm the hypothesis that people seem to have lost interest in elections.

THE SOCIAL LEFT AND THE POLITICAL LEFT IN KERALA: DIVERGENCES AND CONVERGENCES

The political history of Kerala since the 1980s reflected the growing divergence between the social left and political left. The parliamentary left appears to have been fully adapted to the changed socio-political environment in which a single-party majority is simply impossible. A coalition is the best possible mechanism to govern in collaboration with those parties with more or less identical ideological preferences. When the left agreed to follow the parliamentary path of democracy as the best available means to bring about social change, it aimed at radically reorienting the parliamentary left toward governance and revolution simultaneously. It was accepted that a parliamentary democratic system and democratic rights were really valuable and gave the masses a chance of advancing to their goal through sweeping socio-economic changes. In its 1964 Party Program, the CPI (M) thus announced:

[The Party] strives to achieve the establishment of people's democracy and socialist transformation through peaceful means. By developing powerful mass revolutionary movement, by combining parliamentary and extra-parliamentary forms of struggle, the working class and its allies will try their utmost to overcome the resistance of the forces of reaction and to bring these transformations through peaceful means.[76]

For the parliamentary left, parliamentary-democratic means appear to be most effective in providing immediate relief to the downtrodden. A socialist revolution seems to be a distant goal. Hence, the best possible option is to utilize the available instrument of political authority toward fulfilling the genuine socio-economic needs of those who are socially and economically peripheral. It was evident in an announcement that the CPI (M) made on the eve of joining the UF in Kerala:

The CPI (M) policy towards participation in state government is because people's democratic government gave the revolutionary fillip and strengthened the mass movement, but did nothing to solve the fundamental economic and political problems of the nation. All they could hope to achieve was "immediate relief" to the people.[77]

To fulfill its new pledge to the people, not only did the parliamentary left participate in democratic elections, but it also formed the government when an opportunity arose. They identified the Congress Party as their foremost enemy in this contest for parliamentary power and charted their course of politics keeping in view Kerala's specific socio-economic profile in which caste and communal considerations remain most crucial in public choice. It is also felt that the parliamentary left may not have adequate numerical strength in the assembly to form a government on its own. Hence the idea of coalition gains salience in the discussion within the party justifying a partnership with likeminded political parties or with those having a more or less identical pro-people socio-economic and political agenda. So, it was a pragmatic choice that the parliamentary communists made in the absence of a full-fledged communist administration in its substantial sense.

The usual pattern of class polarization in a society based on changes in the economic mode of production is a precondition for revolution in classical Marxism. In case of Kerala, the situation was not exactly favorably disposed toward class polarization in the classical Marxist sense given—presumably because of well-entrenched socio-economic interests—caste and communal considerations. The national movement was generally an all-inclusive movement against one common enemy, namely the British. The caste-related social reform movements in the same period also helped delay and appeared to have halted the processes of strong polarization of Kerala society along class lines. In such a context naturally the educated middle class of the upper and lower castes spoke in favor of internal and external reforms. Hence an explanation couched neither exclusively in caste nor class terms does not seem be persuasive in understanding the growth and gradual consolidation of the parliamentary left in Kerala; a large number of non-class factors—such as ethnicity, region, education, among others—were decisive in the formative stages of the Kerala variant of Indian communism. What is thus needed is to conceptualize such a complex texture of left politics in Kerala by drawing on equally complex processes whereby caste and class seem to have been enmeshed in a social reality that cannot be grasped, let alone understood, within the available conventional tools of analysis. With the acceptance of election as a mode of change, voters' social identities became an important consideration. It was not surprising that voters also sought to be mobilized by appealing to the caste/religious affiliation, underplaying significantly their class identities. The importance of the individual vote in elections contributes to a new conceptualization of political representation in which caste and class, instead of being mutually contradictory, seemed to have acted in tandem to reinforce each other. Realizing this social context, the communists revised their strategy from revolution to participation in democratic elections and finally to agreement to share power with political parties having more or less similar ideological priorities since the 1950s. But the gradual abandonment of class politics and revolution in the classical Marxist–Leninist sense by the left parties points out the complex milieu of identity formation in Kerala in the last century. The parliamentary left, being complacent with its electoral success, did not appear to pay much attention to class issues, which was responsible for the growth of a specific socio-economic structure in which religion and caste remained critical to one's self-identity, demonstrating perhaps the failure of the party to act as an agency of change. The party is absorbed in the system in such a way that it seems to have lost its vitality as a vanguard of the people in the Leninist sense of the term.

The growth and gradual consolidation of the parliamentary left in Kerala is also attributed to the increasing numerical strength of the middle class. It was the consequence of a number of radical reforms and struggles led by the communists and a large number of welfare policies in education and health under their initiative. This middle-class formation and its socio-cultural features were completely a product of the political left. In view of its hegemonic presence in the party, the party appears to be a hostage of the middle class. The middle class, representing the bourgeois values and preferences, tends to underplay, if not scuttle, the radical policies meant for the underprivileged, just to maintain its class privileges. Caught in a dilemma, the parliamentary left, which is ideologically favorably disposed toward the underprivileged, is unable to push most of the radical policies presumably because of the class limitations of the leadership. The party has thus no alternative but to situate its politics in a middle-class–dominated society, which is enlarging its sphere of influences while clinging onto some of the fundamental principles of classical Marxism–Leninism in accepting the parliamentary path merely as a transitional phase toward a socialist revolution. The religious/caste polarization and class issues have attained newer meaning in the middle-class–dominated society. The new polarizations happening in the "left-leaning" middle-class society is certainly weakening the Marxist–Leninist foundation of the parliamentary left by forcing it to accept more and more social democratic policies tilted heavily in favor of the middle class and its cohorts.

The emerging new middle class, which cannot be vulnerable to the political party divisions, has become a problem as well as an opportunity for the left politics in the state since the 1990s. The experience of the 1980s shows that the political coalitions formed then did not represent the right-left division of the social sphere. By the 1980s, when the coalition government proved to be a successful experiment at least in providing the state with political (ministerial) stability, the link of the parliamentary left with the grassroots did not appear to be as strong as before, presumably because of the articulation of politics exclusively in election mode. Gone are the days when the communist cadres were intimately connected with the daily struggle that the people at the grassroots always waged for their mere survival. So, the parliamentary left seems to have been "bourgeoisfied" by being appreciative of the liberal democratic path of socio-economic and political changes.

From a typical social point of view, there are two interrelated phases that the parliamentary left confronted in Kerala. First, concerted attempts were made to form class-based organization in a society that is divided across various forms of social identity, including identities driven by caste, region, and religion, which always remained very critical, if not prominent. Having created a stable vote bank for the left in the state, the parliamentary communists seemed to have developed an acceptable ideological platform against a common enemy regardless of differences around one's primordial loyalties, like caste or religion. Second, the next phase began after the euphoria of snatching power from a bourgeois party (Congress) through the ballot was over. It was realized that no substantial socio-economic transformation was possible so long as the parliamentary left concentrated on election as the only mode of change. Moreover, the acceptance of a coalition with other parties despite being ideologically incongruent further diluted the distinctive radical character of the parliamentary left. So, coalition partners were chosen not on the basis of ideological compatibility but on the basis of sheer political calculations for amassing a majority in the assembly to form the government. Ideology is thus generally bypassed to constitute a majority by drawing upon politically expedient arguments. This is true of the parliamentary left and its bête noire, the Congress Party and other political parties with a bourgeois ideological dispensation.

Realizing this, the left political parties, mainly the CPI (M), redefined their strategy and formed a broader front seeking to unite the left and other progressive political forces having rightist inclination, especially those fighting against various forms of social injustice within the typical Gandhian parameters of nonviolent peaceful movements. An important factor that sustains coalition governments comprising not exactly ideologically compatible partners is the articulation of some common socio-political agenda that remains critical in policy formulation once in governance. By making "the liaison committees" integral to their functioning, both the LDF and UDF have sought to institutionalize the practice of consultation and compromise among their constituents.[78] This was the reason that the parliamentary left accepted the nomenclature "left front," which is far more flexible than mere "left" to accommodate a variety of political forces even with conflicting ideological interests to form a coalition of seemingly compatible socio-economic interests. For the parliamentary left, this is perhaps the most difficult challenge: by being tuned to Marxism–Leninism, the parliamentary communists, on the one hand, cannot entirely abdicate class struggle between the rich and the poor; on the other hand, the desire to keep its bête noire UDF out of power necessitates the acceptance of partners for the coalition that are not ideologically similar and also not incompatible. Justification of a progressive politics of pragmatism that focuses on non-class issues is a far more difficult task now for the leading partner of the LDF, CPI (M), than in the past when the communists were devoted to violent class struggle to eradicate the context-driven class differentiations with the support of the peasants and workers. Now, in the context of coalition politics, the class basis appears to have been completely diluted because the parliamentary left does not seem to be rigid in choosing its partners in its struggle for power through ballot. So, the fundamental challenge that the parliamentary left confronts today is not to maintain its ideological purity but to chart out a pragmatic course of action to win elections and form the government. One of the reasons for growing factionalism in the CPI (M) is probably the declining importance of ideology that has become a mere label without much substance in the era of "the politics of accommodation" aimed at maximum political dividends.[79] In the context of the growing acceptance of the neoliberal path of development, the response of the parliamentary left does not seem to be very different from its bourgeois partners. Unlike its West Bengal counterpart, the Kerala left did not show enthusiasm in welcoming the private investors, though there is hardly an innovative left critique of the neoliberal onslaught in its distinctive ideological perspective. Not only is this indicative of the failure of the parliamentary communists to provide a contextual interpretation of neoliberalism and its adverse impact on the people in the periphery but also far more severe consequences of the left being absorbed in the bourgeois system of governance devoting its energy not for its replacement but for making it stronger and more durable.

CONCLUDING OBSERVATIONS

Over a period of seven decades, left politics in Kerala has shown several signs of transition. First, the parliamentary left has undergone significant transformation in Kerala presumably in response to the changing socio-economic reality in which mere ideological claims do not appear to be an effective instrument for political mobilization. What was critical was the delivery of services to the people, and in that respect the left governments seem to have reinvented the processes of parliamentary democracy in which the prevalent political institutions became, at least in popular perception, effective instruments for meaningful socio-economic changes at the grassroots. Of all the major administrative steps, the first was land reform, which not only sought to redistribute the available land but also, more significantly, to abolish landlordism by challenging its ideological basis. The second administrative step was the guarantee of rights to the wage workers, including the hutment dwellers (*kudikidappukars*). The final major step was making the basic services for survival and dignity, especially health and education, which were in shambles in the past, easily available. Second, it is now evident that the parliamentary left may not be adequate to bring about radical socialist revolution; nevertheless, by raising pertinent socio-economic issues and by pointing out the sources of socio-economic difficulties confronting the masses, the parliamentary left, even when in opposition, helped to create a space for public debate and democratic struggle involving various social strata. It is thus not an exaggeration to suggest that the parliamentary left has succeeded in Kerala primarily because the citizens here are "active and organized and also [because] horizontal forms of associations prevail over vertical (clientelistic) forms of association [that always support] encompassing demands that promote the public interest over narrow and fragmented demands of state patronage (rents)."[80] Third, appreciative of Bernsteinian social democracy, the parliamentary left in Kerala continues to remain politically viable presumably because of its success in adopting significant policy decisions that dramatically alter prevalent class relations in favor of the marginalized. This is not a mean achievement in a state that is not demographically as homogeneous as West Bengal or Tripura. Fourth, the ideological support base of the parliamentary left has been less "a function of its governance capacity than its mobilizational capacity."[81] Having found itself periodically in the opposition, the CPI (M) and its allies maintained their grassroots connections through their cadre-supported frontal organizations to continually "reinvigorate [their] mobilizational base and [their] political agenda." To remain politically viable at the grassroots, the parliamentary communists thus "busied themselves with the task of occupying the trenches of civil society, building mass-based organizations, [raising] demands, and cultivating a noisy but effective politics of contention."[82] Finally, in the building of contemporary Kerala, the contribution of the parliamentary left is as critical as its bête noire, the Congress-led UDF. The oft-quoted Kerala model, based on higher social indicators (of longer life expectancy, less infant mortality, higher literacy rate, among others), is a trajectory of experience, driven by "public action"[83] against, in the words of Amartya Sen and Jean Dreze, "the sources of unfreedom," drawn on the considerations of caste, class, and capability deprivations. Public action plays "a central role in economic development and in bringing social opportunities within the reach of the people as a whole."[84] It has been sustained by "The radical commitments of left-leaning governments, on the one hand and of [the] activists . . . , on the other, have done much . . . to guarantee widespread social opportunities in many crucial fields."[85] Besides a well-entrenched public action tradition, Kerala has also special cultural and historical characteristics that remain critical in conceptualizing the social transformation that the state has undergone. Kerala has been fortunate, argue Dreze and Sen, "in having strong social movements that concentrated on educational advancement—along with general emancipation—of the lower castes," and this has been "a special feature of left-wing and radical political movements in the

State."[86] In such a context, political process has also "played an extremely important role in Kerala's development experience, supplementing or supplanting the inherited socio-cultural dynamics."[87] So unlike its counterparts in West Bengal and Tripura, the parliamentary left in Kerala was placed in a socio-historically uniquely textured milieu,[88] sustaining and consolidating the social-democratic zeal of that section of communists that was ideologically persuaded to fulfill their ideological mission through liberal political institutions.

The parliamentary left has also undergone qualitative changes. Gone are those days of ideological discussion and social struggles, which were integral to the left in the past, to put across relevant issues for further debates. Ideology is important so long as it reinforces a political strategy or bolsters the support base. Politics of confrontation of the past is now replaced with (petty) struggles for survival and reform in the present. In this struggle for survival, ideology and memories of a revolutionary past also occasionally appear as important but not as a catalyst. What is thus critical for the leadership is to devise appropriate strategies to gain maximum political mileage in competitive parliamentary politics. So, the poll outcomes are not reflective of an ideological battle but are mere indications of how effective a particular strategy became in a specific context. As will be shown in chapter 4, since the elections are now primarily strategy driven, the role of party managers has suddenly become very significant. By making effective strategies to attract votes for the party, these managers remain most critical during the preparation of the election manifesto, which invariably ignores the grassroots inputs to accommodate the strategy-driven statements. There thus appears an unbridgeable gulf between the organization and the leadership, which is apparently being swayed by the party managers and conveniently disregards the genuine socio-economic inputs from the grassroots. The result is evident in the growing decline of the parliamentary left as an ideology-driven effective political force that, instead of being engaged in radical social, economic, and political transformation, concentrates on securing political power through the ballot.

3

Parliamentary Left in West Bengal: Organizational Hegemony Established through an Ideological Churning

THE PARLIAMENTARY LEFT captured political power in West Bengal in 1977 and ruled the state until 2011 when it was trounced by a united opposition, led by All India Trinamul Congress. On the basis of their pro-people legislative measures, especially tenurial security to the sharecroppers, besides adopting various ameliorating measures for the marginalized, the Left Front government maintained its popularity among the voters, especially in rural areas. Given its special care for the villagers, the ruling party never become popular in urban West Bengal, which always preferred political parties other than their left counterparts. In the context of globalization, especially since 1994, the parliamentary communists agreed to private investment for industrial development, which, it was believed, would ensure jobs for the urban youth and generate income for the state. The adoption of the 1994 industrial policy that allowed land acquisition for industrialization was governed by this consideration. The result was evident in the poll outcome of the 2006 state assembly election when the Communist Party of India (Marxist; CPI [M])-led Left Front not only trounced its opposition almost completely, it also won more than two-thirds of the seats in the assembly. This was the best electoral performance of the parliamentary left in Indian elections held so far. This chapter, by making an in-depth analysis of the 2006 election results, seeks to provide a detailed account of the processes that acted critically in sustaining the electability of the parliamentary left and in expanding its support base in urban areas where it failed so far. The aim here is to understand the changing nature of the left in Indian politics that did not appear to be initially enthusiastic about neoliberal economic reforms since they were contrary to the classical Marxist–Leninist ideological position. In the changed environment of globalization, the left however did not find it ideologically incongruent to welcome private capital if it contributed to the rejuvenation of the economy, which meant new sources of income and improved well-being for the people. Hence, for the left, there was hardly a contradiction between the copybook ideology and invitation to private investors, which paid rich dividends to the ruling left conglomerations for a record seventh time in a row.

The 2006 Assembly election in West Bengal is also remarkable at least for two fundamental reasons. First, the outcome of the poll clearly shows the invincibility of the Left Front conglomeration in West Bengal in the light of perhaps the fairest election conducted in the state so far, under the surveillance of the Election Commission of India. Second, the 2006 election will also be remembered because this was the poll in which the Left Front political leadership redefined Marxism by adapting to the neoliberal design of development to accept foreign direct investment (FDI) as nothing inimical to fundamental Marxist principles. The redefined Marxism paid perhaps the richest political dividends to the Left Front candidates in terms of votes that is also suggestive of its acceptability among those who matter in elections, namely, the voters. A contrast with Kerala may not completely be out of place because Marxist-led Left Democratic Front (LDF) in Kerala that won the 2006 election continues to uphold the classical Marxist paradigm and thus the acceptance of FDI amounts to dilution of the basic ideological belief. Ideology may not have been decisive in Kerala because the electoral victory of the LDF is also attributed to the anti-incumbency factor that ruined the chances of the incumbent Congress-led United Democratic Front government in 2006. This chapter is not merely a study of the election in West Bengal; its aim is also to show the growing popularity of the Left Front coalition due to a specific ideological twist that the Marxists had articulated while campaigning for votes in their favor. By drawing on the processes of election and its outcome, the chapter also concentrates on the specific texture of the political at the state level with reference to the issues that may not acquire salience, let alone viability, either in different states or at the national level. This chapter is therefore significant not only in terms of its content but also in arguing that the texture of the political can never be uniform in India presumably because of the well-entrenched diversities shaping the country's society, economy, and polity.

SETTING THE SCENE

The 2006 elections in five states in India (West Bengal, Kerala, Tamil Nadu, Assam, and Pondicherry) confirm that the texture of Indian politics had undergone radical changes. It was established beyond doubt that the era of single-party rule was over though the juggernaut of the Left Front was unstoppable in West Bengal. Besides almost completely decimating the opposition in the state, the Left Front constituents, especially its leading partner, the CPI (M), made significant inroads in Calcutta and other peripheral towns across various age groups. In Kerala, the LDF replaced the Congress-led United Democratic Front by following the rules of musical chairs as it were. The voters' preference was for a coalition government, led by the LDF in the 2006 assembly election. In Tamil Nadu, the Dravida Munnetra Kazhagam–led conglomeration that included the Congress as well swept the polls, reducing the ruling coalition's numerical strength in an assembly of 234 seats to only sixty-nine. The story was not different in Assam where the Congress-led alliance defeated the competing alliance, led by the Asom Gana Parishad. The poll outcomes clearly cannot be grasped in a uniform way. Because the socio-political economic context differs from one state to another, explanations also vary. Nonetheless what the poll outcome had confirmed was the growing importance of coalitions as the most critical factor in electoral victory.

By being most durable, the Left Front was a class by itself. Besides its ideological compatibility, what cemented the bond among the Left Front partners was their opposition to the "communal" Bharatiya Janata Party (BJP) and its allies. Here lies a chord of unity with other coalitions of parties that fought the elections in four different states other than West Bengal. Although regional parties remained crucial in these assembly elections, they were clearly divided according to their affiliations with the two pan-Indian political parties, namely, the BJP and the Congress. The electoral scene in West Bengal was different in the sense that the Left Front, despite being part of the Congress-led United Progressive Alliance (UPA) in Delhi, was opposed to the Congress in the state. The 2006 West Bengal poll outcome was more or less well anticipated. Yet, this election was a watershed in West Bengal politics with far-reaching political consequences not only for the Left Front leadership but also for the state that seemed to have eschewed the orthodox Marxist state-directed development paradigm. In theoretical terms, the Left Front was closer to the western European social-democratic path as some major policy decisions regarding industrial revival in the state of the newly elected government clearly indicate. This did not happen overnight because the poll outcome was also indicative of the ideological salience of the ruling conglomeration in contrast with other contending political parties though the results might not be a perfect index of popularity of the winning group due largely to the obvious limitations of the application of the "majority principle" in the electoral verdict.

THE PROACTIVE ELECTION COMMISSION OF INDIA

The 2006 West Bengal Assembly election was not at all different from earlier elections since the electoral outcome remained identical. The Left Front returned to power with a comfortable majority. Yet, this election was perhaps most dramatic in a number of ways. First, for the first time, the Election Commission took charge of the election in the state in an unprecedented manner. The state government was largely, if not completely, bypassed for its alleged partisan role in elections. Two reasons account for such an "abusive role." The first reason was that the incumbent Left Front government was charged with manipulating the voters' list, and hence those opposed to the ruling authority called upon the Election Commission to intervene. One of the charges that gained currency was the inclusion of "bogus" voters. The Election Commission found a large number of them in various districts. During the clean-up operation, an observer found 1.3 million false names[1] in the list of voters and struck them off. Hence the charge seemed authenticated, and the media thus attributed the sustained electoral victory of the Left Front to these "bogus voters." The stringent measures that the Election Commission undertook however alienated a large number of people who found them "unwarranted" and "undemocratic" because in correcting the voters' list, the commission acted in a "high-handed" manner. One commentator noted, "The state was virtually under the control of the EC [Election Commission]. Imported police and para-military personnel penetrated all parts of the state; route marches by them were organized in every constituency, sometimes twice a day."[2]

The Election Commission seemed to have left no stone unturned to conduct a free and fair poll in the Left Front–ruled West Bengal. The Election Commission was made to believe that the law and order situation in West Bengal was as bad as that of Bihar. Given its remarkable success in Bihar, the commission resorted to the same strategy to contain "electoral malpractices" that appeared to have contributed to continuous Left Front victory.

The second reason that the commission was charged with playing an abusive role in the election was that, to hold a free and fair poll, the commission decided to conduct the poll in five fairly dispersed dates stretching across almost two months. Again, the Bihar formula was accepted in the sense that the election was held under strict surveillance of the coercive instrument of the state. The commission requisitioned police and para-military forces from outside the state simply because the state police did not appear to be reliable. Because the dates were dispersed, it was possible to get an adequate number of them to supervise the voting on the day of the election. The state was under seige as it were. It is true that, due to their presence, this election was almost free from electoral violence involving any of the contending political parties. Voters cast their votes without any threat.

Second, this election was unique from previous elections because voters were disturbed by the difficulties associated with accommodating the large contingent of these forces before the election. A large number of public buildings, including schools, colleges, and libraries, were taken over, disturbing the normal life of the areas in which elections were held. Even the National Library in the capital city of Kolkata was not spared. Instead of raising hopes, the very presence of such a huge contingent of coercive forces caused consternation and anger among the common voters. In fact, the existence of these forces was never appreciated by the voters; the very idea of being disciplined by force disturbed Bengali sensibilities, as an on-the-spot survey reveals. The voters expressed resentment on the grounds that "the entire Bengali *jati*" was blamed for the misdeeds of a handful of miscreants.[3] The highhanded manner in which the Election Commission dealt with the poll preparations created an impression that it considered the people of West Bengal "a suspect species." Perhaps this also contributed to the close to 7 percent increase over 2001 in the number of people who voted. They voted, as Ashok Mitra euphorically suggested, "with their feet against the innuendoes dropped by the commission."[4]

The continuity of the Left Front government in West Bengal for more than three decades seems to have fed the allegation for "electoral malpractices." This was what drove the commission to intervene. Following the discovery of "bogus voters" in various parts of the state, the apprehension that the voters' list was manipulated gained currency. It was also discovered that, with its enthusiasm for a free and fair poll, the Commission also struck off names of a large number of genuine voters who surfaced only during the election.[5]

How was it possible for the commission to emerge as a "messiah" in a state that is politically conscious and largely free from prejudices, linked with ascriptive identities? One of the reasons was surely the media hype that arose once the commission-appointed observers emerged on the scene. Wherever the observers went, the leading newspapers gave extensive coverage of what they discovered as "bogus voters."[6] The purpose was to authenticate the allegation of "manipulation" of the voters' list. By so doing, the media actually upheld the charges of the parties in opposition that the sustained electoral popularity of the Left Front was largely possible due to "extraordinary corrupt practices at all levels" that made "scientific rigging," as it is euphemistically defined, possible. The local bureaucracy was held responsible. As a former bureaucrat argues, "Either they slipped up negligently or more probably they connived stealthily with the interested political groups to manipulate the voters' list in their favor."[7] That the commission was persuaded was evident by the guidelines that it issued: These were as follows: (i) a state where the proportion of the registered voters is higher than the national average is likely to have more bogus voters; (ii) if the proportion of votes cast to the aggregate number of votes registered in a constituency or a polling station is higher than the national average, the poll in these constituencies or polling booths requires careful attention; and (iii) if a candidate obtains votes of 85 percent to 90 percent in any constituency or polling booth, the counting must be done most rigorously, and, if necessary, a repoll may be advised.[8] Despite strong criticism of these guidelines by the Left Front leadership, what drove the commission while formulating them was the desire to eradicate the alleged electoral malpractices, which had presumably gained ground during the long tenure of the Left Front government in West Bengal. The 2006 assembly election was thus a clear break with the past in two ways: (i) the deep involvement of the commission in conducting the poll was unprecedented and provoked mass consternation both during the campaign and its aftermath for having created "conditions of severe surveillance" in which elections were conducted; and (ii) as a result, elections that always were "a joyous celebration of democracy" hardly remained so because "the EC [Election Commission] was determined to smother that joy."[9]

THE POLL OUTCOME

The 2006 election was historic, if for nothing else, for "the zeal shown by the Election Commission in monitoring this election [lent] the result a special meaning."[10] There were three major coalitions of parties in the electoral fray. Besides the Left Front, the other two coalitions of parties were the Trinamul-led alliance and the conglomeration that formed around the Congress. As the results show, the Left Front was far ahead of other contending political parties both in terms of the number of legislative seats and the share of votes. In fact there had been a steady increase in these counts since 1996.[11] Unlike the Left Front, the opposition experienced "a poll debacle," as it were, because of the dramatic decline both in numerical legislative strength and share of votes. This was certainly a significant factor in the last West Bengal assembly, which radically altered the political landscape of the "left bastion" in India. Table 3.1 is illustrative.

As the tally of seats and percentage of the share of popular votes in Table 3.1 reveals, the Left Front victory was most impressive though the most spectacular win was the 1987 assembly election when, in a tally of 251 seats of the Left Front (out of a total of 294 assembly seats), the CPI (M) won as many as 187 seats. Yet, the 2006 poll results evoked

TABLE 3.1

The 2006 West Bengal Assembly Results

Parties	Seats Won, 2001	Seats Won, 2006	Percentage of Votes, 2001	Percentage of Votes, 2006
Left Front	199	235	48.4	50.2
CPI (M)	143	176	36.6	37.0
CPI	7	8	1.8	2.1
AIFB	25	23	5.6	5.7
RSP	17	20	3.4	3.7
WBSP	4	4	0.7	0.7
RJD	–	1	0.7	0.1
DSP		1	0.4	0.1
Independent (LF)		2	0.4	0.1
Congress	26	21	7.9	15.0
Trinamul Congress	60	30	30.7	26.3
GNLF	3	3	0.5	0.1
JKP (N)	–	1	0.2	0.2
Independent	9	4	5.0	3.8

Notes: CPI (M) = Communist Party of India (Marxist). CPI = Communist Party of India. AIFB = All India Forward Bloc. RSP = Revolutionary Party of India. WBSP = West Bengal Socialist Party. RJD = Rashtriya Janata Dal. DSP = Democratic Socialist Party. Independent (LF) = Independent (Left Front). GNLF = Gorkha National Liberation Front. JKP (N) = Jharkhand Party (Naren).

Source: Drawn from *The Hindu*, 16 May 2006; *Frontline*, 2 June 2006: 6.

surprise because of the dramatic decline of the opposition parties. There was hardly an opposition worth its name.

THE POSSIBLE EXPLANATION

The poll outcome in West Bengal was not dramatic in the sense that it was more or less anticipated. What was surprising was the dramatic decline of the numerical strength of the opposition parties. The stringent measures of the Election Commission to ensure "a level playing field for all" in the state—resulting in the highest voter turnout—denied the opposition the chance "to explain away the defeat by pointing to the election malpractices."[12] From the point of view of the Left Front, the verdict was, as commonly defined, both a change and continuity. Given the retention of power in the Writers' Building (the state secretariat), the 2006 poll was clearly a continuity. But with the growing importance of the new leadership in the Front following the retirement of the previous chief minister, Jyoti Basu, in 2000, this election had also endorsed its new face. Not only was the new leadership critical to the coalition, the newly first-time elected members of the assembly became crucial in sustaining the Front government as an effective pro-people instrument. The challenge before the parliamentary left was to retain the new constituencies of support along with its traditional social base.

THE INVINCIBILITY OF THE PARLIAMENTARY LEFT IN RURAL BENGAL

The CPI (M)-led Left Front's reformist orientation enabled it to pursue some "redistributive programs"[13] without fundamentally alienating property-owning productive groups. As a system of governance, panchayats had radically altered the structure of power in rural West Bengal where 70 percent of the state's population lives. With the presence of the Left Front activists in every key institution at the grassroots—ranging from the governing bodies of credit societies to the primary schools—the government was able to build and sustain a well-entrenched network among the rural population. This led to the consolidation of what was identified as "governmental locality" that signified "the presence of government in a locality as an institution [and the] locality's presence in government as a process." Such governmentalization of rural localities "generated a new and innovative correspondence within and between village representative bodies and tied them with the Assembly House and the Writers' Buildings."[14] In such a symbiotic network between the villagers and the Front activists[15] lies the explanation as to why the Left Front retained its grip in rural West Bengal without sustaining any substantial losses.

The situation in rural West Bengal was not as extreme or dismal as some of the political commentators seem to think. Much of the economic change in rural West Bengal since 1977 was made possible because of a significant political process, initiated and carried forward by the Left Front government through legislative action. Important here was the devolution of power—including considerable financial powers—to the elected panchayats. The achievement of the Left Front in the rural areas in particular—its land reform measures, the registration of sharecroppers (*operation barga*), and the panchayati system—ushered in a significant process of radical changes in the political layout of the state.[16] Of these two major legislative steps, the operation barga was "a milestone, a wise strategic investment, which . . . became the fulcrum of the Left Front's continued existence at the helm of power."[17] With the protection of tenurial rights of the 1.3 million (almost 96 percent) out of a total of 2 million sharecroppers in the state[18] and formal devolution of power to the institutions of governance at the grassroots, the left rural support base was consolidated further. As the outcome of the 1978 panchayati elections shows, the Left Front won 69 percent of seats with a share of more than 54 percent of total votes. The change was also visible in the leadership: the landlords, rich peasants, and moneylenders who "had been the bedrock of the erstwhile Congress rule" were replaced by "marginal farmers, primary and secondary school teachers, landless agricultural labourers, women and Dalits."[19] The parliamentary left thus gave the sharecroppers a legal identity that was further consolidated by breaking the age-old domination of landlords in rural governance. Undoubtedly, it was an effective piece of legislation that unleashed the processes whereby the underprivileged started reclaiming their rights with dignity—the impact of which was evident in the gradual metamorphosis in the rural power structure that pushed out the wealthy to accommodate the newly awaken marginalized sections.

So, Operation Barga, together with a strong political commitment to implementing land reforms, ushered in a process of genuine democratic participation by the rural poor in the remaking of their lives and their socio-economic environment. Although the enactment of the Seventy-Third Amendment Act was a significant step toward revamping the panchayati institutions in the country, the Left Front initiated the process as early as 1977–1980 by giving pachanyats substantial power for local development.[20] Since the programs for poverty alleviation, sponsored by the union government in New Delhi or other agencies, were closely supervised through the party hierarchy, they were better implemented in West Bengal than in any other states. Such a supervisory role developed and sustained a constant interaction with the people at the grassroots which, inter alia, accounted for the consolidation of the Left Front in rural Bengal. Furthermore, with its long tradition of political mass mobilization and struggles—in championing the cause of the working class, urban and rural workers, the poor peasants, and the middle-class employees—not only did the Left Front sustain but also gradually expanded its organizational network within the state.[21] Table 3.2 shows that the Left Front appeared invincible in rural Bengal.

It is thus evident that Operation Barga and the panchayati raj system of governance set in motion "a process of building indispensable political tools"[22] that ensured continuous electoral success for the party so long as the opposition remained fractured and disunited. This is one side of the coin. The story of the Left Front ascendancy can also be told in a different way. The fact that the ruling party candidates had won unopposed in a large number of panchayat constituencies[23] was indicative of a dangerous political

TABLE 3.2

Share of the Left Front Votes in the Panchayats and Zila Parishads

Year	Gram Panchayat	Panchayat Samiti	Zila Parishad
1978	70.3	77.0	71.5
1983	61.2	66.2	62.2
1988	72.3	79.0	73.5
1993	64.4	72.8	65.7
1998	56.1	67.1	58.1
2003	65.8	74.1	67.2

Source: Computed from the data available from *Paschim Banger Panchayat Nirvachan Tathya O Samiksha* (1978–2003), Bharater Communist Party, Paschim Banga Rajya Committee.

trend that hardly allowed opposition to crystallize simply because they would not dare "to provoke a situation in which they would dare the combined wrath of the [party] cadres and police."[24] Furthermore, contrary to the Left Front claim, as a study reveals, the downward devolution of power gave way to the rising middle sections of the rural society who now controlled the panchayats. As a result, these bodies became "synonymous with the elected popular bureaucracy."[25] What it suggests is the concentration and centralization of power in the panchayats in the name of ushering in an era of participatory democracy in the real sense. Despite the overwhelming electoral and organizational presence of the poorer sections of rural Bengal, the process that seemingly crippled the panchayats seemed to have been strengthened presumably because of the rigid party control over these rural centers of democratic administration. Governed by what is known as a political-organizational perspective, the CPI (M), for instance, justified hegemonic control of the party in terms of an ideological goal of "democratic centralism." That the party cannot be bypassed is clearly spelled out by the CPI (M) state committee:

> Democratic participation [does] not mean acting at will. It means [that] the activation of panchayats in accordance with the principles of and ideals of the party. The basic issue involved here is giving party leadership to panchayats. This leadership consists of (a) political leadership and (b) organizational leadership. . . . The political leadership of the party is established only when people in their own experience accept the political perspective of the party as their own. Even though decisions may be correct, they are not automatically translated into actions. We need to activate our activists and the masses for carrying out our decisions. . . . The party has a definite aim. Panchayat activities should be conducted in such a way that they conform to the basic goals of the party.[26]

There is thus no doubt that the panchayats in West Bengal were governed by the party in power. To translate the party perspective, the CPI (M) State Committee constituted, at the level of panchayats, a guiding cell (*parichalan committee*) that was entrusted with the task of steering the panchayats in accordance with the directives of the party high command. The party therefore commanded:

> All elected party members of panchayat samiti and zila parishad will act under the respective committees. Generally the local and zonal committees of the party will look after the gram panchayat samitis. The final decision at each level will be taken by the Parichalan Committee of the party, although the elected members of the party may offer views if they are not satisfied with the decision.[27]

The growing hegemony of the party provides, on the one hand, the organizational support to the panchayats; it also, on the other, strengthens the party functionaries who, despite being "outsiders," continued to remain significant in the panchayat bodies simply because of their assigned role in the party directives. So, centralization of power actually strikes at the very root of the devolution of power. What thus emerged gradually was the politics of patronage and populist policies. Furthermore, because political parties competed in panchayat elections and the winner had direct control over the substance of the village level plan and the selection of the beneficiaries, "the panchayat system [invariably] indulges in politicization of the planning process and the implementation of the public projects."[28] This probably explains the story of death and malnutrition in Amlashole in West Midnapur; in the tribal belts of Purulia, Nadia, and eastern part of Murshidabad; in the tea-garden areas of Cooch Bihar; and the fringe areas of Dinajpur. Panchayats failed and the party functionaries appropriated these grassroots institutions to fulfill their selfish goal, as an important Left Front cabinet minister confessed that "the local panchayat leaders squandered the Central government funds for development to buy liquor and build club houses."[29] Apart from these specific examples, the overall economic conditions of the state did not appear to be very impressive, as the 2004–2005 India Development Report shows in Table 3.3.

In electoral terms, the human development index, as shown in Table 3.3, does not seem to be significant. The juggernaut of the Left Front seemed unstoppable, as the poll verdict suggests. In fact, the Left Front had further consolidated its position in rural Bengal. In the economically backward districts of Bankura and South Dinajpur, the Left Front trounced other contending parties by winning all the thirteen and five seats, respectively. Even in the district of Burdwan that always remained the center-of-left consolidation, the poll verdict hardly made a dent in the left support base. The Left Front increased its tally from twenty-one in 2001 to twenty-three out of the twenty-six seats, with the CPI (M) alone capturing twenty-one. The poll outcome was an upshot of sustained pro-people activities that the Front government undertook since it captured power in 1977. By using the state power for the social transformation of the marginalized classes, a commentator thus argues, "the government has created a climate of security [for these classes] and has provided more for the poor than other Governments have."[30] What explains the

TABLE 3.3

Economic Conditions of West Bengal

	1993–1994				1999–2002			
	Extremely Poor	Very Poor	Moderately Poor	Poor Below Poverty Line	Extremely Poor	Very Poor	Moderately Poor	Poor Below Poverty Line
West Bengal	1.4	13.6	27.6	41.2	1.1	10.8	20.9	31.7
All India	2.0	14.7	22.1	36.8	0.8	8.2	18.3	26.5

Source: Kirit S. Parikh and R. Radhakrishna, eds., *India Development Report, 2004–05* (New Delhi: Oxford University Press, 2005).

continuity of the Left Front is the success in integrating the governmental ameliorating pro-people policies with the strategies of political mobilization. By contextualizing the Marxist ideology, The CPI (M)-led coalition shifted its social base from "being a party of the industrial proletariat" to that of marginal farmers, sharecroppers, and the landless poor. This class base was "carefully stitched together to forge a coalition of socially marginalized groups that included Dalits, Adivasis and Muslims." The sustained viability of the Left Front for more than three decades can be attributed to "this unique class-community coalition" that made the Left Front invincible in rural Bengal.

THE BRAND BUDDHA[31] IN URBAN BENGAL

Apart from its land reform programs, the Left Front appeared to have created a permanent base in urban (and in rural) areas by drawing upon the federal arrangement, which is tilted in favor of the center. As the states have to depend largely on financial grants from the center for most of their developmental plans, they are reduced to mere structural units of a union "that cannot be federal simply because it is rooted in the imperial 1935 Government of India Act."[32] Constitutionally approved agencies add to the process of the concentration of power in the central government. For instance, the Planning Commission is a centralizing agency with hegemonic control over the finances. The governor is another constitutional agency, acting largely on behalf of the central government. Seeking to review the center–state relations, the Left Front government undertook a campaign when it came to power in 1977. One of the outcomes of this campaign was certainly the appointment of the Sarkaria Commission in 1980. The issue of the center–state relations has however gradually lost its significance in the Left Front poll campaign presumably because none of the post-1989 central governments had the numerical strength in the Lok Sabha to completely ignore the state governments. The situation appears to be favorable for a thorough review of the center–state relations with the installation of a coalition government at the center following the 1999 Lok Sabha poll in which the support of the constituent regional parties was crucial for its survival.

The 2006 outcome was illustrative of the success of the Brand Buddha in expanding the Left Front support bases even among those who never stood by the left. The results in Kolkata demonstrated that the poll verdict was clearly tilted in favor of the beleaguered left. Kolkata was never the left stronghold, and the anti-incumbency factors always remained critical in voters' preference. In 2006, the Front victory in ten constituencies in Kolkata and its suburbs translated to growing popularity among urban voters. Similarly, results in the industrial belts of Howrah and Hooghly where the Left Front obtained a majority of the assembly seats confirmed its popularity. In Howrah, the Front won fourteen out of sixteen seats, out of which CPI (M) captured eleven. Of the nineteen seats in Hooghly, the Left Front obtained seventeen, of which the CPI (M)'s share was thirteen.

There is no denying the importance of the party organization in the Left Front victory. What was new in the 2006 election was the proactive role of the chief minister, Buddhadeb Bhattacharjee, the new face of the Front and symbol of continuity and change. The efforts at industrialization and securing investments for the state by Bhattacharjee seemed to have paid electoral dividends to the Front that he led. The message that the new leadership gave by focusing more on industrialization, urban infrastructure, and urban middle classes had "kindled the hopes and aspirations of the new voters."[33] In fact, the principal aim of the new government was to adopt policies and programs for developing both the rural and urban Bengal to arrest the economic degeneration of the state that remained the industrial hub of the country in the recent past.

While delineating his priorities as the chief of the Front government, Bhattacharjee provided a blueprint for the future that he prefaced by saying, "The message that the people have given us with their verdict is that we should give even more importance to what we are doing and we have to succeed."[34] In this press meeting, he identified three important tasks that the Front had to accomplish to fulfill the expectation of the voters: first, to continue to accord importance to agriculture sector because that was what sustained the economy in a big way; second, to match the improvement in agriculture by similar growth in the industrial sector, which was possible if equal importance was given to industrial growth and investment in industries that created jobs and contributed to state's overall economic growth; and third, to ensure an overall growth of the state and to take care of those who were still below the poverty line.[35]

It was a tightrope walk for the chief minister who was clearly following an ideological path that resembles the European social-democratic practices. By adopting a guarded approach to liberalization, Bhattacharjee was trying to strike a balance between those hardcore supporters who dismissed "economic liberalization" as bourgeois conspiracy and revisionists who were willing to endorse the neoliberal ideology so long as it contributed to the economic well-being of the state. This was evident in his first press meeting after the announcement of the poll results. Emphatically arguing that "not everything about liberalization is right," Bhattacharjee further elaborated that "we are against the policy of hire and fire of labour and arbitrary privatization." Despite his firm commitment to socialism, that he was a pragmatic leader was evident when he mentioned that "we cannot avoid liberalization because we live in a time where we have to work according to the market conditions."[36] He was in favor of inviting "private capital" for industrial rejuvenation of West Bengal because "this is the mandate [that] the Left Front cannot ignore."[37] He was critical of "isolationism," which was, according to him, responsible for the breakdown of the former Soviet Union. In conformity with "the Chinese reformist ideology," Bhattacharjee never found any contradiction between the private or even the foreign sector with the state sector when the primary mission was to "ensure economic well-being of the people." Besides his social-democratic economic stances, he was favorably inclined toward multiparty democracy which was, according to him, most appropriate in a diverse society like India. Believing in the dictum of "let hundred flowers blossom," the chief minister redefined the CPI (M) ideology by being critical to "rigidity and parochialism" in the party,[38] which explained its success in urban areas, particularly in Kolkata and its vicinity. As the poll results show, in greater Kolkata, out of a total of forty-eight seats, the Left Front increased its tally to thirty-three in contrast with its tally of twenty-two seats in the assembly election that was held in 2001. The main loser was the Trinamul Congress, which was routed in as many as twelve constituencies where it won in the 2001 election. Now, the Mamata-led Trinamul Congress retained only eleven seats from greater Kolkata. One of the reasons for such a reversal was certainly a clear vote swing away from the Trinamul Congress.[39]

There was thus no doubt that the Brand Buddha reinvented the CPI (M)-led Left Front by seeking to adapt the governmental ideology to the changed environment.[40] This electoral victory was a significant turning point for the Left Front that could not afford to be an ideological monolith in the radically altered global circumstances with the apparent triumph of "the end of history phase." The Front's ascendancy was also indicative of peculiar state-centric social, economic, and political processes that perhaps explain why only the parliamentary left had survived in the midst of the strong storms of anti-incumbency that swept the rest of the country.[41] Also, the unassailable popularity of Buddhadeb Bhattacharjee was also evident by the fact that he created history by trouncing his opponent by a massive margin of 58,130 votes that also shows the growing importance of the Brand Buddha in West Bengal politics.

AN OVERALL ASSESSMENT

The sustained electoral victory of the parliamentary left in West Bengal was illustrative of its ability to sway the voters, both in rural and urban areas, toward the constituent of the Left Front government. Historically, the left rose to prominence by taking up agrarian issues. Naturally, land reforms and rural development were on the top of the agenda when the Left Front came to power in 1977. These two—identified as the policy of "walking on two legs"—were closely interrelated, and the success in one depended crucially on the success in the other. Appreciative of a developmental social democratic ideology, the left emphasized "the preservation of democratic institutions on the one hand and the use of state power for facilitating 'development with redistribution' on the other."[42] By being "reformist," the left sought support of both the middle peasants and rural poor by simultaneously focusing on fair agricultural prices and marginal land reforms. Operation Barga was not a radical agrarian measure but an effort to register the *bargadars* (sharecroppers) so that they enjoy the protection of the prevalent legislations, including security of tenure and modified rents. This was an intelligent legal enactment that instantaneously created a solid base for the left among the numerically strong middle peasants who also worked as sharecroppers to make both ends meet. There was hardly any backlash from the propertied section presumably because they had neither the government support nor the resources to take on the rising middle peasants. Operation Barga involved registration of 1.4 million *bargadars,* and through such a reformist measure, about 1.1 million acres of land was permanently brought under the control of *bargadars* and their right to cultivate was secured.[43] So, the left became unassailable because of a tactical move to control the propertied and inspired the middle peasants with legal entitlements "to pursue incremental reforms within the constraints of democratic-capitalism."[44]

There is no doubt that the sustained left rule in West Bengal was largely due to the ability of the parliamentary left to penetrate the rural areas and forge much deeper organizational links with the vast majority at the grassroots. Not only did the legal endorsement of Operation Barga accord permanent rights to the sharecroppers, it also made them integral to the local political leadership. It has thus been argued:

> The Marxists' mass support seems rather to have been a result of the manner in which they sought to form their political authority. It seems to have been a matter of the Marxists' ability not only to penetrate the rural areas as organizations, but their ability to establish themselves as major actors in what may be seen as traditional village politics.[45]

With the establishment of the left rule in West Bengal, the socio-politically marginalized sharecroppers seemed to have found a powerful ally in the left parties who gradually became their "patrons" in their fight against socio-economically vested interests in rural West Bengal. In sustaining the patron–client network, the role of the cadres remained most critical. By encouraging them to work under the overall direction of the party, the cadres were expected to take up "local issues, issues that agitated the peasants, and to exploit these for mobilizational purposes."[46] So, the parliamentary left represented a kind of politics that was "both new and old at the same time"[47]—new because it created a new political platform for the sharecroppers to stand out in rural power set-up and old because it also encouraged the cadre-sponsored leadership to act as patrons to those supportive of the left diktat. Furthermore, the left hegemony was consolidated by "a powerful literate section in rural society" comprising primary and secondary school teachers who hold a distinctive place in rural politics because of their locational advantages; these school teachers almost always "placed themselves in various committees, established personal contacts and developed interests, not always consistent with the declared goals of the party."[48] With the consolidation of constituencies of support, the left, especially the CPI (M), sustained an organizational grip over the rural voters. Unlike the Congress Party, which the left replaced in 1977, the sustained popularity of the parliamentary left in at least electoral politics was thus an account of the left endeavor "to develop the network of patron–client relationship among the state government employees, trade unions, the intelligentsia and academics, the panchayats and cooperatives [that] established a monolithic identity for the party in power."[49] Besides incremental land reforms that did not disturb the class balance in rural West Bengal, the parliamentary communists maintained their hegemony by creating parallel institutions of political authority through the party, which always acted as a bridge between the leadership and the supporters at the grassroots. There is no doubt that, by reorganizing the rural power structure, the incumbent Left Front government empowered a specific section of the rural population that developed vested interests over a period of time, and, in view of their critical role in the party organization, the leadership was restrained to take any step to undermine their importance, which ultimately led to dissent not only within the party but also among the supporters. Furthermore, the party's well-defined policies for those having connections with land as sharecroppers led to deradicalization of the objective for which the left fought. Given the hegemonic presence of the sharecroppers and those supporting landed interests, it was not possible for the parliamentary left to pursue some of its radical goals. It has thus been argued that the left ensured its electability in rural West Bengal at an ideological cost:

> [By] tenurial security and creating opportunities for peaceful negotiation for the rural poor along with more transparent and participatory modes of distributing scarce resources and benefits (such as credit, production inputs, employment and various subsidies) ... [the parliamentary left] had to shear off some of its more extreme political goals [to] tune itself to the principal requirements of bourgeois democracy.[50]

Nonetheless, there is no doubt that in comparison with the bourgeois parties that held power in West Bengal, the parliamentary left created circumstances in which, besides those having fixed tenurial rights, the rural poor also felt connected with governance presumably because of its pro-people distribution of benefits without bias.

THE ELECTION MACHINERY

Furthermore, the success of the Left Front parties in elections was also attributed to well-tuned election machinery.[51] The CPI (M) nurtured a strong organization with a wide network to maintain a firm grip on both its cadres and voters.[52] Furthermore, employees in the formal sector constituted an important source of strength for the Left Front, especially the CPI (M). There were approximately three million industrial workers belonging to the CPI (M)-led Centre of Indian Trade Unions. The frontal organizations—the All Bengal Teachers' Association, West Bengal College and University Teachers' Association, and the West Bengal Government Teachers' Association—control the teaching profession in the state. The Coordination Committee was one of the biggest and perhaps most powerful trade union organizations controlling the government employees. By securing benefits, these frontal organizations gained enormous respect among their supporters. Furthermore, Krishak Sabha, with its huge membership among the peasantry, was the "live wire" of the CPI (M) support base in rural West Bengal. Unlike other contending parties, which were revitalized once the poll dates were announced, these frontal organizations always remained active in their respective fields. By linking the government and the governed, they provided inputs to the policymakers that were not otherwise available. The government thus never remained a distant agency to those at the grassroots, which undoubtedly consolidated the ruling party's support base.

While the Left Front drew on the support of the frontal organizations in normal times, during the election campaign a structure probably unmatched by any other electoral democracy in the world, as elaborately shown in Table 3.4, was created to effectively mobilize voters for the Left Front. Managed by the full-time party cadres, these committees played crucial roles both in the selection of the candidates for the assembly segments and in the campaign during the election. Operating within specified geographical boundaries, the activities of these committees were coordinated by the district committee, the apex body in the district, which is under the state-level committee, located in Calcutta (now Kolkata). Although during the elections their activities were geared toward the elections, they continued to function even in the aftermath of elections as permanent local units of the Left Front parties, involved in the day-to-day life of the people living in particular localities. In other words, they acted as a link between the localities and the provincial party machinery, which provided the basic input to the Left Front government in adopting the appropriate policies. By linking them with "the election cell" in the party headquarters, which also runs a propaganda cell for publicizing the views of the party on various social, economic, and political issues, the Election Committees remained a critical unit especially during the election.

The left bastion was thus well maintained over the years due to a well-entrenched election machinery. This was certainly a significant factor in its consistently impressive electoral performance. Neither the Trinamul Congress nor the Indian National Congress had succeeded in evolving an organization to match the Left Front. While for the former, political mobilization began and perhaps ended with the election, the Left Front remained engaged in a continuous dialogue with the voters that perhaps was translated in votes during the election.

TABLE 3.4

Election Committee for Assembly Segment	
Urban Areas	Rural Areas
Ward Committees	Area Committee
Booth Committees	Anchal Committee
Station or Sub-Station	Branch Committee
Street-In-Charge	Booth Committee
Campaign Workers	Campaign Units for Groups of Households

Source: Available from District Committee, South Calcutta.

THE FRAGMENTED OPPOSITION

The left juggernaut seemed to be invincible because there was hardly an organized opposition to match the left's high level of organization, supported by trained cadres and an election machinery with its tentacles reaching even into the remote areas of rural Bengal. Apart from remaining divided, the anti-left political parties had neither "any leader" worth the name nor any organization capable of competing with "the mass fronts of the parties constituting the Left Front."[53] The decline of the opposition began in the 2004 Lok Sabha election when out of a total of forty-two parliamentary seats, the Left Front won thirty-five, the Congress captured six seats (14.6 percent of votes) against one seat for the Trinamul Congress (21 percent of votes). The explanation has to be located in the failure of the opposition parties to come together against the perhaps the most well-organized political party in India. In other words, compared to its fragmented opposition, the Left Front was a homogeneous unit made up of partners who were willing to put aside differences for the sake of the coalition. The outcome of the 2006 assembly election was thus predictable. It is not surprising that the Left Front secured more than 50 percent of the popular votes, which is better than any of the contending parties. While the Trinamul Congress obtained 26 percent of the popular votes, the share of the Congress and the BJP was 15 percent and 2 percent, respectively. So the fragmented opposition was no match for the organized left. A study reveals[54] that one of the principal reasons for the Left Front victory was the vote split among voters who supported the opposition against the left. Had there been no division of opposition votes, the number of the Left Front seats in the legislative assembly would certainly have been less. In a number of constituencies, the Left Front candidates won by default since votes were divided among the parties opposed to the ruling conglomeration. If there was a *"mahajat"* (grand collation) of three major anti-Left Front political parties—namely, the Congress, the BJP, and the Trinamul Congress—the CPI (M)-led coalition would have seen a reversal in a large number of constituencies.

Given the fractured opposition, is it fair to attribute the massive Left Front victory to the lack of unity among the opposition parties. Hence, the victory of the Front candidates was not indicative of pro-left sentiments but an inevitable outcome of the lack of unity and factional squabbles among the contending parties. In fact, the failure to form an electoral coalition against the Left Front cost the opposition parties as many as seventy seats because votes split between the Trinamul and Congress candidates enabled the Left Front candidates to win. Whether one can attribute this poll debacle of the anti-left political parties to "a serious strategic failure" is debatable. But there is no doubt that the opposition parties in West Bengal were largely crippled by internal feuding and a lack of leadership. Of the three major parties, the Trinamul Congress emerged as an alternative, though it, argues a commentator, "self destructed," thanks to its creator, Mamata Banerjee, who destroyed "the hopes by her whimsical behaviour that hardly inspires a great deal of confidence."[55] Furthermore, though she is "an excellent rabble rouser," underlines another analyst, "she is unable to think or execute any coherent programme for either the administration or the state [simply because] she is too temperamental."[56] Besides her own folly, the organization that she leads had shown serious cracks due largely to factional fights among her colleagues. Furthermore, what disturbed the Bengali sensibilities was perhaps her fickle-mindedness in selecting coalition partners. At one point of time, it was the BJP; at another time, it was the Congress. The Congress was a weak link because of its failure to rise above factional fights,[57] and the BJP lacked organization and the popular support, besides its failure to strike a chord with the politically minded Bengalis, presumably because of its endorsement of a so-called communal ideology. In contrast with all these contending parties, "the Left Front vote bank remains stable—with the Bengali electorate left with no option but to accept the [Front] as something better than others."[58] The new leadership seemed to have swayed the majority of the voters by appropriate socio-economic programs for rejuvenating the state economy and revamping its infrastructure.

The 2006 election was not at all different, since there was hardly a serious threat to its continuity in any of the past state assembly elections. Even in the 2001 assembly poll when Mamata Banerjee's political stock was "at the highest," the Trinamul Congress captured only sixty of the 294 assembly seats, which was far below the required number of seats in the legislature to form a simple majority. Besides her mercurial temperament and whimsical politics, Banerjee seemed to have alienated a large number of urban voters because of her "mindless opposition" to anything that the state government proposed, including the large-scale foreign investment for development in the state in general and generation of employment in particular. The decline of Trinamul seats in Kolkata and its vicinity was perhaps the outcome of the growing disenchantment of the middle-class voters who turned their back on her for being "anti-development." It is therefore not surprising that the Trinamul Congress lost its grip due largely to a significant vote swing away from the party, as Table 3.5 makes evident.

TABLE 3.5

Electoral Performance of Trinamul Congress, 2006

Region	Seats Won	Vote Swing
Greater Kolkata	12	−5.7
North Bengal	1	−6.5
South East	8	−2.4
South West	9	−3.4
Total	30	−4.3

Source: Computed on the basis of data available from *The Hindu*, 16 May 2006.

Although the vote swing of 1.2 percent in favor of the Left Front was not terribly significant, the Trinamul Congress, as Table 3.5 shows, undoubtedly suffered a serious setback in West Bengal. The voters reendorsed the Left Front for another term presumably because it was perhaps the only conglomeration that was capable of providing a stable government with reasonably persuasive economic programs and a political agenda, which both the major contending parties miserably lacked. Hence, an enthusiastic supporter of the Left Front sarcastically concludes that "to ensure free and fair elections in West Bengal, it was not enough to import poll personnel, poll observers and paramilitary security guards from elsewhere, one must also import voters from other states!"[59] There is no denying that in some constituencies the Front witnessed a reversal, which it had contained by gaining new constituencies. The Left Front, especially its leading member, CPI (M), seemed to have acquired the characteristics of a "catch-all party" that was willing to adopt "reconciliatory stances" (even at the cost of its core ideological beliefs) to expand its support base. Whether this was likely to rattle "core supporters" or adapt them to the reformed party was not easy to meaningfully address, at least when the euphoria over electoral victory was high.

CONCLUDING OBSERVATIONS

The trend that was evident in the 2004 Lok Sabha poll continued in the 2006 assembly poll. As the outcome of the Lok Sabha poll shows, of a total of 112 seats contested, the left parties won in sixty-one constituencies of which the leading partner of the Front, CPI (M), captured forty-three seats. Thirty-five of these seats came from West Bengal, which had been ruled uninterruptedly by the CPI (M)-led Left Front government since 1977. One of the cementing factors of this sustained coalition government is certainly the fact that the CPI (M) held a majority in the Assembly of 294 seats. The withdrawal of support by other coalition partners, including the Communist Party of India, the Forward Bloc, and the Revolutionary Party of India, therefore made no difference to the dominant party within the coalition. For the CPI (M), the decision to lead the coalition government stemmed from its commitment to champion the left cause,[60] articulated through radical programs and policies involving people at large. Furthermore, the hegemonic presence of the CPI (M) ruled out the possibility of any threat by the Front partners to its stability. It was therefore strategically appropriate for the constituents to remain within the Front to avoid political extinction in the state. By being accommodative, the leading partner, CPI (M), also gained an image of being "a trustworthy ally."[61] Also, the fact that the CPI (M) by itself had a majority in the legislature strengthened the coalition presumably because the smaller parties, even if they were united, were incapable of mustering the required numerical majority to replace the leading partner, the CPI (M).[62] This perhaps supported the continuity of the coalition in West Bengal. For the big brother, CPI (M), coalition was a process of coming together of political forces with more or less common socio-economic and political goals.[63] Small parties were drawn to the coalition because (i) it was an articulation of their opposition to both the Congress and other political forces that were inimical to the ideology that they represented; and (ii) by their participation in the government, the constituents of the coalition, however small, continued to remain politically viable. The Left Front was therefore a unique experiment of coalition government that is particularly not catholic in its ideological commitment but pragmatic while responding to the new compulsions of prevalent socio-economic circumstances. Its continuity for more than two decades is illustrative of a coalition that survived more or less without trouble underlining the importance of broad ideological compatibility in cementing a bond among the constituents willing to share power with like-minded partners. Its agreement to support the Congress-led UPA shows that what governed the left front was its opposition to the BJP-led National Democratic Alliance. This may appear puzzling since in West Bengal, Tripura, and Kerala where the left parties had strongholds the main opposition was invariably the Congress. Their coalition with the Congress at the center was justified as a "strategic alliance" to contain "the communal BJP and other parties supporting its communal agenda."[64] By declining to join the UPA government, the CPI (M), it seems, reflected "the frog-in-the-well strategy." The party did not want to venture into the unknown and bigger world for fear of losing its bases in West Bengal, Kerala, and Tripura since their overwhelming significance in national politics in the aftermath of the fourteenth Lok Sabha poll derived directly from the strong social base that the parliamentary left had built over the years. Without their bases intact, the CPI (M) would be seen in New Delhi as no more than a "ginger group." Hence the strategy of supporting a Congress-led coalition at the center may be bewildering unless linked with the broader ideological campaign against the BJP's so-called communal agenda. Furthermore, the decision to stay away from the UPA government was also defended by the argument that by joining the ruling coalition in governance, the Left Front would concede the space of opposition to others, especially the Sangh Parivar. So the coalition era redefined the ideological contour of the left forces in India in a fundamental way: by adopting a less catholic and more pragmatic ideological vision, the left parties also had their roles in consolidating a consensus politics in India by avoiding contentious issues and agendas. The continuity of the Left Front in West Bengal for more than two decades is thus illustrative of a coalition that survived more or less without trouble due largely to a broad ideological compatibility among the constituents willing to share power with the like-minded partners. Apart from ideology, the common minimum program, always devised and approved by the Front Committee, remained immensely vital in sustaining the left coalition by avoiding those issues and programs that were likely to be divisive. So, the West Bengal coalition had an advantage on both counts—ideological congruence and the common minimum program—that put this experiment in a class by itself.

Furthermore, endorsement of disinvestment policy by the coalition government in West Bengal suggested a significant change in its ideological perspective. Seeking to re-invent its existence in the changed neoliberal environment, the Front appeared to have redefined, if not diluted, its ideology by responding creatively to the new social and eco-nomic inputs, which were rooted elsewhere. Whether this step was illustrative of "prag-matism" or ideological eclipse is debatable; what was significant, however, was the ability of the Front constituents to adjust with the changed environment where the market was a decisive player in the decision-making process. The Left Front support for selective ap-plication of disinvestment was the outcome of a threadbare discussion with the coalition partners, which approved the strategy as seemingly the most appropriate in today's con-text. Although the Front as a collective was agreeable to the policy of disinvestment, it was not accepted by those involved in the trade union struggle, and it was likely to cause mass retrenchment of the people working in various public sector units, which were hailed in the past as instruments for change so long as the state-led development strategy was appreciated. Nonetheless, the astounding victory of the parliamentary left in the 2006 assembly election also shows the success of social democracy as an ideology. With a massive electoral support in West Bengal, the left, instead of self-assessing, took the poll outcome as an endorsement of its socio-economic programs, which rather than con-solidating actually severely dented the social base that it had been nurturing over de-cades. What was most paradoxical was the failure of the parliamentary left to guard its traditional social base that sustained the Left Front government in the state for more than three decades. In the course of time, the growing mass disillusionment with the left created a base for the opposition, which soon was evident, first in the 2009 national poll and later in the 2011 state assembly election when the left lost its hegemony after being in power for more than three decades. So, for the parliamentary left, the 2006 assembly poll was a watershed because, while it reinforced the popularity of the left, it also set in motion processes that led to its downfall, as the 2011 election results show, which will be discussed in the chapter that follows.

4

Parliamentary Left in West Bengal: A Nemesis Failing to Rekindle the Old Charm in Globalizing India[1]

THE CONTINUITY OF the parliamentary left in governance in West Bengal for more than three decades is a record not only in India but also in the context of electoral politics anywhere in the world. Besides ensuring steady agricultural growth with effective land reforms, the left coalition maintained its strong presence in the state through a carefully managed organizational spread of disciplined left parties and their increasing mass base across the state. West Bengal was, under the left rule, thus a unique example of democratic governance where political stability was not the result of low levels of political mobilization but an outcome of sustained organizational efforts involving stakeholders in both urban and rural areas. Parallel to the prevalent bureaucratic structure of the government, the party organizations gradually became the principal instruments for distribution of public provisions, from getting a hospital bed to selection of beneficiaries in targeted government schemes. People too approached the party to settle private and even familial disputes. It is therefore difficult to understand the long duration of the Left Front government without appreciating the critical role of the party-sponsored organization. While it gave society a sense of coherence, it also made the left, in its anxiety to be acceptable, socially conservative. Nonetheless, the parliamentary left under the leadership of Jyoti Basu, the longest serving chief minister in an elected democracy, remained electorally unassailable since 1977, which itself is a record in India's recent political history. With Basu resigning from office in 2000, the leadership of the Left Front government in West Bengal was bestowed on his younger colleague, Buddhadeb Bhattacharya, who became the chief minister. By decimating the opposition in the 2006 state assembly election under the stewardship of Bhattacharya, the West Bengal left created another record by establishing its hegemony in urban areas as well. This remarkable poll outcome was attributed to the decision of the left government for rapid industrialization through neoliberal economic policies. The parliamentary left, by eschewing the orthodox Marxist paradigm of state-driven planned development, clearly favored the West European social-democratic path of development, which did not seem to auger well with its supporters in the state. As soon as the government took steps to acquire land to form Special Economic Zones (SEZ) for rapid industrialization, it became clear that the situation was not exactly in its favor. The forcible acquisition of land by the state created circumstances that brought the previously fragmented opposition together. With a clear mandate in its favor, the parliamentary left did not seem to read the popular signals correctly and dismissed the voicing of opposition to the land acquisition policy as a mere ripple. What began as a seismic vibration became a tsunami in the course of time, and the Left Front regime that was considered unassailable collapsed like a house of cards. The popular grievances were articulated in the 2009 Lok Sabha poll in which the Left Front received a severe blow: in comparison with its 2004 tally of thirty-six Lok Sabha seats, the Front constituents won only fifteen seats. The trend that was evident in 2009 continued in the 2011 assembly election with the defeat of the Left Front candidates in more than two-thirds of assembly constituencies. While identifying the specific reasons for its decline, this chapter also examines the evolving socio-economic and political processes in the state that may have contributed to the Left Front's changing electoral fortunes. In broad conceptual terms, it is argued that the Left Front appeared to have been caught between the contrasting imperatives of adapting to changing socio-economic conditions in liberalizing India and attempting to remain true to its traditional communist ideology and support base. It has also failed to address the changing socio-economic grievances of people at the grassroots. The left leadership also appeared to be fragile, especially following the consolidation of the leader-based factions that remained unaddressed since there was not an acceptable patriarch to replace the previous chief minister, Jyoti Basu, who passed away in 2010. How the Left Front approach reconciles these contrasting imperatives in the future is thus a critical area of inquiry to understand the ideological metamorphosis of India's parliamentary left, if in fact it can transform itself. Nonetheless, it is clear that the parliamentary left is no longer unassailable in a state that the Left Front had governed for over three decades.

THE 2011 STATE ASSEMBLY ELECTION

A tsunami, called Mamata Banerjee, swept the longest-serving elected communist government in West Bengal (India). The Left Front government, led by the Communist Party of India (Marxist; CPI [M]), remained in power for thirty-four consecutive years since 1977. So with the defeat of the Left Front in 2011, the All India Trinamul

Congress (AITMC) made history. The AITMC–Congress alliance won 227 of the total 294 Assembly seats while the Left Front managed to win only sixty-two seats in comparison with its tally of 235 seats in 2006 Assembly election. The leading partner of the winning alliance, the Trinamul Congress, won 184 seats, enough to form the next government on its own. The landslide victory of the Trinamul Congress–led alliance is indicative of mass resentment of CPI (M), which became completely alienated from the people, given the growing hegemony of what is commonly known as the "cadre raj," where the administration became virtually subservient to well-entrenched party machineries at various levels of governance. By opposing the Left Front for its alleged anti-people activities, the AITMC became a "movement" that provided a platform to an alternative voice in the state. There is no doubt that the support base that made the left in West Bengal apparently invincible was largely due to ameliorating legislative measures, including radical land reforms that it had adopted once in governance. This support base was however then maintained in a typical Stalinistic fashion by the well-entrenched party that also controlled the opposition by coercive means. The result was evident: not only did the AITMC reap the benefit, the Left Front was almost decimated in areas of its strongholds, and its major partner, CPI (M), failed to win even a single seat in three districts—Kolkata, Howrah, and Darjeeling—that had always remained favorably disposed toward the communist government in the past. This sound defeat created an avalanche that swept through perhaps the most well-organized party in India—a party that had its tentacles in every nook and cranny of West Bengal, which was considered one of most politically conscious states of India. This election is therefore historic because the Left Front experienced a tremendous defeat at the hands of the AITMC, which had broken away from the Indian National Congress just thirteen years earlier in 1998.

THE POLL OUTCOME

As is evident, the dramatic decline of the leading partner of the Left Front, the CPI (M), led to the avalanche of losses in the 2011 election; none of its partners were able to retain the seats that they had won in the earlier election of 2006, as Table 4.1 shows.

For the CPI (M), the decline in West Bengal is most dramatic: from 176 Assembly seats won in the 2006 election, the CPI (M) reduced its number of wins to only forty-two seats in 2011, while its principal rival, the AITMC, increased its tally from thirty to 184 and its electoral ally, the Congress, enhanced its share of seats from twenty-one to forty-two. The decrease in the tally of the constituent parties of the Left Front and the corresponding increase of seats of the opposition can be regarded as a "debacle" for the former, which is also reflected in the significant decline of their share of popular votes. A perusal of the district-wise poll outcomes confirms further the failure of the

TABLE 4.1

Comparing the 2011 and 2006 West Bengal Assembly Results

Parties	Seats Won, 2011	Seats Won, 2006	Percentage of Votes, 2011	Percentage of Votes, 2006
AITMC–Congress	226	–	42.9	0.0
Left Front	62	235	39.1	50.2
CPI (M)	40	176	39.1	41.9
CPI	2	8	1.8	2.1
AIFB	11	23	5.6	5.7
RSP	7	20	3.4	3.7
WBSP	1	4	0.7	0.7
RJD	–	1	0.1	0.7
Congress	42	21	15.0	7.9
Trinamul Congress	184	30	44.1	26.3
Gorkha Janmukti Morcha	3		0.5	
Others	7	18	5.0	3.8

Note: AITMC–Congress = All India Trinamul Congress–Congress alliance. CPI (M) = Communist Party of India (Marxist). CPI = Communist Party of India. AIFB = All India Forward Bloc. RSP = Revolutionary Party of India. WBSP = West Bengal Socialist Party. RJD = Rashtriya Janata Dal.

Source: Drawn from *The Hindu*, New Delhi, 16 May 2011; *Hindustan Times*, New Delhi, 17 May 2011; *Ananda Bazar Patrika*, Kolkata, 16 May 2001; *Ananda Bazar Patrika*, Kolkata, 18 May 2011; and *Bartaman*, Kolkata, 18 May 2011.

Left Front leadership to meaningfully address the popular grievances that had been gaining steam over the years. The decline of the left is visible throughout the state, including those areas that were considered to be left strongholds in the past, as Table 4.2 illustrates:

TABLE 4.2

West Bengal Assembly Election Results by District, 2011

District Name	Left Front	AITMC Alliance	Others
Bankura (12)	3	9	–
Bardhaman (25)	14	11	–
Birbhum (11)	3	8	–
Cooch Behar (9)	6	3	–
Darjeeling (6)	–	3	3[a]
East Midnapore (16)	1	15	–
Hooghly (18)	2	16	–
Howrah (16)	–	16	–
Jalpaiguri (12)	5	6	1[b]

TABLE 4.2

Continued District Name	Left Front	AITMC Alliance	Others
Kolkata (11)	–	11	–
Malda (12)	2	9	1[b]
Murshidabad (22)	9	13	–
Nadia (17)	3	14	–
North 24 Parganas (33)	2	31	–
North Dinajpur (9)	3	6	–
Purulia (9)	4	5	–
South 24 Parganas (31)	4	27	–
South Dinajpur (6)	1	5	–
West Midnapore (19)	8	11	–

[a] Independent.

[b] Gorkha Janamukti Morcha.

Notes: The Left Front comprises the Communist Party of India (Marxist), Communist Party of India, Revolutionary Socialist Party of India, All India Forward Bloc, Revolutionary Communist Party, Samajwadi Party, Democratic Socialist Party, Biplabi Bangla Congress, and Workers Party of India. The AITMC alliance consists of All India Trinamul Congress, Indian National Congress, and Socialist Unity Centre. Figures in parentheses show the total number of seats in the districts.

Source: Prepared from *Ananda Bazar Patrika* (Kolkata), 14 May 2011; *Bartaman* (Kolkata), 14 May 2011; and *The Telegraph* (Kolkata), 14 May 2011.

The dramatic victory of the AITMC is an expression of accumulated public anger against the outrages committed by the Left Front's—particularly the CPI (M)'s—arrogant leaders, cadres, and panchayat heads in rural areas who ignored genuine grievances of those allegedly belonging to the opposition camps. This was also a challenge to the hegemonic control of the well-entrenched CPI (M) that developed a mechanism that affected every aspect of life in West Bengal. There was no escape route, and the price of opposing the ruling authority was terribly high. The poll reversal was dramatic but not entirely unanticipated given the growing opposition to the Left Front since the last state assembly election in 2006 in which the Left Front registered an almost landslide victory, decimating the opposition parties to almost nonentities in the Assembly. What, in broad terms, accounts for the near debacle of the Left Front is probably the failure of the government to meaningfully address the socio-economic grievances at the grassroots. As a former CPI (M) activist laments, "Despite constant warning, the CPI (M) leadership never bothered to take us seriously often 'dismissing' our apprehension as entirely 'overstretched' and reflective of 'political immaturity.'"[2] Whether the interpretation of the leadership is correct, the fact remains that an almost 11 percent vote swing against the ruling coalition in West Bengal cost them more than two-thirds of the seats that it had won in the 2006 state poll while an almost 13 percent vote swing for the AITMC increased their seats from thirty to 184. The shift in voters' preference is thus quite visible. Interestingly, the issues—security in land rights and livelihood—that catapulted the Left Front to the center stage in 1977 seem to have swayed the West Bengal voters in the 2011 Vidhan Sabha poll, especially in rural areas, in favor of the AITMC and the Indian National Congress and against the ruling Left Front. In other words, what became critical in the victory of the AITMC–Indian National Congress combination was the successful application of the pro-people "leftist" rhetoric to galvanize opposition to the Left Front government.

BEGINNING OF A NEW PHASE

The 2011 landslide victory of the AITMC–Congress alliance does not appear to be as dramatic given the indications of the breakdown of the Left Front's social base, which started showing cracks in the 2009 Lok Sabha poll when the share of Lok Sabha seats of the Left Front was reduced to fifteen in comparison to its tally of thirty-five in the 2004 Lok Sabha poll. Of the Left Front constituents, the CPI (M) bore the brunt of the mass disenchantment as it succeeded in retaining only nine seats in the Lok Sabha poll in contrast with its earlier tally of twenty-six. The ascendancy of the main partner of the AITMC–Congress alliance was confirmed in the 2010 Kolkata municipal poll when the Left Front lost miserably. With ninety-three seats in the Kolkata Corporation, the Trinamul Congress defeated the former ruling coalition, the Left Front, which has only thirty-nine seats. Besides the Kolkata Corporation outcome, the Trinamul Congress had won in a large number of municipal elections in West Bengal. So the writing on the wall seems to have indicated the downfall of the Left Front and rise of its bête-noir, the AITMC, in a state that was considered to be a left bastion since 1977 when the left parties came to power for the first time after ousting the Congress Party from power. The achievement of the Left Front in the rural areas in particular—its land reform measures, the registration of sharecroppers (Operation Barga), the panchayati system—had ushered in a significant process of radical changes in the political layout of the state.[3] Much of the economic change in rural West Bengal since 1977 was made possible because of a significant political process, initiated and carried forward by the Left Front government. Important here was the devolution of power—including considerable financial powers—to the elected panchayats. This step, together with a strong political commitment to implementing land reforms, ensured a process of genuine democratic participation by the rural poor in the remaking of their lives and their socio-economic environment. Although the enactment of the Seventy-Third Amendment was a significant step toward revamping the panchayati institutions in the country, the Left Front initiated the process as early as 1977–1980 by giving panchayats substantial power for local development.[4] Since the programs for poverty alleviation, sponsored by New Delhi or other agencies, were closely supervised through the party hierarchy, they were better implemented in West Bengal than in any other states. Such a supervisory role developed and sustained a constant interaction with the people at the grassroots which, inter alia, accounts for the consolidation of the Left Front in rural Bengal. Furthermore, with its long tradition of political mass mobilization and struggles—in championing the cause of the working class, urban and rural workers, the poor peasants, and the middle-class employees—the Left Front not only sustained but also gradually expanded its organizational network within the state. The Marxists' mass support was probably largely due to their success in "entering into a reciprocal relationship with their supporters [that] secured for the latter the protection and acknowledgment that had so far been wanting."[5] The Left Front, which built its support base by sustained pro-people activities at least in the initial years of its rule, seemed to have crumbled, especially since the 2006 Assembly election, primarily due to the arrogance that accompanied the Left Front administration by virtue of having a two-thirds majority in the Assembly. The erosion of the left support base was a gain for the AITMC, especially in rural Bengal. Given the visible breakdown of law and order because the administration was subservient to the power-hungry local CPI (M) leaders and cadres and due to the pervasive corruption in the operations of the public distribution system, it was easier for the AITMC leader, Mamata Banerjee, to sway the rural masses in her favor. Urban voters were equally disillusioned with the left presumably because of its inability to revamp the economy to create jobs and other avenues for productive engagement of the youth without dislocating people from their habitat. In addition, Mamata's campaign against forcible acquisition of land for industrialization instantaneously created a support base for AITMC.

Voters rejected a thoroughly discredited Left Front government. Two slogans were critical in translating popular resentment against the Left Front into votes. Since the 2009 Lok Sabha poll, the leader of the Trinamul Congress, Mamata Banerjee, appeared to have gained considerable political mileage by resorting to the slogan *Ma, Mati O Manush* (Mother, motherland, and people). Banerjee became a symbol of protest against injustice and misgovernance across the state. What contributed to her rise was also her image as a "girl-next-door" that immediately gained her attention as a pro-people leader. To take on this image, she dressed in a crumpled sari, wore cheap flip-flops, and lived in a humble house in a crowded middle-class locality. Seeking to establish *Ganatantra* (democracy) to get rid of *Dalatantra* (party rule), the winning coalition appealed to voters for *paribartan* (change) as against *pratyabartan* (return to power) of the Left Front. The other slogan of the AITMC—*badal chhai badla noi* (we want change and not revenge)—seemed to have swayed the voters in favor of the non-left coalition. The slogans were effective in garnering support for the AITMC–Congress alliance; what accounted for the growing alienation of the Left Front was its failure to understand the popular mood in the state at large. It is clear that forcible acquisition of land for industrialization by the former ruling authority alienated a significant section of its traditional voters. This remained a significant issue in this election. The electoral victory of the winning coalition can thus be attributed partly to the visceral anti-CPI (M) sentiments and partly to the mass hope for *paribartan* or change in terms of better governance, education, health facilities, and employment. However, the battle between *paribartan* and *pratyabartan* soon moved into other areas. The CPI (M) candidates, including senior leaders, left no stone unturned to defame the AITMC–Congress alliance. Gautam Deb, one of the senior CPI (M) leaders and a senior minister, accused the Trinamul Congress of using black market money in its election campaign and questioned the source of the coalition's enormous funds. Both the contending parties got involved in a war of words that extended to leveling baseless charges against each other. On occasions, the CPI (M) activists made obscene remarks against Trinamul Congress leader Mamata Banerjee. These drew widespread condemnation, and incumbent chief minister Buddhadeb Bhattacharjee publicly censured his colleagues to avoid further damage. The story of the avalanche that swept the Left Front thus reflected two major electoral trends: (i) a negative vote that rejected the Left Front and (b) a positive vote for the promise of better governance at the behest of the AITMC–Congress coalition.

The first significant issue that severely dented the social base of the Left Front was undoubtedly the ill-advised land acquisition policy for quick industrialization. Not only did the 1994 new industrial policy defending land acquisition provoke severe criticism from within the Left Front, it also led to serious dissent within the CPI (M), which forced the central leadership to bring out a communique in its defense. Justifying the decision to transfer lands to the private investors for industrialization, the central leadership argued that it would create jobs and thus produce income for the state. Given the constitutional embargo on the state to generate income in accordance with its priorities, the Left Front government had no other alternative but to encourage private investment for industrial growth. With its acceptance of private investment, the parliamentary left made a conscious choice that it believed would rejuvenate the industrial health of the state.[6] There is no doubt that a critical proportion of its traditional supporters walked away because of the crass insensitivity that the Left Front exhibited on the issue of land acquisition for industrialization under private patronage. What was most bizarre was the inability of the party leadership to comprehend the growing disenchantment of the supporters who by casting votes against the Left Front had actually expressed their ire against the incumbent ruling authority, which had completely failed to address their genuine socio-economic grievances in the changed environment of globalizing India. By championing the grievances of those who lost land due to the Left Front's land acquisition policy, the AITMC reaped rich electoral dividends in recent years. The AITMC led protests against land takeover for industry, injecting the slogan that the time for change had come in West Bengal; in the process, it consolidated the anti-incumbency vote against thirty-four years of envious uninterrupted left rule. To counter the campaign, the Left Front spoke about its achievements in the agriculture and agro-business industries. It also drew on the investment that the Left Front government made to regain the voters' confidence.

That the mass rage that was evident in the 2009 Lok Sabha poll had not abated was confirmed by the results of the 2010 local elections in West Bengal, held in May 2011. This election gave a clear edge to the Trinamul Congress and its partner, the Congress, over the ruling Left Front. The constituents of the Left Front did not appear to have even understood the rising tide against the government that was soon to engulf the state. Quite simply, the poll outcome was largely shaped by local issues and the success of the incumbent government to deliver. The key to the left success in West Bengal was undoubtedly the radical land reforms that helped consolidate its social base in rural areas. In the changed environment of globalization with the rising expectation of the voters, the incumbent government seemed to have failed to gauge the popular mood, which was reflected in demands for better primary education, health-care facilities, nutrition, agricultural and nonagricultural wages, compensation for displacement, and regular supplies as well as proper distribution of food through the public distribution system. The failure to meaningfully address these issues surely caused a dent in the Left Front support base, which the government had been consolidating since 1977 by adopting revolutionary land legislations. The Left Front treated the 2006 landslide victory as an endorsement for rapid industrialization and took its rural support for granted. The grand plans to seize large tracts of fertile land for Tata's Nano car factory became the Achilles heel for the incumbent government. The movement against forcible land acquisition spread like wildfire, and the Left Front did not appear to recognize the severity of public resentment, which was translated into votes in the 2011 Assembly election.

THE SEZ CONTROVERSY

What accounted for the dip in the popularity of the Left Front government was forcible acquisition of land for quick industrialization in the state. True to his election pledge, the chief minister of West Bengal, Buddhadeb Bhattacharjee, took steps to acquire a large swath of land in Nandigram, in the district of Midnapur, to establish a mega Indonesian chemical hub, for which land acquisition was necessary. The state government defended the decision by arguing that industrialization would provide new sources of livelihood to the people of the area as income from land has considerably shrunk for a variety of reasons, including massive fragmentation of land. Nandigram as an SEZ would have fulfilled the twin goals of contributing to the economic wealth of the state and providing alternative sources of income to the local population. The argument did not make sense to those for whom it was intended to convince, namely, the rural population. The resulting turmoil brought together the government's political foes regardless of ideology, led by the Trinamul Congress, to endorse one platform.

Similar to Nandigram, the decision of the Left Front government to acquire land for Tata's Nano car factory in Singur in the district of Hooghly antagonized its supporters among the rural poor. A nonpolitical platform—Bhumi Ucched Partirodh Committee (Land Eviction Resistance Committee)—was formed, organized by those opposed to the forcible land acquisition policy. The real winner was the Trinamul leader, Mamata Banaerjee, who undertook a twenty-five-days hunger strike in December 2006 to champion the cause of those farmers in Singur who were reluctant to hand over their land for the factory. What did she gain besides drawing national (or perhaps international) attention? The most obvious gain was her return to the center stage of West Bengal politics, which was politically very rewarding especially given her massive electoral failure in the 2006 Assembly election. She "whipped the land acquisition fear into frenzy." It was "a primeval insecurity guaranteed to make every farmer rise in revolt."[7] The Singur campaign reestablished her reputation as the prime mover of anti-left political mobilization. Banerjee's opposition to the land acquisition was also reflective of her political maturity, which was not evident in movements that she led in the past. Most of her campaigns were anti-CPI (M) or anti-government. This was the first time that she had a well-defined pro-people issue involving the farmers of Singur who lost their land to "forced" industrialization of the state.

The controversy over acquisition of land from the farmers in West Bengal for indus-tries clearly suggests that the top-down mode of governance is hardly effective in India's highly politically mobilized state of West Bengal. The chief minister's zeal for quick in-dustrialization not only provoked strong criticisms from his Left Front partners but also allowed the opposition parties to bolster their anti-government campaigns. The decision to forcibly acquire land for a car factory in Singur in the vicinity of Kolkata and for the SEZ[8] in Nandigram alienated a significant section of grassroots supporters who were drawn to the Left Front primarily because of the radical land reform measures that the state government undertook after it came to power. The leading partner of the Front, the CPI (M), appeared to have ignored its commitment to "the tiller of the soil," given Bud-dhadeb Bhattacharjee's enthusiasm for rapid industrialization. As a bewildered sup-porter articulated his disenchantment, "The only party we have known all our life is CPM. For years, we heard leaders spew anti-industry speeches. Now, there is a sudden turnaround. I don't understand."[9] Bewilderment led to anger when the state police re-sorted to violence, killing fourteen protestors in Nandigram on the occasion of a protest march opposing the SEZ on 14 March 2007. Justifying the SEZ as the only effective ec-onomic instrument to "reverse the process of de-industrialization," the Left Front lead-ership dismissed the incident as "a stray-one, engineered by outsiders."[10]

The situation however took a radical turn when the Nandigram firing remained in the limelight and caused a fissure among the Front partners. None of the constituents, in-cluding the three major partners—the Revolutionary Socialist Party, the CPI, and the Forward Bloc—supported the government's uncritical endorsement of the SEZ. De-scribing the incident as "unexpected, unbelievable and traumatic," the CPI squarely blamed Bhattacharjee for running the Left Front government as "a government of CPM [*sic*] alone keeping the allies in the dark."[11] Critical of land acquisition by force, even a former CPI (M) minister expressed disappointment over the Left Front strategy of quick industrialization based on private capital with large state subsidies without taking the landowners into consideration.[12] The people's tribunal that looked into the March 14 police shooting in Nandigram also came out sharply against the government by insinu-ating that "the motive behind this massacre seemed to be the ruling party's wish to teach a lesson to the poor villagers by terrorizing them for opposing the proposed SEZ."[13]

The Bhattacharjee-led Left Front government was in a tight spot because of its failure to secure land for the proposed chemical hub. This not only threatened to dishearten pro-spective investors but also extended a moral boost to the coalition of forces that came to-gether to scuttle the government's blueprint for the rapid industrialization of the state. Given its numerical hegemony in the Left Front government, the CPI (M) did not seem to swallow "the defeat," as what followed in Nandigram in November 2007 confirmed. The well-planned "recapture" of Nandigram from anti-land acquisition forces by armed cadres was a clear testimony of how ruthless the party could be, despite leading a government with more than a two-thirds majority in the legislative assembly. Justifying the intervention of the armed cadres and the refusal to call in the police, government sources contended that the police were not sent for fear of a repeat of the March 14 incident. The consequences were disastrous; many innocent people were killed, and those who were opposed to the SEZ were forced to leave Nandigram. Bhattacharjee, the chief minister, seemed to be happy when these armed cadres barged into the village to "reclaim" the lost ground because the protesters, as he emphatically stated, "have been paid back in their coin."[14] The Left Front government thus won the first round of the battle by following what can only be described as a quintessentially Stalinist formula in settling the Nandigram problem. Even those sympathetic to the Left Front found it difficult to accept that CPI (M), long regarded as a friend of the poor, could have been so ruthless. More appalling was the application of brute force that was applied to make some of India's poorest people surrender the piece of land that gave them identity. Seeking to redefine its ideological priority in the changed circumstances of globalization, the Left Front government seemed to have charted a new course of action despite significant opposition to it, both in West Bengal and elsewhere in the country. The CPI (M) leadership thus defended the violent takeover by the cadres by saying that if the party cadres had not acted in Nandigram, then the entire process of industrialization would have purportedly stalled. This created a clear fissure among the grassroots supporters that brought back the Left Front government to power in 2006 with a massive majority. Singur and Nandigram were, argues a perceptive commentator, "the last straw on the camel's back that provided the trigger for the popular explosion of anger and frustration across the state."[15] The popular disillusionment was visible in the 2008 panchayat election when the Left Front, for the first time in three decades of its hegemonic presence, lost four Zila Parishads to the opposition parties.[16] While the Trinamul Congress captured East Midnapur and South 24 Parganas, the Congress retained North Dinajpur and won in Malda though it lost Murshidabad to the Left Front.[17] Murshidabad seemed to be the sole and biggest revenge on the opposition since the Left Front won the district back from the Congress, which failed to retain the district due probably to infighting within the district Congress Committee.

EROSION OF THE SOCIAL BASE

Besides the forcible land acquisition by the state, what had alienated the ordinary voters was the establishment of cadre raj that unleashed the "reign of terror" in rural areas. No redressal was available to the victims presumably because of the complicity of the administration with the cadres who belonged mostly to the leading partner of the Left Front, the CPI (M). There is no doubt that the left fortress was built on a formidable party machinery that was all pervasive. Over the years, the CPI (M) developed a machinery that became privy to the detailed information about each household in the villages, including the ideological inclination of their members. With the revamping of the panchayats, it was possible for the party to tighten its grip over the recalcitrant villagers. The government machinery became an appendage to the parallel party machinery. The CPI (M) rode on these newly created parallel centers of power that appropriated the governmental authority thanks to the endorsement by the top leadership in the Alimuddin Street headquarters of the party. The grip of the party was so complete that nothing could happen without the party's approval. As a result, many of the party activists turned into extortionists. As an affected farmer, Sheikh Sukur of Birbhum articulates, "The party started imposing illegal taxes. We had to pay a tax before rowing and harvesting." Even a social occasion, like a wedding in the villages, was not free from CPI (M) control. Sukur further comments, "During my daughter's wedding three years ago, I paid Rs. 750/- to the CPM for permission to throw a feast."[18] There are many instances when the local CPI (M) activists went on rampage when they were opposed. Jamal revealed that he was severely thrashed by the party members when he refused to pay a tax. As he narrated, "Two years ago, when I wanted to repair the leaking thatched roof of my small mud hut, the party demanded Rs. 500/- saying that if I had money to repair the roof, I had had money to pay them as well. When I refused, their cadres beat me up and I had to ultimately pay Rs. 300/-."[19] This is not a stray example. There are many victims of "the dreaded party machinery" that also made rather a large number of committed activists redundant. Safiq Hussain, drawn to CPI (M) because of the pro-people Operation Barga,[20] became totally "disillusioned" with the growing importance of "the goons" in the party. He expressed his feeling unambiguously when he stated, "My comrades were only interested in making money. Lots of funds were siphoned off. I protested many times, but no one listened. I dissociated myself from the party."[21] It was therefore not surprising that the party machinery that the CPI (M) cadres so assiduously built over three decades of the Left Front rule failed to garner votes for the party in power. The opposition certainly gained because of the mass resentment and dissociation of those frustrated with the rather dictatorial functioning of the party functionaries. The party that held power in the state by its ideological commitment to the downtrodden seemed to have lost its pro-people stance due probably to "its arrogance" for being "unassailable" in elections.[22]

The story of Sukur and Jamal is also indicative of the erosion of the left base among the Muslims in West Bengal. So far, the Left Front sustained the image of being pro-Muslim and its candidates won in most of the Muslim-dominated constituencies simply because of large-scale Muslim support. This was not the case this time, as Table 4.2 shows. The Sachar Committee report shows that, despite "the rhetoric of secularism, the state of Muslims in West Bengal was among the worst in the country,"[23] which undoubtedly resulted in an erosion of the left support base among the West Bengal Muslims. It has also been observed that the underprivileged sections of the numerically significant Muslim minority (25 percent of the total population according to the 2001 census) did not receive social and political support from the state in contrast with their Hindu counterparts. Muslims in West Bengal were surely "on the margins," deprived of state patronage.[24] They also felt betrayed when the state chief minister, Buddhadeb Bhattacharjee, exhorted people to launch a campaign against Madrassas in 2007 as supposed "dens of terrorism."[25] It might have been a strange coincidence because those dispossessed in Nandigram were largely Muslims and Dalits. Furthermore, it was alleged that while seeking to combat bird flu in villages in Birbhum and Murshidabad the CPI (M) cadres culled the seemingly affected birds belonging to the Muslim families without adequately compensating them.[26] It is therefore not surprising that the Left Front candidates lost miserably in districts like North and South 24 Parganas, Nadia, Murshidabad, Malda, and Birbhum, all of which have a high proportion of Muslim population. The total insensitivity displayed by the Calcutta police while handling the brutal murder of a Muslim graphics teacher (Rizwanur Rahman) in Calcutta further increased the sense of disillusionment of urban Muslims. The top CPI (M) functionaries were reported to have influenced the investigation to save the local industrialists charged with the murder.[27] Like the Muslims, the disadvantaged sections, especially Dalits and agricultural laborers, shifted their loyalty away from the left forces. One of the major factors for this withdrawal was also likely the failure of the implementation of the 2006 National Rural Employment Guarantee Act. A field interview of villagers in Birbhum confirms this apprehension. The villagers were given work under this centrally sponsored scheme only after the local wing of the party approved. Also, they were deprived of their income if they were reluctant to pay "the tax" for the party.[28] The official authority appeared to be a mute observer on most of the occasions. The dismal performance of the state government led the Paschim Banga Khet Majoor Samity, a nonparty-registered trade union of agricultural workers, to file public interest litigation in the Calcutta High Court on nonimplementation of the one hundred days of work guarantee schemes in West Bengal.[29]

DISILLUSIONMENT OF THE EDUCATED MIDDLE CLASS

Besides the Muslims and Dalits, the educated sections appeared to have been rattled with "the tyrannical functioning" of the party and the failure of the government to contain such tendencies. Pursuing a culture of patronage and clientelism, the party bosses or party managers, as some commentators prefer to call them,[30] maintained their hegemony through "a calibrated network of dependence, patronage, benefits, rewards, punishments and threats."[31] More important, the party functionaries became the principal, if not indispensable, arbiter in the lives of the people. In villages, they regularly held "*salishis* or arbitration hearings, mediating family and social disputes—marriage, property issues, morality codes or social customs." It was resented by the people because

No longer an outsider, the party moved into the inner circle of families, becoming part of them; people relied on its skills and powers as facilitators when needing access to health, education, finances and employment. . . . [Party] thus became a brand, a vehicle to upward mobility, access to privilege and concessions [which put in place] a whole economy of rewards and punishments, of pleasure and power, on the one hand, and violence and exclusion, on the other.[32]

West Bengal thus became the Orwellian animal farm where Snowballs are relegated to nothing except to fulfill the partisan Napoleonic political design in the name of an ideological war against the bourgeoisie and their cohorts. A voice of protest, instead of taking it at its face value, is thus violently suppressed since it is regarded as a challenge to the authority of the party and hence cannot be tolerated. It was indeed a suffocating situation in which the party hegemony was maintained by a Stalinist feudal mindset that seemed to have gripped the parliamentary left in West Bengal largely because of its long tenure in governance that it maintained through massive electoral support from among the voters for more than three decades. By being sensitive to the basic socio-economic needs of the people, the left created a space that it gradually lost presumably due to the failure of the leadership to counter this Stalinist feudal mindset and its failure to contain the cadres who not only became "disconnected" from the rural masses but became individual instruments of authority even to the extent of disregarding, on occasions, the party directives.

Everybody, from remote villages to the city of Kolkata, was thus for *Parivartan* (change). In fact, the banner of *parivartan chai* (we want change) was displayed all over Kolkata and its vicinity before the 2011 assembly election in West Bengal. Once drawn to CPI (M) for its ameliorating ideology, the city's intellectuals were shocked with the way that the CPI (M) cadres "reclaimed" Nandigram by force. This led to a spontaneous protest in the city in which the leading writers, educationists, and people belonging to art and culture participated. In other words, the turmoil over land acquisition became the rallying point for those opposed to the Left Front. The opposition was handed an issue on a platter that became most critical in binding the previously disparate groups together. People from different walks of life joined hands to dislodge the party in power. For instance, Shaonli Mitra, a pro-left leading theater personality, was drawn to the campaign because she failed to comprehend how the CPI (M), which led progressive cultural movements in the past, could be so ruthless to those opposing the Left Front by democratic means.[33] Another artist of repute, Shuvaprasanna was more analytical when he argued that they were thus far misled by the CPI (M)-sponsored skilled propaganda. Whatever anti-people actions the state government took in the larger commitment to the ideal of equality "were not aberrations [but] were essential mutilations wrought by too much power."

Today we know that the CPI (M) has no commitment to ideology, but is an arrogant force that will go to any extent to grab power. Anybody who disagrees is brutally silenced; if you are not with them, you are against them. . . . We felt the might of the state [when we protested over the happenings] in Singur and Nandigram; we were abused by slander campaigns, our theatres were shut down.[34]

As evident, the Left Front lost its appeal among the electorate largely due to a dip in its popularity that cut across various social groups. The Trinamul–Congress alliance gained because of the left failure to address the genuine socio-economic grievances of the people at the grassroots. The alliance may not have given a well-defined program, but its slogan—*Ma, Mati O Manus* (Mother, motherland, and people) seemed to have articulated a powerful sentiment against the Left Front, which translated into votes. This was a vote against the distortion of the "social democratic line," which catapulted the Left Front constituents to the center stage of Indian politics in 1977 and sustained its continuity since then. The dramatic win of the AITMC seems to have repeated history because the Left Front that came to power for the first time in 1977 consolidated its base by addressing the genuine socio-economic grievances of the rural masses. What the voters did not appreciate was the attempt to push neoliberal policies in the name of development and industrialization at their cost. The strategy of compulsory land acquisition of even highly arable land to facilitate industrialization under private auspices was, argued a former CPI (M) cardholding member, "ill-founded and worse in its implementation."[35] The state witnessed spontaneous mass mobilization against land acquisition that cut across political boundaries. The clinching event was the "gruesome violence" that the arrogant state government resorted to during the recapture of Nandigram in March 2007.[36] Even a hard-core CPI (M) supporter was bewildered at the aggressive state-sponsored attack on the farmers to acquire agricultural land for neoliberal industrialization. For instance, to Islam Ali of Madhaipur, a small hamlet close to Siuri of the district of Birbhum, the way the CPI (M) cadres reclaimed Nandigram was "reflective of 'the big brother' arrogance which was responsible for its unprecedented electoral debacle since the assumption of power by the Left Front in West Bengal in 1977."[37] Even a top CPI (M) functionary attributed the rapid decline of the Left Front to "the big-brother attitude" in the 2011 assembly election.[38] As evident, the forced land acquisition ruptured the organic link that the Front government had with the rural masses, including those belonging to the CPI (M) and other constituents of the Left Front. Such a situation was not merely indicative of but pointed to the overall disenchantment of the voters in West Bengal with the ruling authority, which translated into votes in the 2011 Vidhan Sabha poll.

APPROPRIATION OF PANCHAYATI RAJ INSTITUTIONS

The Front had built a strong base in rural West Bengal primarily because of meaningful land reforms that benefitted the marginal sections of the population. The various reforms that radically altered agrarian economy were "effectuated through the use of mobilized supporters more than the administrative machinery."[39] The gain was consolidated by the establishment of panchayati governance in which people participated in policy decisions at the grassroots by overcoming the rules and hurdles of a bureaucratic administration. The Left Front had thus been able to penetrate the countryside without depending on the large landowners. It has thus been argued that the CPI (M)-led Left Front regime, along with the panchayati raj institutions, "thus represents two interlinked patterns of political change: an organizational penetration by the 'center' into the 'periphery,' and a simultaneous shift in the class basis of institutional power."[40] This is therefore not surprising that the landless and socially and educationally backward sections constitute a strong base for the left.[41] The support base gradually became invincible with the institutionalization of panchayati raj governance at the grassroots that also consolidated a clientelist relationship between the party and its supporters. The clientelist relationship has its flipside as well because these panchayats gradually degenerated into "institutions dominated by local CPI (M) and other Left Front party leaders and apparatchiks who diverted the government funds from investment in social welfare for the villagers to build party offices and their own houses."[42] Those opposed to the ruling party in the panchayat are deprived of the benefits of the governmental schemes for the rural population.

A clientelist equation probably explains the story of death and malnutrition in Amlashole in West Midnapur; in the tribal belts of Purulia, Nadia, and the eastern part of Murshidabad; in tea garden areas of Kochbehar; and the fringe areas of Dinajpur. The highly publicized starvation deaths are attributed to the politicization of administration that resulted in a patron–client relationship where certain sections were excluded from vital public policy schemes in times of distress. As is evident, the politicization of the administration largely accounts for a lackadaisical attitude of the local government. Amlashole voted for Kailash Mura of the CPI (M) in the panchayat election in which the Jharkhand Party won a majority. The Jharkhand Party had to operate within other local institutional structures—Zila Parishad and the Panchayati Samiti—that were controlled by CPI (M). Thus the villagers of Amlashole suffered in two ways for their political affiliation. First, they were discriminated against by the Jharkhand Party–dominated panchayat because the villagers opted for a CPI (M) candidate. Second, they were discriminated against by the CPI (M) administration because their village was located in an opposition-controlled panchayat.[43] Panchayats in Amlashole allowed starvation deaths to happen presumably because of the arrogance of the party activists that appeared to have crippled the party over time. These grassroots institutions were no longer available for the goal for which they were created in the first place, and the party functionaries appropriated them to fulfill their selfish goals; an important Left Front cabinet minister confessed that "the local panchayat leaders squandered the Central government funds for development to buy liquor and build club houses."[44] Furthermore, panchayati raj institutions ceased to be forums for discussions given the hegemonic role of the party in its governance. Decisions adopted in the party meetings were only presented "as fait accompli at the official panchayat meetings,"[45] and there was hardly any serious political discussion on this presumably because "individual panchayat members are not elected by the people qua individuals but as representatives of a party that selected them as candidates."[46]

It is not therefore surprising that the panchayati raj institutions that brought hope to the people at the grassroots were subject to trenchant criticism by those who found them the most effective form of rural governance when they were introduced in West Bengal. The reasons are not difficult to find. A large sample survey carried out in 2006 confirms that the credibility of those at the helm of affairs was wanting. That most panchayat members were corrupt was confirmed by the survey that further indicates "a pervasive distrust in the moral authority of those who claim to mediate, on political grounds, the contending claims of livelihood, fairness and dignity."[47] It is this "popular distrust" that accounts for the gradual decline of the left forces in rural West Bengal. The rot seemed to have begun earlier because a party document, released as early as 1985, warned:

> The Left Front have not been able to meet the aspirations of the people . . . [and] there is considerable slackness, and corruption has put a halt to the implementation of pro-people social programmes. Vested interests [thus] take advantage of these lapse . . . and help the opportunist elements to strike roots in the party.[48]

While this distrust causes a clear dent in the Left support base, it has also alienated the poor, especially the Dalit and the tribal population from the institutions of panchayat governance. If these institutions cannot innovate ways to accommodate the poor, they may, warns an analyst, "create space for various 'forbidden forms of claim making' that have little regard for the existing democratic norms."[49] The growing consolidation of "ultra-radical extremist forces" appeared under the guise of the Bhumi Ucched Partirodh Committee (Committee against eviction from land) in Singur and the People's Committee against Police Atrocities in Lalgarh, which represented the grassroots endeavor to pursue a course of action opposed to what the ruling Left Front has so far followed to ameliorate the conditions of the poor.[50]

THE *MAHAJOT* (GRAND ALLIANCE)

The Left Front seemed to be invincible before 2009, partly because there was hardly any organized opposition to match its cast-iron organization, supported by trained cadres and well-oiled electoral machinery extending to even the most remote areas of West Bengal.[51] The opposition's particularly poor electoral performance in the 2006 assembly poll—out of 295 seats, the Left Front captured 235 seats while the AITMC's share was only thirty seats—made it seem that the Left Front was virtually invincible. The outcome of the 2006 election also validated the apparently hegemonic political dominance of the Left Front in West Bengal. In this election, the Left Front secured more than 50 percent of the popular votes with two-thirds of Assembly seats. Thus what attributed the landslide victory of the Left Front was the vote-splitting among supporters of the anti-left opposition.[52] The scene changed dramatically before the 2009 Lok Sabha poll when the anti–Left Front opposition parties, spearheaded by the AITMC and the Congress, formed a grand alliance, which was characterized as a *mahajot*.[53] Since the AITMC was an offshoot of the Congress, its supporters were easily persuaded to accept the alliance because there was little ideological difference between the two. A former partner of the BJP-led National Democratic Alliance, the AITMC accepted the Congress as a pre-poll ally in the 2011 election to project its secular character. The AITMC was also impressed with the ruling United Progressive Alliance coalition's record of good governance at the center. The alliance was finally clinched through the intervention of the Congress high command, which justified the creation of a coalition in West Bengal as the only possible way to defeat the CPI (M) and its allies in the Left Front. For the Congress, the *mahajot* was a strategic alliance against the ruling party, which was likely to pay electoral dividends for itself in view of the growing popularity of the AITMC. On the whole, the AITMC-led alliance became lethal because it succeeded in translating anti-left voices into votes at the 2009 Lok Sabah poll, followed by the 2011 assembly election. The alliance won because it succeeded in providing a united forum for disenchanted voters of West Bengal, which was evident in the large-scale participation of voters in the election. The West Bengal election witnessed a record voter turnout, close to 85 percent. This turnout was unprecedented, as the data reveal that in certain areas as many as 90 percent of voters cast their votes. Also, with the presence of the para-military forces, voting was made easier, and there was hardly a single charge of rigging, which reportedly occurred at the behest of the ruling authority in the past elections.

As the electoral outcomes show, the clear winner of the 2011 election, similar to the 2009 Lok Sabha poll, was the AITMC, which won 184 seats out of 229 seats that it contested. Its electoral partner, the Congress, fielded candidates in sixty-six constituencies and captured forty-two seats. The loser was certainly the Left Front, including its leading partner, the CPI (M), which won fewer seats (forty) than the Congress Party. What is most striking is the dramatic decline of the Left Front in areas that were considered its strongholds and the defeat of twenty-nine of the Left Front ministers by relatively unknown AITMC–Congress alliance candidates.

Mass disenchantment was evident in the fact that the CPI (M) lost miserably in most of the districts in West Bengal. There is therefore no doubt that the left base had been considerably eroded, especially its major constituent, the CPI (M), which no longer remained unassailable as it had in the past. Not only did the left candidates lose in predominantly urban areas, but their plight was not different in predominantly rural constituencies. The loss of the left was the gain of the *mahajot*. The AITMC–Congress alliance earned a convincing victory and the Left Front was humiliated.

The dramatic decline of the parliamentary left that was evident in the 2011 Assembly election was also visible in the 2013 polls to the local bodies in which the Left Front lost miserably to its bête noire, the AITMC. The Trinamul supremo, Mamata Banerjee, recognized

TABLE 4.3

Share (Percentage) of Gram Panchayats, Won by Major Political Parties, 1978–2013

	1978	1983	1988	1993	1998	2003	2008	2013
Left	90	76	90	87	88	87	69	24
Congress	10	23	9	11	5	9	13	8
AITMC	–	–	–	–	5	2	16	55
Others	–	1	1	2	2	2	2	11

Note: AITMC = All India Trinamul Congress.

Source: Dwaipayan Bhattacharya and Kumar Rana, "West Bengal Panchayat Elections: What Does It Mean for the Left?" *Economic and Political Weekly*, 14 September 2013, 11.

that power in West Bengal was vulnerable until the panchayats and municipalities were seized, for that is "where the muscles of cadres are oiled and massaged."[34] She outsmarted the left at its own game in local elections. As the results show, the Trinamul candidates won 5,098 seats unopposed in south Bengal alone, which is more than double the Left Front's uncontested wins (2,362) of the last elections in 2008. At the district level, the number of seats that AITMC had won unopposed was fifteen, which is almost double that of the Left Front's wins in 2008. Nonetheless, the trend was clear: the rural voters supported the Banerjee-led AITMC spontaneously to bring about a change in rural power structure, as Table 4.3 demonstrates.

The defeat was ironic for a cadre-based organization that held power in West Bengal for more than three decades. The poll outcome of 2013 is almost a repetition of the 2003 results with the players in reverse positions. In 2003 the leading partner of the Front, the CPI (M), won unopposed in a considerable number of seats, which provoked the AITMC to charge the incumbent state authority of "mass scale rigging" or "terrorizing the Trinamul supporters." In 2013, the nature of the complaint was the same, but the complainants were reversed: the parliamentarians belonging to the Left Front protested against large-scale rigging and terrorizing their voters by holding a sit-in-dharna in front of parliament. The charge that the incumbent Trinamul government utilized the state machinery to consolidate the hold of the party may have some substance though there is no denying that the support base that Banerjee had built was largely the outcome of the deficit of governance and the zealous acceptance of the neoliberal economic reforms by the parliamentary left at the cost of those associated with land. The decrease of the left vote surely confirms the popularity of the Banerjee-led Trinamul Congress, which the organized parliamentary left failed to scuttle. The failure of the left to retain its base in rural West Bengal seems to have exposed the weaknesses of the supposedly invincible cadre-based organization of the left, which took on a largely mythical character and was unnecessarily hyped in the public eye.[55] So, the defeat of the parliamentary left and the victory of the AITMC in local polls reinforced the public's faith in the democratic processes for substantial political changes in which the role of the voters seems to be far more critical than what is usually construed. This is the most important outcome of the local polls: it not only demolished the mythical strength of the cadre-based organization but also highlighted the significance of individual charisma in persuading voters to vote for a particular ideological wave that Banerjee represented in her opposition to the parliamentary left since the formation of the AITMC in 1998.

The cadre-Raj that the parliamentary left had built in Stalinistic fashion had shown cracks in the 2009 Lok Sabha poll and finally collapsed in the 2011 assembly election. The outcome of the 2013 local election further reconfirmed its demise. It is ironic that a well-entrenched party that gradually spread its tentacles across various social strata in the state lost its base rather dramatically. The AITMC has built its organization by drawing on the majority of the former cadres of the constituent parties of the Left Front, which was visible in the 2013 election to the panchayats in which the CPI (M) and other partners of the Left Front lost ignominiously.

CONCLUDING OBSERVATIONS

It is somewhat ironic that the Left Front, hailed as a savior of the rural poor in the aftermath of the Emergency (1975–1977) because of its large-scale land reforms, including Operation Barga, has increasingly been falling out of favor with most sections of Bengali society. The successive victories of the CPI (M)-led Left Front in West Bengal, even after the growing disenchantment with its performance since the 1990s, were, as suggested by a former sympathizer of the Left Front, "due to party's judicious mixture of coercion and persuasion"[56] that did not work in the 2011 election. The Front's tactics failed for two reasons: (i) the alert Election Commission, aided by the central security forces, left no stone unturned to put the coercive elements, regardless of party affiliation, in check, and (ii) the CPI (M)'s persuasive appeal did not yield results in light of its past anti-people deeds. The left treated its electoral victories in the 2004 Lok Sabha poll and 2006 assembly election as an endorsement of its plan for rapid industrialization. It took its rural support base for granted in its "grand plans to seize large tracts of fertile land for setting up factories, establishing special economic zones [and] expanding urban "territories."[57] Even after the land acquisition policy backfired, there was hardly any retrospection on the part of the leadership. Instead, the chief minister firmly announced his determination to pursue his policy of industrialization.[58] The CPI (M) preferred to sustain its social base by drawing on "conspiracy theory" that was a driving force behind its attack on the opposition. It was ironic that a party that came to power by seeking to fulfill mass expectations tended to explain the situations of crisis and predicaments in terms of plots and undercover players out to destroy the people-driven Left Front government. It was almost as if the party is infallible and those challenging the government on policy issues were not driven by genuine differences of opinion but "conspiratorial motives of revenge and destruction."[59]

The large-scale defeat of the Left Front candidates was also illustrative of the extent to which "the Leninist organization in the Stalinist mold" may not always be adequate to forcibly gag the voice of protest. There is no doubt that the sustained Left Front rule was attributed to "a well-entrenched party machinery [that] manages conflict and [also] co-opts the aggrieved through its patronage network"—a carefully devised strategy suggestive of how the party changes at the local levels in pragmatic ways to remain constantly in the reckoning.[60] This had worked in the past, and the Left Front government resorted to coercive methods, including police shootings, to establish its authority against aggrieved masses with legitimate claims and demands. The long-suppressed history of Marichjhampi massacre in 1979, exactly two years after the Left Front came to power for the first time, confirms that the Singur and Nandigram episode is a continuity of the past. On an assurance of the government, a few thousand refugee families who had earlier been sent to Dandakaranya in Madhya Pradesh by the earlier Congress government arrived in Sundarban areas to settle there. Contrary to its commitment to the refugees, the government retaliated by arresting those who refused to return to their habitat. Despite government efforts, a large number of these families managed to evade police surveillances and reached Marichjhampi, an island in the northernmost forested part of the Sundarban, where they gradually settled down by making the place habitable by dint of hard work. It was not easy for the Left Front to swallow the opposition, and the settlers were accused of violating official laws like the Forest Act and threatening the lives of the famous Royal Bengal Tigers. When persuasion failed, the government started on 26 January 1979 "an economic blockade of the settlement with thirty police launches . . . in an attempt to deprive the settlers of food and other essential items for survival."[61] The government launched a police operation to forcibly remove the recalcitrant families in May 1979, which led to "a war between the two groups of people, one backed by state power and modern paraphernalia, the other dispossessed and who had only their hands and the spirit of companionship."[62] The outcome of such a rivalry was obvious: "out of the 14,388 families who deserted for West Bengal, 10,260 families returned to their previous [habitat] . . . and the remaining 4,128 families perished in transit, died of starvation, exhaustion and many were killed . . . by police firing . . . [and] their bodies were allegedly dumped into the river."[63] Scared of mass resentment, the government declared Marichjhampi out of bounds for journalists essentially to stop the flow of news from the affected areas on government atrocities. So what happened in Singur and Nandigram appears to be a continuity of the past, confirming how draconian the left parties could be if their authority was challenged. So the left response in Singur and Nandigram was not merely an endeavor to forcibly acquire land for industrialization but also reflective of political arrogance of the Left Front largely because of the hegemonic organizational control that it had in the state for more than three decades!

Furthermore, the Left Front report card on health and education in the state is appalling: as the 2004 Human Development Report suggests, the figures from West Bengal are far below the national average in regard to immunization, antenatal care, nutrition among women, and number of doctors and hospital beds per lakh (100,000). What is most staggering to note is the fact that "the percentage of rural house-holds not getting enough food every day in some months of the year is highest in West Bengal (10.6%)," worse than Orissa (4.8 percent), and is perennially in the grip of death due to hunger.[64] After three decades of sustained Left Front rule in West Bengal, the 2011 poll reversal is also indicative of intellectual bankruptcy of the Marxists that remain "locked into their textbooks" blocking completely "indigenous innovations" like their Latin American or European counterparts.[65] Marxism that the Left Front endorses is "an archaic one, being practised in the 1960s" that has lost its viability in the twenty-first century in which the world has radically changed.[66] So, the party appeared to be ill-equipped to address the genuine socio-economic grievances of the masses despite having agreed to address "the organizational defects" in its 10–12 June 2011 Central Committee meeting in Hyderabad by admitting that "its mistakes in Singur and Nandigram had proved costly leading to the worst-ever debacle in West Bengal Assembly election."[67] Also, it may sound paradoxical that the AITMC–Congress alliance gained political dividends on these mistakes in the 2011 Vidhan Sabha (Assembly) poll confirming the far-reaching, if not devastating, consequences of a clear disconnect between ideological belief and strategic calculations in a parliamentary form of political competition.

PART II

Maoism: Articulation of Left-Wing Extremism in India, written with Rajat Kumar Kujur

ON 25 MAY 2013, Maoists ruthlessly ambushed a convoy carrying people for an election campaign through the forests in the district of Bastar in Chhattisgarh, which resulted in the killing of twenty-five individuals, including some of the top leadership of the Congress Party. The main target was Mahendra Karma who was brutally killed in the attack for having founded an armed civilian vigilante group, known as Salwa Judum, in the state comprising the tribal youth who are familiar with the terrain, dialect, and the local population. This attack was also the Maoist retaliation for the government's activities in the so-called Maoist districts in West Bengal, Jharkhand, Chhattisgarh, and Andhra Pradesh in which a large number of Maoists, including some top leaders, were recently gunned down. The number of Maoist attacks in May during the past four years seems to point to a direct link between the increase in temperature and the frequency of attack in the affected districts. According to experts, there is logic behind the spur in such violence during the pre-monsoon period. May is the preferred month as it falls during the middle of the Maoist five-month (March–July) annual tactical counteroffensive campaign. During the month of May, the trees and bushes shed leaves, which allows the attackers better visibility and thus a clear tactical advantage during the attack.[1] The season suits them because by the time the security force scramble to launch "a counter-offensive,"[2] the monsoon starts, which makes the terrain almost completely inaccessible. The Maoists go deeper into the forests where the forces cannot enter until the heavy downpours come to an end. Mobility is not easy during the monsoon given the topographical difficulty in Dandakaranya, which is spread through Chhattisgarh, Orissa, and Jharkhand. Hence the Maoists undertake a tactical counteroffensive campaign most often during the month of May to inflict maximum damage to the government security forces.

In regard to this planned mindless killing, what motivated the Maoists was a heartfelt long-drawn desire of revenge against the creator of the armed vigilante, Salwa Judum, and to demonstrate their capacity to strike in the so-called red corridor. Hence, the May Maoist guerrilla ambush is characterized as "a piece of the larger phenomenon of the violence of the oppressed which is always preceded and provoked by the violence of oppressor."[3] This is thus not a stray incident given the fact that Maoism is an ideologically charged political design to seize power in India. Spreading over sixteen Indian states running through the center of the Indian hinterland from the Nepal–Bihar border to the Karnataka–Kerala borders, Maoists, by being involved in their daily struggle for existence, appear to have developed organic roots among the people in this area. As an anonymous police source confirms, some 19,000 square kilometers in the region represent "a free zone," where the Indian state had ceased to exist and no government official dares to enter; in the red corridor, not only do the insurgents run a parallel government, they also politically indoctrinate the local habitats to sustain and expand their ideological appeal.[4] In the context of large-scale land acquisition by industrial houses in what is a mineral-rich region—especially in the district of Dantewada, Bastar, and Bijapur in Chhattisgarh—the Maoist violent response seems to be a natural outburst. Even the government report confirms the mass-scale displacement of the local people due to "the biggest grab of land after Columbus," which was initially "scripted by Tata Steel and Essar Steel who want seven villages or thereabouts each to mine the richest lode of iron ore available in India."[5] The result was disastrous: a local tribal who lost his small piece of land graphically illustrates this effect by saying that before the land acquisition he had a source of sustenance that was complemented by the forest produce, a lifeline for thousands like him in the Bastar forests. With the transfer of land to private operators, he now became "a daily wage contract labourer who remains without food if there is no work."[6] This story is typical of Dandakaranya area where thousands of tribals feel deprived in their own land where there is a clear deficit of governance in view of the excesses, perpetrated by private moneylenders and junior government functionaries in the revenue and forests departments.

What then is Maoism? The simple answer is that it is a brand of radical ideology drawing on the political ideas of Mao besides the classical Marxism. At a rather complex level, it is an ideological response to India's journey as an independent nation that followed a specific path of development. Hence Maoism is also an ideological package seeking to articulate an alternative with roots in both orthodox Marxism and the Chinese variety. That Maoism goes beyond "the armchair revolutionaries" to inspire "the have-nots" under the most adverse circumstances to fight for their cause also reveals its meaningful role in galvanizing those at the grassroots. As an ideology, Maoism addresses the genuine socio-economic grievances of the people in the affected areas by mapping out an exploitation-free social order, which remains the primary goal of the movement. The aim may remain unfulfilled though there is no doubt that the Left-wing Extremists (LWE) are inspired to believe that the Maoist objective of an equitable society will surely be attained.

Maoism in India has thrived on the objective conditions of poverty, which have various ramifications. Undoubtedly, high economic and income disparity and exploitation of the impoverished, especially "the wretched of the earth," contribute to conditions that are conducive to revolutionary and radical politics. India's development strategy since independence was hardly adequate to eradicate the sources of discontent. The situation seems to have been made worse with the onset of globalization that has created "islands of deprivation" all over the country. As the state is being dragged into the new development packages that are neither adequate nor appropriate for the "peripherals," Maoism seems to have provided a powerful alternative. The tribals veer toward ultra-left-wing extremism for the failure of the state to provide "food, clothing, education, basic health care and legitimate rights over the land that is theirs."[7] The argument, drawn on poverty, is strengthened by linking the past deficits with the disadvantages inherent and perceived in the present initiatives for globalization. The Orissa (and Chhattisgarh) case is an eye-opener because Maoism has gained enormously due to the "displacement" of the indigenous population in areas where both the state-sponsored industrial magnates and other international business tycoons have taken over land for agro-industries. Here is a difference between the present Maoism and the Naxalbari movement. In case of the latter, it was an organized peasant attack against peculiar "feudal" land relations, particularly in West Bengal whereas the Maoists in Orissa and Chhattisgarh draw on the "displacement" of the local people due to the zealous support of the state for quick development through "forced" industrialization

The steady expansion of Maoist influence is therefore attributed to its success in persuading "the exploited masses" to take part in the movement as possibly the only way out of their subhuman existence. The grassroots situation is so appalling that there is hardly a difference of opinion between the Naxalites espousing a violent path to create a new social order and the government officials involved in combating "the red menace." Justifying the armed revolution to overturn the prevalent exploitative system, Ajit Buxla, a Maoist responsible for mobilizing the tribals in Malkangiri, a district in Orissa, did not find it incongruent to resort to violence. In his words, "When you see death taking tolls on your near and dear ones and you know their life could have been saved had they been given proper and timely medication, you are forced to believe that the existence of state has nothing to do with the life of poor and marginalized."[8] Corroborating the feeling, Bidhu Bhusan Mishra, the former Inspector General of Police, Government of Orissa, was more categorical; explaining the increasing influence of Maoism in rural Orissa, he said, "The lack of development, grievances of the tribals and poor, and the absence of administration have been conducive to the spread of left wing extremism in Orissa."[9] Two important points come out of these two statements, made by individuals with completely different aims: first, in view of the terrible plight of those in the periphery due to stark poverty, Maoism seems to have gained enormously by ideologically articulating an alternative to the prevalent inequitable world, and, second, the failure of the state to reach out to the marginalized continues to baffle the administrators and the governed. As an official confirms, "Naxalites operate in a vacuum created by inadequacy of administrative and political institutions, espouse local demands and take advantage of the prevalent disaffection and injustice among the exploited segments of the population and seek to offer an alternative system of governance which promises emancipation of these segments."[10] It is not therefore surprising that the prime minister of India in his address to the 2007 Chief Ministers Conference suggested that without meaningfully addressing "development needs of the affected people," the Naxalism cannot be effectively combated. As he argued,

> Development and internal security are two sides of the same coin. Each is critically dependent on the other. Often, the lack of development and the lack of any prospects for improving one's lot provide a fertile ground for extremist ideologies to flourish. . . . At the same time, development cannot take place in the absence of a secure and stable environment. . . . I have said in the past that the Left Wing Extremism is probably the single biggest security challenge to the Indian state. It continues to be so and we cannot rest in peace until we have eliminated this virus.[11]

The basic thrust of the argument made by the prime minister relates to the realization that the conventional coercive methods do not seem to be adequate unless the genuine socio-economic grievances of those sustaining the Naxal campaign are meaningfully addressed. This line of reasoning is endorsed by the reports submitted by the Expert Committee of the Planning Commission and the Second Administrative Reforms Commission. By making a comparative survey of twenty severely Naxal-affected districts in five states—Andhra Pradesh, Bihar, Chhattisgarh, Jharkhand, and Orissa—with twenty nonaffected districts in the same states, the committee found a direct correspondence between the rise and consolidation of left-wing extremism and lack of development. One of the major factors that accounts for the consolidation of Naxalism is undoubtedly the lack of faith of the rural masses in the government machinery that is invariably geared to protect those relatively better placed in socio-economic terms. There are areas where the government functionaries are hardly visible and the funds, earmarked for welfare schemes, are mostly appropriated by those in complicity with the government officials. While commenting on the role of the paramilitary and police forces, the committee found that these combative forces needed to be sensitized to the human needs to effectively challenge "the red menace." The second Administrative Commission that submitted its report entitled "Combating Terrorism" in June 2008 puts the Naxals on par with *jihadis* clinging to "religious fundamentalism."[12] Like the Expert Committee, the commission also agreed that the roots of Naxalism were located in the development trajectory of these Indian states where large sections of population continued to suffer due to distorted economic growth. The commission thus recommended a multi-pronged strategy based on political consensus, good governance, socio-economic development, and respect for the rule of law. What is remarkable is the fact that the government of India, while articulating its response, took into account the major recommendations possibly to reorient its policies vis-à-vis Maoism in those areas where it has evolved as an organic movement.

To review and monitor different mechanisms of the Naxal problem, the government of India constituted an Empowered Group of Ministers, a Standing Committee of Chief Ministers of Concerned States, Coordination Centre, a Task Force under Special Secretary (Internal Security), and an Inter-Ministerial Group, headed by an additional secretary (Naxal Management). By evolving a two-pronged strategy, the government seeks to address "the Naxal menace" at two levels: while it is necessary to conduct proactive and sustained operations against the extremists and put in place all measures required for this, it is also necessary to simultaneously give focused attention to development and governance issues, particularly at the cutting-edge level. The Ministry of Home Affairs in its annual reports lists several schemes—including the Backward Districts Initiatives, Backward Regions Grant Fund, the National Rural Employment Guarantee Scheme, the Prime Minister's *Gram Sadak Yojna* (rural roadways), the National Rural Health Mission Scheme, and *Sarva Siksha Abhiyan* (universal education), among others—to meaningfully articulate the role of the government in eradicating poverty at the grassroots. In fact, it was agreed upon by those involved in the anti-Naxal cell of the government of India that so long as the masses were stuck in poverty Maoism was likely to flourish because of its success (i) in projecting an exploitation-free world after the revolution and (ii) in dismissing the role of the government in ameliorating the conditions of the poverty-stricken people given their historical failure since independence. Maoism is therefore not merely a law-and-order problem; it is also an ideological battle underlining serious lacuna in India's development strategy since independence. With various welfare schemes in place, the government initiatives are likely to yield results in due course of time, which will perhaps be a serious threat to Maoism drawing on "lack of development" as perhaps the most effective agenda in the Maoist campaign.

It is true that Maoists have drawn on the genuine socio-economic grievances of the poverty-stricken masses for political mobilization in favor of their ideological campaign. This is one side of the story; the other part addresses how they seek to fulfill their aim. As true Maoists, Naxalites unhesitatingly resort to violent means to change the inequitable society. An unconfirmed source suggests that the People's

Liberation Guerrilla Army that was formed in 2000 has more than ten thousand armed cadre nationwide, twenty-five-thousand members of the people's militia, and fifty thousand members in village-level units.[13] In absolute terms, the military strength may not be so alarming. What is worrisome, as the government underlines, is "the simultaneous attack at multiple locations by large number of Naxalites in a military type operations . . . looting of weapons at Giridih (Jharkhand), detention of a passenger train in Latchar (Orissa) [and] looting of explosives from the NDMC magazine in Chhattisgarh."[14] There are reasons to believe that the Naxalite guerrilla army has so far not only succeeded in sustaining its grip in the so-called liberated zones but has also brought new areas under its control by following a completely different kind of tactics to overpower the government paramilitary forces. On 29 June 2008, the Maoists, for the first time, showcased their ability in marine warfare when they chose to attack a motor launch inside the Balimela reservoir in the Malkangiri district of Orissa, which left thirty-four people dead. The official combatant force comprised members from the specially created paramilitary wing, known as the Greyhound commandos. The incident took place in the area that is claimed by the Naxals as the Liberated Zone, the area where the Malkangiri district of Orissa shares a border with the Bastar area of the Chhattisgarh and Khammam districts of Andhra Pradesh. Malkangiri is separated from Andhra by the Sileru River and from Chhattisgarh by the Saberi River. Besides the Sileru and Saberi, there is another interstate river, the Mahendrataneya, between Orissa and Andhra. Operationally, this is the area where Naxals recently raised a boat wing to facilitate faster movement of their cadres and weapons.[15]

Similar to a typical Leninist organization, appreciative of democratic centralism, the entire Maoist activities are governed by a centralized leadership that so far remained free from factional feuds. The killing of Swami Laxmananda Saraswati, a Vishwa Hindu Parishad leader, and four other associates in Kandahmal in Orissa on 23 August 2008 however led to the rise of a powerful faction condemning the act because of the probable repercussions on intercommunal relations in this small Orissa town with a sizeable section of Dalit Christians. The merciless killing of Saraswati and his associates that triggered attacks on Christians in Orissa have split the Communist Party of India (Maoist; CPI [Maoist]) on religious lines for the first time, with many Hindu members breaking away to form a rival group. As the media reports confirm, the new group calls itself IDGA–Maoist, the acronym for Idealist Democratic Guerrilla Army of CPI (Maowadi). According to the police sources, this group, also known as M2, is made up of Hindu Maoists, who were appalled by the murder of the eighty-four-year-old Laxmananada Saraswati in Kandhmahal in August 2008. "The content of M2 leaflets prove beyond doubt that Saraswati's murder has divided the Maoists which has people from both Christian and Hindu faiths. . . . M2 criticizes conversions and quotes Lord Krishna's sermons in the *Bhagwad Gita*," sources said. Although the extremists profess that they don't work for a religious ideology and that they target all exploiters, Saraswati's killing appears to have provoked a debate on intercommunal relations, according to police sources. Whatever be the outcome of the debate, the fact that such an issue gained prominence reveals that Maoists are not as free from religious prejudices as they so vociferously claim.[16]

Divided into three chapters, this part is devoted to the analysis of the rise and consolidation of Maoism in India focusing on its distinctive ideological appeal in the context of globalization resulting in the massive displacement of the tribals in the name of rapid industrial development. Beginning with the genesis of Maoism, this part also dwells on the Maoist blueprint for future India in accordance with fundamental tenets of Marxism–Leninism and the thought of Mao Tse-Tung, which, to fulfill the ideological mission, clearly encourages unbridled violence as perhaps the only means to work toward the establishment of a classless society in the future. Furthermore, based on a thorough probing of the prevalent socio-economic circumstances confronting the indigenous population, it has also been shown how the widely acclaimed state-led development paradigm became vacuous in its claim by its failure to bring about inclusive development in India.

5

Genesis of Maoism in India

FROM A REBELLION for land rights to a socio-political movement critiquing India's state-led development paradigm and finally to a serious threat to the country's internal security, the Maoist movement has indeed come a long way. This Maoist journey has been the most unusual one as it traveled from an unknown village of Naxalbari in West Bengal to reach 509 Police stations comprising seven thousand villages in eleven states, namely, Andhra Pradesh, Chhattisgarh, Bihar, Jharkhand, Orissa, Maharashtra, Uttar Pradesh, Madhya Pradesh, West Bengal, Tamil Nadu, Karnataka, and Kerala.[1] The level of violence is significant in the affected districts of Andhra Pradesh, Chhattisgarh, Jharkhand, Bihar, Maharashtra, and Orissa. There were reports that the Naxals are fast targeting some regions in Uttaranchal and Haryana. As per the 2006 data, 40 percent of the country's geographical area and 35 percent of the country's total population is affected by the problem of Naxal violence. This is no simple mathematics, as it implies that the problem of Naxalism is more acute than the problems in Kashmir and in the northeast.[2] In January and February 2007 the Communist Party of India (Maoist; CPI [Maoist]) conducted its Ninth Party Congress, which signaled yet another phase in the cycle of Maoist insurgencies in India. For the Naxal leadership, this came as a grand success since the Maoists were holding a unity congress after a gap of thirty-six years— their Eighth Congress was held in 1970. The Maoists claim that the congress resolved the disputed political issues in the party through debates and discussions in which both the leaders and the led participated with mutual respect to one another.[3] This claim is politically significant in two ways: not only does this formally recognize the preva-lence of inter/intra organizational feuds among the ultra-radical outfits, it is also a

TABLE 5.1

Profile of Naxal/Maoist Violence in the Affected States, by year, 2008–2012

States	2008		2009		2010		2011		2012	
	Incidents	Deaths	Incidents	Deaths	Incidents	Deaths	Incidents	Deaths	Incidents	Deaths
AP	92	46	66	18	100	24	54	9	67	13
Bihar	164	73	232	72	307	97	316	63	166	44
Chhattisgarh	620	242	529	290	625	343	465	204	369	109
Jharkhand	484	207	742	208	501	157	517	182	479	162
MP	35	26	1	–	7	1	8	–	11	–
Maharashtra	68	22	154	93	94	45	109	54	134	41
Orissa	103	101	266	67	218	79	192	53	171	45
UP	4	–	8	2	6	1	1	–	1	–
WB	35	26	255	158	350	256	92	45	6	–
Other States	14	4	5	–	4	–	6	1	8	–
Total	1,591	721	2,258	908	2,212	1,003	1,760	611	1,412	414

Notes: AP = Andhra Pradesh. MP = Madhya Pradesh. UP = Uttar Pradesh. WB = West Bengal.

Sources: Compiled from the reports prepared by the Ministry of Home Affairs, Government of India, *Annual Report, 2012–13* (New Delhi: Ministry of Home Affairs, Government of India, 2013). Online: http://www.mha.nic.in/sites/upload_files/mha/files/AR%28F%291213.pdf.

persuasive testimony of the Maoist efforts to sort out differences through meaningful dialogues among themselves.

The data provided by the Union Home Ministry, given in Table 5.1, are not just a statement but an astounding revelation of a grave danger, a shadow of which looms over the whole system of India's democratic governance. It is not only the number of deaths but also the loss of the country's physical territory that is even more worrisome. It leaves no room for romanticism. In no unclear terms it reveals that the Naxal threat is real. Furthermore, in comparison with other extremist outfits in northeast India and Jammu and Kashmir, the left-wing extremist groups are reported to have committed more than 80 percent of violent acts and killings, as Table 5.2 shows.

What are the reasons that have kept this movement alive for a period of about four decades? Despite all the tall claims made by successive governments, people in the Naxal-affected regions continue to lead a miserable life. The metamorphic growth of violence and the inability of the state to come out with a well-thought strategy have entirely paralyzed the rural administration in the Naxal-infested regions. The ill-represented national government, nonresponsive state governments, failed institutions of local self-government, and the establishment of Naxal Janata Sarkar[4] particularly in the Naxal-dominant regions have led to the formation of a vicious nexus between bureaucrats, politicians, contractors, and the Naxals not to assist the downtrodden but to make Naxalism a lucrative business. On the other hand, throughout all these decades the Naxal movement has never been able to prepare a development formula for the people for whom it claims to have a waged a war against the state. Also there is little hope that the Naxal rank and file would ever come closer to the level where policies are made or programs are implemented. The aim of the chapter is to acquaint the readers with the organizational evolution of Maoism in its contemporary articulation in India. Drawn on Marxism–Leninism and Mao's political ideas, Maoism is an undoubtedly a continuity of the previous Naxalbari movement. In fact, the similarity is obvious given the

TABLE 5.2

Left-Wing Activities since 2009			
Year	Incidents involving Left-Wing Extremism	Incidents in Northeast India	Incidents in Jammu and Kashmir
2009	2,258 (908)	1,297 (306)	499 (150)
2010	2,212 (1003)	773 (114)	488 (116)
2011	1,760 (611)	627 (102)	340 (64)
2012	1,412 (414)	1,025 (111)	220 (30)

Note: Figures in parentheses indicate the number of killings during the year.

Source: Ministry of Home Affairs, Government of India, Annual Report, 2012–13 (New Delhi: Ministry of Home Affairs, Government of India), chapter 2, 11–21. Online: http://www.mha.nic.in/sites/upload_files/mha/files/AR%28E%291213.pdf.

compatible ideological roots. This is probably the reason why Maoism is also identified as Naxalism in the contemporary political discourses that also include the official characterization of the movement. Despite semantic differences in the nomenclature, Maoism and Naxalism seem to be broadly ideologically identical. In the contemporary literature, both these expressions are therefore interchangeably used to mean the ultra-left-wing extremism in India that appears to be pervasive in the red corridor.

ROOTS OF MAOISM

To understand the current phase of Maoism we need to understand different aspects of organizational transformation that occurred within the Naxal movement during the last decade or so because the Naxal movement is a reflection of continuity and change. Drawn on Marxism and Leninism and Mao's political thought, the present incarnation of this movement is undoubtedly continuity at least in ideological terms. That the nature of the movement differs from one district to another is suggestive of the extent to which the local socio-economic circumstances remain critical in its articulation. For instance, in the tribal districts of Orissa, Maoism consolidates its support by concentrating on tribal rights over forest products. In nontribal districts, the movement draws on challenging the feudal land relations. In other words, Maoism is adapted to the prevalent socio-economic issues while setting its agenda for "the downtrodden." Dandakaranya is the area in which Maoism seems to have developed organic roots by generally involving the socio-economically deprived tribals. This is an area in central India encompassing thirteen districts of five states of Andhra Pradesh, Chhattisgarh, Madhya Pradesh, Maharashtra, and Orissa. Their ideological activities are largely confined to Adilabad, Khammam, East Godavari, Vishakhapatnam (Andhra Pradesh), Dantewada, Bijapur, Kanker, Narayanpur, Bastar and Rajnandgaon (Chhattisgarh), Gadchiroli, Chandrapur and Bhandara (Maharashtra), Balaghat (Madhya Pradesh), Koraput, and Malkangiri (Orissa). Operating in an area of nearly eighty thousand square miles, which has thick forests, rivers, and rivulets, Maoists move around these districts almost freely because of their well-entrenched organization, which is detrimental to any state-led preemptive measures to detain them. With a population of roughly twenty-two million, this is also a tribal-preponderant area, which remains the permanent habitat of the Gond, Madia, Govari, Kondh, Konda Reddy, Nayakapu, Dorla, Muria/Koya, and Oriya tribes of Puruja, Gudijursa, Butar, and Durva.[5] These tribals are not nomadic but settlers, and their association with the forest and hills is most intimate not only because they provide a livelihood but also a definite cultural mooring that shapes their existence in these God-forbidden places that suddenly have attracted the attention of the corporate mafia presumably because of the huge reserve of precious natural resources.

Despite having drawn ideological impetus from the same source, Maoists are highly fragmented and are prone to factional squabbles to settle personal scores among themselves. The fragmented character of the movement gave rise to all possible trends and groupings, thereby paving the way for new avenues of organizational conflict. Due to its fragmented character the movement witnessed many past leaders and cadres making a comeback as though from oblivion. This aspect of Naxal organizational politics is very important to understand as it also enabled the reemergence of a whole range of questions that were supposed to have been already resolved once and for all.

A PRELUDE TO THE GROWTH OF THE NAXAL MOVEMENT IN INDIA

To understand the genesis of the Naxal movement one needs to locate it within the framework of the communist movement in India. To be more specific, any study of the Naxal movement cannot overlook the importance of the rise and fall of the Telangana movement (1946–1951). For Indian communists, the peasant movement in Telangana would always remain the glorious chapter in the history of peasant struggles. It was "a simple peasant movement against feudal oppression and Nizam's autocracy [that] had grown into a partisan struggle for liberation."[6] In that sense, the Telangana movement was the first serious effort by sections of the Communist Party leadership to learn from the experiences of the Chinese revolution and to develop a comprehensive line for India's democratic revolution. Despite the role of the committed activists, the movement remained confined to districts of Warangal and Nalgonda where the communist leadership implemented the ideological program. This limited success seemed to have "convinced the CPI leadership that Telangana was soon going to be the pattern all over the Nizam's state and then for the rest of the country."[7] That these signals were too deceptive to take seriously was evident when the movement was finally withdrawn in 1951, just two years after it began, for parliamentary politics in which the Communist Party of India (CPI) enthusiastically participated. Nonetheless, the Telangana experiment facilitated the growth of three distinct lines in the Indian communist movement. First, the line promoted by Ranadive and his followers rejected the significance of the Chinese revolution and advocated the simultaneous accomplishment of the democratic and the socialist revolutions based on city-based working-class insurrections. The group drew inspiration from Stalin and fiercely attacked Mao as another Tito.

The second line mainly professed and propagated by the Andhra Secretariat drew heavily from the Chinese experiences and the teachings of Mao in building up the struggle of Telangana. The Andhra leadership successfully spearheaded the movement against the Nizam; however, it failed to tackle the complex question of meeting the challenge of the government of India. The Nehru government embarked on the road to parliamentary democracy, conditioning it with reforms like the "abolition of Zamindari system." All these objective conditions facilitated the dominance of a centrist line put forward by Ajay Ghosh and Dange. This line characteristically pointed out the differences between Chinese and Indian conditions and pushed the party along the parliamentary road, which articulated the third line in the Indian communist movement. The third ideological line was translated in 1957 when the communists succeeded in forming a government in Kerala, which, however, was soon overthrown. Following the India–China war in 1964, the party split into two: the CPI and Communist Party of India (Marxist; CPI [M]). While the CPI preached the theory of "peaceful road to non-capitalist development," the CPI (M) followed the centrist line. Though there were serious differences on ideological and tactical lines, both the parties went ahead with their parliamentary exercises and formed the United Front government in West Bengal.

ASSESSMENT OF PAST MOVEMENTS

One can draw two conclusions on the basis of careful reading of the socio-political processes in which these two movements—Tebhaga in West Bengal and Telangana in the erstwhile princely state of Hyderabad—were organized.[8] First, these movements were politically organized by political parties drawn on Marxism–Leninism and Maoism. It is true that these movements failed to attain the goal of radical agrarian reforms for a variety of reasons. Yet, by raising a powerful voice against feudal exploitation, they seemed to have begun a process of social churning that became critical for the future movements. Second, these movements also articulated an alternative to the state-led development paradigm, which was hardly adequate to get rid of the well-entrenched feudalism. These movements were watersheds in independent India's political history and powerful statements on the failure of the state to redress peasant grievances due to reasons connected with the ideological priority of the ruling authority that replaced the colonial power following the 1947 transfer of power. Despite their failure, these movements had undoubtedly sensitized Indian society to the desperate efforts made by the rural poor to escape the intolerable conditions of economic oppression and social humiliation. There is also no doubt that the Naxalbari movement served as a catalyst in West Bengal where it made its first appearance following the introduction of "land reforms" by the Left Front state government, which had been ruling West Bengal uninterruptedly for more than three decades since 1977.

On the backdrop of political uncertainty of far-reaching consequences, one particular incident that took place in an unknown location involving unknown people hugely transformed the history of left-wing extremism in India. In a remote village called Naxalbari in West Bengal one tribal youth named Bimal Kissan, having obtained a judicial order, went to plow his land on 2 March 1967. Goons associated with the local landlords attacked him. Tribal people of the area retaliated and started forcefully reclaiming their lands. What followed was a rebellion, which left one police subinspector and nine tribals dead. This particular incident acquired a larger appeal in about two months on the basis of the open support that it garnered from cross sections of communist revolutionaries belonging to the state units of the CPI (M) in West Bengal, Bihar, Orissa, Andhra

Pradesh, Tamil Nadu, Kerala, Uttar Pradesh, and Jammu and Kashmir. Though the United Front government of West Bengal, steered by two communist parties, the CPI and the CPI (M), with all repressive measures, was able to contain the rebellion within seventy-two days, these ultra-radical units regrouped in May 1968 and formed the All India Coordination Committee of Communist Revolutionaries (AICCCR). "Allegiance to the armed struggle and non-participation in the elections" were the two cardinal principles that the AICCCR adopted for its operations. However, differences cropped up over how the armed struggle should be advanced, and this led to the exclusion of a section of activists from Andhra Pradesh and West Bengal, led, respectively, by T. Nagi Reddy and Kanai Chatterjee.

On the issue of the annihilation of the class enemy, the Kanai Chatterjee group had serious objections to the view that the annihilation of the class enemy should only be taken up after building up mass agitations. However, the majority in the AICCCR rejected this, and the AICCCR went ahead with the formation of the Communist Party of India (Marxist–Leninist; CPI [ML]) in May 1969. This led Chatterjee to join the Maoist Communist Centre (MCC). The CPI (ML) held its first congress in 1970 in Kolkata, and Charu Mazumdar was formally elected its general secretary.

THE NAXALBARI MOVEMENT (1969–1972): A REVIEW

The Naxalbari movement was a short-lived "spring thunder" that helped reconceptualize political discourses in India. This was primarily an agrarian struggle against brutal feudal exploitation that led to a massive anti-state confrontation. Hailing the Naxalbari movement, the *People's Daily*, the mouthpiece of the Chinese Communist Party, thus commented:

> A peal of spring thunder has crashed over the land of India. Revolutionary peasants in the Darjeeling area [in West Bengal] have risen in rebellion. Under the leadership of a revolutionary group of the Indian Communist Party, a red area of rural revolutionary armed struggle has been established in India. This is a development of tremendous significance for the Indian people's revolutionary struggle.[9]

Challenging the status-quo state, the movement inspired a large section of Indian youth to undertake even "armed struggle" for seizure of political power. When it was launched, the center of gravity of the movement was rural West Bengal that later shifted also to urban areas in various Indian states. In terms of its geographical expanse, the movement was not as widespread as its contemporary incarnation, namely Maoism. Nonetheless, there is no doubt that the Naxalbari movement provided the ideological impetus to Maoism that is a contemporary response to the prevalent socio-economic imbalances in the globalizing India.

The Naxalbari movement was not "suddenly created in 1967, [nor] did it fall from heaven by the grace of God, nor was it a spontaneous outburst."[10] It was the culmination of long-drawn-out anti-feudal struggles in the Indian state of West Bengal that began with movements against "illegal extortion" of *jotedars* (landlords). It was therefore argued in the *People's Daily* that the Naxalbari movement was "an inevitability . . . because the reactionary rule has left with [the people] no alternative."[11] At the outset, this was an agrarian struggle that "combined both institutional and noninstitutional means of exercising power as [the participants] developed some kind of a disciplined peasant militia, comprised mainly of tribal Santal, Oraon and Munda communities, with traditional arms like bows and arrows."[12] In course of time, the movement that was likened to "a prairie fire" lost its momentum for variety of reasons: primary among them was the failure of the leadership to sustain "the revolutionary enthusiasm" of the masses, as Kanu Sanyal, one of the top Naxal leaders, admitted, saying,

> After we went underground during 1967–68 and later during 1969–72, most of us lost touch with the reality of the situation on the ground; unfortunately we learnt much later that what was being dished out by our top leaders and others including the party organs were either distorted or highly exaggerated accounts which suited "the high command's dictates" and in the process the revolutionary potential suffered incalculable damage.[13]

There are two important reasons for the gradual decline of the Naxalbari movement, as Sanyal underlines. First, what caused the breakdown of the movement was a tactical failure to build an ideology-driven organization of the exploited classes. Unable to form "a revolutionary front of all revolutionary classes" comprising "poor and landless peasants and also the workers," the CPI (ML) leadership insisted on guerrilla war for "the seizure of power." Emphasizing guerrilla warfare waged by the peasantry "as the only form of struggle in the present stage of revolution," the party ignored "the need for mass organizations or for an agrarian programme as a concomitant of peasant struggle." Holding Charu Majumdar, the main ideologue of the party, responsible for such a futile tactical line, Sanyal further argues that not only did Majumdar reject "the ideas of a mass organization," he also advocated "the building of a secret organization through which the poor and landless peasants can establish their leadership of the peasant movement."[14] Despite strong opposition by his colleagues, Majumdar was hardly persuaded because in his opinion revolution was possible only "by organizing guerrilla war by poor and landless peasants. . . . Guerrilla war is the only tactic of the peasants' revolutionary struggle [that] cannot be achieved by any mass organization through open struggle."[15] The second tactical line that caused irreparable damage to the movement was "the battle of annihilation" as Majumdar characterized. Appreciating the battle of annihilation as "both a higher form of class struggle and the starting point of guerrilla war," Majumdar supported the annihilation campaign even to the extent of alienating his colleagues, arguing,

Only by waging class struggle—the battle of annihilation—the new man will be created, the new man who will defy death and will be free from all thought of self-interests. And with this death-defying spirit he will go close to the enemy, snatch his rifle, avenge the martyrs and the people's army will emerge. To go close to the enemy, it is necessary to conquer all thought of self. And this can be achieved only by the blood of martyrs. That inspires and creates new men out of the fighters, fills them with class hatred and makes them close to the enemy [to] snatch his rifle with bare hands.[16]

The annihilation line caused consternation among both the leaders and the rank and file of the movement. Characterizing the annihilation line as "a terrorism of a very low kind," Ashim Chatterjee critiqued Majumdar by saying,

This was nothing more than secret assassination by small armed groups. Such actions do not in any way raise the class consciousness of workers and peasants or enthuse them to organize on a class basis. Rather they inhibit their natural feelings of class hatred within the bounds of individual revenge and retribution. . . . All communists recognize that by . . . annihilating individual capitalists or individual landlords, the capital or the system of feudal exploitation will not be eliminated, nor will a proletarian dictatorship or the rule of workers and peasants be created. It is natural for those at a low level of political consciousness to go for the apparently simple solution of annihilating the individual capitalist or the individual landlord.[17]

Not only was the annihilation line criticized by Chatterjee, it was condemned by the Naxal activists at the grassroots. In his appraisal of the Naxalbari movement, Prabhat Jana, an activist in Orissa, found annihilation totally incompatible with Marxism–Leninism. As he argued, "Individual terror—secret assassination of individuals—does tremendous harm to the cause of revolution instead of helping it in two significant ways: first, it diverts the Party from the path of class struggle, from the path of people's war. It is petty-bourgeois subjectivism [dreaming] to create mass upsurge through individual terror by a handful of militants." Second, the annihilation line is suicidal because "a handful of militants isolated from the people can easily be suppressed by the enemy." As such, "it belittles the enemies' strength from the tactical point of view."[18] The annihilation campaign, instead of contributing to the cause of the movement, damaged its future to a significant extent. While a large section of the people were "antagonized, thousands of cadres tortured, maimed and imprisoned and several hundreds—both leaders and cadres—died."[19]

Besides clear tactical failures, the movement was also handicapped due to lack of proper ideological guidance. For instance, to do away with the bourgeois cultural traditions, the party instructed the cadres to burn the portraits and deface and destroy the statutes of "the heroes" of the Bengal Renaissance in Calcutta and elsewhere. This step, instead of fulfilling the ideological aim of the movement, alienated the urban middle class to a significant extent. Supporters were bewildered because instead of ideologically combating the influence of the bourgeois cultural traditions, the party resorted to easy means that shocked "the middle class that [was] brought up to revere the pro-imperialist and cultural leaders."[20]

Besides the ideological bankruptcy, the Naxalbari movement received a serious jolt when its ideological mentor, the Chinese Communist Party, threatened to withdraw support and came out strongly against the Naxal leadership for having deviated from Marxism–Leninism. As the present stage of revolution in India was "people's democratic revolution" in which the principal task was to overthrow feudalism and the domination of imperialism and to distribute land among the peasants, the Chinese leadership, particularly Chou En-Lai, insisted that the Indian revolutionaries should, as a strategy, build a united front of the exploited classes even with some of the exploiting classes, including the capitalists. It was also pointed out that the Naxalbari movement lost its "vitality" because it failed to mobilize "the peasant masses" since it lacked a well-defined agrarian program. The Indian leadership was also criticized for mechanical application of the Chinese model of revolution to contemporary India that was undoubtedly a failure to creatively articulate Marxism–Leninism disregarding the prevalent socio-economic milieu. Peeved with the annihilation line that drew on Charu Majumdar's dictum that "one who has not smeared his hands red with blood of the class enemy is not fit to be called a communist," Chou En-Lai was reported to have asked the Indian communist leadership to withdraw the campaign for such "secret assassinations." Also, the slogan "China's chairman is our chairman" displeased the Chinese leadership to a significant extent since it meant that the movement was controlled and guided by a foreign power, which was certain to alienate "any sensible human being with self-dignity and pride in one's national identity."[21] Although this slogan never became very popular, it appears to have reflected a genuine weakness of the left-radical movements in India since the formation of the Communist Party in 1923 by those charged in the Meerut conspiracy case. Initially, it was the Communist Party of Great Britain that, through its emissaries, almost dictated the CPI during the nationalist struggle. The most disappointing course of action by the CPI was undertaken during the Second World War. So long as the former Soviet Union had a pact with the Hitler's Germany, the war was "an imperialist war." Following Hitler's attack on Moscow, the war became a "people's war." When the Soviet Union joined hands with Britain against Hitler, Indian communists found it ideologically appropriate not to oppose the British war effort in India. As a result, they did not participate in the Congress-led Quit movement in 1942 since it would have weakened the British government (and thus the people's war), which was involved in a historic battle against fascism in the Second World War. The stance that the Indian communists had adopted in this context was perhaps ideologically tenable though it was "a betrayal" for the nationalists fighting for independence despite adverse consequences. The Indian communists later realized that, by supporting the colonial government, they alienated the masses. Nonetheless, history was repeated and those involved in the Spring Thunder almost two and a half decades after the 1942 open rebellion uncritically accepted the hegemonic role of a foreign communist leader even as the Chinese Communist Party strongly voiced its annoyance and later disapproval.

THE NAXALBARI MOVEMENT AFTER CHARU MAJUMDAR

The history of the post–Charu Majumdar Naxal movement is characterized by a number of splits brought about by personalized and narrow perceptions about the Maoist revolutionary line and attempts at course correction by some of the major groups. Even Kanu Sanyal, one of the founders of the movement, was not free from this trend. He gave up the path of "dedicated armed struggle" by 1977 and accepted parliamentary practice as one form of revolutionary activity.

It was during 1974 that one influential group of CPI (ML), led by Jauhar (Subrata Dutt), Nagbhushan Pattnaik, and Vinod Mishra, launched a major initiative that they referred to as a "course correction." This group renamed itself as CPI (ML) Liberation in 1974, and, in 1976, during the emergency, it adopted a new platform that called for the continuation of armed guerrilla struggles along with efforts to form a broad anti-Congress democratic front, consisting of both communist and noncommunist parties. The group also suggested that pure military armed struggle should be limited and that there should be greater emphasis on mass peasant struggles in an attempt to provide an Indianized version of Marxism–Leninism–Maoism. However, during the next three years, the movement suffered further splits with leaders such as Kondapalli Seetharamaiah (Andhra Pradesh) and N. Prasad (Bihar) dissociating themselves from the activities of the party. This led Prasad to form the CPI (ML) Unity Organization, and Seetharamaiah started the People's War Group (PWG) in 1980. Seetharamaiah's platform also sought to restrict the "annihilation of class enemies," but the PWG's emphasis was on building up mass organizations, not on developing a broad democratic front. Since then, the principal division in the Naxalite movement has been between these two lines of thought and action, as advanced by the CPI (ML) Liberation and the PWG. While Liberation branded the PWG a group of "left adventurists," the PWG castigated the Liberation group as "revisionists" who imitated the CPI (M). On the other hand, the growth of MCC as a major armed group in the same areas created the scope of multifarious organizational conflicts among the Naxal groups. The Liberation took a theoretical stand of correcting the past mistakes of "completely rejecting parliamentary politics." However, the PWG and the MCC completely rejected the parliamentary democratic system of governance and vowed to wage a "people's war for people's government." In the process while the Liberation group registered its first electoral victory in Bihar in 1989, more Naxalite factions such as the CPI (ML) New Democracy, the CPI (ML) S. R. Bhaj-jee Group, and the CPI (ML) Unity Initiative were formed in that state.

The Naxalbari movement saw different turns and twists in the 1990s. First, intra-organizational conflict and rivalry among different groups touched several high points resulting in the loss of a considerable number of cadres to rival groups. Second, despite the large-scale inner conflicts, there was always an exercise going at various levels working toward unity. Third, in 1990 the affected state registered a considerable growth in violent incidents, and at the same time a considerable change in policy approach at the government level was also witnessed. If the Naxal movement is mostly characterized by fragmented groups and innumerable splits, successive governments at the national and state level were never able to follow a uniform approach to deal with the problem of Naxalism. All these have had a marked impact in the growth of the Naxal movement.

NEW THREADS IN CONTINUATION WITH THE PAST

There are three major outfits through which Naxalism operates: the CPI (ML) Libera-tion, the PWG, and the MCC. Although these groups draw on more or less the same ideological principles, they differ from one another in regard to certain tactical lines which are as follows:

- The analysis of the first phase (1967–1971) of the Naxalite movement and the line of annihilation that was followed.
- The position that armed struggle is the principal form of struggle and that the armed guerrilla squad is the primary unit of struggle.
- Because the principal form of struggle is armed struggle, the entire activity of the agrarian struggle should be underground.
- Whether the contradiction between feudalism and Indian masses is the princi-pal form of contradiction in Indian society or whether India has emerged as a capitalist state and, hence, the contradiction between capitalism and the general public is the principal contradiction.
- Whether forming a united front with various forces and movements like the Dalit movements, farmers' movements, ethnic and regional movements, eco-logical movements, and so on is advisable.[22]

There is a note of caution, however. Despite having separate nomenclature, these out-fits have identical roots since they all were associated with the CPI (ML) when it was formed in 1969. Several groups later emerged either due to factional feuds within the or-ganization due to ideological differences or due to personality clashes that culminated in the division within the party. This resulted in weakening of the movement that was ideo-logically innovative but was not politically as attractive as was expected at the beginning.

This is a paradox in India's communist movement that, despite being ideologically creative, never became a pan-Indian political force due to organizational weaknesses and the failure to address these weaknesses meaningfully. Nonetheless, the Naxalbari movement stands out because of the legacy that it left behind.

[It brought to the fore] the political urgency of the agrarian revolution in India, of the militant organization of the small and landless peasantry to accomplish this revolution, of the systematic expansion of the sphere of people's power as a preparation for, and not merely as a hypothetical consequences of, the seizure of power.... Naxalbari is not simply the story of a few brave lives lost in a futile battle. It represents a political task which must be achieved.[23]

CPI (ML) LIBERATION

Historically speaking, the origin of CPI (ML) liberation dates back to 1974. However, the post-emergency phase of 1977, when most leaders of the communist movement were released from the jail, was the time when the activity of liberation was first noticed. The Party Central Committee, in a move to unite the splinter groups owing their origin to CPI (ML), called a meeting from 30 January to 2 February 1981. However, the meeting could not derive the expected results. "From this point onwards whereas the [Party Central Committee] group goes on to become irrelevant and splits up into various factions, the M–L movement begins to polarize between the Marxist–Leninist line of CPI (ML) Liberation and the anarchist line of CPI (ML) People's War (PW)."[24] During 1982 Indian People's Front was launched in New Delhi at a national conference. In due course of time, the Indian People's Front became the party's open political platform that actively intervened in national politics. At the end of the year, the Third Party Congress took place at Giridih, Bihar, where the issue of participation in election was clinched. This shift in the outlook of CPI (ML) Liberation proved to be vital in designing a later course of action within the Naxal movement. As one scholar observes, "Even though the Liberation group considers itself the true inheritor of the CPI (ML) legacy, its political line has changed dramatically from that of the original CPI (ML)."[25] With this strategic shift in functioning the CPI (ML) Liberation recorded its first electoral victory under the banner of the Indian People's Front in 1989, and Ara (one Lok Sabha Constituency in Central Bihar) sent the first "Naxalite" member to Parliament.[26] In a special conference that convened in July 1990, the party decided to resume open functioning. This decision was formalized at its Fifth Congress in December 1992. In 1994, the Indian People's Front was disbanded. The Election Commission recognized the party in 1995, and since then the CPI (ML) began contesting successive elections at the national and state levels.

The CPI (ML) Liberation, though functioning above ground within the parliamentary democracy set-up, has not completely disbanded the path of armed rebellion.

> The Party does not rule out the possibility that under a set of exceptional national and international circumstances, the balance of social and political forces may even permit a relatively peaceful transfer of central power to revolutionary forces. But in a country where democratic institutions are based on essentially fragile and narrow foundations and where even small victories and partial reforms can only be achieved and maintained on the strength of mass militancy, the party of the proletariat must prepare itself for winning the ultimate decisive victory in an armed revolution. A people's democratic front and a people's army, therefore, remain the two most fundamental weapons of revolution in the arsenal of the Party.[27]

This again points out the dilemmas within the ultra-left movement, which is very often reflected in the unpredictable character of the Naxal movement.

People's War Group (PWG)

The PWG is the most important among all the splinter groups representing the Naxal movement because today the dominant line within Naxal politics is the PWG line of thought. Though it is popularly known as PWG or PW, its official nomenclature is the Communist Party of India—Marxist–Leninist (People's War). If Naxalism today is being considered as the greatest internal security problem and if today Naxals claim to be running a parallel government in different parts of the country, its credit mostly goes to the PWG. "The CPI (ML) (PW) was formed on Lenin's birth anniversary on April 22, 1980."[28] Kondapalli Seetharamaiah, one of the most influential Naxalite leaders from Andhra Pradesh and a member of the former Central Organizing Committee of the CPI (ML), is the founding father of PWG; ironically however he was later expelled from the group. While elaborating the ideological program of the party, it was proclaimed:

> The Programme of our Party has declared that India is a vast "semi-colonial and semi-feudal country," with about 80 percent of our population residing in our villages. It is ruled by the big-bourgeois big landlord classes, subservient to imperialism. The contradiction between the alliance of imperialism, feudalism and comprador-bureaucrat-capitalism on the one hand and the broad masses of the people on the other is the principal contradiction in our country. Only a successful People's Democratic Revolution i.e. New Democratic Revolution and the establishment of People's Democratic Dictatorship of the workers, peasants, the middle classes and national bourgeoisie under the leadership of the working class can lead to the liberation of our people from all exploitation and the dictatorship of the

reactionary ruling classes and pave the way for building Socialism and Communism in our country, the ultimate aim of our Party. People's War based on Armed Agrarian Revolution is the only path for achieving people's democracy, i.e. new democracy, in our country.[29]

Rejecting the parliamentary democratic system and branding individual annihilation as individual terrorism, PWG declares that a people's war is the only path to bring about a people's government in the country. It is clear that there was a set of organizational, strategic, and tactical conflicts going on within the CPI (ML), which paved the way for the split and creation of a more radical party. Broadly speaking the party programs of CPI (ML) Liberation were mostly focused on the cause of peasants, while the group led by K. Seetharamaih wanted the party to be a platform for peasants, workers, tribals, and other weaker sections of the society. It was the prime agenda of Liberation to build up a political front focusing on peasant struggles, whereas PWG was more interested in the formation of mass organizations instead of a democratic front. One of the renowned guerrilla leaders of the former PWG summarizes the essence of the conflict between CPI (ML) Liberation and CPI (ML) PW by stating:

> In the Liberation group, which at one time was one of the strong groups defending Charu Majumdar's revolutionary line, after the martyrdom of Comrade Johar, with the leadership falling into the hands of Vinod Mishra, they began betraying the Indian revolution. As part of a conspiratorial plan, a once revolutionary party was gradually changed into a revisionist party, like the CPI and CPM. The armed resistance struggles against the state's attacks, taking place under the then leadership of Liberation, was ended. The armed struggle to crush the feudal private armies was made a secondary task. In this way, they diverted the entire group away from the basic path outlined by the unified CPI (ML), and particularly of its founder, Com. CM—that of protracted people's war—into becoming agents of the ruling classes, by surrendering them to the parliamentary path. They converted the Comrade Johar–led Liberation, from being a revolutionary movement, into a legalist, reformist and parliamentary movement; and changed the underground organization into an open opportunist and revisionist organization.[30]

The above two official statements of PWG clearly suggest that the birth of PWG, which resulted due to another split within the CPI (ML) Liberation, was mostly designed due to the dynamics of conflict among lots of its cadres. For a considerable period after its birth PWG's activities were limited to Andhra Pradesh only, whereas CPI (ML) Liberation continued to hold its turf in Bihar. It was during this period another organization came into existence on 1 January 1982. It was named CPI (ML) Party Unity, which came into existence as a merger between CPI (ML) Unity Organizations and the

Central Organizing Committee CPI (ML). Hereafter the left-wing extremism in India witnessed some of the worst ever conflicts, which again forced many of the organizations to take a position and adopt new tactics. Bihar has always remained a strong battle-ground for Naxal operations, and ironically Bihar witnessed most of the clashes were between CPI (ML) Party Unity and CPI (ML) Liberation in the past, as Table 5.3 illustrates:

TABLE 5.3

Left-Wing Activities in Bihar

Year	Number of Clashes	Number of Deaths
1994	5	8 (PU 5, Lib 3)
1995	16	13 (PU 8, Lib 5)
1996	36	24 (PU 5, Lib 19)
1997	21	16 (PU 3. Lib 3)

Notes: PU = Party Unity. Lib = Communist Party of India (Marxist–Leninist) Liberation.
Source: Times of India (Patna), 7 December 1997.

When these conflicts were taking a toll on the cadres of both sides, another develop-ment was taking place simultaneously. In August 1998, Party Unity merged with CPI (ML) PWG and the group came to be known as PW. "The merger of the two parties is the culmination of the unity process which began in March '93 and continued for over five years during which differences on several political, ideological and organizational questions were resolved through thread-bare discussion."[31] The statement continues,

> The emergence of the united Party—the Communist Party of India (Marxist–Leninist) [PW]—does not mark the completion of the process of unification of the genuine communist revolutionary forces in India. The newly Unified Party will continue its efforts in right earnest to achieve this unification. We also call upon the other genuine revolutionary elements in the various M-L parties in India who are being led astray by both right and left opportunist leadership, to fight against these deviations and rally under the banner of the United Party. The United Party pledges itself to avenge the death of thousands of martyrs who fell in the course of the ongoing democratic revolution in India paved with blood by these martyrs until their cherished goals are accomplished. This is the era of Revolutions.[32]

By this merger PWG became another force to reckon with in Bihar and in other areas where the United Party had a presence. Further developments suggest that with this merger the armed rebellion path of the Naxal movement became stronger, while with its parliamentary practices Liberation was losing its turf to PWG. The same Liberation that once controlled the whole of Central Bihar was losing its territory and supporters to

PWG and MCC. Not only in Bihar but everywhere, Liberation was being systematically reduced from the map of Naxalite politics. By participating in electoral methods and by not being able to make an impressive mark the Liberation movement became weak and the PWG's armed operation started gaining momentum.

So when the Liberation with its changed modus operandi was being reduced to the status of any other small political party, the PWG in the same period managed to register its presence outside Andhra Pradesh and gradually made strongholds in different areas of Bihar, Orissa, Madhya Pradesh, Jharkhand, Chhattisgarh, and Maharashtra. Of course, due to this conflict between the Party Unity and Liberation, both the groups suffered in terms of loss of a considerable number of their cadres, but, as we saw, this conflict also resulted in the merger of Party Unity and the PWG and ultimately resulted in the violent consolidation of the movement.

The formation of the PW also resulted in tactical changes in several aspects of the Naxal movement in general. "In our agenda for a new democratic revolution, there are two aspects—the agrarian revolution and fight for nationality."[33] This statement shows the amount of organizational change witnessed by the Naxal movement in all those years. In 1967, it started in the name of agrarian revolution, which gradually took the stance of replacement of the parliamentary form of government, but the question of nationality was never asked. This reflects the pattern of conflict between PW and Liberation. By questioning nationality, PW wanted to make it clear that it wanted a broad revolutionary pattern, and "land to tillers" could be a program but not the sole agenda of the revolution.

During 15–30 November 1995 the PW conducted an All India Special Conference in some unknown locality of Dandakaranya. There it adopted two important party documents. The "Party Program" as adopted in the conference reads,

India is a semi-feudal, semi-colonial society; here the New Democratic Revolution (NDR) has to be completed victoriously paving way to the Socialist Revolution and to advance towards the ultimate goal of Communism. The Indian people are weighed down by three big mountains: feudalism, imperialism and comprador bureaucrat capital; these are the targets to be overthrown in the present stage of NDR. The four major contradictions in the present-day Indian society are: the contradiction between feudalism and the broad masses; the contradiction between imperialism and the Indian people; the contradiction between capital and labour and the contradiction within the ruling classes. While the first two are fundamental contradictions to be resolved through the NDR, the contradiction between feudalism and the broad masses is the principal contradiction at the present stage. India is a multi-national country—a prison-house of nationalities and all the nationalities have the right to self-determination including secession. When NDR is victoriously completed, India will become a voluntary and genuine federation of all national people's republics.[34]

The second adopted in the conference was the document on the "Strategy and Tactics." It reads:

The political strategy to be pursued in the present stage of NDR in India is one of forming a broad united front of all the anti-feudal, anti-imperialist forces—the working class, the peasantry, the petty bourgeoisie and the national bourgeoisie—under the leadership of the working class to overthrow the common enemies—feudalism, imperialism and comprador bureaucratic capital. The military strategy or the path of Indian Revolution is the path of protracted people's war, i.e., liberating the countryside first through area wise seizure of power establishing guerrilla zones and base areas and then encircling the cities and finally capturing power throughout the country. The unevenness in the economic, social and political development of Indian society calls for different tactics, i.e., forms of struggle and organization, to be pursued in different regions of the country, while the political tactic line throughout the country remains the same. In urban areas the political and mass work should be carried out observing utmost precaution and the organizational work should proceed keeping in view the long-range perspective. Caste is a peculiar problem in India; and appropriate forms of organization and struggle should be evolved vigorously to fight out untouchability, caste discrimination and to finally root out the caste system. The tactics of boycott of elections have to be pursued for a long time in the prevailing conditions in India; and participating in parliamentary and assembly elections under any pretext only weakens the class struggle.[35]

These two documents containing different organizational aspects of PW makes a clear-cut demarcation for the issues pertaining to organizational conflict between Liberation and PW. PW, on the basis of its assessment of the people's level of preparedness for an armed struggle, discarded total annihilation of "class enemies" as the only form of struggle and stressed on floating mass organizations. It established several front organizations. During the 1980s, the Radical Students' Union and Rayatu Kuli Sangham emerged as organizations with an impressive mass following, and most of the PWG's present base and political cadres had developed through that practice. However, during the 1990s, growth of militarization became the characteristic feature of the PWG. The formation of the People's Guerrilla Army (PGA), special guerrilla squads, Permanent Action Team, and Special Action Team were the distinctive features of PWG activities for quite some time before it merged with the MCC to form the CPI (Maoist).[36]

Maoist Communist Centre (MCC)

The next important group within the broad spectrum of Naxal movement is the MCC. Among a number of organizations it stands apart as, conventionally speaking, it never was part of the CPI (ML), which many claim as the mother of all Naxal organizations.

"The MCC, while supporting the Naxalbari struggle, did not join the CPI (ML) because of some tactical differences and on the question of Party formation."[37] The MCC was formed on 20 October 1969, during the same time when the CPI (ML) was formed; however, during those days it was known as Dakshin Desh. In 1975 the group renamed itself as the MCC. In 2003, the MCC merged with the Revolutionary Communist Centre of India–Maoists to form the Maoist Communist Centre–India (MCC–I).

Right from its inception, the MCC stood for taking up armed struggle as the main form of struggle and waging a protracted people's war as the central task of the party. This position of MCC has been repeatedly expressed and emphasized by the Maoists while decoding their strategy. As the *Red Star*, the MCC weekly, firmly declares,

> This armed revolutionary war is the war of the armed people themselves; it is "Protracted People's War" as shown by Mao Tse Tung. The concrete economic and political condition of India leads to the very conclusion that the path shown by the great leader and teacher, Mao Tse Tung, the path of the Chinese Revolution, that is, and to establish a powerful people's army and people's militia and to establish dependable, strong and self-sufficient base areas in the countryside, to constantly consolidate and expand the people's army and the base areas, gradually to encircle the urban areas from the countryside by liberating the countryside, finally to capture the cities and to establish the state system and political authority of the people themselves by decisively destroying the state power of the reactionaries—this very path of the protracted People's War is the only path of liberation of the people of India, the path of victory of the new democratic revolution.[38]

CPI (Maoist)

The Naxal movement in India entered into yet another phase of organizational transformation with the merger of two of the principal armed organizations: the PW and the MCC–I, which resulted in the formation of the CPI (Maoist).

> The formation of the unified Communist Party of India (Maoist) is a new milestone in the history of the revolutionary communist movement of India. A unified Maoist party based on Marxism–Leninism–Maoism is a long delayed and highly cherished need of the revolutionary minded and oppressed people of the country, including all our ranks, and also all the Maoist forces of South Asia and internationally. Now, this long-aspired desire and dream has been transformed into a reality.[39]

This statement, given by the first secretary of CPI (Maoist), Ganapathy, assumes a great deal of importance as it reflects the organizational politics that was going on all these years between these two organizations representing the Naxal movement.

The exalted aim of the CPI (Maoist) as announced on the occasion of its formation is to establish a compact revolutionary zone stretching from Nepal to Bihar to Andhra Pradesh and beyond. While continuing its goal of people's democracy, the ultimate aim of the CPI (Maoist) is to seize power through protracted armed struggle. According to the press statement issued on the event of announcing the merger,

> The immediate aim and programme of the Maoist party is to carry on and complete the already ongoing and advancing New Democratic Revolution in India as a part of the world proletarian revolution by overthrowing the semi-colonial, semi-feudal system under the neo-colonial form of indirect rule, exploitation and control.[40]

This revolution will remain directed against imperialism, feudalism, and comprador bureaucratic capitalism. This revolution will be carried out and completed through armed agrarian revolutionary war, that is, a protracted people's war with the armed seizure of power remaining as its central and principal task, encircling the cities from the countryside and finally capturing them. Hence the countryside as well as the Protracted People's War will remain as the "center of gravity" of the party's work, while urban work will be complimentary to it. According to the same press release, the CPI (Maoists) "will still seek to unite all genuine Maoist groups that remain outside this unified party."[41]

It is important to examine the significance of the merger particularly when earlier attempts were not successful. In fact, the merger is largely seen as a result of the gradual convergence of views of these two groups on areas such as the role of the party, approaches to revolution, and the adoption of strategies and tactics. In the formative years, Charu Mazumdar and Kanhai Chatterjee represented two irreconcilably different lines and approaches to "revolution." At the time of the formation of the CPI (ML) in 1969, the Dakshin Desh, an earlier form of the MCC, remained opposed to the process due to sharp differences with the CPI (ML) over issues such as formation of a communist party, existence of revolutionary mass struggle, and preparedness of the people to participate in it. The joint press statement released by the former general secretaries of PW and MCC–I highlighted the essence of the merger.

> In the past history there were many splits within the M–L movement. But splits are only one side of the coin; the brighter side was that there were continuous efforts to unify the revolutionaries. The CPI (ML) ([Party Unity]), though it had its origins in Bengal, it spread and was strengthened by unifying several revolutionary groups. The CPI (ML) (PW), though it originated in Andhra Pradesh and Tamil Nadu, unified with revolutionaries in almost all the states where it was working. The MCC, too, had originated in Bengal, unified many revolutionary groups in it in many States and became the MCCI.[42]

This statement underlines the continuous process of organizational politics within the broad spectrum of Naxalite movement in the process, which resulted in organizational conflict.

Looking back, the need for a joint unified platform was felt by the leadership of both the parties as early as 1981.

The PW and MCC began unity talks from their very first meeting in 1981. However, the reason for the delay in the process was the lack of continuity of leadership. The arrest of Comrade Kondapally Seetaramaiah (KS), the leader of the PW, and later the internal crisis of the PW and split in the Central Committee (CC) delayed the unity process for several years. In the early eighties, the MCC lost its two top leaders Comrades Amulya Sen (AS) and Kanhai Chatterjee (KC), which had some negative impact, resulting in further delay in the unity process.[43]

However, this is not to suggest that the formation of CPI (Maoist) is the final stage of the Naxal movement. As one official Maoist document puts it, "Revolutions never proceed in a straight line. The history of all successful revolutions shows this. The path is zigzag, there are ups and downs, there is victory and defeat repeated a number of times . . . before final victory. Of course, there is no final victory until the stage of communism is reached."[44] The above-mentioned analysis makes a forceful plea that more than anything the Naxal movement essentially is a political problem and that it needs to be examined from the perspective of organizational politics.

The merger of the CPI (ML) (PW) and MCC–I that resulted in the birth of the CPI (Maoist) also successfully brought the dominant faction of CPI (ML) Janashakti into its fold. Amidst speculations of the merger, both the Janashakti and CPI (Maoist) presented a united front in 2005. A death toll of 892 persons in 2004 was largely believed to be a result of the merger which reportedly gave the Maoists effective striking power in their encounter with police and para-military forces. The Naxal movement, however, continued to conquer new territories in 2006–2007. Other than the escalation in violence, the later part of 2006 also witnessed significant changes in the operational ways of the Naxal movement.

The honeymoon between the CPI (Maoist) and the Janashakti did not last longer than a year, and in 2006 it became apparent that both were clearly going different ways to occupy operational areas. During the open session of the CPI (Maoist), held in December 2006, the Janashakti was asked to make clear its stand on its political aims and programs; the Janashakti, however, chose not to attend the session. Consequently, the CPI (Maoist) withdrew the partner status from the Janashakti and decided to provide need-based support only in the case of police actions. The conflict between the CPI (Maoist) and the Janashakti became public only recently, when the Orissa Janashakti group led by Anna Reddy killed three forest officials on 31 January 2007. The CPI (Maoist) state leadership immediately distanced itself from the killings. Subsequent police inquiry confirmed the involvement of the Janashakti group in the gruesome act.

Of course, things are at a formative stage today; the setting is ready for a possible realignment of the Maoist forces. In Karnataka, which is largely viewed as the new Naxal target, the CPI (Maoist) recently suffered a major setback as a number of cadres in the state, who disagreed with the Maoist agenda of intensifying the revolution in rural areas first and then spreading it to urban centers, have floated a new party: the Maoist Coordination Committee. It should be noted that the political cracks in Karnataka have now started to extend to other states.

From the above discussion we can derive the following conclusions. First, the history of the Naxal movement is the history of a continuous process of organizational conflicts, splits, and mergers. Second, the Naxal movement essentially represents the simultaneous but not necessarily peaceful coexistence of many streams, and looking from this angle the movement does have a presence in all parts of the country. Third, the growth of the Naxal movement is closely linked with the ongoing process of organizational conflict. The ultimate political objective behind all this organizational exercise, according to the statements of various senior Naxalite leaders, is to build a leftist alternative and mobilize people on issues such as increased "imperialist intervention" and "pro-imperialist policies" pursued by the union government in support of "revolutionary war" based on Chinese leader Mao's theory of organized peasant insurrection. Similarly, the history of the Naxal movement right from its first phase of 1967 demonstrates that even if there has been a continuous evolution in terms of the movement's understanding of the Indian situation, focus of the movement, character, fighting capabilities, and financial resources of these groups, they have remained more or less consistent as far as their core ideology is concerned. Barring Liberation they all reject parliamentary system of governance and want to bring about a fundamental change in the nature of the Indian state. For this they have adopted the strategy of protracted armed struggle, which entails building up bases in rural and remote areas and transforming them first into guerrilla zones and then into liberated zones, undertaking area-wide seizures, and encircling cities, and finally seizing political power and achieving nationwide victory. Fourth, the history of the Naxal movement so far has been the history of conflicts and splits; however, one cannot deny that it also represents the history of mergers.

CONCLUDING OBSERVATIONS

Maoism is a contemporary manifestation of the ultra-left movement in India although it would not be wrong to characterize the movement as a historical continuity simply because of the broad ideological compatibility with the past movements that drew on Marxism–Leninism and Maoism. Besides the Naxalbari movement in the late 1960s and early 1970s, the Telangana liberation struggle (1946–1951) and the Tebhaga movement (1946–1949) also mobilized the marginalized against the so-called feudal forces that stalled land reforms and other ameliorating social and economic measures for the majority.

What distinguishes the Tebhaga and Telangana upsurges from the past movements was that these were politically inspired and supported by a well-entrenched organization, under the guidance of the undivided CPI. The Tebhaga movement, as its nomenclature suggests, demanded the reduction of the share of the landlord from one-half of the crop to one-third. The leadership came from the Kisan Sabha, a peasant front of the CPI. This Bengal-based movement gradually spread in Dinajpur and Rangpur in north Bengal and twenty-four parganas in south Bengal. Despite its temporary success, the movement gradually petered out in the face of an organized government-sponsored counteroffensive. Yet, the movement forced the ruling authority to introduce the Barga-dar Act, which legalized the demand of the sharecroppers to retain two-thirds of the harvested crop. Unlike the Tebhaga movement, which mobilized Bengal peasants in se-lective districts to enhance their share of the produce, the Telangana movement was a genuine agrarian liberation struggle to get rid of feudal landlordism and dynastic rule of Nizam in Hyderabad. The movement however lost its momentum with the 1947 inde-pendence when Nizam's rule came to an end. There were some in the Communist Party who wanted to continue the movement against the Indian government, but a majority of them were in favor of withdrawal. In 1951, the movement was formally withdrawn. In a rather superficial sense, the Telangana movement succeeded because Nizam lost his au-thority in the changed environment of free India after the 1947 transfer of power. Yet, it would be appropriate to suggest that the movement raised a voice against feudal atroci-ties, which was articulated differently in independent India, resulting in ameliorating land reform measures.

The Naxalbari movement was an ideological continuity of the past movements that sought to organize peasants against feudal exploitation. The name is derived from Nax-albari, a nondiscrete place in the northern part of West Bengal. Mobilized by those who formed the CPI (ML) in 1969, one of the primary aims of the "spring thunder, " as it is metaphorically characterized, was to bring about radical changes in the prevalent agrar-ian structure that endorsed "feudal exploitation" of perhaps a very primitive nature. As a 1969 political resolution of the party suggests,

> The increasing concentration of land in the hands of a few landlords, the expro-priation of almost the total surplus produced by the toiling peasantry in the form of rent, the complete landlessness of about 40% of the rural population, the back-breaking usurious exploitation, the ever-growing evictions of the poor peasantry coupled with the brutal social oppression—including lynching of "harijans," remi-niscent of the medieval ages—and the complete backwardness of the technique of production clearly demonstrate the semi-feudal character of our society.[45]

What is distinctive about Naxalbari is that a majority of peasants are tribals. Exploited by the landlords and their agents, they were employed on a contractual basis, and, in most cases, they did not even get the government-fixed wage for their work in the fields. The movement failed to attain its goal. Nonetheless, it had a far-reaching impact on the entire agrarian scene throughout India. It was like a "premeditated throw of a pebble bringing forth a series of ripples in the water."[46] The uprising, though ephemeral in exis-tence, was widely publicized and inspired the rural poor in other parts of the country to launch militant struggles against feudal exploitation and the failure of the state to evolve an equitable economy. While the immediate and spontaneous demand of the peasants involved in the Naxalbari movement was the fulfillment of some economic demands, it also led to a long-ranging struggle for "the ultimate seizure of political power" that not only survived but also expanded despite internal factional squabbles and an organized state counteroffensive.

There are two fundamental ideological points that remained critical in the Naxalite approach to revolution: for the Naxalites, the rent-seeking landlords were the main class enemies and the bourgeoisie or capitalism was not the main enemy, since the agrarian sector in India was still semi-feudal and semi-colonial. In view of the well-entrenched feudal land relations, supported by landlords, progress toward capitalism was thus difficult, if not impossible. Hence the primary duty of those involved in radical social change was to liquidate the landlords and landlordism. It was against these large landed but supposedly noncapitalist proprietors that "the Naxalite people's" war was waged by a United Front of all revolutionary classes, and all revolutionary groups engaged in the armed struggle against feudalism.[47] By following the Maoist idea of "national democracy," the immediate ideological objective of the Naxalites was to form a multi-class political platform involving social groups with contradictory class interests (e.g., rich peasants, middle peasants, poor and landless peasants) and to establish a national democratic regime as a possible step toward fulfilling the ultimate socialist goal.

Notwithstanding obvious similarities, the Maoist movement differs from the Spring Thunder of the 1969–1972 period on a variety of counts. First, Maoism seems to have struck an emotional chord with the tribal population, unlike the Naxalbari movement, which shifted its center of gravity to the urban and semi-urban areas and drew support from the educated middle-class youth. It is difficult to clearly identify the class background of the Maoists though there is no doubt that the participants are "not romantic, middle-class babus, as was the case generally during Charu Majumdar's quixotic misadventure of 1969–72 period especially in West Bengal."[48] Second, unlike their Naxal counterparts, Maoists are "better-organized" and "well-equipped" with sophisticated firepower, as it was evident in the series of successful attacks on the police and paramilitary armed forces in Bihar, Chhattisgarh, and Orissa. There are official reports that Maoists are regularly trained in a military style in areas where the government seems to have lost control. Finally, Maoists are ideologically more closely knit than those involved in the Naxalbari movement. One of the major factors that led to the collapse of the Naxalbari movement was internecine feuding not only among the leaders but also among the grassroots activists. According to Kanu Sanyal, one of the top Naxal leaders, what led to the downfall of the Naxalbari movement was "an atmosphere of disrespect and expression of arrogance by the leaders that [resulted in] reducing the Communist revolutionaries in India to groups and sub-groups."[49] What crippled the Naxalbari movement was the emergence and consolidation of two contradictory trends. On the one hand, "the urban-based leadership, cloaked in a more sophisticated ideology, claimed superior

knowledge and status with regard to the manner in which the movement should be conducted."[30] Opposed to it was, on the other hand, "the co-opted indigenous leadership"[31]
that followed the principle of democratic consultation at every level of the organization
before arriving at a decision. While the first trend is illustrative of an "elitist leadership"
that Charu Majumdar consolidated by developing a centralized organization with concentration of power at the top, the Kanu Sanyal–led rural wing of the leadership sought
to democratize the organization by meaningfully involving the activists at various levels
of the leadership. The movement lost considerable momentum largely due to the division
among the leaders, which not only weakened the organization but also caused confusion
among the followers. The present-day Maoists seem to have learned a lesson from the
past that was translated into reality when out of four different Maoist outfits emerged
the CPI (Maoist) in 2005. Undoubtedly, this merger is a milestone in India's left-wing
movements since most of the radical outfits fizzled out in the past due to factional fighting. The formation of the CPI (Maoist) is therefore a watershed insofar as the consolidation of those clinging to Maoism are concerned. The gradual but steady expansion of the
red corridor since the 2004 merger is also a powerful testimony to the growing importance of Maoism as a political means to get rid of the well-entrenched socio-economic
imbalances at the grassroots.

Maoism is thus an ideological continuity with the past, and yet this is a contextual
response to the peculiar Indian reality that differs radically from one place to another. In
the past, ultra-left movements seem to have uncritically accepted the "one size fits all"
approach by accepting classical Marxism–Leninism as sacrosanct. Given the socio-
economic and cultural diversity of the continental variety, India can never be comprehended in a single axis. By being sensitive to this well-entrenched diversity, Maoism has
reinvented Marxism–Leninism in a non-European milieu. Even within India, the issues
that Maoists raise differ radically from one state to another. In Andhra Pradesh, Maoism
draws, for instance, on anti-feudal sentiments whereas in the tribal belt of Orissa and
Chhattisgarh, rights over forest produce remains the most effective demand for political
mobilization. This context-driven articulation of Maoism is certainly a critical factor in
its rise as perhaps the most effective ideological voice of the downtrodden notwithstanding the adverse consequences.

It is difficult to predict the future of Maoism though there is no doubt that it has succeeded, so far, in expanding the red corridor by involving mainly the peripheral sections
of society in an area stretching across almost half of India. This itself is suggestive of the
historical limitations of the state-led development programs that failed miserably to take
care of the basic needs of a vast population. The situation seems to have worsened following the acceptance of neoliberal economic reforms in the wake of a serious domestic
fiscal crisis in the early 1990s. The government design for rapid industrialization seems to
have received a serious blow because of organized opposition by those who lost their land
to industrialization. The idea of Special Economic Zones did not auger well with the
people at the grassroots, who felt betrayed by the government policy of transferring land

owned by many small peasants to a single, privately owned company. In areas where Maoism was hardly a force, the forcible eviction of peasants from land for Special Economic Zones leads to circumstances in which Maoists are accepted by those fighting for their rights as a natural ally. In other words, the economic reforms, despite being middle-class friendly, seem to have consolidated the class division in India's rural areas by creating a path of development that is clearly tilted toward foreign capital and its Indian collaborators. Given the appalling socio-economic circumstances in which the vast majority of the Indian population stays alive, it may not be an exaggeration to suggest that Maoism is likely to strike roots since it provides the struggling masses with a powerful voice defending their rights for survival. Maoism is therefore not merely an articulation of ultra-extremist ideology; it is also a well-designed scheme for mobilizing those who remain historically underprivileged for reasons connected to India's interventionist economic strategies under state-led development planning since independence.

6

The Maoist Blueprint for the Future India

MAOISM IS AN articulation of left-wing extremism in India. It has evolved historically following the formation of the Communist Party of India (Marxism–Leninism; CPI [ML]) in West Bengal in 1969 that led the Naxalite movement. Initially confined to West Bengal, the Naxalbari movement gradually spread across the length and breadth of the country. Despite its failure to seize state power, the movement was a sharp comment on India's state-led development program, which was hardly adequate to bring about uniform economic development in India. Maoism is thus a continuity of left radicalism in a meaningful way. Like its past counterpart, Maoism draws on the reinterpretation of Marxism–Leninism by Mao Tse-tung in the context of agricultural China. The aim of this chapter is to acquaint the readers with the organization and organizational network of the ultra-left-wing CPI (Maoist). This chapter elaborates the principal theme in two ways. First, it will focus on the overall structure of the party and the provisional government (the Janathana Sarkar) that it has established in the so-called liberated zones in India. Second, it will attempt a possible explanation for the temporary lull in the Maoist movement in various parts of India by focusing on its internal dynamics as well as the success of the state-sponsored counterinsurgency measures in liquidating some of the top Maoist leaders.

MAOISM AND "ACTION"

Maoism sustains its support base by and thrives on "action." As the brutal attack on the police station in Gadchiroli in Maharashtra on 1 February 2009 killing fifteen policemen reveals, the only mantra that sustains Maoism is "organize and strike back." To remain in the reckoning, the secretary of the CPI (Maoist), Satyanarayana Reddy (alias Kosa), wrote a letter to his cadres to hit back at the government-sponsored police forces to fulfill their ideological aim of seizure of power. Persuading his followers, Reddy expressed his anxiety over their failure in "materializing the revolutionary aim" in the division by saying,

> There has been hardly any output from Gadchiroli division. We have been on the back-foot for quite some time. Why has there been a dearth of recruits for the People's Liberation Guerrilla Army in Gadchiroli Ambush after ambush failed. I would want companies and platoons from Dandakaranaya Special Zonal Committee (DSZC) to join hands with those in Gadchiroli and strengthen our base. The enemy (government) has been carefully devising strategies. And through their policies of development they have tried to gain favour of people [sic]. We have had some setbacks. We need to gear-up in Gadchiroli. And we need to do that fast.[1]

The letter is a testimony to how important the leadership is in conducting the Maoist operation in the remote areas. Once the decision is made by the leadership, it is invariably executed by the cadres who are responsible for "action." There are however reports that decisions are made after discussions among the key members of the Zonal Committee that, in principle, take into account the inputs from the grassroots activists before arriving at a plan of action. In fact, the ambush on the police camp in Gadchiroli that followed the circulation of the above letter confirms that the attack was both an outcome of police atrocities in the peripheral areas of the district and illustrative of the Maoist capability of inflicting irreparable damage to the administration. What is however most disturbing is the increasing number of deaths of civilians in such encounters between Naxalites and the security forces, as Table 6.1 illustrates.

Since Table 6.1 is drawn from the "official data," the interpretation may not always be authentic without cross-checking with comparable data available from other sources.

TABLE 6.1

Outcome of Left-Wing Activities

	2003	2004	2005	2006	2007	2008
Civilians killed	27	20	26	39	24	15
Policemen killed	6	6	18	3	3	6
Naxalites killed	8	4	3	22	7	11
Naxalites arrested	278	155	300	79	123	112
Naxalites surrendered	95	100	83	65	39	146

Source: Data received from the Intelligence Bureau and Rajesh Pradhan, superintendent of police, Gadchiroli District; reproduced in the Hindustan Times, 8 February 2009.

One can however identify trends insofar as Maoist violence is concerned. Civilians suffered most, as the table clearly indicates; the role of the security agency in arresting the Naxalites is quite effective, and the growing number of the Naxalites who had already surrendered is perhaps indicative of the disillusionment of a large section of Maoists in the district with the path of violence. Nonetheless, one cannot gloss over the fact that Maoism is a force to reckon with in contemporary India with its influence over at least one-fifth of India's total number of districts, and one in India's six citizens seems to have been swayed by its ideological appeal.

SHAPING THE ORGANIZATION

The CPI (Maoist) is, as the foreword to its constitution underlines, "the consolidated political vanguard of the Indian proletariat." Inspired by Marxism–Leninism and Maoism, the party strives to "carry on and complete the new democratic revolution in India as a part of world proletariat revolution" by overthrowing the exploiting classes. The new democratic revolution will be "carried out and completed through armed agrarian revolutionary war [that will be complemented] by the parallel rise of the Maoist cadres in cities and towns."[2] After spelling out the fundamental guiding principles in the foreword, which is just like a preamble to the constitution, the CPI (Maoist) constitution, in as many sixty-one provisions, provides a detailed exposition of a constitutional arrangement seeking to replace "the bourgeoisie order." Since the Maoists are committed to overthrow the class-divided state, they are very careful when selecting party members. There are two requirements that are stringently followed in this regard: (i) the uncritical acceptance by the prospective party members of Marxism–Leninism–Maoism, and (ii) the public pledge of the new recruits to the effect of "subordinating their personal interests to the interests of the party and people." In fact, the whole party "shall follow the principle that the individual is subordinate to the organization, the minority is subordinate to the majority, the lower level is subordinate to the higher level, and the entire party is subordinate to the Central Committee."[3] In chapter six, the constitution spells out steps to maintain party discipline, which is most critical for any revolutionary organization. As Article 26 stipulates, "Without iron discipline, no revolutionary party will be able to give capable leadership to the masses in the war and fulfill the responsibility of revolution." Although the party is the motivating ideological force, the role of the people's army is nonetheless significant in pursuing the goal of new democratic revolution. Under the strict guidance of the party, the Maoist army will, according to Article 54, engage in "rousing, mobilizing, organizing and arming the people in carrying out the task of revolution."[4]

As shown, the constitution is an ideological document motivating the Maoists to organize themselves for the final assault on the state power. Guided by the Leninist principle of democratic centralism, the Maoists appreciate "democracy under centralized guidance" and hence the Party Central Committee "decides when and on what questions debates and discussion should be allowed" to avoid wastage of time and energy.[5] So, democracy has a restrictive meaning presumably because of the adverse circumstances in which the party is functioning. Nonetheless, the debates within the party were allowed for constructive purposes, as the party leadership agreed in the 2007 Ninth Congress. For the Maoists, democracy is an initiative to ensure the involvement of the party cadres in what they undertake as part of the revolutionary masses. Therefore,

> [Initiatives must be] demonstrated concretely in the ability of the leading bodies, the cadres and the Party rank and file to work creatively, in their readiness to assume responsibility, in the exuberant vigour they show in their work, in their courage and ability to raise questions, voice opinions and criticize defects, and in the comradely supervision that is maintained over the leading bodies and the leading cadres.[6]

Maoism is not merely a sporadic articulation of mass grievances; this is also a serious ideological endeavor to sustain a movement challenging the prevalent state power that seems to have lost its claim over a vast section of socio-economically excluded rural masses. There is no doubt that the movement has gained momentum to the extent of being the biggest threat to India's democracy. One may be persuaded by the argument that Maoism has flourished due presumably to the failure of the post-colonial state to address the genuine socio-economic grievances of the peripherals. So, Maoism has a natural appeal to the downtrodden in perhaps the most backward regions of India, which are otherwise rich because of a rich depository of valuable minerals. The story remains incomplete because the ideological appeal is also meaningfully articulated by a sustained campaign, backed by an adequately organized party. The CPI (Maoist) is organized following the idea of Mao Tse-tung. It is not surprising therefore that there is an uncanny similarity between the Mao-led Chinese Communist Party and its Indian counterpart if one examines the constitutional provisions guiding the party, as the following discussion demonstrates:

Chapter 7 of the constitution of the party deals with "party's organizational structure," which is well-elaborated in three articles (Articles 29, 30, and 31) with eighteen clauses.[7] Suggesting the basic principles of organization, Article 29 mentions that "the party organization shall be formed according to geographical division or spheres of production." According to Article 30, which is a further elaboration of the party structure, the party congress shall be the highest organ and set the tone and tenor of the party. Structurally, the central committee is the highest executive authority and is supported by (i) a special area committee/special zonal committee/state committee, (ii) a zonal committee/district/divisional committee, (iii) a subzonal/subdivisional committee, and (iv) area committees/local level committees–village/*basti* (slum)/factory/college committees. The primary unit of the party is the cell, defined as "the nucleus of the organization" that can be formed area-wise, profession-wise, or production-wise. As the nucleus of the organization,

> The party cell is a living link between the broad masses of an area and the party.... The cell will lead the revolutionary war of broad masses of people with full initiative. It shall make relentless effort to bring the masses of factory, locality and peasant areas close to the political line and aims of the party. [It will involve the] militant activists and party followers in the revolutionary war against autocratic semi-colonial, semi-feudal state system. It will stress from the very beginning to educate the masses to function secretly, illegally according to the strategy and tactics of the Protracted People's War. [The cell] is also responsible for educating and training those cadres who are entrusted with the task of ideologically preparing the masses for People's War.[8]

The Maoist party organization[9] that seeks to combine democracy with centralism is also a replica of the Chinese Communist Party. It is not therefore surprising that the CPI (Maoist) share a lot of characteristics with the Mao-led Chinese Communist Party. The constitutional provisions relating to CPI (Maoist) draw heavily on the report prepared by Mao Tse-tung for the sixth plenary session of the sixth central committee that was held in October 1938. Hence there are a lot of similarities, both in ideas and language, between the actual provisions of the Constitution of the Indian Maoists and the 1938 report of Mao Tse-tung. For instance, in regard to three important areas—the policies governing the cadres, party discipline, and party democracy—the Maoist constitution resembles the 1938 report of Mao Tse-tung.[10]

Since the CPI (Maoist) is a party for revolution, the organization is structured to achieve its twin goals of (i) spreading the left-wing ideology and (ii) preparing the masses for "action" against the class enemies, as its structure clearly stipulates: at the helm of the organization remains the central committee, which has two major wings: a political wing and an action wing. The political wing comprises (i) the state committee; (ii) the district committee; (iii) the zonal committee; and (iv) the *sangham*, the action wing, which is structured around (i) the armed zonal committee, (ii) the regional committee, (iii) the *dalam* (squad) committee, and (iv) the *dalam*. As the ideological wing of the party, the political wing is entrusted with the task of spreading Maoism at the grassroots. The armed zonal committee is directly involved in military operation against "the enemy." The *dalam*, consisting of at least ten armed and trained cadres, is the basic building block of the Naxalite military wing. A member is chosen to join the *dalam* only after a long apprenticeship as a *sangham* member where he or she is monitored by the party to ascertain his or her capability in armed encounter. *Sangham* members are involved in distribution of pamphlets and carrying messages. They are also used to collect information on those suspected to be police informers. Arms training is given only to members of the *dalam,* which also includes two or three female participants. Each *dalam* has a commander and a deputy commander. The *dalams* generally approach the target area on foot and make their escape on foot. A *dalam* looks after around fifty villages. For large-scale operations, several *dalams* join together; otherwise, they operate independently.

At the primary level, young *sangham* members are involved in activities for dissemination of Maoist ideology by distributing pamphlets in earmarked areas. Their role is crucial in identifying "the police informers" in the villages. Only after they discharge their responsibilities according to the expectation of the *dalam* committee, they are admitted to a *dalam*. In other words, only after the successful completion of training, the *sangham* members are allowed to be recruited for the *dalam*. In this sense, the *sangham* is the preparatory ground for the *dalam*. Hence those who are sympathetic to the Maoist cause are generally welcome, provided the Zonal Committee of the political wing has no objection. Theoretically, this is a foolproof mechanism, and yet, given the factional feud among the *sangham* members, there are occasions when the so-called unwanted elements figure even in the *dalams*, resulting not only in infighting among the members but also, in extreme cases, in disintegration.

The Naxal superstructure is said to resemble a batch of concentric circles: the innermost is the most powerful leadership, located in the remotest forests, forever on the move. The zone, area, and range commanders occupy the middle levels of the classic pyramid management structure. These are reportedly the backbone of the organization, the hands-on, day-to-day direct leaders to the cadres, leading assaults and tracking the goings-on in the villages on their watch. The outermost circles comprise sympathizers who do not wear uniforms, freely interface with the outside world on the basis of their identity of the average villagers, but are the "eyes and ears," the runners for the "brothers" inside. When police claim that they have killed or arrested Naxals, it is believed that they are mostly these outermost cadres. Of course, the Naxals claim that the police arrest or kill only the innocent people.[11]

MAOIST ORGANIZATION IN THE DISTRICTS

The districts in which the Naxalites have total control (with almost complete decimation of the civilian authority) are organizationally divided into "guerrilla zones" and "liberated zones." It was easier for the ultra-leftists to carve out liberated zones in those districts that share borders with two or three states. Illustrative here is Gadchiroli, which is one of those few districts in the Vidarbha region of Maharashtra that shares a border with Chhattisgarh where the Maoists have become a strong ideological force given their role in highlighting "the popular misery" due to government indifference to the increasing number of farmer suicide, in the entire area.[12] Sandwiched between the Naxalite-dominated areas of Rajanandagaon, Kanker, Dantewada, and Bijapur in Chhattisgarh and Karimnagar and Khammam in Andhra Pradesh, Gadchiroli is a strategic location in which the security forces do not have easy access because (i) it is a difficult terrain that remains beyond reach unless the local inhabitants provide logistic help and (ii) it remains inaccessible because the Naxalites have strongholds in the adjacent districts that always act as a buffer in case the security forces wage a combined operation. As the inputs available from the local sources suggest, the district of Gadchiroli is divided into three operational divisions: south Gadchiroli, north Gadchiroli, and north Gondia. Each division has under its command more than twenty guerrilla squads and platoons.[13] Though the Naxalites earlier operated in *dalams* of fifteen and twenty cadres, they have switched to a military-style hierarchy now of local guerrilla squads, platoons, battalions, and divisions.[14] There is no doubt that the Maoists have, over the years, built a well-knit organization in the district to support their ideological goal. According to the official sources, this increasing influence is largely attributed to the government's reluctance to initiate punitive measures against those Naxalites who took shelter in 1980 in Gadchiroli when the security forces came down heavily against them in the neighboring districts in Andhra Pradesh. As a police officer who spent almost his entire career in the Naxal-dominated districts of Andhra Pradesh and later Maharashtra admits, "When the Naxalites entered Maharashtra from Andhra Pradesh, our government chose to see it just as 'a spillover' and decided not to pay attention [and] we are paying the price now."[15] As the police report suggests, a large section of the People's War Group (PWG) that was founded by legendary Naxalite leader, Kondapallu Seetharamaiah, in Andhra Pradesh "infiltrates Gadchiroli of Maharashtra after a police crack down on Naxalites in Andhra Pradesh in 1980."[16] Those who are active in the Maoist movement now are either politically baptized by the PWG or are inspired by its cadres. In this sense, the police contention that, had the movement been nipped in the bud, it would not have had a devastating proportion now appears to have an objective basis.

ORGANIZATION IN URBAN AREAS

Unlike the past, the Naxalites now pay adequate attention to the urban areas where a stable party organization is necessary to accomplish the final goal of the movement, that is, seizure of political power. As Ganapathy argues, "Unless the urban India is drawn to the struggle for the seizure of power, our revolution will remain incomplete."[17] In its Urban Perspective Plan, the party therefore provides a detailed discussion of the party structure that must be developed to complement the revolutionary activities in rural areas. The aim is "to harass the state machinery not only in the villages, but also in towns and cities to attack 'the reactionary demon' from all sides."[18] The principle governing the party organization in urban areas seeks to combine "political centralization" with "organizational decentralization." Such a peculiar admixture of two principles is explained in the Maoist document by stating that the combination of these two principles means that "all [Party Members] and all bodies, particularly at the lower level, should have solid ideological-political foundations, so that they are able to independently find their bearings and take the correct organizational decisions according to the political line of the Party." This is particularly important in the urban areas because (i) it is difficult to maintain close and constant links between secret higher bodies and those at the lower levels engaged in direct open work given the openness of urban space and (ii) with the availability of technological gadgets for communication to the state, delay may cause damage to the works in which the party is engaged to advance the cause of revolution.

Controlled by the party's high command, the urban wing of the party is divided into (i) the cell, (ii) the area party committee, (iii) the part-timer party committees, (iv) the party factions, and (v) the layers. The cell is the primary committee that is entrusted with the task of both expanding its organization and ideologically indoctrinating the fence sitters. The cell can be formed on the basis of unit of production: for the workers, this could be factory, shop, department, shift, production line, industrial estate, and so on; for students and middle-class employees, this could be college, school, institution, office, and so on. For effective functioning and operation of the cell, cells are advised to unite with other cells if there are less than three units in a particular segment. While identifying the basic tasks of the cell, it was suggested that the tasks "include organizing masses, politicizing them, educating the advanced elements and recruiting them into the party, and preparing its members and other activists to go to the countryside to work for the success of the agrarian revolution." Out of the effective cells, a professional revolutionary cell can be created to provide advanced political training to those cell members who have shown potential to take a bigger responsibility for the party by such activities which the party high command deems fit. The second rung consists of the area party committee; two or more cells operating in a locality or unit of production may form the area committee to undertake and monitor the activities in the segment in which they are located. Accordingly, one can think of a factory committee, a college committee, or a basti (slum) committee, among others. The area committee may also consist of part-time members who, despite being sympathetic to the Maoist cause, may not have adequate time to involve themselves full time in party work. Nonetheless, these committees play a critical role in sustaining the organization in urban areas by being continuously involved in development-centric activities and raising issues that are critical to urban areas. The Maoists are aware that unless a careful selection process is devised, these committees will provide easy access to their activities, which will harm the organization and the goals of the organization. Hence, it was forcefully mentioned that while setting up such committees, the party should take care of the "reliability" of the members by thoroughly scrutinizing the past of the probable recruits; otherwise, the entire purpose stands defeated and may result in irreparable damage to the party. Besides the cell and party committees, the party sets up factions in various nonparty organizations to spread the Maoist messages in a discreet manner. The aim is to (i) unite the splinter group around the basis of a common goal and (ii) to ascertain the possibility of working together against a common enemy (i.e., the state). This is likely to pay dividends because exposure to nonparty organizations in urban areas will enable party cadres to mingle with a large group of people who are otherwise neutral in the sense of not belonging to a particular party. The formation of a faction is contingent on the circumstances; if the members feel that the party committee is adequate to handle the responsibility, there is no need of a faction; however, if the party feels otherwise, factions may be constituted as and when necessary. In the urban party structure, layers refers to "the various Party organization like city committee, area committee, factory/slum/college committees, cells as well as the links to the mass organizations of the activists and factions." Layers are responsible for maintaining the liaison among the units of the party at various levels. In this sense, their role is critical in sustaining the organization through links with various units located at the various levels, and, given the adverse circumstances in which the party functions, layers cannot be bypassed and party functionaries are instructed accordingly.

The Naxalites are aware that without a proper coordination among all the units both in urban and rural areas it will be difficult to advance their cause. Also, given the centrality of rural party units in agrarian revolution, the ideological activities of the party in urban areas need to be coordinated and led from the rural areas. This arrangement is justified because of (i) the lack of adequate number of party cadres who are capable of discharging the responsibilities and (ii) the presence of the various state-sponsored coercive agencies to scuttle the Naxalite efforts. Hence, it was suggested that the urban units should "unite with those organizations involved in struggles against the ruling classes" regardless of the ideological compatibility. This includes "the formation of various tactical united fronts as well as building worker-peasant alliance which is the basis of the strategic united front." Drawn on the Maoist idea of new democracy, the effort is meaningful and justified and involves (i) building a basic working-class unity, (ii) mobilizing the peasantry, and (iii) uniting other revolutionary classes such as the semiproletariat and petty bourgeoisie and (iv) the national bourgeoisie and ruling organizations with a people-friendly agenda. From the strict ideological point of view, the Maoist formula of unity with even the ruling class organizations may not find favor with orthodox Marxists though its strategic utility cannot be underestimated. The Maoists appear to be alert to this possibility that this strategic alliance may cause a dent among the committed cadres who may not appreciate such a strategic dilution. Hence there is a clear direction as to when and how this unity is useful from the point of the Maoist primary ideological goal. Three suggestions are made. First, unity with a ruling class organization is possible in the industries because the goals that they seek to achieve are the same as the Maoists; furthermore, the unity is justified to avoid a split among the workers. So, the identical locations lead to unity notwithstanding the ideological incompatibility among those working for the same cause. Second, the Maoists favor issue-based unity with organizations, not strictly ideologically identical, for sustaining the momentum for people's struggle for genuine socio-economic demands. The aim is to build joint fronts with those organizations involving masses for a cause. This is perhaps the most effective strategy when the Maoist organization is not at all strong in urban areas. By adopting a slightly flexible approach for a long-term gain, the Maoists are favorably inclined to coordinate with other communist revolutionary camps, the large number of democratic organizations ventilating the mass grievances, and various other sporadic non-political formations seeking to champion the cause of the people. Third, possible unity can be achieved with the coming together of the Naxalites with other organizations that are working in particular geographical areas with compatible socio-political aims. Characterized as the area unity, this form of alliance creates unity among those confronting identical problems in a specific location. Issues vary from sanitation, water, and transport to safety and security against hooliganism. In the context of growing mass disenchantment with the state-sponsored globalization, the area-based approach seems to have provided the activists with different ideological inklings, offering them with a broad platform to voice their protest. This will not only give the Maoists an opportunity to assess the potential of other democratic organizations to address mass grievances but also provides exposure to those issues that may have escaped their attention while formulating the ideological agenda presumably due to their rural bias.

There are two basic points that have emerged out of this detailed elaboration of the party structure in urban areas. First, to establish a new democratic regime in India, the Maoists cannot afford to ignore the cities and towns. Unless there are complementary efforts from the urban areas, it will be difficult to achieve the goal. Hence the organization in urban India is as important as it is rural India. Second, a sincere endeavor in grasping the urban grievances will also acquaint the Maoists with the urban-centric issues, which would be inconceivable if the focus is confined to rural areas. This is an opportunity for the Maoists in three ways. First, it helps the Maoists to create a constituency in the urban areas by their ideological appeal. Second, it enables them to assess the striking capacity of the ruling class coercive agents who may not be visible in rural areas but are responsible for framing policies and suggesting various ways of combating the "red menace" elsewhere. Finally, a strong organization in the urban segment will complement the efforts of the People's Guerrilla Army in the final war against the Indian ruling class, which will not only be isolated but also terribly crippled due to the breakdown of the network of support.

THE PROVISIONAL GOVERNMENT: THE JANATHANA SARKAR[19]

In the liberated zone of Dandakaranya in Chhattisgarh, the Maoists are reported to have formed a provisional government that may not be effective in governance terms but provides adequate inputs to throw light on the Maoist governmental structure. Located in the area (village) level, the Janathana Sarkar (people's government) is the first stage of governance seeking to articulate an alternative form of public administration. Ideologically inspired by Mao's idea of new democracy, the provisional government can be formed in areas with a population of five hundred to three thousand. The constitution provides that the government will be formed by the people's assembly comprising those who are elected on the basis of adult suffrage. The term of the assembly is for three years. So far, the Sarkar in the selected areas have been formed through consensus among the elected representatives to the people's assembly though the constitution allows the central committee to dictate in cases of gridlock when members fail to arrive at a consensus. While those who are eighteen and above are eligible to vote, the minimum age for contesting the election for the assembly is twenty. Elections have so far been held on camera, given the adverse circumstances in which the Naxalites are functioning. Nonetheless, the classified government documents indicate that those who are sympathetic to Maoism seem enthusiastic when the election was supposedly held. As the operation is so secretive, no alternative sources are available, although interaction with the tribals in the specified areas reveals that, in the safe zones, elections are held regularly.

One may not get first-hand information regarding the election, but what is striking is the availability of well-written documents in the public domain on the structure of government. On the Maoist website, the Janathana Sarkar is reported to have eight departments of finance, defense, agriculture, judiciary, education and culture, health, forest protection, and public relations. The Maoist document elaborates the specific functions and responsibilities of these departments. Since power emanates from "the barrel of a gun," the People's Liberation Guerrilla Army (PLGA) occupies an important position in Maoist thinking. Formed by a dedicated group willing to sacrifice everything for an ideological cause, the PLGA is reportedly constituted by the "love and trust of the people" in the liberated zones. On the basis of a rough scan of the effective Maoist attacks on Indian security forces, one can reasonably be convinced of the PLGA's striking capacity. How do they draw people into the PLGA? In an interview, the general secretary, G. S. Ganapathy, attributed the popularity of the Maoist army to the spontaneous mass support to the PLGA based on their commitment to the establishment of a classless society in which everybody will have his or her share of national wealth.[20] Besides its fight for a mission, the PLGA reportedly attracts people by propagating the cause as a fight until the end. A widely circulated pamphlet in Dandakaranya thus makes a persuasive appeal:

> Once you join the army, you will not get any salary but food, clothes, personal needs will be fulfilled and families would be helped by the Sarkar. What you will earn will be love and affection of the people. Whereas those who join government armed forces will get salary, and rights to loot, kill and rape, but also earn undying hatred of the people and you will not be remembered. Instead your death will be celebrated.[21]

Another pamphlet makes fun of different government forces by equating the given names of the soldiers, not being treated as human beings, with animals because "the government does not regard [the soldiers] as anything more than animals; indeed no better than slaves: sometimes you are called dogs [because they are part of a force called Greyhound], sometimes snakes [by being part of Cobra] and sometimes cats [by being constituent of Black Cats]."[22] Besides these campaign strategies, what seems to have attracted the tribals to the PLGA, despite adverse consequences, is its image of fighting for protecting the basic rights of those who are being displaced by the government policy of transferring "the mineral wealth of Dandakaranya forests to multinationals and foreign capitals."[23] For the tribals, land is not merely a source of their sustenance but it is also a source of their identity; once the land is lost, they become destitute in their own land. So, the PLGA is, for them, a shield to defend their rights over land, which has suddenly become most attractive given the discovery of precious mineral resources.

There are two other departments, namely forest protection and people's judiciary, which deserve mention because the functions of other departments correspond with the conventional knowledge of government departments in any political system. Seeking to protect the forest-dependent communities, the forest department is entrusted with three important tasks, which are enumerated in detail in the document: (i) it will regulate the trading of forest products for profit; it will oppose procuring of herbs, fruit trees, and other valuable trees that are helpful for medical services in methods that would destroy them; (ii) it will strive for developing forests; it will stop illicit timber business; it will arrest those involved in illegal timber business and those who help them; and (iii) it will challenge the government for its policy of displacement and dispossession of the natural heir to the forests by giving away land to the outsiders for anti-people business ventures. Like the forest department, the people's judiciary is very popular in the areas, controlled by Janathana Sarkar. Following the class-sensitive principles of justice, the judiciary avoids punitive measures unless they are absolutely necessary. The Naxal courts, known as Jan Adalat, are expected to administer justice in line with "the customary traditions of the area" while upholding the ideological importance of Marxism–Leninism– Maoism. Two specific methods are generally followed by Jan Adalat: (i) for the class enemies, like landlords, agents of semi-colonial and semi-feudal forces, and those supporting anti-people activities, the courts are not hesitant to adopt stern measures after having given them a chance to defend themselves; and (ii) while settling disputes, these courts need to be sensitive to "those various forums," which the Adivasis have developed over generations. The Jan Adalat is expected to strengthen these people-oriented forums, drawn on the local/customary traditions, to fulfill its people-centric role.

Notwithstanding the reported excesses, committed by Jan Adalat, there is no doubt that the people's judiciary is one of the most popular organs of the provisional government, just like the forest department. The reason is not difficult to understand. The government courts take years to dispense justice while the Maoist courts resolve disputes relatively quickly, as various media reports confirm.[24] "When there is a dispute," an eyewitness account reveals, "the Jan Adalat call the parties together and the punishment is given right away." The villagers seem to like it very much because little time is wasted.

Besides delivering justice without much delay, the Maoists seem to have gained acceptance because the people's courts are generally anti-landlords except on rare occasions. This has given confidence to the tribals because "if you go to the police, they will invariably support the landlord."[25] As the discussion shows, the Janathana Sarkar, however rudimentary in its form, is most significant in the articulation and sustenance of the Maoist-led ultra-extremist movement in India in two ways. First, the Janathana Sarkar has projected the capability of the Maoists to provide an alternative form of governance, based on Marxism–Leninism–Maoism, and translated into reality its commitment to a new democracy. Because this is emotionally gratifying, it will undoubtedly help the Maoists to gain political mileage. The idea is gaining ground at least in the so-called liberated zone where the government is vulnerable to the left-wing extremists. Second, the formation and the continuity of the Janathana Sarkar, despite severe state repression, also suggest the extent to which it has organic roots in the area. One of the reasons supporting its growing strength is certainly due to its success in addressing the genuine socio-economic grievances of the people. Besides providing "instant justice" to the aggrieved tribals, the meaningful role that the provisional government plays, as a report of its developmental activities in five villages in Chhattisgarh underlines, in adopting and supporting schemes contributing to the well-being of the people in the area under its purview seems to have brought the government closer to the people. Accordingly, the government agrees, for instance, to financially endorse collective farming as perhaps the only meaningful device for the survival of those who are subject to near-famine conditions almost every year. This appears to be a top priority of the provisional government; as the party declares, "we must take up the development of agriculture and production as the main political task. . . . We have to develop irrigation, develop organic manure for augmenting agricultural production." The party is also aware that "this development is not possible merely with local adivasi support." What is thus required is to invite those who are sympathetic to the Maoist cause to help "guiding and training the local people for building ponds, canals and other developmental activities [that cannot be] postponed and has to begin now."[26] Besides seeking ways to develop agriculture, the Sarkar (government) appears to have gained enormously in those areas where it is seriously engaged in providing medical aid to those who cannot afford treatment. The Medicine Committees are constituted by the government to provide care to the disease-affected tribals. Although the quality of treatment that these committees provide may not, for obvious reasons, approximate to the standard to the nontribal areas, the effort is both meaningful and symbolically empowering for those who usually surrender to the "supernatural forces or obnoxious black magic" for healing and cure.

With its pro-people activities, the Sarkar seems to have created an alternative power center in the vast Dandakaranya forest area. It is true that in the face of the forcible takeover of tribal land for the big corporations, the Maoist government provides support to those struggling to keep the land in their possession; it is also true that there are cases of excesses in the implementation of the Maoist diktat in the absence of a counterbalance in these affected districts. Nonetheless, the Sarkar seems to have developed organic roots by challenging the government plan to squeeze the tribals further for partisan goals; hence, it has been sarcastically stated that "when their land is wanted by corporation, the government talks of development."[27] Here lies the reason for the success of the Maoist Sarkar: by linking the partisan government with the well-off and associating it with the reckless policy of taking over land from the genuine owners at the cost of the marginalized, the Maoist government has succeeded in not only creating but also consolidating its pro-people image among the hapless in the remote areas where the state so far remains just an expression with no significant meaning.

DECODING THE MAOIST REVOLUTIONARY POTENTIAL

Maoism is both an ideology and a movement: as an ideology, it seeks to build an egalitarian society free from exploitation and prejudices; as a movement, it has endeavored to fulfill its ideological mission by undertaking an armed revolution. The Maoist ideology continues to remain viable since it is an alternative and also a persuasive conceptualization of radical socio-economic changes involving those at the lower rung of society. However, the Maoist movement has shown signs of numerous cracks, including those which are linked to the internecine factional feuds within the Maoist ranks. One of the principal reasons for the decline of earlier left-wing extremist movements in India was the failure to come together despite having more or less identical ideological lineage. As shown already, the state could control the Naxalite movement rather easily because of irreconcilable differences among the top leader over "the annihilation line," which weakened the organization beyond repair. In other words, it was easier for the state-led coercive forces to combat "the Naxalite menace" since the red radicals failed to resist the combatants in unison. This was not an exception. History shows that both the Tebagha upsurge in the early 1940s and the 1946–1951 Telangana movement also failed to sustain the mass momentum for radical socio-economic changes in the face of state brutality. Nonetheless, they raised important issues affecting people's lives that independent India's state could not ignore while being in the saddle of power. One can thus make an argument that, despite their failure in attaining the ideological goal of creating an exploitation-free society, these movements can never be ignored because of their role in forcing the state to take care of those issues that would not have otherwise received so much attention. On the basis of a thorough scan of the left-wing extremist movements since independence, one also discovers a consistent pattern in their evolution and decline, which is critical in grasping left-wing extremism as an ideology-driven alternative discourse. As is evident, these movements, despite being immensely popular at the outset presumably because of the issues that they raised, gradually declined due to their failure to sustain the momentum that they generated when they first appeared on the scene. The aim here is to understand the processes and also to identify the factors that account for the decimation of left-wing-extremist movements in India irrespective of the validity of the issues that they articulated while pursuing a specific ideological mission.

Maoists are a well-knit group with tremendous striking power, which was witnessed in their regular encounter with the police and para-military forces in recent times. As shown above, by developing their own administrative networks in those areas that they control, they have not only established an alternative form of governance but also have articulated their vision of an egalitarian society that seeks to abolish the class hierarchy. The question that needs to be asked is what these efforts mean to those who are reportedly the beneficiaries. Based on ethnographic data from West Bengal, Orissa, and Chhattisgarh, one is drawn to the conclusion that for the hapless majority in remote hamlets in tribal India, the Maoists provided them with a voice that did not thus far reach those presiding over India's destiny. As a result, the differentiated segment of India's population usually remained "outsiders" largely because of the well-entrenched vested interests in vast tracts of India's tribal land, which was always lucrative for forest and other natural resources. For instance, those who collected tendu leaves (a commercially rewarding item since they are used for making *Bidis*, an indigenous version of cigarette) were always given less than what they should get as per the Government of India's minimum wage policy. Only after the Maoists intervened, the contractors agreed to pay the minimum wage that had been, thus far, denied. This had an electrifying effect among those who always remained at the mercy of the contractors for their bare survival. Similarly, the decision to extract bauxites from the Niyamgiri hill in Orissa provoked mass consternation because of the threat of displacement and the apprehension of losing sources of livelihood out of forest products once the forest disappeared following the excavation for minerals. Here, too, the Maoists' help in mobilizing the victims of land acquisition for an alumina refinery by the London-based Vedanta group of companies acted in the local residents' favor. The project was finally withdrawn when a majority of the *Gram Sabhas* (elected village administration) of the Niyamgiri areas opposed the excavation in response to an order of the Supreme Court of India that directed the Government of Orissa to consult them over mining.[28] These illustrations are indicative of how the radical militants gain ground in these areas, which, as the Planning Commission admits, "remained backward even after six decades of independence."[29] So, the Maoists were welcomed by the local tribes because they "help them get their rights, protect them from exploitation and redress their grievances."[30] The Maoists chased "away forest guards, improving [the tribals'] access to the forests [and] secured a fifty-percent increase in the price of tendu leaves," which was undoubtedly a great leap in their income.[31] In exchange, the insurgents are supported by "Advasis (tribals) who provide them with the resources they [need] to undertake insurgency, such as food, shelter, intelligence and foot soldiers."[32] By being part of their daily struggle in this godforsaken land, the Maoists evolved, in course of time, an emotional chord with the hapless tribes, which helped them to build a solid organization in support of their ideological mission.

Advasis and the Maoists are bound together in a symbiotic relationship in which the tribals see the Maoist insurgency as "basically a fight for social justice, equality, protection and local development."[33] As elaborated by a surrendered Maoist commander from Chhattisgarh, Badrana, the Maoists became popular not only because they gave the innocent tribal a voice of protest but also because they brought about radical social changes in tribal society. According to him, many women joined the ranks in response to the battle that the Maoists had waged against superstitious beliefs. In tribal society, menstruation was considered some kind of curse. Once their menstrual cycle commenced, the women were forced to stay in a separate house on the outskirts of the village and were required to hide and not to show their face to a man in case he happened to pass by. The other custom was to get women married to much younger men. This was to ensure an extra hand for work. Once the women grew old, the man— still young—would remarry, leaving his wife in the lurch. By being persuasive and when necessary coercive, the Maoists gradually convinced the village elders to discontinue these evil practices, which made the Maoists immensely popular among the women, and many of them joined the rank to escape social atrocities emanating from patriarchy and feudalism.[34]

The Maoist onslaught on the Indian state that was considered to be the single biggest security challenge has however seen a reversal in recent years, and the Red Terror does not seem as disturbing as in the past. While analyzing the Maoist strength or weakness as an effective political movement, there is no denying that during the last three years since 2011 Maoists suffered heavily in their strongholds of Abujmad (Chhattisgarh), Saranda (Jharkhand), and Lalgarh (West Bengal). However, what is more worrying is that they have added several new territories to their map that do not necessarily fall under the category of conventional Maoist areas. Maoists have always made it very clear that their ultimate political aim is to replace the parliamentary democracy in India and establish their own model of People's Government, and for this they need a pan-Indian presence; they are systematically working toward that goal.

Maoism appears to be losing its grip even in areas that were considered their strongholds in recent past; as mentioned, the Red militants had built a strong organization among the deprived sections of the rural population by raising those pertinent issues that were integrally linked with their mere survival. Besides the state-led ruthless coercive operations, the Maoists lost ground due to their alienation from the villagers who no longer protected their former saviors. The indiscriminate killing of innocent villagers on suspicion of being informers was certainly a definite factor that made the Maoists despicable in those areas. The Jan Adalats (people's court), which was once appreciated, became an instrument to justify the Maoist atrocities; there were instances where justice was miscarried, and innocents were severely punished, including amputation of limbs, gouging out of eyes, and even killing.[35] The other means to which the Maoists are reported to have resorted recently is kidnapping of innocent workers who work for their survival in sand-mining, for instance, in Jamui in Bihar to pressure private contractors for extortion money. There are instances when the refusal of the contractors to heed the demand for ransom money has led to the killing of those kidnapped workers.[36] All this led to a distrust of the Maoists among the people who had so far remained with them despite police atrocities. Not only did the people in some affected districts withdraw support, they on some occasions also resisted the Maoists for "their terroristic design" against the hapless tribals. A resolution was accordingly adopted in a meeting, held in July 2010, which was attended by more than ten thousand villagers in the district town of Jhargram of Jhargram district in West Bengal. They were largely village women who gathered to protest the Maoist atrocities in their villages. They expressed their anguish by waving "belligerently weapons which included no fire arms, but stout sticks made from tree branches, bamboo staves, and sharp tools used for chopping and cutting in the kitchen or harvesting crops."[37] The Maoists, instead of addressing the root cause of such mass resentment, replied by killing a local schoolteacher who was reportedly the mastermind behind this mass protest. Similarly, the Andhra Maoists no longer remained as protected as they were before because of the withdrawal of mass support especially in tribal villages. To resist the Maoist terror, the villagers came forward to support the government para-military forces despite being aware of the adverse consequences. In the context of the indiscriminate killing of village headmen, the widespread laying of landmines, the recruitment of minors, the sabotage of all means of communication, and the ban on employment-generating public works, the Maoists not only became estranged from their supporters but were also despised by them. All these circumstances led to "a wedge between the party and its tribal sympathisers in the liberated zones."[38] For the Maoists, violence was endemic in the context of a brutal state, which because of its obvious class prejudices could never be an instrument for substantial socio-economic changes. The Maoist violence, it was further justified, "is only to put an end to all the violence in the rotten system and to bring peace to our country and people."[39] So, it became a vicious circle in which the Maoists got entrapped, which however caused irreparable damage to the organization that came into being to establish an exploitation-free society by following the Maoist version of classical Marxism–Leninism.

There is thus now a clear dent in the Maoist movement, which no longer remains as unassailable as in the past due to reasons that are internal to the organization and its leadership and the government's developmental initiatives. Maoism is on the wane especially in areas where they had built well-knit organizational networks to sustain the movement even in the face of coercive assault by the state. Besides being disenchanted with Maoism, the tribal population in the affected districts seems to have found a meaningful alternative as the Government of India has undertaken several measures to address their genuine socio-economic grievances. As will be shown below, the Maoist decline in recent years has not happened suddenly but gradually due to a complex interplay of factors including the dramatic attitudinal changes of the state in recognizing the Maoist assault not solely as a law-and-order problem but also a developmental challenge.

CRISIS OF LEADERSHIP AND ITS IMPLICATIONS

The past few years have seen a significant loss of cadre and leadership by the CPI (Maoist), and this has been a major concern for them. The politburo, the highest decision-making body of its organizational structure, originally had sixteen members, of which two have been killed and seven are now in custody. As of now the politburo is left with just Muppala Lakshman Rao alias Ganapathy, the party General Secretary, Prashant Bose alias Kishan Da, Nambala Keshavarao alias Ganganna, Mallojula Venugopal Rao alias Bhupathi, Katakam Sudershan alias Anand, Malla Raji Reddy alias Sathenna, and Misir Besra alias Sunirmal—all of them are underground but active. Similarly, out of thirty-nine members in the Central Committee, which also includes the politburo, eighteen have been neutralized, five have been killed, and thirteen are in custody. Those killed include Sande Rajamouli, Wadkapur Chandramouli, Patel Sudhakar Reddy, Azad, and Kishenji. Among those arrested include Sumanand Singh alias Sumanda, Kobad Ghandy alias Rajan, Sridhar Krishnan Srinivasan alias Vishnu, Balraj, Chintan, Varanasi Subrahmanyam alias Sukanth alias Srikanth, Vijay Kumar Arya alias Yashpal alias Jaspal, and Jantu Mukherjee alias Sahebda alias Ajay.[40] The most fatal blow that the CPI (Maoist) suffered in the recent past was the death of legendary Cherukuri Rajkumar alias Azad and Malojula Koteshwara Rao alias Kishenji, respectively considered to be the voice and face of contemporary Maoist movement in India.[41] As per their own estimate, the Maoists have lost at least 150 of their leaders at various levels just within past few years. The most recent of these losses was Mohan Vishwakarma, a senior member of the Maoist's Central Technical Committee and Technical Research and Arms Manufacturing Unit, who was arrested in Kolkata (West Bengal) on 26 July 2012. The past few years have also witnessed a large number of Maoist cadres either being arrested or surrendered in different parts of the country. As per the available statistics, 905 Maoists were arrested in 2012, in addition to 1,003 arrests in 2011, 1,281 in 2010, and 836 in 2009. Similarly, 414 CPI (Maoist) cadres surrendered in 2012, 227 in 2011, 150 in 2010, and 73 in 2009.[42] Some of them surrendered in exchange for very favorably disposed government packages, which not only guaranteed them protection from jail sentences but also ensured a peaceful life for them and their family; there were some who, being disillusioned with the Maoist path of violent revolution, opted for parliamentary means of socio-political changes. After surrendering, two former Maoist commanders of Palamu and Chatra (in Jharkhand), Kameshwar Baitha and Ranjan Yadav, who took part in the 2014 Lok Sabha poll, for instance, felt that radical socio-economic changes were possible "not through an armed revolution, but through parliamentary means."[43] Similarly, Gudsa Usendi alias G. V. K. Prasad left the life of a guerrilla along with his partner, Santoshi, because of serious ideological differences with the leadership over the course of revolution. Opposed to "the destruction of school buildings and indiscriminate killing of adivasis in the name of destroying the informer network," Usendi was showcased and later expelled from the party allegedly for being "a traitor" who was also accused of "moral misdemeanour."[44] In view of his serious ailment, which needed immediate medication, and "a generous surrender and rehabilitation packages by the Andhra Pradesh government for Maoist cadres,"[45] Usendi willingly opted out of his fugitive life in the jungles.[46] These examples show that Maoism does not seem to be as effective an ideology now as in the past. This has caused irreparable damage to the movement, which lost a considerable amount of its appeal at the grassroots possibly due to the surrender of those who had, over the years, built the organization in the red corridor.

All these losses definitely had an impact on the course of Maoist movement. This is also one of the critical reasons for a significant decrease in the volume of Maoist violence. West Bengal saw an extraordinary upsurge in Maoist violence under the leadership of Kishenji; his killing in 2011 was a severe blow to the Maoist movement in general and particularly in West Bengal where he not only spearheaded the campaign but also held different splinter groups together for a common ideological mission. While showing concern over the increasing number of deaths of the most trusted comrades, the Maoist leadership attributed "the success of the enemy [to] their failure of understanding the counter-insurgency strategy."[47] Admitting that "the loss is phenomenal," efforts are under way to regroup "the red revolutionaries . . . to bring about radical socio-economic transformation in India"[48] as perhaps the only way to sustain the mass momentum that the earlier leadership had generated.

INTER-ORGANIZATIONAL AND INTRA-ORGANIZATIONAL CONFLICT

Inter-organizational and intra-organizational conflicts are also responsible for the decline of this decade-long Maoist movement in India. This is manifested in the rising dissent within the CPI (Maoist) and creation of several new factions within the broad tradition of Maoism. As per available statistics, Jharkhand is one state that has seen the emergence of at least eight such splinter groups in the recent past; most prominent among them are the Tritiya Prastuti Committee, the People's Liberation Front of India, and the Jharkhand Jana Mukti Parishad.[49] Inter-organizational and intra-organizational feuds apart, the cycle of competitive violence has sucked into it the entire state of Jharkhand, which has undertaken specific steps to contain the red menace in the state. The internal friction between various rival left-wing extremist groups in Jharkhand is the principal reason for alarming Maoist violence in the state. Recently the Telugu leadership of CPI (Maoist) came under severe attack from the top Orissa Maoist leader Sabayasachi Panda. On 1 June 2012, Panda wrote two letters to CPI (Maoist) General Secretary Ganapathy, politburo members Prashant Bose, Narayan Sanyal, and other Maoist leaders. In the two letters, which ran to thirty-nine pages, he leveled serious allegations of mindless violence, dictatorship, financial irregularity, tribal exploitation, sexual harassment, big-brother attitude of the Andhra Orissa Border Special Zonal Committee, discrimination against minorities and Christians, and so on against the party leadership. Instead of addressing the charges that Panda hurled against the top leadership, he was summarily expelled because of his alleged involvement in anti-party activities following which he, in an audio tape released to the media in early 2013, declared to have severed all ties with the CPI (Maoist) and announced the formation of his Orissa Maovadi Party. Since then the Maoist movement in Orissa has been experiencing certain new conflict dynamics, which could have serious implications in the future course of the movement. Nonetheless, the tussle between Panda and the party's Telugu-dominated Central Committee reveals an inner tension substantiating the charge that "the leadership of the movement that aspires to transform India into a 'people's democracy' is not remotely representative of the vast diversity of India."[50] As is evident in the composition of the Central Committee, nearly half of the thirty-two members are just from one of India's 650 districts, which is Karimnagar of Andhra Pradesh; there are very few tribals and women in this highest forum of decision-making. Panda's revolt and subsequent expulsion were thus a testimony to the fact that "the domination of Andhra militants is causing friction and regional fissures within the movement," which, thus far, did not receive leadership's serious attention.[51]

THE GOVERNMENT STRATEGIES

It has been agreed at the highest level of decision-making that the root of Maoism is India's distorted development strategy that failed to address the genuine socio-economic grievances of the people across the country. As the former prime minister Manmohan Singh confessed,

> We cannot overlook the fact that many areas in which such extremism flourishes are under-developed and many of the people, mainly poor tribals, who live in these areas have not shared equitably the fruits of development. . . . It is incumbent upon us to ensure that no area of our country is denied the benefits of our ambitious developmental programmes.[52]

By devising the principle of "walking on two legs," which combines "the stick" of proactive and sustained military assault with "the carrot" of development and governance, the Indian state sought to combat the red menace.[53] As a result, the state's counterinsurgency focused both on coercive and developmental means; while for the former, the Government of India unleashed Operation Green Hunt, which meant deployment of the central paramilitary troops into the forested and hilly terrain of eastern and central India to flush out the Maoists, the carrot strategy was articulated in evolving various developmental schemes for these affected areas. A new combative force, known as the COBRA (Commando Battalion for Resolute Action) was created in early 2009 to take the Maoists head on. Launched in 2009, Operation Green Hunt is a massive and nationally coordinated coercive drive "to crush the centers of Maoist power and adivasi rebellion, especially in the forested regions of the Red Corridor,"[54] which led a commentator to characterize the operation as "a furtive declaration of war" by the state on India's indigenous population.[55] Operation Green Hunt was supported by the parallel efforts on the part of those states in which Maoism was most well-entrenched: the state government of Andhra Pradesh developed, for instance, an elite police force, christened as Greyhounds, for this purpose. Created in 1989, the Greyhounds are an elite unit of the Andhra Pradesh Police trained in guerrilla warfare. With higher pay, subsidized housing, and insurance by the government, this elite police force is sent to "the remote forest and hilly regions where Maoists are suspected to be active."[56] This feat is repeated in other states as well. For instance, by launching "Operation NGO [Nongovernmental Organizational] Hunt," the Jharkhand government is determined to outlaw those nongovernmental organizations that are alleged to be "the sympathisers of Naxalites." In their effort to empower the villagers, mobilize them, and fight to protect their constitutional rights, these organizations have unleashed a campaign to make the rural folk aware of their rights and entitlements, which has contributed to protest movements that were embarrassing to the government. So, Operation NGO Hunt is basically a preemptive movement.[57] Similarly, the state government of Chhattisgarh created a vigilante force, Salwa Judum, to equip those opposed to the Maoists with arms and ammunition. Five thousand Salwa Judum special police officers played a critical role in counterinsurgency in the state.[58] The result was soon evident. Following the indiscriminate killings of the Maoists or their sympathizers, the movement appears to have lost its momentum to a significant extent.

Nonetheless, it has now been accepted that Maoism is not merely a law-and-order problem as was conceived earlier but also a "developmental challenge," and the affected provinces require "a combination of political, developmental and perception management responses as a part of a holistic strategy" to address the serious issues of lack of productive employment, education, and adequate health care.[59] Accordingly, after imposing a ban on CPI (Maoist) in 2009, the Government of India thus set a tone for a coordinated approach against the Maoists. All along the Ministry of Home Affairs, the Government of India has emerged as the principal state actor in the Maoist conflict. Under the leadership of the Ministry of Home Affairs, the Government of India has now devised an integrated approach combining security and development to defuse the Maoist crises. It was a conscious decision at the government level to go beyond the traditional law-and-order approach. The Government of India has taken a stand that the governments of the affected state will deal directly with the issues related to left-wing extremism in their state while the union government will monitor, coordinate, and supplement the efforts of the states. In a significant decision taken in 2010, the Government of India identified thirty-five Naxal-infested districts from nine states for special attention on planning, implementation, and monitoring of development schemes. As a part of its Focused Area Approach, the Government of India's major

flagship programs such as the Pradhan Mantri Gram Sadak Yojana, Forest Rights Act
2006, National Rural Employment Guarantee Act, Rajiv Gandhi Grameen Vidyuti-
karan Yojana, National Rural Drinking Water Supply Programme, Sarva Sikshya
Abhiyan, and Indira Awas Yojana are being seriously pursued to address the socio-
economic grievances to undermine the Maoist endeavor to recruit new members from
the affected areas. With the union government adding eighteen more Naxal-infested
districts in 2011 for the implementation of the Integrated Action Plan, the total numbers of such districts have now become seventy-eight. A sum of Rs. 1,500 crore was released to the concerned districts during 2010–2011. Another Rs. 1,090 crore was released in the first part of 2011–2012. In 2011 the Ministry of Home Affairs recommended
a sum of Rs. 10,700 crore for the Ministry of Road, Transport and Highways to implement the Road Requirement Plan for the Maoist-infested districts. The union government has also allocated funds on a 100 percent grant basis for the affected districts for
establishment of hostels for Scheduled Tribe girls and boys as well as Ashram schools
in tribal subplan areas. In tune with the Government of India's developmental initiatives, the state government of Andhra Pradesh has also combined "counterinsurgency
efforts with a strong focus on rural development."[60] Seeking to bring about inclusive
development, formerly adopted government programs such as the Remote and Interior
Areas Development, Integrated Novel Development in Rural Areas and Model Municipal Areas, and Jalayagnam (irrigation project) were implemented. With the stringent monitoring by the government of these programs, they became instruments for
radical socio-economic changes at the grassroots.

While implementing the government programs, the staff on the ground faced difficulties because of the stringent and archaic forest laws. In a significant decision, the Minis
try of Environment and Forest announced some relaxation in its provisions to enable
smooth implementation of government flagship projects in the forest areas. It allowed the
diversion of forest land, once approved by the local panchayats, in the Naxal-affected
areas for projects such as schools; dispensaries/hospitals; electrical and telecommunica-
tion lines; drinking water; water and rain water harvesting structures; minor irrigation
canals; nonconventional sources of energy; skill up-gradation and vocational training
centers; power substations; rural roads; communication posts; police establishments such
as police stations, outposts, border outposts, watch towers in sensitive areas; and laying of
optical fiber cables, telephone lines, and drinking water supply lines. In addition, the
Ministry of Panchayati Raj has constituted a committee under the Chairmanship of
Member Planning Commission to look into the aspects of minimum support price, value
addition, and marketing of minor forest produce in the Fifth Schedule Areas.[61] During
the financial year 2011–2012, an amount of Rs. 20 crore was allocated to the Central
Armed Police Forces to undertake the Civic Action Programme in the Naxal-infested
states. The Ministry of Rural Development has always been involved with the implementation of development projects in the Naxal-infested areas. To implement the prime minister's Rural Development Fellowship Scheme, the ministry undertook several steps,

including land acquisition, seeking to reach out to the deprived sections in rural areas even in the face of stiff opposition of the vested interests. Undoubtedly, it was a change of strategy that yielded positive results in a context in which the Maoists were usually projected as saviors in the almost near-absence of government-sponsored developmental activities in most of the remote hamlets in the red corridor.

With all its mega-plan and high-profile visits in the Maoist-infested areas the union government may have shown its keenness for resolving the crisis of governance in the Maoist-infested areas, but, as far as the implementation level is concerned, the government still has to match its own perception levels. The Mahatma Gandhi National Rural Employment Guarantee Scheme, which is portrayed by the government as one of its trump card in counter-Maoist strategy, is marred with corruption charges from almost all the states. As per the information provided by the Sarpanch (head of the elected village administration) of village Hitameta, Dantewada, Rs. 1 crore was spent on four nonexistent stop dams, and 122 workers out of the total 145 listed workers never worked at the site. The master roll even brought six deceased villagers back to life, listing their names under the workers who have collected wages. As per information provided by a senior government officer on the basis of anonymity, nearly 40 to 50 percent of all government expenditure in Dantewada is lost in corruption.[62] This is just one of so many instances of corruption involving the Mahatma Gandhi National Rural Employment Guarantee Scheme projects. The details released by the Ministry of Home Affairs on the Integrated Action Plan funds until the end of 2011 reveal an altogether dismal picture. Of the 68,173 development projects taken up across the country, only 27,687 have been completed.[63] This raises some serious concerns over the developmental aspect of the government's two- pronged strategies involving developmental plans and coercive measures. What is important is to ensure the proper implementation of the program at the grassroots rather than simply announcing mega-developmental projects with no serious intention for their execution. Left-wing extremism shall therefore remain an effective ideological alternative at the grassroots so long as these poverty-alleviation programs are not meaningfully implemented for those who felt betrayed by India's state-led planned development.

POLARIZING THE POLARIZED: THE MAOIST DILEMMA

What led to the consolidation of left-wing extremism in India was the failure of the Indian state to be adequately sensitive to the genuine socio-economic grievances of those on the periphery. India's social map always remains fractured along class, caste, and ethnicity axes. By being integrally connected with the marginalized in their daily struggle for existence, the Maoists almost instantly created a space for themselves among the wretched of the earth. Over a decade or so, they also became India's serious domestic threat because they had waged a war against the ruling authority to fulfill their pledge for an exploitation-free society. In the face of the well-equipped Indian state, the weaknesses of the red militants are not only exposed but also utilized to crush them in a most violent manner. Not only have the Maoists succumbed on occasion, but also their capacity to rise again is considerably restricted by the steady weakening of the organization due to internecine factional feuding and the thinning of the support base because of the ruthless Stalinist design in eliminating summarily those who are suspected to be an impediment for revolutionary new democracy. The result is visible: the Maoist movement is fast losing its momentum even in their stronghold areas. The question that needs to be asked now is whether Maoism shall have the same fate as the previous versions of left-wing extremism that galvanized a generation and also disappeared as fast as they had emerged on India's political scene. Despite doubts about the forms of protest movements, one is sure of the fact that left radicalism continues to remain relevant because of "the widening crisis in much of rural India, and the never ending exploitations of class, caste and ethnicity [which means that] revolutionary forces shall always find new areas for bases, no matter how many times they have been defeated or driven out of their earlier strongholds."[64] It is true that the effective use of "security-centric (counterinsurgency) and people-centric (development) policies"[65] by the state have positive results and Maoism does not seem to be as lethal as in the past. There is no doubt that sustained security operations across their areas of influence have forced the Maoists to retreat. Since the beginning of Operation Green Hunt in 2009, their grip over certain guerrilla zones has loosened. Maoism is certainly on the wane, but as several instances of ambush with the military and paramilitary forces, including the 11 March 2014 assault in Chhattisgarh, killing fifteen of the security personnel, reveal,[66] they are still able to launch lethal attacks on the state and inflict severe damage.

Maoism cannot thus be completely wiped out so long as the context contributing to left-wing extremism remains. The situation appears to be grim, especially now when the neo-liberal developmental model that the Indian state has endorsed has become "synonymous with depriving the poor of their livelihood resources" by allowing the multinational companies to excavate precious minerals in the vast tract of India's tribal land for private gain.[67] In the process, the hapless adivasis are caught and crushed between two larger forces, the Indian state and Maoists beyond their control. Tribals in all the Maoist-hit areas thus live in constant fear. As an eye-witness account reveals, they are bound to provide shelter and food whenever the *annalu* (as the Maoists are called in local parlance) visit them. Such visits are soon followed by police teams to draw out from them the whereabouts of the extremists.[68] The Maoists kill them on charges of being police informers while the security forces leave no stone unturned to extract information, inflicting inhuman torture and killing them when other methods of discipline fail. They are thus sandwiched between a ruthless state, which to completely wipe out the red menace goes to extremes to establish its hegemony and acts ruthlessly coercive toward the local inhabitants, and the Maoists, who, by resorting to indiscriminate killing, have also become suspect to those who helped them build and sustain the organization even in the most adverse circumstances.

This is paradoxical that the Maoists have dug their own grave in areas where people defended their cause by being participants in the movement that they launched for a new democratic revolution. The internecine factional feuds leading to indiscriminate killings continue to plague the organization that does not seem to have received serious attention by the Maoist leadership. In fact, it is not far-fetched to argue that the CPI (Maoist) is likely to face the same fate as its former left-wing extremist colleagues who lost their zeal for radical socio-economic changes not merely because of the state-driven counterinsurgency efforts but also because of the factional rivalries among the groups with identical ideological missions. After having studied left-wing extremism in India, an analyst has drawn a parallel between the Indian Maoist movement and the Sendero Luminoso (Shining Path) movement in Peru, which the Communist Party led in 1980 to capture state power through a violent revolution.[69] By the mid-1990s, the campaign was ruthlessly contained by the Peruvian army with most of the activists indiscriminately killed. One of the reasons that led to its downfall was the "lethal retribution" by the red militants in Peru not only against those opposed to the movement but also against "neutral civilian population with no direct connection to the conflict."[70] With the growing disillusionment of the villagers with the Maoists because of their misdirected endeavor at liquidating class enemies, like its Peruvian counterpart, the Maoist movement that represented hope and a surge for radical socio-economic transformation seems to have lost a considerable amount of its appeal in the red corridor. Is this indicative of a complete decimation of left-wing extremism in India? It is unlikely, because as long as the socio-economic imbalances are encouraged and sustained by an exploitative state, left-wing extremism will remain the most sought-after option for those who are unjustly discriminated against in a regime that claims to have adopted an egalitarian constitution.

CONCLUDING OBSERVATIONS

Maoism is a powerful ideological movement with organic roots in India's socio-economic reality. The spread of the movement shows that the ideology of Maoism is well conceived and the tactic is sound. There is no doubt that Maoism has struck an emotional chord with a significant section of India's indigenous population. For those suffering due to abysmal poverty, Maoism is an empowering ideology that inspires them to launch an assault on the state power despite the adverse consequences. The state appears to have failed to provide the basic facilities for human existence to the forest-dependent tribals. It seems that they are destined to suffer because the state is either invisible or, where it exists, it is just a mute observer and appears to be absolutely crippled in its attempts to meaningfully attack the age-old system of exploitation at the behest of the government-sponsored agents. The ground reality is appalling, as a report in *The Economist* underlines:

> In one area [in Chhattisgarh], there is a hand-pump, installed by the local government, but the well is dry. There are no roads, water pipes, electricity or telephone lines. In another village, a teacher does come, but, in the absence of a school, holds classes outdoor. Policemen, health workers and officials are never seen.[71]

The vacuum is filled by the Naxalites, looking after the villagers within their limited capacity. It is conceivable that the Maoists cannot match the government in providing what is required to ameliorate the conditions of the poor; but their endeavor to extend support to the villagers whenever need arises has led to a symbiotic bond with the local people. The belief that the Maoists are fighting for the tribals has gained ground particularly in areas producing tendu leaves with their success in enhancing the rates by almost 200 percent for the collection of non-timber forest produce, especially tendu leaves. Adivasis, who are grueling in the state of penury, are persuaded to accept that the Naxalites are their saviors in distress. So, the success of the Naxalites can safely be attributed to the stark poverty in which tribals are forced to survive, if that is possible. The aggrieved tribals gravitate toward Maoists who hold out the promise of fighting their cause. Unless a long-term solution to the endemic poverty is meaningfully pursued by the state, the objective conditions supportive of the left-wing extremism continue to thrive. A long-term solution lies in an honest attempt to address the basic causes arising from poverty, land alienation, unemployment, corruption, displacement and dispossession of tribals, and poor governance. True, these problems cannot be solved overnight. But if the state could at least give an impression that "their severity is being mitigated every year, that itself would go a long way in building confidence among [the affected] people."[72]

The story remains incomplete without commenting on the organizational network that the Naxalites have developed over the years. Undoubtedly, the 2004 merger of three well-entrenched Naxalite outfits into the CPI (Maoist) is a significant event in the evolution of the left-wing extremist movement in India. The Maoists are now an organized lot. What is revealing in contrast with its past incarnation is the consistent effort by the Maoists to build an organization to pursue their goal. Unlike the previous Naxalbari movement of the 1960s, the present campaign is primarily rural-based with influences in specific cities and towns. One of the reasons for the decline of the Naxalbari movement was its inability to sustain its momentum in the villages once it began flourishing in specific metropolitan cities and selective towns. Besides other major factors that were responsible for the degeneration of the Naxalism as an ideology, the movement was derailed particularly because of its failure to evolve a mechanism of choosing "the committed cadres" from among those joining the outfit to advance their personal agenda. So, the organization was unable to remain true to its goal due to an unstable foundation and presumably due to the incongruity of purposes among its members. The present-day

Maoists appear to have learned this lesson, as the organization's recent modus operandi suggests. Although there is no reason to believe that the Maoist organization is set in stone and not impregnable, the blueprint that the Maoists have prepared is illustrative of the future road map insofar as the organization is concerned. Here too, the present-day Naxalites are clearly different from their former counterparts: while the former were constantly engaged in refining the organization in line with the prevalent socio-economic circumstances and organizational requirements, few serious efforts were made to build a well-entrenched organization to sustain the movement. In other words, the Naxalites of the past depended on the spontaneous outburst of those inspired by radicalism of the Marxist variety while contemporary Maoism seeks to build on that spontaneity to create a sustainable organization to support left-wing extremism in India.

What is evident is that Maoism is not a passing phase. It has acquired a base and a capability to hit the Indian state where it is weakest. Thriving on the government failure to deliver basic services to those who need them most, the Maoists appear to have created a space for themselves in India's recent political history. The possibility of capturing state power by the Maoists is certainly remote, though they have the power to deter investment and development in some of India's poorest regions, which also happen to be among the richest in some vital resources such as coal, iron, and other useful mineral resources. So, the movement, backed by effective striking power, has the effect of "sharpening inequity which many see as the biggest danger facing India in the next few years and which is the Naxalites' recruiting sergeant."[73]

7

Maoism: A Utopia or "Jacobean" Reign of Terror?[1]

᠌

MAOISM IN INDIA has thrived on the objective conditions of poverty that has various ramifications. Undoubtedly, high economic and income disparity and exploitation of the impoverished, especially "the wretched of the earth," contribute to conditions that are conducive to revolutionary and radical politics. India's development strategy since independence was hardly adequate to eradicate the sources of discontent. The situation seems to have grown worse with the onset of globalization that has created "islands of deprivation" all over the country. As the state is being dragged into the new development packages, which are neither adequate nor appropriate for the "peripherals," Maoism seems to have provided a powerful alternative. The argument, drawn on poverty, is strengthened by linking the past deficits with the disadvantages inherent and perceived in the present initiatives for globalization. The Orissa (and Chhattisgarh) case is an eye-opener because Maoism has gained enormously due to the displacement of the indigenous population in areas where both the state-sponsored industrial magnates and other international business tycoons have taken over land for agro-industries. Here there is a difference between the present Maoism and the Naxalbari movement. The latter was an organized peasant attack against specific "feudal" land relations, particularly in West Bengal whereas the Maoists in Orissa and Chhattisgarh draw on the displacement of the local people due to zealous support of the state for quick development through forced industrialization. So, issues that are critical to the Maoist organization vary from one context to another. The aim of this chapter is therefore to focus on major contextual issues and their articulation by the Maoists in specific socio-economic milieu in which they appear to have become politically purposeful and ideologically significant agents of socio-economic changes. This will be done in two ways. First, rather than dwelling on context-specific issues, the chapter deals with those critical issues in which the Maoist movement is being articulated in different parts of India. Second, the chapter examines the impact of ultra-left-wing extremism on government policy, both in terms of its response to the Maoist movement and its preparedness to address the socio-economic issues that the movement has raised.

MAJOR CONTEXTUAL ISSUES

It is true that the land question continues to remain significant in the consolidation of left-wing extremism in India. What however triggered the present radical Maoist movements were primarily forest rights of the tribal population, forcible land acquisition for industrialization, and the setting up of Special Economic Zones (SEZs). In a significant way, globalization seems to have disturbed the economic balance in the country. With the adoption of the policy of economic liberalization of the Indian economy and its interaction with the processes of globalization, the rural market has now been integrated with urban commerce, producing in the process "new structures of power based on land and capital" that will further marginalize the rural poor. By creating SEZs, the state seems to have created investment opportunities in industry and trade for the national and global capital. This process has begun to threaten the marginal farmers and those drawing on land as their only source of survival. Money cannot compensate for their dispossession and displacement from the land presumably because they are emotionally linked with land and because it will be difficult for them to adopt any other means for livelihood other than farming.

Maoism is a contextual response to the socio-economic grievances of the peripheral sections of society who, despite the euphoria over a state-directed Soviet model of planned economic development, remain impoverished. Maoism is Marxism–Leninism in an agricultural context where national and global capital are strongly resisted by drawing upon an ideological discourse that has been creatively articulated to take care of the indigenous socio-economic and political forces as well as local traditions. In Orissa, Maoism has struck a chord with the indigenous population. Tribals are opposed to the denial of their rights over forest lands, and their opposition to the state is largely due to the "complicity of the state" with the industrial magnates (both national and global) in taking the forests away for agro-business. Those opposing the corporate-led industrialization are considered "unlawful" and often accused of "disloyalty" and "treason." What is implemented in the name of development is a model of development for private profit that ignores the basic requirements of the indigenous population. A report of the People's Union for Democratic Rights on three mining projects in Orissa's Kalahandi and Rayagada districts confirms the extent to which local people are marginalized due to "the application of such a model of development." The report underlines "the total dependence on depressed agriculture . . . low irrigation facilities . . . worsened by inequitable land relations, token and partial land reforms and extremely low educational and health facilities provided by the state. It is in these conditions that these mining projects are pushed through." The local people are shown "the carrot of vague oral promises of permanent jobs and large salaries" by the company and local administration. To silence the voice of protest, the government resorts to all kinds of punitive measures, including "regular flag marches through peaceful tribal villages, beatings, threats, arbitrary warrants and arrests, to firing and killing of protestors." The regions in which the mining projects are under way "live under the constant shadow of a draconian state."[2] This is the main source of tension in the tribal areas. Yet the influence of the Maoists varies because the "development failures" may not uniformly affect various social groups at the grassroots. This explains why Maoists are more popular among the Adivasis and less among those with clear landed interests. Nonetheless, what is deplorable is the lack of basic facilities for the tribals in those areas in India in which the Naxalites roam around rather freely presumably because of their active engagement with the local people while combating the Indian state for a better future. In a public appeal, Binayak Sen, the medical practitioner who was arrested for his alleged link with the extremists in Chhattisgarh, attributed the rising popularity of the extremism to the failure of the state to provide basic human requirements. He thus argued that the state should immediately undertake "a specific series of measures directed at relieving the humanitarian situation on the ground." As an immediate priority, the problems to be addressed would include food and water, shelter and livelihood, health care, and transport and infrastructure.[3] This public appeal reveals the appalling circumstances in which the indigenous population survives in the affected areas. Even the state-driven, recently introduced Integrated Action Plan in the districts affected by left-wing extremism is far from being effective presumably because most of the programs are decided not by the local village councils (gram panchayats) but by "the trio of district collector, superintendent of police and the forest officer."[4] The growing expansion of the Maoist influence can thus be said to be an outcome of a socio-economic reality, which is partly historical and partly due to the mindless application of neo-liberal developmental packages.

THE MERGER SIGNALING A NEW THRUST

If the September 2004 merger of several Naxal groups signaled a new beginning in relation to the course of the Maoist movement in India, January and February 2007, when the Communist Party of India (Maoist; CPI [Maoist]) conducted its Ninth Party Congress, signals yet another phase in the cycle of Maoist insurgencies in India. The Naxal leadership views this congress as a grand success since the Maoists were holding a unity congress after a gap of thirty-six years—their eighth congress was held in 1970. The Maoists claim that the congress resolved the disputed political issues in the party through lively, democratic, and comradely debate and discussion. This Maoist claim hints at the new developments within the politics of Naxalism. It is also significant for the admission of the existence of inter- and intra-organizational conflict within the political gamut of CPI (Maoist).

The merger of the CPI (Marxist–Leninist), People's War, and the Maoist Communist Centre–India that resulted in the birth of CPI (Maoist) also successfully brought the dominant faction of CPI (Marxist–Leninist) Janashakti into the fold. Amidst speculations of the merger, both the Janashakti and CPI (Maoist) presented a united front in 2005. A death toll of 892 persons that year was largely believed to be a result of the merger. The Naxal movement, however, continued to conquer new territories in 2006, though it witnessed only 749 deaths, fewer than the previous year. In 2005, Naxal violence was reported from 509 police stations across eleven states, while in 2006, 1,427 police stations in thirteen states came under the shadow of the red terror. Other than the escalation in violence, the latter part of 2006 also witnessed significant changes in the operational ways of the Naxal movement.

The honeymoon between the CPI (Maoist) and the Janashakti did not last longer than a year, and in 2006 it became apparent that both were clearly going different ways to occupy operational areas. During the open session of the CPI (Maoist), held in December 2006, the Janashakti was asked to make clear its stand on political aims and programs; the Janashakti, however, chose not to attend the session. Consequently, the CPI (Maoist) withdrew partner status from the Janashakti and decided to provide need-based support only in the case of police actions. The conflict between the CPI (Maoist) and the Janashakti became public when the Orissa Janashakti group led by Anna Reddy killed three forest officials on 31 January 2007. The CPI (Maoist) state leadership immediately distanced itself from the killings. Subsequent police inquiry confirmed the involvement of the Janashakti group in the gruesome act.

Of course, things are at a formative stage today; the setting is ready for a possible realignment of the Maoist forces. In Karnataka, which is largely viewed as the new Naxal target, the CPI (Maoist) recently suffered a major setback as a number of cadres in the state, who disagreed with the Maoist agenda of intensifying the revolution in rural areas first and then spreading it to urban centers, have created a new party named the Maoist Coordination Committee. In addition, the political cracks in Karnataka have now started to extend to other states. Internationally, in 2006, though the CPI (Maoist) and Communist Party of Nepal (Maoist; CPN [Maoist]) suffered an estranged relationship, Naxals were, during the same period, successful enough to establish a link with the powerful Russian armed mafias.

The long years of Naxal presence in India underline certain distinct characteristics. First, Naxal history has been a history of conflicts and splits; one cannot deny, however, that it also represents the history of mergers. Second, the Naxal movement essentially represents simultaneous, albeit not so peaceful, coexistence of many streams, and, viewed from this angle, the movement has a presence in all parts of the country. This implies that the inseparable character of organizational conflict has actually helped the movement to grow in different areas. Third, the growth of the Naxal movement is closely linked with the ongoing process of organizational conflict. The ultimate political objective behind all this organizational exercise is to build a leftist alternative to capture political power through the process of revolutionary war.

The formation of the CPI (Maoist) was not the final stage of the Naxal movement; the ultimate aim of the Naxal movement is the seizure of state power, and in the process the movement need not always take a linear route. With new national and international variables taking shape, the politics of Naxalism is bound to accommodate these changes; hence, it is necessary that the government take notice of these changes at an early stage. While the Naxal movement has always surprised others with its adaptability, the government responses so far have been mostly predictable. In view of the Maoist claim of a "deciding phase," the government must think resourcefully, speculate on the new forms that will emerge, and construct new frames of reference that will serve as the foundation for strategy formulation and policy implementation. The success of future counter-Naxal programs will depend on successful integration of intelligence, law enforcement, information operations, targeted military force, and civil affairs.

REVEALING THE CAPABILITY TO STRIKE

One can recall the 2004 Naxal attack in Koraput, the 2006 Naxal attack in R. Udayagiri, or the 2008 Nayagarh Naxal attack; incidents of this nature reveal that Orissa has always offered Naxals a safe haven to test their abilities. On 29 June 2008, the Naxals showcased their ability over water when they attacked a motor launch carrying sixty-six people across the Balimela reservoir in the Malkangiri district. These included sixty-one police officers from Andhra Pradesh—mostly Greyhound commandos, two from the Orissa police, and three others. Twenty-eight out of these sixty-six persons swam to safety but the rest are missing. Massive search operations are under way that have so far resulted in the recovery of eighteen bodies, with some twenty more persons yet to be accounted for.

Initial reports from the Naxalite zone reveal that the water ambush was masterminded by Chenda Bhushanam (alias Naga Raju, Katru, Bali Reddy), Kakuri Pandanna (alias Pasanna, Jogan), and Ravi, all established guerrilla leaders of the Andhra–Orissa Border Special Zonal Committee (AOBSZC). It is also reported that the State Militia Commission, a recently constituted force of the CPI (Maoist), engineered the attack. The professionalism that the Naxals displayed leaves no doubt that they had all the information needed about the movement of this force. The Naxals were waiting for the security personnel to fall in their trap at Alampaka, a small mountain inside the reservoir. They fired from here using LMGs, SLRs, AK-47s, and rocket launchers. Earlier in the day, the Naxals captured another passenger boat that they used after the incident to flee to Janbai from where they managed to reach their safe territory of Papluar and Manyamkonda.

The Naxals in the border area of Orissa, Andhra Pradesh, and Chhattisgarh have been used inflatable boats for some time; recently the Malkangiri police seized a motor that was attached to an inflatable boat. The Liberated Zone claimed by the Naxals is the area where the Malkangiri District of Orissa shares a border with the Bastar area in the Chhattisgarh and Khammam districts in Andhra Pradesh. Malkangiri is separated from Andhra by the Sileru River and from Chhattisgarh by the Saberi River. Besides the Sileru and Saberi, there is another interstate river, the Mahendrataneya, between Orissa and Andhra. The Naxals have now raised a boat wing to facilitate faster movement of their cadres and weapons. S. K. Nath, deputy inspector general of police, southwestern range, Orissa confirmed the Naxal activities down these rivers.

Orissa has been witnessing a steady increase in incidents of Naxal violence. In fact, the provisional data through 1 July 2008 reveals that Orissa has suffered the most casualties among the Naxal-affected states. Orissa recorded a total of ninety-nine deaths in this period, which includes fifty-seven security personnel, twenty-eight Naxals, and fourteen civilians. In this same period, Chhattisgarh recorded ninety-four deaths; Jharkhand, eighty-two; Bihar, forty-four; and Andhra Pradesh, thirty-eight. Since 2006, the government of Orissa has banned the CPI (Maoist) and seven of its front organizations. The ban order was accompanied by a comprehensive surrender and rehabilitation package for the Naxals. However, the violence graph after the ban shows that the government has not been able to impose the ban successfully, nor has its surrender and rehabilitation package yielded many results. Unfortunately, the government is taking too long to realize that a ban is no solution; the government needs to effectively coordinate its military offensives with socio-economic measures to make the ban effective.

While the Naxals in Orissa are becoming increasingly stronger, the government claims to be suffering from acute shortages of infrastructure and personnel. Of course, the state has every right to ask for central para-military forces and central funding for security measures; it cannot fight the Naxals effectively with twelve thousand vacancies in the state police. Orissa has only ninety-two police officers per one lakh population, whereas the national average is 142 police officers. With extensive industrial and mining activities, the state government constantly boasts about its financial achievements; hence, finance is not a problem to meet its security needs. Given the extraordinary situation in the Naxal-affected areas, Orissa needs a joint command to direct its anti-Naxal operations. The democratization of the development process and modernization of the military process must proceed together in all anti-Naxal policies and operations in Orissa. Anti-Naxal measures (security and socio-economic) need good delivery mechanisms (political, administrative, and police) to win over the people, which alone can end the ongoing Naxal violence.

THE MAOIST CAPABILITY

On 8 September 2006, the Andhra Pradesh Police recovered 600 unloaded rockets, 275 unassembled rockets, 27 rocket launchers, 70 gelatine sticks, and other explosives belonging to the CPI (Maoist) from the Mahabubnagar and Prakasam districts. This largest-ever arms haul included two tons of spare parts to make sixteen rocket launchers, high-tensile springs used to propel explosives, fins that could be attached to shells, five hundred live 0.303 rounds, detonators, wire, an electronic weighing scale, and two digital thermometers. The ammunition was shipped from Chennai in May 2006 and reached Vijayawada and Proddatur, where it was redirected to Achampet and Giddalur.

Since its inception in 2004, the CPI (Maoist) has been working on a terror strategy and has emerged as the most sophisticated armed group in India. As revealed in Naxal literature, the CPI (Maoist) now has around ten thousand cadres who are adept in guerrilla warfare, with another forty-five thousand over ground cadres. Over the years it has built up an arsenal of twenty thousand modern weapons, which includes INSAS, AK-series rifles, and SLRs, mostly looted from security forces. Use of fabricated rocket launchers has added to their firepower. Though the Naxals have not yet gained access to RDX, they have frequently used gelatine sticks and improvised explosive devices.

In addition, the Naxals have a huge number of country-made weapons, which they procure through a chain of underground arms production units. There are over 1,500 illegal arms manufacturing units in Bihar alone, mostly located in the Nalanda, Nawada, Gaya, and Munger districts. Recently, Gorakhpur and Ghazipur in Uttar Pradesh have emerged as Maoist centers for the production and distribution of illegal arms. Naxals also have an undetermined number of arms manufacturing units in the dense forests of Saranda (Jharkhand), Redhakhol (Orissa), and Dandakaranya (Chhattisgarh). A recent study conducted jointly by Oxfam, Amnesty International, and the International Network on small arms estimated that forty million guns out of the estimated seventy-five million illegal small arms worldwide are in Central India with the Naxals active in Bihar, Chhattisgarh, Jharkhand, Orissa, Madhya Pradesh, and Uttar Pradesh. The report reveals that along with the mafias, the Naxals have become buyers of assault weapons like Kalashnikovs and M-16s.

The People's Liberation Guerrilla Army of the CPI (Maoist) has developed into an efficient guerrilla force trained on the lines of a professional armed force. The CPI (Maoists) have an elaborate command structure; at the apex is their Central Military Commission followed by five regional bureaus. Under each regional bureau there is a Zonal Military Commission, which is responsible for executing armed operations. The people's militia is at the bottom of this structure. Naxals now run at least eighty training camps all over India, and each camp has the infrastructure to train three hundred cadres at one time. Naxals, particularly in Andhra Pradesh, have been using wireless scanners, which can tap into the frequency of police communications. The big question is: Who is providing such high-tech equipment and training to the Naxals? Though the government is hesitant to provide information, it is speculated that the United Liberation Front of Assam and some retired Indian Army officials are involved in training the Naxals. For a long time, the United Liberation Front of Assam has been a major source for automatic weapons for Maoist cadres.

The recent violent operations of the Naxalites, it seems, leave no space for ideological commitment. Indiscriminate violence in the name of revolution cannot be countenanced. The Naxals have repeatedly stated that "armed struggle" is nonnegotiable. This position does not make sense. "Armed struggle" may be the means to the end, but it cannot be an end in itself. The Naxal brand of politics may highlight the evils of the Indian socio-political framework, but it will not able to eradicate these evils. On the other hand, the state cannot escape the blame for inflicting more violence and suffering upon its civilian population through counterviolence.

In recent years, many high-level meetings have been held to finalize a strategy to deal with the red terror. A number of decisions were made in these meetings, but the fundamental realities have not improved; rather, they have worsened. In most Naxalite-affected states there is absolutely no coordination among the police and administration. The frequent Coordination Committee Meetings convened by the union government may provide a broad understanding of the problem, but greater coordination is needed between the police and civil administration at the ground level for effective implementation of government decisions made at the highest level.

THE OFFICIAL ASSESSMENT OF THE RED TERROR

In May 2006, the Indian Planning Commission appointed an expert committee headed by D. Bandopadhyay, a retired Indian Administrative Service officer instrumental in dealing with the Naxalites in West Bengal in the 1970s, along with Prakash Singh, former deputy general of police of Uttar Pradesh and an expert on Naxal issues; Ajit Doval, former director of the Intelligence Bureau; B. D. Sharma, a retired bureaucrat and activist; Sukhdeo Thorat, University Grants Commission chairman; and K. Balagopal, a human rights lawyer, as its members to study development issues and address the causes of "discontent, unrest and extremism." The committee submitted its report in early June, 2008 and it is now available on the Planning Commission's website.[5]

The expert committee has done a commendable job in underscoring the social, political, economic, and cultural discrimination faced by the scheduled castes and scheduled tribes across the country as a key factor in drawing large numbers of discontented people to the Naxalites. The group compared twenty severely Naxalite-affected districts in five states—Andhra Pradesh, Bihar, Chhattisgarh, Jharkhand, and Orissa—with twenty nonaffected districts in the same states to establish a correlation between certain human development indicators and their link to social unrest. On the basis of this assessment, the committee established lack of empowerment of local communities as the main reason for the spread of the Naxal movement. Choosing its words carefully, the report states, "We have two worlds of education, two worlds of health, two worlds of transport and two worlds of housing."

The expert committee delved deep into the new conflict zones of India, including the mines and mineral-rich areas, steel zones, and the SEZs. The report holds the faulty system of land acquisition and a nonexistent rehabilitation and resettlement policy largely responsible for the support enjoyed by the Naxalites.

> Even those who know very little about the Naxalite movement know that its central slogan has been "land to the tiller" and that attempts to put the poor in possession of land have defined much of their activity and the notion of a SEZ, irrespective of whether it is established on multi-cropped land or not, is an assault on livelihood.[6]

On the other hand, the committee makes a forceful plea for a policy and legal framework to enable small and marginal farmers to lease land with secure rights and to protect the landless poor occupying government land so that they are not treated as encroachers.

For the first time in the history of the Naxal movement, a government-appointed committee has put the blame on the state for the growth of the movement. Providing statistics of 125 districts from the Naxal-affected states, the committee finds that the state bureaucracy has pitiably failed in delivering good governance in these areas. The committee has also severely criticized the states for their double standard in making panchayats truly the units of local self-governance. Findings of the report recommend rigorous training for the police force not only on humane tactics of controlling rural violence but also on the constitutional obligation of the state for the protection of fundamental rights. Coming down heavily on the civil war instrument of Salwa Judum, the committee asked for its immediate suspension.

Making a departure from the usual government position, the expert committee concludes that the development paradigm pursued since independence has aggravated the prevailing discontent among the marginalized sections of society. The report also points out the administration's failure "to implement the protective regulations in scheduled areas, which has resulted in land alienation, forced eviction from land, dependence of the tribals on the money lenders—made worse often by violence by the state functionaries."[7] While the government failed to address the grievances of those who lost their land to the money lenders, the Naxalites in the forest areas of Chhattisgarh, Vidarbha region of Maharashtra, Orissa, and Jharkhand have led the Adivasis "to occupy forest lands that they should have enjoyed in the normal course of things under the traditional recognized rights, but which were denied by government officials through forest settlement proceedings."[8] Naxalites seem to have developed organic roots in these areas presumably because of their success in securing the minimum wage for the tribals and the abolition of "the practice of forced labour under which the toiling castes had to provide free labour to the upper castes." Furthermore, the role of the people's court, as the report underlines, in resolving "disputes in the interest of the weaker party" seems to have created a space in which Naxalites flourished naturally. In the assessment of the Expert Committee, the Naxalites have gained considerably due to (i) the failure of the state to address the genuine socio-economic grievances of the indigenous population and (ii) their success in evolving a parallel and alternative order that has benefitted the poor, especially the Dalits and Adivasis.

The report can be termed as an honest attempt to look into the problem of Naxalism from a wider perspective. While many find the report "refreshing" for making a forceful plea to depart from a security-centric view of tackling Naxal violence, there is a danger of misinterpreting security measures in the context of the Naxal movement. Many believe in a law-and-order approach to tackle Naxalism while others consider Naxalism as the reflection of the prevalent injustice in the society. Naxalism is a security challenge, and only an inclusive growth formula will minimize the legitimate dissent of the people. Naxalism is a case in which policing and development cannot be separated. An adequate police force combined with a proper agenda for development can ensure the success of an anti-Naxal policy. Dealing with Naxalism needs a holistic approach with development initiatives as an integral part of the security approach. Security here must be understood in its broader perspective that includes human development in its scope, because human security is an inseparable component of any human development formula, and vice versa.

THE CREATION OF A COMPACT REVOLUTIONARY ZONE

In August 2001 the idea of establishing a Compact Revolutionary Zone (CRZ), from the forest tracts of Adilabad (Andhra Pradesh) to Nepal, traversing the forest areas of Maharashtra, Chhattisgarh, Jharkhand, and Bihar, was conceptualized at Siliguri in a high-level meeting of the Maoist leaders from India and Nepal. The primary aim of the CRZ is to facilitate the easy movement of extremists from one area in the proposed zone to another. The concept of the CRZ was essentially seen as a prologue to the further expansion of left-wing extremism in the subcontinent. Looked at from this angle, the notion of the CRZ seems to be moving in the right direction, for there has been a remarkable Maoist growth between 2001 and 2007 in both India and Nepal. While the CPN (Maoist) joined the interim government of Nepal, their Maoist counterparts in India carved out several guerrilla zones in different parts of the country. What was once an utopian concept, the idea and reality of the CRZ in India has indeed made big strides.

While the Maoists were busy executing their mega plan of a CRZ, the economic policy of India made a dramatic shift when the government of India announced the setting up of SEZs in its Export–Import Policy 2000. As per the SEZ Act of 2005, SEZs are geographical regions that have different economic laws than the rest of the country to facilitate increased investments and economic activity. The politics engulfing the whole issue of SEZs has definitely acquired a Maoist flavor, as can be clearly ascertained from the happenings of Kalinga Nagar in Orissa, Singur, and Nandigram in West Bengal.[9] The recent happenings on the SEZ front show that the idea of SEZs, which was originally formulated as a development strategy, has now become a rallying cry for left-wing extremism.

During their 2007 Ninth Unity Congress, the top-ranking Maoist leadership from sixteen Indian states decided to launch violent attacks on the SEZs and the projects that displace people. The Annual Report of the Central Military Commission of the CPI (Maoist) outlines the Naxal plan of creating disruptions at several proposed infrastructures, mining projects, and steel plants. The potential Naxal targets as mentioned in the report are the bauxite mining project of the Jindals in Visakhapatnam; the Polavaram irrigation project; steel plants proposed in Chhattisgarh by Tata, Essar, and Jindal; the center's proposed railway line on the Rajhara–Raighat–Jagdalpur sector; Posco's steel plants under construction in Orissa; power plants proposed by the Ambanis; a proposed steel plant in Jharkhand by the Mittal Group; and the Kosi irrigation project in northern Bihar. In the name of development, the tribals are always betrayed, as the Naxal commander Ramgam argued, saying that, when the government began mining,

> The iron ore are there, it had promised to employ the locals. Did that happen? No. The iron ore is shipped from Bailadila to Vishakhapatnam from where it is sent to Japan. The locals go far and wide for livelihood. Because of that experience, people elsewhere refuse to part with their land.[10]

The Naxal concept of the CRZ and their brand of politics over the issue of SEZs is something that needs to be taken seriously. The Naxal intentions are clear: they want to use SEZs as the most powerful weapon for the complete realization of the CRZ. The link between the Naxal concept of the CRZ and the new development mantra of SEZs is no coincidence. The Naxals have grown stronger in the tribal districts of Chhattisgarh, Orissa, Jharkhand, Karnataka, and Maharashtra, attracting US$85 billion of promised investments, mostly in steel and iron plants and mining projects. Ironically, all these investments and projects are of no benefit to the locals. In fact, in most cases, in the absence of a credible rehabilitation and resettlement policy, the locals are forced to lose their lands, which are crucial for their survival. The Naxals have been quick to realize this and reflect it in their agenda.

After the state was forced to withdraw the SEZ from Nandigram in West Bengal due to a popular outburst challenging its imposition, the union government was forced to take stock of the issues related to SEZs. Recently, after including a few changes in the SEZ Act, the Central Government's Empowered Group of Ministers on SEZs approved eighty-three new proposals in addition to the already approved sixty-three projects. The head of the government has already declared that SEZs are a reality. SEZs in themselves are not a bad idea, but the problem lies with their poor implementation. Rehabilitation and resettlement hold the key to the successful realization of SEZs in India. The government needs to show that SEZs as a development strategy would result in equitable distribution of its gains.

There is no denying that India is growing, but certain sections are being continuously denied a share in this growth. Except for symbolic tokenism, such as the employment guarantee scheme, the fundamentals of delivery are missing from most of the plans and projects. It is this tokenism that has given an opportunity to the Naxals to hijack the issue of SEZs in their favor. Today, the Naxals have realized that the Spring Thunder of 1968 failed to give the desired results owing to wide differences in Indian and Chinese conditions. Accordingly, they have reformulated their premises of Maoism. Unfortunately, the government is taking too long to realize that, though its SEZs policy is based on the Chinese model, its success depends primarily on its application to Indian conditions.

THE 2007 NINTH UNITY CONGRESS AND MAOISM

The Ninth Unity Congress of CPI (Maoist) is an ideological milestone for Maoism in India. Besides evolving specific strategies for combating the state power in India, the congress also prepared a blueprint for the seizure of power. In his address to the participants, Mupalla Lakshmana Rao, popularly known as Ganapathy, the general secretary of the party, exhorted,

> The 9th Unity Congress affirmed the general line of the new democratic revolution with agrarian revolution as its axis and protracted people's war as the path of the Indian revolution that had first come into the agenda with the Naxalbari upsurge. . . . It set several new tasks for the party with the main focus on establishment of base areas as the immediate, basic and central task before the entire party. It also resolved to advance the people's war throughout the country . . . and wage a broad-based militant mass movement against the neo-liberal policies of globalization, liberalization, privatization pursued by the reactionary ruling classes under the dictates of imperialism.[11]

Two important ideas were articulated. On the one hand, the Maoists are favorably disposed toward a militant mass movement to usher in a new era of people's power; they are also exhorted, on the other hand, to take "the guerrilla war to a higher level of mobile war in the areas where guerrilla war is in an advanced stage and to expand the areas of armed struggle to as many states as possible."[12] Ganapathy also pledged "to mobilize masses against the conspiracies and treacherous policies of the rulers to snatch land from people and hand it over to the [multinational corporations] and big business houses in the name of development through the creation of hundreds of SEZs."[13] The militant campaign against the government efforts to acquire land for SEZs in Orissa, West

Bengal, or Andhra Pradesh is being largely seen as part of a larger Maoist endeavor to resist the government agenda on the SEZs, as Ganapathy further argued: "We shall be in the forefront of every people's movement. The Congress has decided to take up struggles against the SEZs which are nothing but neo-colonial enclaves on Indian territory where no laws of the land can be applied."[14]

There were only a few violent incidents during the Naxal call for an economic blockade, but what is more important is the change in the Naxal game plan, which the government completely failed to read, following which it watched helplessly as the Naxals targeted trains, communication and transportation networks, and mining companies. On 26 June 2007, the Naxals tried to blow up a BSNL communication tower in the Malkangiri district of Orissa. For the third time in a month, the Naxals targeted BSNL communication towers in the district, having earlier tried to blow up such installations at Kalimela and MV-79 village. Biramdih railway station in West Bengal's Purulia district was raided by about fifty guerrillas who set the stationmaster's cabin on fire and totally destroyed the signaling system. In Bihar, the Naxals reportedly blasted a railway control room near the Mehsi railway station in East Champaran. Andhra Pradesh was relatively calm, though the Maoists did set a bus on fire.

Jharkhand, on the other hand, incurred a loss of around Rs. 1.5 billion. Rs. 300 million was reportedly lost by the railways due to cancellation of goods and passenger trains. The economic blockade disrupted coal and iron ore production and transport, amounting to a loss of around Rs. 600 million. Similarly, traders from the import and export business were forced to bear a loss of around Rs. 500 million. Another Rs. 45 million was lost as buses and trucks remained off the road. In the Bastar region of Chhattisgarh, two Salwa Judum leaders were reportedly killed, while the guerrillas also managed to halt the transportation of iron ore from the Dantewada District's Bailadila hills to Visakhapatnam by damaging railway tracks. Hundreds of trucks were seen standing idle on the national highways as transporters decided to keep their vehicles off the road. While the Naxals forcefully made their presence felt, life came to a stand still in the Narayanpur, Bijapur, Bastar, Kanker, and Dantewada districts of the Bastar region.

Just a week before the Naxals imposed this economic blockade, the top-ranking police officers of the four Naxal states of Andhra Pradesh, Chhattisgarh, Orissa, and Jharkhand met at Vishakhapatnam to discuss the changed strategy of the Naxals. However, during the Naxal blockade the police were completely on the back foot. Other than patrolling, there was nothing that the police could do, and even patrolling could not prevent the Naxals from going ahead with their agenda. Of course, the police may claim that there were no major casualties reported, but bloodshed was not on the Naxal agenda. As part of their changed strategy, Naxals wanted to create maximum impact with minimum damage.

It has been quite some time since the Naxals realized that in the wake of massive force deployment by the government, they could not continue with the traditional methods of guerrilla war. They, therefore, decided to adopt "mobile war" as their new strategy.

Ganapathy himself is the chief of the "mobile operations," and Ganesh, the secretary of the AOBSZC, is his deputy. As part of their changed strategy, the Naxals aim to paralyze normal life by attacking the communication, transportation, railway, and other essential establishments. They have also learned that the economic development strategy of the country has created a sense of alienation among certain sections of society and have eyed such alienated groups. The government must try to win over these sections before it is too late. Time-bound development with target-orientated implementation would definitely fill the gap, which so far has only provided a breeding ground for the extremists. Similarly, police modernization should not be limited to the procurement of arms and ammunitions; security agencies must work on their intelligence network, and a unified command for the forces at the ground level would solve much operational confusion among the various agencies. While a genuine relief and rehabilitation policy with guaranteed implementation is the need of the hour, it is, nonetheless, time to end failed initiatives like Salwa Judum.

MAOISM AND HINDUTVA[15] POLITICS

In a shocking but rare interview given to a private television news channel in Orissa, secretary of the CPI (Maoist), Orissa State Committee, Sabyasachi Panda[16] claimed that it was the CPI (Maoist) that had killed Vishwa Hindu Parishad leader Swami Laxmanananda Saraswati and four others in Jalespata Ashram in Kandhamal District. In the same interview, the mastermind of many Naxal attacks in Orissa also warned that they would kill around a dozen people whom he alleged were responsible for the communal tension in Kandhamal unless they stopped their activities. Sabyasachi Panda deserves to be taken seriously for his close proximity with Ganapathy and other top leaders of the Central Committee and Central Military Commission of the CPI (Maoists).

The one-time close associate of the maverick Nagbhushan Patnaik, Sabyasachi Panda, later developed serious differences with him and in 1996 revolted against the party to form Kui Labanga Sangha and Chashi Mulia Samiti, which later became the frontal organizations of the People's War Group in Orissa. Sabyasachi Panda is one of the founder members of the AOBSZC of the CPI (Maoist) and was in charge of the dreaded Bansadhara Division for quite a long period. Before assuming the charge of secretary of Orissa State Committee of CPI (Maoist), Sabyasachi Panda formed the People's Liberation Guerrilla Army in the state.

Since 23 August 2008, the day when Swami Laxmananda Saraswati was killed, Orissa's Kandhamal district has witnessed an unprecedented and unrelenting attack on Christians. With four thousand houses burned, three hundred villages set on fire, sixty thousand refugees, and over thirty people dead, Kandhamal attracted global attention. In this chaotic situation the interview of Sabyasachi was aired on 5 October, which made many ask why it took so long for the top leader of CPI (Maoist) in Orissa to speak to the media and take responsibility? Some may also wonder what Naxals gain by killing an old Hindu priest? Yet others may also suspect his claim on the grounds that Naxals have no history of interfering in religious matters. As the reports (based on evidence) pour in, it is clear that the root cause of the sordid incident in Kandhamal is the ethnic division between the relatively better-placed Kandhas (Hindus) and the Panas (Dalit Christians).[17] Maoism is not a significant political force in this district, though by condemning the alleged Hindu attack on the Dalit Christians they are trying to create a space for themselves. Maoists have sympathy for the Panas not because they are Christians but because they are subject to social atrocities by being Dalits. Interestingly, Maoists have not paid adequate attention to this social texture of the Oriya society presumably because the presence of Christians is very negligible in areas in which they have strong grassroots support.[18]

Sabyasachi claimed in the interview, "Naxals had left two letters claiming responsibility for the murders, but the state government suppressed both." There seems to be some truth in his claim, because within half an hour of the gruesome murder of Swami Laxmananda the then-deputy general of police of Orissa told the media that the government suspected Naxal involvement in the incident. A few days after the incident, the superintendent of police of Sambalpur, Sanjay Kumar, revealed that Naxals Prasanna Pal (alias Pabitra) and Ranjan Rout (alias Robin), who were brought on remand from Jagatsinghpur, had confessed to the Naxals' plan to eliminate Swami Lakshmanananda Saraswati. The job was taken up by the Bansadhara division of the banned ultra-left outfit headed by Sabyasachi Panda and the decision was made after the communal flare-up at Brahmanigoan, Kumar added. All these facts substantiate Sabyasachi's claim.

The politics of Naxalism understands neither religion nor does it understand caste; however, growth of Naxalism in Bihar may mainly be attributed to caste factors. For some years now, the issue of conversion and reconversion has become a driving force in Orissa politics. Naxals may not have interfered in religious issues in the past, but that does not prevent them from entering into the arena of communal politics. Naxalites aim at liberating the country by creating an atmosphere of chaos, terror, and suspicion. "The tribals are not Hindu. They are nature worshippers. There are now five lakh (half a million) Hindus in Kandhamal and this number has grown because of these forces," Sabyasachi alleged. This statement gives a clear indication of Naxal involvement in Swami Laxmananda's murder. The Naxal movement in Orissa claims to be strong in tribal pockets; however, over the past few years Swami Laxmananda had become an icon among Hindu tribals in and around Kandhamal. There was obvious pressure on the Naxal leadership to expand its support base in nontraditional Naxal areas, and it is for this that the Naxals could have killed Swami Laxamananda to spread their message. There are also reports that a few top-ranking leaders of the CPI (Maoist) from the neighboring states of Andhra Pradesh and Chhattisgarh recently complained that Sabyasachi was going soft in Orissa and had confined himself to only the Gajapati and Rayagada jungles. Sabyasachi might well have attacked the symbol of Vishwa Hindu Parishad in Orissa to prove his detractors wrong.

The Naxal brand of politics has changed course many times in the past; today, there does not seem to be any ideology left in their modus operandi. The killing of Swami Laxamananda may be an incident in isolation, or it may also be the signal of new formations within Naxal politics. It is for the investigating agencies to find out the truth. At the moment, however, there are reasons to believe that there is no spokesperson of CPI (Maoist) in Orissa who is more authentic than Sabyasachi Panda.

MAOISM AND CHILD SOLDIERS

It is an established policy of the banned CPI (Maoist) to recruit children above age sixteen. However, the process starts earlier with the recruitment of children in the age group of six to twelve for children's associations called *bal sangams*, where children are trained in Maoist ideology, used as informers, and taught to fight with sticks. Depending on their skills and aptitude, children from a Bal Sangam are "promoted" to other Naxalite departments like *sangams* (village-level associations), *chaitanya natya manch* (street theater troupes), *jan militias* (armed informers who travel with the dalams), and *dalams* (armed squads). In the *sangams, jan militias,* and *dalams*, Naxalites provide weapons training to children with rifles and teach them to use different types of explosives, including landmines. Children in *jan militias* and *dalams* participate in armed conflicts with the security forces. Children in *bal sangams, sangams,* and *chaitanya natya manchs* do not participate directly in hostilities, but are vulnerable to attacks by the security forces during anti-Naxalite combing operations. Children recruited into *dalams* are not permitted to leave and may face severe reprisals, including the killing of family members, if they surrender to the police.

There are police reports suggesting that the Maoists are targeting the children from poor families, promising them "a future to live in dignity." Young girls too join *sangham* to escape being "forced into early marriage and other kinds of exploitation." The police further confirm that "these child soldiers perform several tasks ranging from actual combat to the laying of mines and explosives, tracking combing operations and spying, besides serving as couriers for the Maoist groups."[19] However, the most dangerous and most recent Naxal strategy is the CPI (Maoists)'s formation of a child liberation army. At least three hundred children are being trained in the dense forests of Dhanbad and Giridih in Jharkhand under a crash course in the use of small arms. Apart from jungle warfare these children are trained to collect information about the movement of security forces and pass it on to the outlaw group. "The Maoist rebels use children in their propaganda war against the government and security forces," confirms S. N. Pradhan, spokesperson of the Jharkhand police.[20]

Use of child soldiers in contemporary armed conflicts is not a new phenomenon; it is a common phenomenon in Sierra Leone, Uganda, Mozambique, Nepal, Sri Lanka, and Myanmar. Since 1996, approximately two million children have died in war, at least six million have been injured or physically disabled, and twelve million have been left home-less. However, given the conflict dynamics of the Naxal movement, if the use of children gets institutionalized in its self-proclaimed war against India, and if the state agencies continue to ignore international covenants and conventions on not using child soldiers, it will make the situation worse than before, affecting an entire generation.

THE "CIVILIAN PROTEST": SALWA JUDUM

The sustained Naxalite campaign has provoked a counter-mobilization of people in the form of Salwa Judum, especially in Chhattisgarh. In the local Gondi dialect, Salwa Judum means "purification hunt" and "collective hunting," though the government pre-fers to translate it as "peace march." For the government, this is a spontaneous movement to save the tribals from the evils of Maoism. However, Salwa Judum is, as the evidence from the field suggests, "another card in the game of counterinsurgency, which essen-tially pits groups of state-sponsored vigilante tribals—those frightened by the Maoists as well as those forced by police and paramilitary to herd into special camps—against the Maoist-indoctrinated and controlled tribals."[21] The Salwa Judum has a three-prong ap-proach where, first, the Naxal-hit tribals are marched to the state-run relief camps while the women and children are left behind. Second, the Salwa Judum activities, accompa-nied by the police and security forces, march into the enemy (Naxalite) stronghold areas to conduct meetings and distribute pamphlets condemning the Naxals for having en-dangered the existence of the local population. More important, they hunt for the Sang-ham members who are then asked to surrender or hand themselves over to the police. Third, the government appoints special police officers among the Salwa Judum activists, who are entrusted and armed to protect the camps as well as accompany the march. The special police officers are allowed to conduct raids in the Naxalite villages to capture and kill the dreaded Naxalites.

Contrary to popular belief that the Salwa Judum is a government-initiated anti-Naxal program, Konda Madhukarrao, a little-known schoolteacher from Kutru in the Bijapur police district of south Bastar, first initiated a public campaign against atrocities com-mitted by the Naxals.[22] However, it took an organized form under the leadership of Ma-hendra Karma, the leader of the opposition in Chhattisgarh, and soon the state govern-ment decided to provide patronage to the program. Those who joined the campaign of their own accord are those who suffered due to Maoist atrocities, wealthier Adivasis, local tradesman and contractors, local politicians and panchayat members, and others with regional independent economic interests and power. As the composition suggests, the Salwa Judum is a platform for the "haves" against the "have-nots." On 25 August 2005, the state government announced that it had set up a committee headed by Chief Secretary A. K. Vijayvargiya to extend support to the Salwa Judum in the form of logis-tics, arms, and funding.[23]

What started off as a genuine anti-Naxal movement has instead exposed the tribals to more violence and made them refugees in their own land. As observed by Ajay Sahni of the Institute of Conflict Management, Salwa Judum has exposed the hapless tribals to repeated rounds of violence by the Maoists and had displaced, according to various estimates, as many as forty thousand tribals who are now huddled in ill-equipped government relief camps in the worst conceivable conditions.[24] Reports, based on independent investigation by several civil society organizations and human rights groups, reveal that the Salwa Judum campaign is a "cover-up" government-sponsored counterinsurgency program that, instead of providing relief to those living in the violence-prone areas, has made the situation further complicated by instigating the tribals to fight among themselves. The following report of 2 December 2005,[25] prepared by a group of civil and human rights activists, is illustrative here. The report, which first blew the lid on Salwa Judum, claims,

1. The Salwa Judum is . . . an organized, state-managed enterprise that has precedents in the Jan Jagaran Abhiyans that have occurred earlier under the leadership of the current Dantewada MLA, Mahendra Karma. The Collector himself has been part of the 75 percent of the Salwa Judum meetings and security forces have been backing the Judum's meeting. The main cadre of Salwa Judum are paid and armed by the state, at a rate that is standard in counter-insurgency operations across the country.

2. The Salwa Judum had led to the forcible displacement of people throughout Bhairamgarh, Geedam and Bijapur areas under police and administrative supervision. . . . People have left behind their cattle and most of their household goods. The entire area is being cleared of inhabitants even as new roads are being built and more police and paramilitary stations are being set up. The region is being turned into one large cantonment.

3. When Salwa Judum meetings are called, people from neighbouring villages are asked to be present. Heavy security forces accompany the meeting. Villagers that refuse to participate face repeated attacks by the combined forces of Salwa Judum, the district force and the paramilitary Naga battalion which is stationed in the area. . . . These raids result in looting, arson and killings in many instances. In some villages, the raids continue till the entire village is cleared and people have moved to camps, while in other cases only old people, women and children are left. Many villages are coming to camps to avoid these attacks in the first place.

4. Once in camps, people have no choice but to support the Salwa Judum. Some of them are forced to work as informers against members of their own and neighbouring villages and participate in attacks against them, leading to permanent divisions within the villages. We also come across instances where the Salwa Judum took young people away from the village and their families were unaware of their whereabouts.

5. Salwa Judum members man checkpoints on roads, search people's belongings and control the flow of transport [in those areas supposedly under the Naxal influence]. They enforce an economic blockade on villages and resist coming to camps. They also try to force civil officials to follow their dictat.

6. FIRs (First Information Reports) registering the looting, burning, beatings/torture by Salwa Judum mobs and the security forces are not recorded. We were told of specific instances where security forces threw dead bodies inside or near villages. The intention seems to be to terrorize people not leaving their villages. These killings are not reported, and therefore hard to corroborate. Some report suggests that ninety six people from thirty six villages have been killed. However, the only killings that are officially recorded are those by Maoists. In the period since Salwa Judum started, it is true that the killings by Maoists have gone up substantially and the official figure today stands at seventy. Rather being "a peace mission," as is claimed, the Salwa Judum has created a situation where violence has escalated.

7. Salwa Judum has strong support among certain sections of local society. This section comprises some non-adivasis immigrant settlers from other parts of India, *sarpanches* (village chief) and traditional leaders whose power has been threatened by the Maoists. . . . Both the local Congress and the Bharatiya Janata Party are supporting the Salwa Judum together.

8 We have heard from several high-ranking officials that there is an undeclared war on in Bastar, and we fear that the worst is yet to come. . . . In addition, people are being encouraged to carry arms. Village defence committees are being created, [special police officers] are being trained and armed, and the entire society is becoming more militaristic.

There are reasons to believe that the Salwa Judum campaign may have begun spontaneously, which the government appropriated to combat the Naxalites. It is therefore not surprising that in course of time the government provided support primarily "through their security forces, dramatically scaling up these local protest meetings into raids against villages believed to be pro-Naxalite, and permitted the protestors to function as a vigilante group aimed at eliminating the Naxalites."[26] The growing strength of the Salwa Judum campaign is undoubtedly due to the support of the state government of Chhattisgarh, which claims that the support extended to the "peace mission" is merely intended for "discharging the constitutional obligation of providing security and safety to the tribal population."[27] The idea of supporting the so-called people's campaign can be traced back to the 2005–2006 annual report of the Ministry of Home Affairs directing "the state to encourage the formation of Local Resistance Groups/Village Defence Committee/Nagrik Suraksha Samitis [Civilian Protection Committees] in the naxalite affected areas."[28] With paramilitary forces at their back, the Salwa Judum activists resort to brutal means to terrorize the villagers. As an eyewitness account reveals, "Villages that refused to attend [the Salwa Judum] meetings were automatically assumed to be Naxalite villages, and were burnt, and people were herded into [the relief] camps."[29] Although these relief camps are meant to provide shelter and protection to those seemingly haunted by the Naxalites, they are actually the preparatory ground for the Salwa Judum campaign. While the relief camps in Bastar (Chhattisgarh), for instance, are meant to be "the temporary shelters for the [violence-affected] adivasis, road side signs call them Salwa Judum camps, further obfuscating the boundary between state and Salwa Judum." A fact-finding mission to camps in Bastar found that these camps "were guarded by both uniformed officers [of the paramilitary forces] and also armed civilians."[30] Further exploration reveals that "these camps are in fact largely occupied by a combination of Salwa Judum activists, security forces and Adivasis and serve a variety of purposes beyond (and often contradictory to) that of a sanctuary."[31] These camps, as the report further confirms, "seemingly act as security bases . . . from which counter-insurgency operations are conducted by both official members of the security forces as well as Salwa Judum."[32] These relief camps are nothing but "internment camps" that allow "the security forces to remove and monitor the villagers who are the primary support base for the Naxalites" by forcibly detaining the Adivasis in the name of fulfilling a humanitarian mission.[33]

As evident, the Salwa Judum, instead of meaningfully addressing the genuine socio-economic grievances of the people in the affected areas, is an attempt to forcibly suppress the voice of protest. While explaining the growing strength of movements against Salwa Judum, Rangam, a Naxal commander, thus argues that "with the rich robbing the poor, the poor had begun to organize against their exploitation. This scared the government and it launched this brutal movement (Salwa Judum) so that it could continue to loot."[34] In the name of a counterinsurgency campaign, the Salwa Judum seems to have unleashed "a reign of terror" to scare the Naxalites away. A pattern appears to have developed in whatever the Salwa Judum undertakes to reestablish government authority, as an eye-witness account graphically illustrates:

> Salwa Judum attack and rob villagers. They burn down crops and kill cattle. They forcibly took away young men and women from the villages, made them SPO (Special Police Officer) and told them to fight us. Fearing them, many committed suicide. Salwa Judum men raped village women, murdering several afterward. They cut off their breasts. They slashed the bellies of pregnant women.[35]

The field inputs corroborate that "this so-called 'people's movement' . . . of Salwa Judum has resulted in life being disrupted in nearly 644 villages or over fifty percent of the district, some 150000 displaced, of which 45958 [are] officially in the relief camp as of February, 2006."[36] Dubbed as "state-sponsored terrorism," this campaign has provoked mass consternation involving different layers of society. While deliberating on public interest litigation in February 2009, the Supreme Court of India censured the government for arming the common people by saying,

How are [the members of Salwa Judum] getting arms? Once you give them arms, it will be difficult to retrieve them and we are going to get disastrous consequences. If you continue with the arms, we may have to take a drastic position. We do not underestimate the enormity of the problem. But you cannot encourage the government to arm the common man to fight naxalites.[37]

In the opinion of the apex court, the military solution does not appear to be effective in combating Maoism, the root of which is located elsewhere. Hence, the court insists that the government should "create employment opportunities in the naxal areas under the National Rural Employment Guarantee Act, provide infrastructure and education facilities in the area."[38] A fall-out of the atrocities committed by Salwa Judum was the 2011 judgment of the Supreme Court of India in which the apex court was persuaded to ban this state-sponsored armed security force. In its July 2011 verdict, the federal government and the state government of Chhattisgarh were asked "to cease and desist from using the Special Police Officer [Salwa Judum in local parlance] in any manner or form in activities, directly or indirectly, aimed at controlling, countering, mitigating or otherwise eliminating Maoist/Naxalite activities in the State of Chhattisgarh."[39]

Given the war-like situation in Chhattisgarh, all these security-related measures seem to be necessary. Some may term these measures as "short term." But the government long-term measures would yield results only if the presence of the government is felt in the Naxal-affected regions. To make this happen, the government needs an effective mechanism of scientific planning that would balance the strategic implication with people's aspirations. At the same time, to push its military agenda, the government has to win over the local tribals for which it needs to work out a comprehensive formula of sustainable development. Unfortunately, though everybody is disturbed with the escalation of violence, the government seems to have underplayed the fact that "poverty is the greatest form of human rights violation and violence in the name of development is the greatest form of exploitation." Other than anything else, Chhattisgarh today needs the basic amenities for human existence, including minimum health care, recognition of forest rights, and a credible system of governance involving tribals not only in its articulation but also in framing and implementing meaningful and people-sensitive developmental plans and programs. Only such a comprehensive solution will translate the governmental pro-people agenda into a reality.

The Salwa Judum is not a unique campaign. As evidence from the past shows, attempts were made to undertake counterinsurgency campaigns seeking to combat socio-political movements threatening the state power. During the Naxalite movement in the late 1960s, the West Bengal government was reported to have organized "resistance groups" (*pratirodh bahini* in local parlance) in those districts that were hard hit by the red campaign. Subdivisional police officers were instructed to mobilize "the local goons and anti-social elements" in their efforts to counter the Naxalites. There are reports that, during 1971, district officers conducted raids, inflicted torture, and threatened arrests in the Naxal-affected areas "to force people to join the police-sponsored anti-Naxal cell in the district."[40] Despite assuring government support, it was not possible for the police to form resistance groups in most of the areas, except for a few worse-affected areas in the district of Birbhum in western West Bengal. Similarly, the Shanti Sena (army for peace), which was formed in Orissa in 1998, had the same objective as that of resistance groups countering the Naxalites. The campaign was short lived because of (i) the lack of zeal for vigilante operation from among the local people and (ii) the gradual withdrawal of government support. Recently, in the Naxal-hit district of Malkangiri, the police have started a low-scale program of "community policing" to win over the local tribals and outplay the Naxals in their heartland. Led by the Malkangiri subdivisional police officers, the district police initiated a campaign to reach out to the villagers in remote areas of the district. There are two stages in such mobilization. In the first stage, police officers initiate interaction with the villagers by organizing sports tournaments and cultural events. The second stage involves the creation of a unit consisting of villagers who are willing to take on the Naxalites by organizing campaigns against them. Under the program of community policing, special police officers are appointed from among the villagers who are both in charge of the units and maintain a constant liaison with the district superintendent of police.[41] The program is still in the embryonic stage. Nonetheless, unlike the Salwa Judum, which is a violent campaign, the Orissa experiment is a testimony of a clear change in the attitude of the police while combating the red terror. Violence is not an effective shield against Maoism, which has thrived presumably because of the emotional chord that it strikes with the local communities. By inculcating a meaningful relationship with the people at the grassroots, the Orissa government, through community policing, has shown the extent to which counterviolence is both counterproductive and thus futile.

EXPANDING THE MAOIST DOMAIN

In one significant way, the contemporary Maoist movement in India is different from its past incarnation in the form of the Naxalbari upsurge of the late 1960s. To show solidarity with ultra-left movements elsewhere, the Indian Maoists took steps to form a unified group of the left-wing radical outfits in South Asia. The outcome was the formation of the Coordination Committee of Maoist Parties of South Asia (CCOMPOSA) in 2000. In its second annual conference in 2002, the committee, to underscore a sense of solidarity among the South Asian Maoist groups, declared,

> People's Wars, waged by the oppressed masses and led by the Maoist Parties of Peru, Nepal, India, Turkey, Bangladesh and armed struggle in other countries provide living testimony to this truth. Not only the oppressed countries of Asia, Africa and Latin America, but also the people of imperialist countries are fighting against

globalization and privatization, which has plunged the working class and sections of the people of the imperialist countries into crisis and despair never felt before.[42]

What brought these outfits in different geographical locations together is an ideological affinity: they are drawn on Marxism–Leninism–Maoism. Inspired by the theory of new democratic revolution, the coordination committee seeks to "build a broad front with the ongoing struggles of the various nationality movements in the subcontinent."[43] With the creation of such a coordination committee, Maoism seems to have spread its tentacles in most South Asian countries. For the Maoists, the committee plays a critical role in the consolidation of what they call a "compact revolutionary zone," which is also christened as the "red corridor" by the media and government officials. Whatever its nomenclature, the CCOMPOSA or the red corridor is an articulation of a voice, powerful indeed, that has gained strength particularly in a vast tract of Indian territory with the growing consolidation of Maoism.

In the last week of August 2007 CCOMPOSA successfully concluded its fourth conference at an undisclosed location in Nepal. The conference was attended by the Proletarian party of the Purba Bangla–Communist Center, the Communist Party of East Bengal (Marxist–Leninist), Red Flag, the Balgladesher Samyobadi Dal (Marxist–Leninist; all from Bangladesh), the Communist Party of Bhutan (Marxist–Leninist–Maoist), the CPN (Maoist), the CPI (Maoist), the Communist Party of India (Marxist–Leninist), and the Naxalbari and Communist Party of India (Marxist–Leninist–Maoist). The Communist Party of Ceylon (Maoist), which attended the meeting, is not a signatory to the resolution, thereby indicating that it was invited as an observer to the conference.

At a time when the relevance of the South Asian Association for Regional Cooperation (SAARC) is being widely questioned, the political leadership in South Asia can hardly afford to ignore this Maoist quest for redemption in the region. When SAARC was formed, it was looked upon not only as the unified platform of South Asia in world politics but also as a platform for regional cooperation and development. However, the experience of SAARC in the past few years shows that many things are still lacking in attaining that goal. On the other hand, when CCOMPOSA was formed, it was seen as just another Maoist platform. The last four years, however, show that it has established itself as the principal coordinator of Maoist movements in different parts of the region. The fourth CCOMPOSA meeting, through its political resolution, vowed to strengthen and expand relations among the Maoist organizations in the region and to assist each other to fight the foes in their respective countries.

During the conference, the member representatives took a close look at the reality on the ground and declared unanimously that South Asia has become a "burning cauldron" of revolutionary movements. Even though the political leadership in South Asia is often shy to accept this, Maoist movements have become an obvious geopolitical feature of the region. In Nepal, Maoists have carved out a distinct place for them in the political structure of the country. Similarly, in India, the merger of two major Maoist parties have given them so much strength that even Prime Minister Dr. Manmohan Singh was forced to declare Naxalism as the single largest security challenge before the nation. In Bangladesh, despite divisions in ranks, Maoists have made strenuous efforts to unite and spread revolutionary activity to new areas. In Bhutan "sprouts" of a new Maoist movement have also begun.

While hailing the People's War in Nepal, the conference also provided a suitable platform to restore normalcy in the relationship between the CPI (Maoist) and the CPN (Maoist). Recently, both the Maoist outfits were involved in a statement war with regard to the separate interpretations of Maoism in both countries. During the conference, both the CPI (Maoist) and CPN (Maoist) came out with a joint press statement in which both agreed that all tactical questions being adopted in the respective countries would be the sole concern of the national parties. At the same, the political resolution passed at the conference asserted that the coordination committee would "deepen and extend the links between genuine Maoists of the region and increase the coordination to fight back the enemies in the respective countries."[44]

These recent developments leave one wondering why and how Maoism has prevailed in South Asia. Does Maoism as an ideology suit South Asia or do conditions in South Asia allow Maoism to grow, or is it a combination of the two? The study of specific Maoist movements in South Asia reveals that Maoist forces have proved to be effective in mobilizing and exciting people to commit acts of violence, with the expectation that it will bring about positive social, economic, and political change. However, the use of violence in the name of development cannot be justified as violence itself is the greatest form of human exploitation.

Effectively dealing with Maoist insurrections in South Asia will necessitate the implementation of a policy that brings new ideas, goals, and projects to the peasants and rural poor. In the context of a steady Maoist march in South Asia, the SAARC has a crucial role to play. The SAARC member states should initiate and encourage such consultations to develop counterinsurgency measures through joint strategies, action plans, and cooperative programs. Besides, the region shares common problems such as poverty, unemployment, and population explosion, and successfully tackling Maoism in the region would depend on how these variables are perceived and tackled. A comparison between SAARC and CCOMPOSA may sound unrealistic today, but the political leadership in the region must not allow the Maoists to hijack the notion of regional cooperation. The SAARC nations must ensure that such a situation never arises, or else it would give a completely new dimension to the concept of regional cooperation.

SOURCES OF SUSTENANCE FOR MAOISM

It is difficult to make any firm statement in regard to the sources of income for the Maoists since the inputs are not easily available. On the basis of a Maoist document, *Our Financial Policy*, one can surmise the possible sources of their income. There are "three sources in the main for fulfilling our economic needs," mentions the document. The first source is "the party membership fee, levy and the contributions of the people"; the second one is "by confiscating the wealth and the income sources of the enemy," and the third is "the taxes we collect in the guerrilla zone and base areas by following progressive tax system."[45] In view of the expansion of the movement in new areas which involve new expenditure, it is difficult for the Maoists to take care of the expenses because "there is a huge gap between increase in income and the corresponding expenditure."[46] Hence the Sarkar issued a directive to be economical while managing the resources stating that "to fulfill ever increasing needs of the war, political propaganda and to uplift the life standards of the people, it is necessary to improve the economic resources and regulate expenditure."[47] In light of the Leninist prescription of centralized planning for income and expenditure, the Maoists, while endorsing the idea, also insist on an effective coordination among various departments of the Sarkar. For effective governance with a revolutionary mission in such a vast country like India, it is also incumbent on the local units of Janatam Sarkar to generate resources to become self-sufficient in coordination with the state and zonal committees.

Our Financial Policy is a Maoist policy document setting the guidelines for Janatam Sarkar in the war zones of Dandakaranya. There is no way one can get the exact annual income and expenses that Maoists incur to fulfill their revolutionary commitments. From the three sources mentioned above, the amount that the Maoists collect out of the membership fee and levy is too to meager take care of even a day's expenditure of the Sarkar. Most of the money is collected in the form of "royalty" on tendu leaves, bamboo, tamarind, and other forest products; the wealth obtained through looting of banks and confiscation of property of the wealthy is another important source of income; the imposition of tax on the companies and contractors building roads and other infrastructural facilities in what is described as the "guerrilla zone" provides maximum income to the Maoists. As the discussion reveals, the sources are primarily indigenous though there are unsubstantiated reports that one cannot rule out foreign funding especially in light of high-tech automatic weapons that the Maoists possess.[48]

Unlike their counterparts elsewhere, the Maoists in Orissa seem to have created a corpus fund to sustain and support the movement. There are conflicting reports on the sources of funds. Nonetheless, the CPI (Maoist) in Orissa has at its disposal sources of income that are not likely to dry up in the near future. It is common knowledge that the Naxalites raise funds through extortion from farmers, teachers, contractors, and businessmen. For instance, as soon as a contractor receives a tender for the construction of an overhead bridge, he is charged 10 percent of the total project money, admitted a civil contractor.[49] Other sources of mobilization of funds include "the operation of illegal mines, sale of tendu leafs," and illegal sale of various forest products and narcotics. According to the available inputs,[50] Naxalites are involved in "opium cultivation" at Chitrakonda in the district of Malkangiri. A rough estimate shows that as much as Rs. 60 million worth of opium is produced in this district and the cultivation is controlled by the Naxal cadres in association with the local people. A police report confirms that every year over 10,000 quintals of ganja (marijuana) are produced in the hilly terrain of Orissa–Andhra Pradesh under the Kalimela and Chitrakinda police stations in the district. Despite earnest efforts, the police fail to control the production and marketing of ganja because of the complicity of the local tribals. Furthermore, ganja, packed in small quantities, is smuggled out to the neighboring states of Chhattisgarh, Andhra Pradesh, Bihar, and Madhya Pradesh by the tribals who are well acquainted with the routes in the difficult hill terrain. Neither the police nor the excise department officials are able to track the carriers simply because they are not familiar with area and they are not adequately equipped to counterattack in case they are attacked by the Naxalites.

There is another important source of funds for the Naxalites. The district of Malkangiri, in particular, produces tendu leaves, which are required to make bidi, a country-made cigarette. Bidi has a huge market simply because it is very cheap, compared to cigarettes. The forest department divides the district into fifty units, and tender is invited from among the traders. Once a particular unit is auctioned, the businessman is allowed to take as many bags of tendu leaves as is prescribed for that unit. The plucking session lasts only fifteen to twenty days in a year; the plants do not require special care for the rest of the year but keep on producing leaves with commercial value presumably because of the conducive ecology of the district.

Before the Naxalites intervened, the tribals were never given the minimum wage of Rs 90. per day, as fixed by the government. Those who worked for the businessmen remained at the mercy of the contractors, and because of the nexus between the government officers and contractors, the minimum wage formula was never implemented. In their effort to ameliorate the conditions of the tribals, the Naxals fixed the minimum wage at Rs. 145 per bundle of tendu leaves. As a result, the income of those hired for plucking leaves substantially increased. This step has a long-term effect: not only did the Naxalite succeed in changing an unjust and exploitative system in regard to daily wages for those plucking tendu leaves, it also resulted in creating a strong support base for the Naxalites. There are reports that "people who are living in Naxal-free areas are also inviting naxalites to come to their villages and establish their hold so that the contractors in their areas can also be forced to pay higher wages."[51] The gain that the tribals made with the intervention of the Naxalites was not without a premium. One day's wage is charged from the tribals as the reward for enhancing their wages. The demand is not unjustified, as Ganapathy argued:

> One day's wage is the people's contribution towards the movement and people should give the money voluntarily [because] if we don't support, the tribals would get only Rs. ninety. So their income is enhanced because of our movement and there is nothing wrong in collecting the contribution from their wages in advance [and hence he suggested that the contribution] has to be collected at the tendu-leaf collection centre itself.[52]

Inputs from the field corroborate that the tribals have found this arrangement appropriate for their self-dignity, and survival though the tendu-leaf collection is just a seasonal job. The Maoist intervention was therefore welcome from the very beginning. The support that the Maoists extended for ensuring a better wage not only contributed to the expansion of their organization in remote areas but also sustained their base despite government atrocities. According to a report, published in *The Guardian*, "The Naxalites finance their operation by levying 'taxes' of around twelve percent on contractors and traders."[53] A system appears to have emerged in which the role of the government is almost absent, and the Maoists seem to have evolved an alternative governance following whatever they decide as "appropriate and fit" for the exploited masses. The Maoists claim that they have "brought order if not law to the area—banishing corrupt officials, expelling landlords and raising prices at gunpoint for harvests of tendu leaves."[54] In such circumstances, the system functions rather smoothly and the contractors also abide by the Maoist "dictates"; otherwise, they lose everything. For the Naxalites, the contractors are useful sources of funds, and they cannot be dispensed with. As Ganapathy, the CPI (Maoist) secretary, remarked, "We require money and [the contractors] regularly provide them. Our aim is to collect money for the movement and not to scare them away."[55] The red flag thus continues to remain a powerful symbol of protest not merely because of the ideological commitment of the indigenous population but also due to effective Maoist strategies for mobilizing adequate funds for the movement.

CONCLUDING OBSERVATIONS

This chapter can be concluded by summarizing the discussion in three fundamental points, which are as follows. First, Maoism is constantly expanding its ideological influence, stretching from the Indian border touching Nepal in the north to Tamil Nadu in the south, which is euphemistically described in the official parlance as the "red corridor" and in the Maoist articulation as the "compact revolutionary zone." This is the "biggest internal security threat" to the government because, for those drawn to the extremists, the Maoist movement has given them a voice and a chance to survive with basic human dignity. In fact, the movement survives and gains strength just because of its strong support at the grassroots. The state seems to have "disappeared," and "a parallel authority seeking to establish people's power" has emerged in the compact revolutionary zone.[56]

Second, the Maoist movement is a sharp comment on India's development trajectory. This is an outcome of distorted development programs that were appropriated by the well-off section of Indian society in the name of an equitable share of the fruits of development. Even the prime minister of India, in his address to the chief ministers of the Naxalite-affected states, admitted that "exploitation, artificially depressed wages, iniquitous socio-political circumstances, inadequate employment opportunities, lack of access to resources, underdeveloped agriculture, geographical isolation, lack of land reforms—all contribute significantly to the growth of the Naxalite movement."[57] In other words, the hilly and forest belt and its plains with distressing socio-economic conditions "favour [the Naxalites] with a secure and popular base."[58] Echoing the concern of the highest political authority in India, a human rights activist from Dantawada District of Chhattisgarh confirms that "decades of exploitation, lack of development, poverty and Forest Acts usurping rights of tribals over "*jal, jangle and jameen*" [water, forest, and land] have made the locals suspicious of any government move."[59] He further adds that the gradual decline of government authority had made the situation worse. "There is no administration [and] only a police force which is still not people-friendly," he laments. "After Salwa Judum, the situation has worsened. On the one hand is the terror of Naxals and on the other the terror of Salwa Judum. Tribals are leaving villages and sleeping in forests. Salwa Judum," he emphatically suggested, "cannot be the answer to Naxalism."[60] This is also evident in a 2011 report, prepared by the People's Union for Civil Liberties, which corroborates the concern by stating, "The indignant local tribal communities are trapped in ending cycles of often brutal violence, unleashed consecutively by Maoists, security forces and the vigilante armed civilian groups, such as the Salwa Judum and its incarnations."[61] This is a peculiar situation in which the local tribal inhabitants suffer brutal violence simply by being in the so-called red corridor. There is no one to prove their innocence and hence they undergo, by default, the life of a suspect even in the midst of harrowing struggle for mere survival in circumstances of uncertainty and severe poverty.

In many areas, including those vacated due to the government-sponsored Salwa Judum campaign, "the edifice of the state structure" appears to have crumbled. There is therefore no "recognized authority" except perhaps the one that the Maoists have developed to translate the people's power into a reality. So there is no military solution to the Naxal crisis. The best way to tackle the "red terror" is by developing meaningful and implementable development packages for these areas that remain peripheral despite India's much-hyped remarkable economic growth in the globalizing world. As is well known, there has been no dearth of programs for the peripherals; however, these programs hardly reach those who need them most. Even the application of force by the paramilitary forces can never be adequate to combat the red menace, an army brigadier helping the Chhattisgarh government train the policemen in anti-terror encounter insists, "unless it is supported by the local people." Hence he recommends that "the paramilitary forces need to be constantly on foot visiting the villages with people-friendly operations because people can be the sources of information in the villages." Unless the tribals "are won-over and supplement the activities of the forces by sharing information and other inputs, the military strategy, however advanced it may be, will hardly be effective."[62]

Third, Maoism is a creative experiment of people's power. This is a device through which "the initiative and energy of the masses . . . are released and come into full play."

This is translated into "the active participation of masses in administering their own lives, collectively developing their villages through construction of schools, tanks, hospitals etc. and increasing production, resolving the local disputes by themselves without ever the need to go to the bourgeois-feudal courts, in short, shaping their won destiny."[63] The Maoist parallel government, christened as Janatam Sarkar, is, argues a Naxal cadre, "in an embryonic stage" and is paving the way for the emergence of a full-fledged government with the seizure of power. The government has eight departments: education and culture, finance, law, defense, agriculture, forest conservation, health and sanitation, and public relations. The conspicuous absence of a land reform department is attributed to the fact that the equitable distribution of land among the tribals has completely ruled out land-related disputes and hence the department is redundant. Of all the departments, the law department seems to be most effective and well-respected for its success in resolving, particularly, "family disputes." In fact, the Maoists claim that, during the period of 2006 to 2009, the Jan-Adalat (people's court) "settled about two hundred disputes between brothers, husband–wives, neighbours." With the growing popularity of the people's court, the local police station seems to have become defunct.[64] Whatever the rate of success, these parallel institutions continue to symbolize efforts drawn on an alternative ideological discourse in which the role of "the people" remains most critical. This is what makes the Maoist endeavor interesting to study and comprehend.

Besides empowering people, the Maoists, like their former Naxalite colleagues who forced the government to bring about radical land reforms particularly in West Bengal, play a "catalyst role" in goading the Indian state to concede some pro-people legislations and schemes, such as the Panchayat Extension to Scheduled Areas Act of 1996, which extended self-governance in tribal-preponderant areas of Andhra Pradesh, Chhattisgarh, Gujarat, Himachal Pradesh, Jharkhand, Maharashtra, Madhya Pradesh, Orissa, and Rajasthan; the 2006 Forest Act; and the 2005 Mahatma Gandhi National Rural Employment Guarantee Act. Although not adequate to radically alter the prevalent class relations, these specific legislative stipulations are nonetheless critical steps toward providing definite benefits to the poor in rural India. The 1996 Panchayat Extension to Scheduled Areas Act attempted to shift the balance of power toward the communities by providing a mechanism for self-protection and self-governance. By recognizing that tribal communities are "competent to self-govern," the act recognizes the importance of their way of life, value system, and worldview.[65] Similarly, the 2006 Forest Act, by legally protecting the tribal rights over forest land, which had been denied for decades, is also a revolutionary step because it secures not only the tribal tenurial rights over land but also rights over forest produce, which provides them with an alternative source of income, especially during the lean season when tribals cannot find employment in the areas in which they live. In an identical way, the 2005 Mahatma Gandhi National Rural Employment Guarantee Act, by ensuring one hundred days of employment to the rural people, is another radical step toward fulfilling an ideological goal of creating jobs for all. It is true that a series of progressive pro-people movements created circumstances for such transformative legislation. The role of the Maoists is no less insignificant especially in tribal India where "their presence enables the transformative perspective to remain alive."[66] Besides "goading the rulers towards propagating, even if hypocritically, inclusive growth . . . , the biggest contribution of the Maoists lies [therefore] in establishing that rebellion against oppression is necessary and possible, and is an intrinsic part of the search for a superior alternative."[67] Given the well-entrenched prejudiced class relations, these institutionalized measures, despite being radical, may not be adequate; they nonetheless represent critical steps that not only recognized the problem of economic disparities at the grassroots but also forced the ruling authority to respond to the genuine socioeconomic concerns of the rural masses.

It is true that Maoism is a meaningful statement on the articulation of governance at the grassroots. It is also true that Maoism is dismissed as "another terrorist campaign" seeking to achieve "not the social and economic advancement of the adivasis but the capture of power in Delhi through a process of armed struggle [in which] the tribals are a mere stepping stone or . . . merely cannon fodder."[68] Nonetheless, there is no denying the fact that the Maoists by being integrated with the local population in the remote, difficult terrain of India have gradually become part of the community due partly to their involvement in the day-to-day struggle for existence and partly due to their success in getting what is due to the tribals for collecting tendu leaves for the contractors. This is not a mean achievement, and the image of the Maoists as saviors of the dispossessed has helped them build a base in these areas. What is strikingly missing in the entire Maoist endeavor is the absence of a blueprint for future. Their hostility to the construction of roads, schools, or hospitals in the forest areas or the difficult hilly terrain in Orissa-Andhra Pradesh and the Chhattisgarh border provides credibility to the campaign that the Naxalites are opposed to development. The Maoists admit that roads, schools, and hospitals are necessary for development, but they are not persuaded because the roads will be used to transport police and paramilitary forces, and school and hospital buildings will provide them accommodation. Hence they are determined to scuttle such government projects. This results in circumstances in which the primary sufferers are the tribals who reel from the effects of underdevelopment due mainly to a Maoist-sponsored ideological battle justifying the resistance to development to sustain a campaign that is surely limited in scope and goal. This is perhaps most ironic in Maoism, though the decision is politically comprehensible. In the absence of a clear roadmap for the future, it is difficult to appreciate the Maoist arguments challenging the governmental development strategy that, despite being politically governed, would have radically altered the prevalent socio-economic texture of the remote areas. Here is a major contradiction that the Maoists cannot avoid addressing, except to the detriment of their popularity as an organically evolved ideological group seeking to accomplish a new democratic revolution in India.

Conclusion

⌒——

COMMUNISM IN INDIA records the rise, consolidation, and relative decline of left politics in India since India's independence in 1947. Despite having ideological roots in classical Marxism and its contemporary variants, Indian communism appears to have taken a unique path of development, and it provides an example for understanding left consolidation in socio-economic circumstances similar to those in which other variants of communism developed elsewhere. Following a well-defined social-democratic path, the Indian variety of parliamentary communism does not differ much from its counterparts elsewhere. There is no doubt that communist ideology attracted mass support in India largely due to its universal egalitarian concerns and its endeavor to implement them through effective legislation. It thus became a refreshing ideology, especially in a transitional society like India, which never became a truly liberal democratic polity, given the importance of its caste system. It is difficult to establish that those championing communism are free from caste prejudices; nonetheless, by questioning birth-driven social segregation, they set in motion a powerful argument challenging what was considered to be sacrosanct. Communism thus became an empowering ideology for the vulnerable sections of Indian society that also remained peripheral in an independent polity, which, despite being politically free, was not adequately equipped to meaningfully address the basic human needs for food, shelter, and social security. So the communist parties and those drawing on parliamentary communism fulfilled two goals simultaneously. On the one hand, their sustained political activities at the grassroots gave socio-political outcasts a powerful voice and made them stakeholders in the political processes, thereby creating a powerful constituency that could not be ignored in electoral democracy.

On the other hand, their role was far more significant in exposing the serious limitations of the prevalent liberal democratic arrangement in fulfilling the founding fathers' widely publicized aim of making India free from hunger, poverty, and insecurity. Despite being ideologically different, political parties appreciative of parliamentary communism adopted the Westminster path of democracy to attain their distinctive pro-people socio-economic goals. For the ultra-left-wing communists, also christened as Maoists, the Western liberal democratic forms were neither democratic nor liberal but a refined system of exploitation of the "have-nots" by the "haves." Seeking to replace the system, they thus found in armed revolution a definite means to usher in an era free from exploitation of human beings by human beings.

As is evident, the idea of forcible overthrow of the system appears to have brought together a large section of the Indian population around Maoism, in what is called the "red corridor." This area stretches from West Bengal through Jharkhand, Orissa, Chhattisgarh, and parts of Andhra Pradesh and Maharashtra. Home to millions of India's tribal people, these areas also contain mineral-rich forests, which are dreamlands to the corporate world. So, the so-called red corridor is not merely a geographic expression but also a physical space articulating a major contradiction in the state-led development paradigm, which India adopted immediately after gaining political freedom. Tribals represent a relentless fight against the neoliberal development model that the corporate magnates champion to fulfill a class-driven goal. One cannot simply wish away the association of the majority of Indian tribals with the ultra-left-wing extremists by saying that they are "misguided." This is true especially when they are ready to sacrifice everything, including their lives, for a cause, which, despite being distant, will radically alter their present socio-economic circumstances. Maoism attracts the support of the exploited—whether tribals or others—presumably because the conventional liberal democratic method does not appear to offer a mechanism to root out the sources of class discrimination, due to its inherent ideological tilt toward class exploitation. Furthermore, the fact that Maoism is expanding its sphere of influence, notwithstanding the coercive state apparatus, confirms that the spread is not the mere political adventurism of a group of dedicated "foot soldiers" but an articulation of an ideological voice, drawn on genuine socio-economic grievances[1] and supported by an equally powerful and well-entrenched organization involving people from various social strata and regions of India. The new version of ultra-left-wing extremism has become integral to contemporary Indian politics. By seeking to grasp its transformed texture in a different fashion, this movement has not only redefined India's political discourse but has also challenged the so-called universal appeal of liberal democracy as the most acceptable political form of governance in post-colonial India.

II

As shown, communism is articulated in two diametrically opposite ways in India. On the one hand, by resorting to parliamentary mode, it seeks to achieve the Marxist goal of human salvation; the Maoist version, on the other hand, pursues the violent liquidation of class enemies as the only meaningful method to establishing a classless society with organic roots. Given the manifestation of these two versions of communism, it is thus fair to argue that both of these forms, being context-driven, reflect the specific socio-economic circumstances in which they are enunciated. Maoism is rather easier to conceptualize given its proclivity to accept more or less uncritically the Maoist interpretation of Marxism–Leninism in the context of an agrarian society. The fact that Maoism has expanded its sphere of influence in large parts of India in the face of state brutality confirms that it is inspirational to "the wretched of the earth" and those who have nothing to lose "but their chains." Unlike its earlier incarnation in the Naxalbari movement, the Maoist crusade is undoubtedly a powerful ideological challenge that cannot be wished away as a mere "law-and-order" problem. It is an inevitable outcome of retarded socio-economic development following the acceptance of the state-led development paradigm since India's independence in 1947. Globalization further complicated the situation as the nation-state lost its viability with the increasing importance of corporate magnates in domestic affairs. The primary aim of these global operators is to extract natural resources as quickly as possible even at the cost of displacing the local habitat for partisan gains. For those affected by such selfish outsiders, Maoism is a refreshing voice, strengthening their zeal to challenge the prevalent status quo.

Unlike Maoism, the parliamentary left did not expand much beyond its traditional stronghold areas (West Bengal, Kerala, and Tripura) in India, suggesting perhaps the failure of the Marxist social democracy to ideologically inspire the marginalized. Nonetheless, it is a significant segment of parliamentary politics in India, especially in the coalition era, when even the pan-Indian political parties may require the support of the left parties to form a stable coalition government at the national level. So the left parties that so far remained regional have suddenly become critical in national politics because of their numerical strength. The parliamentary left became indispensable for the national coalition because of its numerical strength in parliament, which it mustered in West Bengal, Kerala, and Tripura by a cadre-based, well-entrenched organization fulfilling a clearly Stalinist design. Ideology is thus a cementing force not only for the cadres; it is also a powerful device to reach out to the nonparty masses. Without adequate organizational support, ideology ceases to become effective. So for a stable ideological social base, organization plays an equally critical role. The long duration of thirty-four years of the Left Front rule in West Bengal is largely the outcome of a very fine enmeshing of ideology and organization. This has paid off in elections since 1977. It was possible for the Left Front, especially the Communist Party of India (Marxist; CPI [M]), to sustain its social base because its political agenda was to meaningfully articulate socio-economic equality regardless of class, clan, and ethnicity. The party's ascendancy, particularly in rural Bengal, was established, comments an analyst, "by the sacrifice and dedication of a group of left leaders who almost always came to the village from outside and mobilized the peasants on some local issues of economic exploitation and social exclusion . . . [which] was both a source of inspiration as well as transformation."[2] What cemented the bond between the party leaders and the led was the simple lifestyle of the former even after they became ministers in the government. This was especially so at the beginning of its rule. For the people, there was hardly a difference between the wielders of power and the governed. This was surely an ideology-inspired behavior that the parliamentary left significantly valued in building a mass-based party. Ideology no longer remained the driving force only for the party but also for the masses who found in ideology an avenue for salvation from injustice and torture. This was translated in the 1977 Left Front victory, which not only replaced the ruthless Congress government but also initiated a new era of people-centric governance. It was a clear break with the past, given the changes it brought about in West Bengal. Not only did the Left Front establish a system of governance based on democratic values and norms, it also gave the poor a sense of dignity through meaningful programs of empowerment. By recognizing the rights of the cultivators over land through Operation Barga, the Left Front government initiated revolutionary changes in rural Bengal, which was consolidated further through the introduction of panchayati governance involving the socio-economically peripheral sections in the decision-making at the grassroots. These radical policy decisions were rather easily implemented not merely because of administrative supportive of the government but also because of the support that the parallel party machinery extended to successfully implement them, as they were ideology driven. The Marxists' political authority was, it is thus argued, "formed on their capacity at least symbolically to break the landlords' power and to take control of the police and administration" to fulfill their ideological goal.[3] This was an ideal example of how organization could be an effective aid to pro-people ideology. The initial popularity of the Left Front in West Bengal was largely attributed to a compatible blending of ideology and organization in which the latter was never allowed to become a Frankenstein presumably because of the hegemonic importance of the former in shaping its politics.

The situation however did not remain the same as successive electoral victories of the Left Front also confirmed the importance of organization in sustaining and consolidating a stable social base. Ideology reduced to certain vacuous expressions with no substantial appeal was no longer valued as it was in the past; the prevalent leadership hardly encouraged debate since they considered it a threat. As long as the Left Front retained power, organizational bankruptcy was not meaningfully addressed. Instead of being the vanguard of the struggling masses, the communist organization was reduced to "a militarist drill of sorts to violently counter political opposition and cultural dissent," which not only made the organization apparently invincible but also gave the leaders the gratifying sense of superiority and fanatical self-confidence without making them realize that a time would come when the classes that they led could become organized and autonomous enough to resist the dictates of the vanguard, as was soon evident in Singur and Nandigram over the forcible land acquisition for Tata's car factory.[4] Thus, giving those running the organization a free hand seemed to have been a deliberate strategy. It gave rich dividends to the party leadership by serving, as a commentator mentions, "a three-fold purpose."[5] First, as an iron-fisted organization, it was able to retain an ideological hold over the party (although it was robbed of its dynamics and reduced to a sterile dogma); second, its subservience to organization resulted in the instrumentalist use of ideology; and, third, this repositioning of the ideology–organization nexus allowed organizational considerations to justify all actions of the party however nefarious and criminal they were. It also endorsed, in a very Stalinist way, the use of unbridled violence for expanding the organization in the face of a challenge.

What is paradoxical was the fact that instead of being complementary to an ideology that created a strong social base for the Left Front, the organization acted in a partisan way by being subservient to the dominant coterie within the party. There was thus a clear schism between the organization and the masses that escaped serious attention, presumably because of the parliamentary left's uninterrupted electoral victories starting in 1977. A process of alienation was set in motion between the party and the followers, but it was never adequately addressed by the party high command largely because the divided opposition never appeared to threaten the continuity of the Front in power. And, also, with its overwhelming majority in the West Bengal legislative assembly, the CPI (M), the leading partner within the Left Front, ignored other constituents of the conglomeration that caused dissension even within the government. The left juggernaut seemed invincible, as the 2006 Assembly election results demonstrated. This not only made the Front, especially the CPI (M), overconfident of its strength but created circumstances in which the coterie supported forcible land acquisition for rapid industrialization, which ran counter to its basic ideological commitment to the agrarian masses in West Bengal. The CPI (M) was thus charged with deviating from its fundamental ideological position vis-à-vis the majority that it always held in contrast with the bourgeois political parties. Paradoxically, the Trinamul–Congress conglomeration that defeated the parliamentary left in West Bengal appropriated the communist concern for the landless after the onset of a forcible land acquisition policy by the left for the private investors in the province. The same ideological goal—land to the tiller—that catapulted the left to the center stage was pursued by its bête-noire, the All India Trinamul Congress, as shown in chapter 4, to create and consolidate its support base in the 2011 Assembly election.[6] The strategy that the leadership felt appropriate for rejuvenating the state's industrial health had thus boomeranged in the context of the massive mass disillusionment with the Left Front. The masses shifted their loyalty gradually to a united opposition, waiting for a chance to prove itself as a viable alternative.

III

Despite being derivative of non-Indian intellectual sources, communism in India is a distinctive contextual response to the pressing socio-economic discomforts confronting Indian masses. At least, the parliamentary form, with its clear contextual roots, provides a unique conceptualization of social democracy in which the role of the organization remains preeminent. The Left Front governments in India, thus argues Atul Kohli, articulate a social-democratic alternative where "well-organized left of centre parties are in a position to assuage the propertied, control the propertyless, and pursue incremental reforms within the constraints of hierarchical societies."[7] The ruling classes never felt threatened primarily because of the social-democratic ideological line that the parliamentary left began pursuing as soon as they became part of parliamentary politics. Even the international agencies, including the World Bank, appeared as benevolent donors to the infrastructural development, particularly in West Bengal, to avoid "a law and order problem . . . and a resurgence of extra-constitutional activities which would have been fatal politically."[8] Given a history of a long-drawn left-wing-extremist movement in the state, the apprehension was not entirely unfounded.

Conceptually, the parliamentary left clung to the European variety of social democracy except, perhaps, in that it sought to be a hegemonic party. In its classical articulation, social democracy amounts to the abdication of "Marxist revolutionary phraseology which is, in fact, out of date [and] building-up of a democratic-socialist party of reform [aiming at] the acquisition of responsible parliamentary government, the development of Free Trade Unions and the cooperatives, and the enlargement of municipal socialism."[9] Furthermore, it was also accepted that socialist values derive "not exclusively from Marxism" but are also rooted in "Christian ethics, humanism and classical philosophy."[10] Drawn on this, the left-wing democrats in France, England, and Scandinavia "built socialist movement and welfare states that helped moderate the inequalities created by unbridled capitalism without sacrificing personal freedoms and individual liberties."[11] A perusal of the nature and functioning of the parliamentary left confirms the extent to which it largely approximates to the classical description of social democracy. This led an analyst to comment that Indian communist parties following the parliamentary path of socio-political changes are "communist in name and organization, but social democratic in ideology and practice."[12] In the context of sterile governance, social-democratic means were revolutionary, and the parliamentary left reaped full benefit especially at the initial stages of its rule because it was believed that "other than limited land reforms, giving relief to the people and using the government to facilitate mass struggles, [the left rule] could not do much under bourgeois democratic state."[13] What it meant was a dilution of its basic ideological faith because the parliamentary communists, instead of being involved in a revolutionary overthrow of the bourgeois order, preferred to utilize the prevalent state machinery for pro-people ameliorating programs. This led a commentator to conclude that "beneath their Stalinist forms, [the Communist Parties of India] have increasingly disclosed a social democratic purpose, primarily concerned with the dexterous management of capitalism rather than its destruction or its transcendence."[14] In contrast with the previous Congress-led bourgeois government, the pro-people agrarian policies that the parliamentary left in West Bengal adopted when in power were undoubtedly revolutionary that sustained its social base, and made the incumbent government invincible. An unhealthy process seemed to have been set in motion that bears an un-canny similarity with the Weimer social democracy just before the rise of authoritarian-ism in Germany before the Second World War. According to contemporary studies, in-stead of being different from the bourgeois governance, social democracy in Germany was reduced to *verbonzung* (bossification), *verkalkung* (ossification), and *verburgerlichung* (bourgeoisification).[15] With the consolidation of these tendencies within the party and government, social democracy lost its fundamental character with the hegemonic pres-ence of a caucus in circumstances where the workers became subservient to the entire processes. The disconnect between the party leadership and the followers was hardly bridged. While explaining the alienation of the social-democratic leaders from their fol-lowers in Germany in the interwar period, Hunt thus argues,

> As they came into broader contact with upper orders of society, as their working-class roots faded farther and farther into the background and automatic reelection guaranteed them life tenure in the socialist bureaucracy [the Social Democratic leaders] developed . . . the physiognomy of prosperous innkeepers [who] could rarely be called to account for their action and tended to develop a contemptuous attitude toward criticism from below.[16]

This is perhaps the most revealing explanation of how the ideological appeal of social democracy gradually lost its momentum in Germany despite its initial revolutionary charm. Two important points stand out. First, the decline of social democracy is attrib-uted, on the one hand, to a clear alienation between the leaders and the led, which also reflected the failure of the former to appreciate the genuine socio-economic issues affect-ing the latter. Second, the arrogance of authority, which was evident in their disdain for genuine criticism, made, on the other hand, the gulf unbridgeable. As early as 1985, within just eight years of its rule in West Bengal, a similar tendency was visible. It was candidly articulated in an official document:

> The Communist Party is no longer seen as a totally different party from other po-litical parties. For the last few years in our role as government, our party workers and leadership have been in close contact with the different levels of bureaucracy. All the aberrations of petty bourgeois class have pervaded our party today. . . . Apart from the lower levels, even the tested leadership is not free from this. . . . The relentless struggles which we should have launched against such aberrations are no longer seen. Our image before the people is blurred.[17]

Despite difference in time and space, the parliamentary left in India had thus the identi-cal trajectory: its rise was meteoric and so was its downfall. Undoubtedly, the agrarian reforms, especially Operation Barga, radically altered the socio-economic complexion of rural Bengal; the panchayati raj governance made the poor a part of administration at the grassroots. The situation, however, dramatically changed when the Left Front sought to consolidate its base among the urban voters by uncritically accepting the neoliberal developmental plans and programs. Like the Congress-led national government, the West Bengal government "having run out of ideas . . . , simply surrendered to the capital and planned their utopia in investments from outside."[18] As shown in chapter 3 (on the decline of the left in West Bengal), what caused a serious dent and later became an Achilles heel in the left social base was "the forcible land acquisition" by the government for rapid industrialization. Similar to its social democratic counterpart in Germany, the parliamentary left, especially in West Bengal, gradually declined, despite having won seven successive assembly elections. This happened largely due to the parliamentary left's inability to creatively assess the new contradictions that emerged in the wake of liberalization; strangely, the opposition that decimated the parliamentary left in the 2011 West Bengal assembly elections consolidated its social base by taking up the causes of those hapless villagers who lost their land due to the ruthless governmental eviction policy for rapid industrialization.

IV

India is perhaps the only example where both the versions of communism—the parliamentary form and its ultra-left-wing articulation—exist simultaneously. It is true that the former is confined to three constituent states—Kerala, West Bengal, and Tripura—while the latter seems to be spreading its influence in various parts of the country. Conceptually, the ultra-left-wing extremism, also known as Maoism, does not differ much from the Maoist-reinvented form of communism. By believing in the forcible overthrow of the bourgeois regime, it simply rearticulates the same version in the Indian context. As is shown in Part II, besides ideological conformity, the Maoist movement is also structured along conventional Maoist instructions. The parliamentary left is however a unique conceptualization of Marxism–Leninism in India that upheld and consolidated liberal democracy in the wake of colonialism. Inspired by classical Marxism, several former nationalists in India were drawn to its revolutionary precepts during the British rule. Being fond of the social democratic appreciation of the parliamentary path, most of them finally gave up violence and found in the election process a great opportunity to substantially alter the existing class relations, which were tilted heavily against the socio-economically underprivileged sections. Is the parliamentary method adequate to fulfill the Marxist vision of human salvation? If Marxism is understood purely in terms of its letters and not spirit, the Indian form of parliamentary communism is a clear deviation from its classical exposition. Is what the parliamentary left represents social democracy at its best and petit-bourgeois politics at its worst? For the parliamentary left, the communist label is what gives them respectability in the absence of substance, as Kohli seeks to prove while assessing the long-drawn Left Front rule in West Bengal.[19] In a similar vein, Bhabani Sengupta did not find the parliamentary left experiment in India innovative at all; instead it reflected an endeavor at short-circuiting the processes of Marxist revolution by suggesting that the parliamentary path was a better option to violent class struggle for bringing about the required socio-economic changes.[20] What is common in the argument that Kohli and Sengupta offer is that they assess the parliamentary left purely from "the classical Marxist point of view" rather than the important context-shaping Marxism. It is true that parliamentary means may not be adequate to accomplish revolution in the Marxist sense. However, it is an effective aid to the struggle for democracy and reform, as the left governments in Kerala, West Bengal, and Tripura have shown. Besides providing "an effective instrument for the efficient and honest government in West Bengal that the Congress failed to provide in the past,"[21] parliamentary communism put forward a meaningful alternative. This was not a mean achievement in the context of severe political instability. Furthermore, in a country like India, where the numbers of people below the poverty line are staggering, parliamentary communism changed the class balance in the countryside through a new institutional network by consolidating the panchayati raj governance. As Kohli himself admitted, "With the comprehensive penetration of the countryside without depending on the large landowners," the parliamentary left in West Bengal has brought a clear shift of institutional power from "the hands of the dominant propertied groups to a politicized lower middle strata."[22] In contrast with the prevalent system of land relations in which the tiller of the soil had hardly any institutional rights over land, this was undoubtedly a revolutionary step that not only changed the socio-economic texture in rural Bengal but also accorded human dignity to "the wretched of the earth." By effectively utilizing the prevalent state machinery in accordance with specific ideological preferences, the parliamentary left also proved how effective the liberal democratic system could be in transforming the institutional base of state power within the liberal democratic framework. Aware of the great difficulty in fulfilling the communist ideological mission, the parliamentary left, while reflecting on its achievement as part of the government in West Bengal, thus made a cautionary remark:

> The aim of our programmes is to alleviate the sufferings of the rural and urban poor and to improve their conditions to a certain extent. We do not claim anything more, as we are aware that without structural changes in the socio-economic order it is hardly possible to bring about any basic change in the conditions of the people.[23]

It is self-evident that, given the well-entrenched socio-economic values and political culture, the fulfillment of the final goal of the communist movement would remain distant though the regime could be effectively utilized to lay out an appropriate context by integrating the masses with the democratic struggle to challenge the roots of class exploitation. A different pattern of development has thus "emerged in a state like West

Bengal, where [the ruling] parliamentary communist party [which was] more social-democratic than communist . . . [was] able to implement modest land reforms [and] with [reasonably consistent] agricultural growth the fruits of economic growth came to be shared widely, bringing down poverty rapidly."[24] By its "non-threatening approach toward property-owning groups whose roles in production and economic growth remain essential for the long-term welfare of the state,"[25] the Left Front government in West Bengal also succeeded in resolving the apparent antipathy between the classes with contradictory socio-economic and political interests. So, the parliamentary method was an innovative design to pursue effectively specific developmental plans and programs involving various strata regardless of contradictory class interests. By catapulting people to the center stage of politics, the communist party, as T. J. Nossiter confirms in his study of Marxist governments in India, reinvented the available liberal democratic political means to demonstrate how effective they could be if they were differently fashioned and molded creatively in different ideological parameters.[26] According to Nossiter, it is easier to dismiss parliamentary communism as "an aberration to the theory and practice of communism" simply because it has its organic roots in a non-European socio-economic milieu. But one should not lose sight of India's contextual peculiarities due to its well-entrenched legacies of colonialism or the nation's very unique caste-divided and ethnically fragmented social fabric. Furthermore, unlike its Western social democratic counterparts, the parliamentary left in India "by trial and error . . . utilized the whole apparatus of liberal democracy, elections, parties, parliaments, levels of governance—from panchayat and municipality to province and federal levels—to advance popular mobilization in ways which were not [available] to Lenin and the Bolsheviks and only hinted by Marx."[27] So, parliamentary communism in India is clearly a creative Marxist conceptualization in non-European circumstances, which cannot be grasped let alone theorized if it is taken out of context. In this sense, the left struggle for democratization and reforms does not appear to be insignificant but is a sure aid to the wider struggle for human dignity regardless of one's socio-economic locations and political predilections.[28]

V

While parliamentary communism is intellectually refreshing because it has reinvented Marxism–Leninism in a transitional India with an inherited liberal democratic framework of governance, Maoism is an articulation of violent class struggle involving the socio-economically marginalized across various Indian provinces. It is true that Maoism shares ideological affinities with former ultra-left-wing extremist movements, including the Naxalite upsurges of the 1960s though it is not identical with the past movements, at least in terms of its social base and organizational texture. Unlike the Naxalite movement, which was largely a middle-class outburst with a limited social base among peasants or workers, Maoism is far more widely spread, especially across India's tribal belt, which has attracted global corporations presumably because of its large deposit of useful minerals. This area is known as the red corridor although, given its huge reserve of precious minerals, it would not be an exaggeration to call it the "mineral corridor." The three tribal-dominated states of Orissa, Chhattisgarh, and Jharkhand are the most productive mineral-bearing states in India, accounting for 70 percent of India's coal reserves, 80 percent of its high-grade iron ore, 60 percent of its bauxite, and almost 100 percent of its chromite reserves.[29] To fulfill the neoliberal developmental goal, efforts are under way to exploit these untapped natural resources, which means displacing the tribals living there. Historically, tribals remain most vulnerable in the face of the so-called developmental endeavor, as a commentator eloquently points out:

> Millions of tribals, who grew up and live in these forests, find themselves dispossessed of their forest land and its produce; before their eyes, [they] have seen their means of livelihood being taken away [with the] mines being excavated on their forest land, earning [millions and millions of dollars] every year for everyone else, but for them.[30]

As a contemporary study endorses, in Jharkhand, one of the worst-affected states in eastern India, 1.8 million tribals have been displaced and 1.5 million acres of land taken away for the sake of development. This allows a free hand to the "corporate mafias" for extraction of valuable minerals and for pursuing "their mindless and essentially partisan model of development."[31] Similarly, the Korean steel magnate POSCO was allowed to extract high-grade iron ore from Khandadhar hills at the cost of the local tribal habitat. The local tribe received a battering from the state when it challenged the POSCO takeover of their land. Similarly, when the tribals who lost their land because of mining in Bailadila in the Dantewada District of Chhattisgarh asked for employment in the mines, they were simply run off by the police.[32] So Maoism is an obvious response to the atrocities meted out to the natural habitat of these areas, which had previously remained off the radar but have increasingly become important purely because of their economic worth in the global market. If the tribals have taken up arms, they have done so, justifies a commentator, "because a government that has given them nothing but violence and neglect and now wants to snatch away the last things they had—their land."[33] For them, the so-called cry for development is a guise to fulfill the partisan mission of the government and its global cohorts waiting to mercilessly exploit India's mineral resources. Hence, the opposition is justified. Is there a parallel or counter Maoist plan for development? The answer is no. Furthermore, it is also alleged that "revolutionary claims for development and liberation of the poor [in the Maoist zone contribute] to a process through which those at the bottom of the social hierarchy . . . remain marginalized," presumably given the hegemonic influence of those at the helm of the rural power structure.[34]

It is true that there is hardly a Maoist vision document on development. Nonetheless, their vehement opposition to the neoliberal development design captures an effort at articulating an argument for inclusive development. This argument is contrary to the prevalent developmental schemes that the Indian state seems to have endorsed by allowing global capital a free hand in India's contemporary development trajectory. As a result,

> A massive land grab by large corporations is going on in various guises, aided and abetted by the land acquisition policies of both the federal and state governments. Destruction of livelihood and displacement of the poor in the name of industrialization, big dams for power generation and irrigation . . . [and] corporatization of agriculture despite farmers' suicide . . . are showing every day how development can turn perverse.[35]

Here lies the root cause of the mass disenchantment with the state, which, to sustain India's consistent economic growth, seems to have completely disregarded the likely human costs given the obvious "disconnect" between the government and the governed at the grassroots. Hence it was not a vacuous response when a Maoist sympathizer in one of the remote hamlets in Dandakaranya forcefully argued that "even if I have to offer my life to stop the government from taking away our land, I will do it because I must ensure that our children do not have to leave this land . . . [which] is our life."[36] The ruling Congress Party does not seem favorably inclined toward sparing land for emotional reasons; land acquisition (and consequently displacement of the habitat) is necessary to the progress of the grand neoliberal design to exploit the natural resources for sustaining India's economic growth. This was forcefully argued by the Union home minister, P. C. Chidambaram, who stated,

> The debate about mining has gone on for centuries. It is nothing new [though] . . . I am completely convinced that no country can develop unless it uses its natural . . . and human resources. Mineral wealth is wealth that must be harvested and used for people. And why not? Do you want the tribals to remain hunters and gatherers? Are we trying to preserve them in some sort of anthropological museum? Yes, we can allow the minerals to remain in the ground for another 10,000 years, but will that bring development to these people? We can respect the fact that they worship the Niyamgiri hill [in Malkangiri in Orissa], but will that put shoes on their feet or their children in school? Will that solve the fact that they are severely malnutritioned? And have no access to health care?[37]

These are two completely different perspectives: on the one hand, tribals consider land to be absolutely inalienable, presumably because of their long emotional attachment, whereas, for the state, on the other hand, land brings about development in its substantial sense. Nonetheless, what comes out of these counterarguments is the fact that Maoism is not merely a law-and-order problem. It has brought out the malice in India's developmental trajectory, being pursued so religiously under the state-led development program. By challenging the very foundation of a planned economic development, which sought to imitate the 1923 Leninist New Economic Program, Maoism has raised a fundamental question about planning and its reliability for inclusive growth. The founding fathers superimposed a half-baked socio-economic formula for uniform growth through an organically disconnected but ideologically viable Nehruvian socialistic model of economic development.

What is common between the former Naxalite movement that rocked India in the 1960s and its twenty-first-century reincarnation of Maoism is the ideological concern for agrarian issues. In both instances, the Indian state had initially dismissed these organically evolved mass movements as just another short-lived attack on domestic security. The state thought that a strong coercive punitive measure was adequate to quell "the much-hyped but politically vacuous movement" at the grassroots. It is a strange coincidence that the state, having failed to gauge the exact nature of mass discontent, undertook coercive strategies to ruthlessly suppress these ultra-left-wing radical movements. This move, instead of being useful, made the situation far more complicated. As a police officer who was in charge of tackling "the Naxalite menace in West Bengal in the 1960s" frankly admitted,

> We witnessed an equally insensitive and unimaginative politico-administrative system grossly misusing the police, para-military and armed forces; it is unfortunate that the latter ... by making their way through like a mechanized brigade ... [seem to have created] many more terrorists, insurgents and revolutionaries than we started with.[38]

Notwithstanding the adverse consequences of such a mindless coercive strategy to combat a rebellion from within, the government counteroffensive to Maoism appears to have been drawn unfortunately on the same assumption, as it was articulated by the union home minister who strongly argued for "a more coordinated effort by the state police to reassert control over territory or tracts of land where regrettably the civil administration has lost control; and for that purpose," he further added, the government of India "will assist them in whatever manner is possible, particularly by providing forces and sharing intelligence."[39]

So there appears to be a complete unanimity in conceptualizing the left-wing extremism in two different historical contexts in the sense that it was seen initially as a mere security threat that could be effectively tackled punitively. In course of time, it was however realized that the movements that caught the imagination of the marginalized needed to be tackled differently. Again, there was a strange unanimity: given the roots of these anti-state political mobilizations in rural inequality, it was therefore decided officially to address the root cause. In the context of the previous Naxalite movement, the official policy was, as a government document clearly stated, "to tackle the Naxalite problem primarily as a socio-economic problem [though] in actual practice, it has been tackled primarily at the law-and-order level that has clearly backfired [because] . . . if there is no effective governmental intervention on behalf of the rural poor against the rural rich, a further radicalization of the rural poor is inevitable."[40] As is evident, the Naxalite movement was primarily rooted in a socio-economically imbalanced society in which the poor continued to suffer despite India being politically free for more than six decades. The same sentiment reverberated in the 2008 report of the expert group, specially constituted by the Planning Commission to investigate the nature of Maoism and why it spread like wildfire in "seven Indian states where the civil administration is almost paralyzed."[41] While recognizing that Maoism is "a political movement with a strong base among the landless and poor peasantry and Adivasis (tribals)," the expert group, in its report entitled *Development Challenges in Extremist-Affected Areas*, forcefully thus argued:

> Its emergence and growth therefore need to be contextualized in the social conditions and experience of people who form a part of it. The huge gap between state policy and performance is a feature of these conditions. Though its professed long-term ideology is capturing state power by force, in its day-to-day manifestation, it is to be looked upon as basically a fight for social justice, equality, protection, security and development.[42]

The report is revealing: besides locating the source of mass discontent in India's development processes perpetuating brutal exploitation of the marginalized in post-independent India, it is also a sharp comment on the deficit of India's governance as well, which led to "a deep sense of exclusion and alienation"[43] among the majority of the tribal population who remain the main pillar of the Maoist movement. It was also found that governance was almost absent in most of the affected areas, and, where it existed, it acted as a shield for "the landowning dominant castes [that] always manipulated governance to their benefit [disregarding] even genuine socio-economic grievances of those at the periphery."[44] So Maoism is not an instant repercussion but a historical outcome of long-drawn social, economic, and political deprivations of identified sections of society who are constitutionally free but in chains because of the class balance that is always tilted in favor of India's well-off sections. Seeking to unearth the roots of mass discontent despite having had a democratic constitution since India's independence in 1947, the expert group thus very astutely observed,

> The development paradigm pursued since independence has aggravated the prevailing discontent among marginalized sections of society. This is because the development paradigm as conceived by the policy makers has always been imposed on these communities, and therefore it has remained insensitive to their needs and concerns, causing irreparable damage to these sections. The benefits of this paradigm have

been disproportionately cornered by the dominant sections at the expense of the poor, who have borne most of the costs. Development which is insensitive to the needs of these communities has invariably caused displacement and reduced them to a sub-human existence. In the case of tribes in particular it has ended up in destroying their social organization, cultural identity and resource base and generated multiple conflicts, undermining their communal solidarity, which cumulatively makes them increasingly vulnerable to exploitation.[45]

Despite his description of Maoism being "the biggest internal threat to India's security," India's prime minister reiterated the concern of the expert group when he confessed,

There has been a systematic failure in giving the tribals a stake in the modern economic processes that inexorably intrude into their living spaces. The alienation built over decades is now taking a dangerous turn in some parts of our country. The systematic exploitation and social and economic abuse of our tribal communities can no longer be tolerated. But the fact is that no sustained activity is possible under the shadow of the gun. Nor have those who claim to speak for the tribals offered an alternative economic or social path that is viable.[46]

There is therefore no doubt that the Indian tribal population remains historically neglected and thus never became integral to the state-led development paradigm. By providing them an avenue for freedom from an age-old system of exploitation, Maoism is surely a refreshing ideological design of salvation and human dignity for the deprived. Like its former counterpart, the Naxalite movement, which built its social base by clamoring for land reform and land distribution, the Maoists fulfill their ideological mission by supporting tribal movements against "the forcible takeover of their sources of livelihood and common resources."[47] Besides their lives becoming untenable when their lands are taken over for mindless mining of precious mineral resources, the tribals are likely to suffer more because of the environmental hazards that are likely once the excavated minerals are processed mechanically for commercial purposes. It was not surprising when a prominent member of the government admitted that "mining has contributed to [Maoism] in the last [four to five decades] because of multi-level displacement, environment degradation and poor implementation of relief and rehabilitation packages."[48] As a contemporary study confirms, there is no environmentally sustainable way of mining bauxite and processing it into aluminum. It is "a highly toxic process that most Western countries have exported out of their own environment because to produce one ton of aluminum, [one] needs about six tons of bauxite, more than several thousand tons of water and a massive amount of electricity . . . and, for that amount of captive water and electricity, [one] also needs big dams which . . . come with their own cycle of cataclysmic destruction."[49] So, mining is a double-edged sword: it results in an obvious displacement of the tribals from their natural habitat, and it also causes irreparable ecological disequilibrium for a product, namely aluminum, which is largely utilized for producing lethal weapons.[50] Based on their human critique of mindless (and indiscriminate) mining in the Dandakaranya area, Maoists have sought to creatively understand the neoliberal development paradigm, which, given its short-term goal, shall strike at the foundation of sustainable and inclusive development. Conceptually revealing and politically sustainable, the Maoist assessment of the situation may not be conclusive in terms of understanding the reality, but it is certainly an effective analytical tool in searching for an answer to India's skewed development record since independence. In other words, Maoism is not merely a political endeavor seeking to transform the existent class relations through a violent seizure of power, but it is also a serious socio-economic discourse that challenges the conceptual foundation of the prevalent developmental paradigm, which is simply inappropriate in a transitional society like India. In this sense, Maoism is a powerful critique of India's development trajectory and a sharp comment on the zealous acceptance of neoliberal economic plans and programs by the ruling authority at the expense of those who remain integral to India's demography but peripheral otherwise. Maoism is thus "a paradox in a democratic socialist India [that] has created new dynamics (and pockets) of deprivation along with economic growth" in the wake of neoliberal onslaught in the twenty-first century.[51] This has also exposed the bankruptcy of the parliamentary left, which, instead of challenging the deliberate neoliberal design of mass-scale "dispossession in the countryside," seems to have welcomed the "corporate mafia" for rapid industrialization through the forcible acquisition of land for Special Economic Zones.[52] Not only is this illustrative of a complete surrender of the parliamentary left to neoliberalism, it also articulates "a desperate effort on their part to survive even by compromising their ideology so drastically that it is impossible to the tell the difference [between] those championing parliamentary communism and other bourgeois parties any more."[53] Furthermore, it is also alleged that the failure of the left governments in the three states of Kerala, Tripura, and West Bengal to meaningfully implement the centrally funded social welfare schemes[54] speaks of their deviation from even the classical Marxist line of pro-people ideological concern. So, the parliamentary left, despite their communistic ideological clinging, actually fulfills the neoliberal socio-economic goal. They have created a vacuum that Maoism has filled with its brand of emancipatory politics. Maoism is thus both a campaign for agrarian reforms and a powerful challenge to the neoliberal economic agenda of dispossessing the rural masses for either agri-business or for mindless mining for rapid industrialization.

What is most striking about the Maoist articulation of genuine socio-economic grievances of those at the lower rung of rural society is the fact that it also entails a persuasive analysis of their roots in the prevalent class relations. It is articulated differently in different circumstances: in the Hindi-speaking areas of Maoist influence, Maoism is an attack on caste atrocities and class exploitation, while in the forests of Andhra Pradesh, Jharkhand, and Orissa, left-wing extremism seeks "to combine class demands with that of self-dignity and autonomy for the marginalized communities."[55] Given its increasing consolidation among the deprived across different Indian states, Maoism seems to have become an effective ideological means for radical socio-economic changes. Hence, the fight against the Maoist violence cannot be conducted, as the Supreme Court argues, "purely as a mere law-and-order problem confronted by whatever means the State can muster [because the root of] the problem lies deep within the socio-economic policies pursued by the State on a society that was already endemically and horrifically suffering from gross inequalities."[56]

As is evident, tribal India is now a tinder box, created by the crystallization of peculiar socio-economic and political processes resulting in a permanent fissure between the "haves" and "have-nots," even to the extent of harboring the determination to liquidate the former by the latter. The state appears to be inclined to silence the voice of protest through coercion. Instead of making the tribals partners in economic development, the military solution further marginalizes the tribals. It has been emphasized at the highest level of decision-making that strong coercive forces are required to completely decimate the "red menace." The government response has been the formation of the Greyhounds, a specially trained commando wing of the Andhra Pradesh police, notorious for its ruthless killings, mostly in fake encounters, of Maoists and their sympathizers. In Orissa, the government seems to have refined its coercive apparatus by forming the India Reserve battalion and the Orissa State Armed Police battalion to deal exclusively with Naxalite and extremist forces. Furthermore, the police department has also launched a public contact campaign in the district of Rayagada and Malkangiri in Orissa to counter the anti-government propaganda carried out by the Maoists. As a strategy, it was welcome and by the police officers though this has not yet yielded impressive results presumably because of the inability of the state government to equip the police forces adequately to combat the Naxalites, who are both trained and have modern firearms at their disposal, as a police officer admitted on condition of anonymity.[57] What is alarming is also the government outsourcing of the responsibility for maintenance of law and order in the Naxal-affected districts to Salwa Judum, a vigilante army and parallel defense administration. Ironically, by arming the civilians, the state government has created a Frankenstein that is simply not controllable. Gun-toting youth—special police officers, in the Salwa Judum parlance—move freely through the countryside, forcing those without guns to fall in line. The circumstances that have emerged consequently are disastrous, as a commentator argues:

> The machismo of revolution is being answered by the machismo of counter-revolution. Call them Sangham organizer or special police officer, the young men [in the affected districts] have been seduced by their new-found—and essentially unearned—authority.... There is thus a double tragedy at work in tribal India. The first tragedy is that the state has treated its Adivasi citizens with contempt and condescension. The second tragedy is that their presumed protectors, the Naxalites, offer no long-term solution either.[58]

Whatever the nature of the campaign—Salwa Judum or Maoist revolutionary violence—the outcome is disastrous for those surviving in uncertainty. The young tribals, as the Supreme Court of India feels, "have thus literally become cannon fodder in the killing fields of Dantewada and other districts in Chhattisgarh."[59] On the one hand, the Salwa Judum supporters have unleashed a reign of terror, while the Naxalites, on the other, retaliate by killing those allegedly working for the state. Families and villages are divided, with "some living with or in fear of the Maoists, others in fear of or in roadside camps, controlled by Salwa Judum." Tribals continue to be harassed on the one side by the state-sponsored Salwa Judum and on the other by the insurgents. They are thus "sandwiched."[60] An Adivasi from the Bastar district of Chhattisgarh expressed his anguish by saying *"Humme dono taraf se dabav hain, ek taraf Naxalyion doosri taraf Salwa Judum, aur hum beech me pis gaye hain"* [Placed between the Maoists and the vigilantes, we Adivasis are being crushed in the middle].[61] The Maoists seem to be "as little concerned about the lives of the non-combatants as is the state."[62] Indiscriminate violence has thus not only made the conditions of the local people most precarious but has also led situations in which development projects in these areas come to a standstill. The state may not be enthusiastic in undertaking programs for development given the circumstances; Naxalites also oppose various forms of development, which, if implemented, are likely to reduce their importance in the eyes of the local tribals given the obvious benefits of the developmental initiatives at the government behest. For instance, roads, if constructed, will speed up the transfer of police and paramilitary forces for controlling the insurgents, while hospital and school buildings will be used to house police and paramilitary forces. The argument may have viability among the Naxalites though it is hardly meaningful to those reeling under massive poverty. The areas in which Naxalites have gained preeminence are among the poorest in India, and there is no dearth of essential demands for schools, electricity, water, health centers, and so on. However, these issues attract little attention presumably because both the state and the Naxalites are engaged in activities, including violent attacks, to prove their points. In the crossfire of purposes, the obvious victim are the tribals, who remain "deprived" on all counts through no specific fault of their own. They become "targets" either way: targets for the state given their alleged complicity with the Naxalites or targets of the Naxalites for their alleged support to the state. So in the affected areas, it is simply impossible "for an ordinary villager to just stay at home and live an ordinary life" given the atmosphere of distrust gripping "the imagination of both the so-called protectors and predators."[63] Given the complicity of the state with neoliberal forces, it is perfectly understandable why the former indulges in coercion to suppress the Maoist onslaught; it is however most perplexing for the villagers to figure out when the Maoists themselves resort to killings of those considered to be renegades by the Maoist courts, which exhibit bias in favor of one faction or the other. Thus "there have been instances where individuals have misused such power for private gain," and it has also been found that "several unprincipled individuals . . . formed gangs after running away from the party and turned against the party itself."[64] The exclusive focus on "the armed struggle [for] the capture of state power involves intense paranoid secrecy and a normalization of wartime mentality"[65] leading to processes whereby the party ceases to be a vanguard of the people but a mere instrumental design for gratifying partisan goals.[66] While assessing the future of Maoism in India, a former Naxalite activist who gradually withdrew from the mainstream Naxalite movement due to his differences over the politics of annihilation of class enemies, thus confessed that "a politics rooted in violence and fear [seems to have become] prominent in the Maoist zone supporting indiscriminate killing on mere suspicion of being informers [illustrating] how profoundly authoritarian the [Maoist] movement has become under the pressure of its overwhelming militarism," and this remains the root cause, as the argument goes, "for growing alienation of the Maoists from their supporters" in areas that were considered their strongholds in the recent past.[67] The fear syndrome causing visible cracks in the Maoist social base seems to have been perpetuated by the capacity for violence. An ethnographic study confirms that "the fear of being ostracized and also killed"[68] provided an extra edge to the Maoist organization, which draws its strength from the tribal sense of confidence from the notion that "the poorest have somebody to support them against the oppressive and exploitative forces of the state or upper castes and classes."[69]

Two important points come out of the above discussion. First, Maoism is a sharp comment on India's democracy, which is not merely seasonal but remains a constantly creative driving force for the peripherals to articulate their demands for justice, equity, and self-dignity. In this sense, democracy in India seems to have unleashed a unique process of inclusive politics. As Nilekani comments, "The move to bottom–up democracy has brought with a far more topsy-turvy politics than we have been used to." But the clamor has, he further argues, "come with more access than ever before, and carries with it an immense potential for change, new answers and better polity . . . Democracy in India has [thus] shifted from being 'essentially foreign' to being, simply, essential."[70] There are various politico-ideological forces, including Maoism, that are crystallized because of the changing boundary of democracy and democratic politics. This is a very interesting juncture in India's post-colonial history. Second, this point relates to the emerging texture of the Indian state, which is now subject to twin pressures that are contradictory in nature: on the one hand, the forces of globalization that seek to integrate the Indian economy with its global counterpart are, on the other hand, being fiercely resisted by various kinds of both violent and nonviolent movements at the grassroots. In such a paradoxical situation, the state, though "omnipresent," is "feeble"; though "centralized" and "interventionist," it is "powerless."[71] Political institutions are in disarray, and the state is constrained by a legitimacy deficit. This is therefore an era of possibilities to relocate the locus of Indian polity, which is no longer confined to the glittery urban world but has shifted to the periphery where political ideology is being articulated through a process of contestation, accommodation, and negotiation. Democracy not only sustains but also refines this mechanism, which is politically meaningful, ideologically innovative, and emotionally gratifying. This is what explains "the continuing survival in India of democracy, ramshackle and battered but still full of life and resilience."[72] Maoism is one of those offshoots, drawing its sustenance from what is described as the "deepening of democracy," giving voice to the voiceless.

VI

Despite their clear differences over the application of Marxist ideologies, there appears to be unanimity between the parliamentary left and the left-wing extremists in regard to their respective social backgrounds. Born out of the frustration of the educated middle classes with the nationalist leadership before political independence in 1947, the Indian Marxists chose to follow the Marxist revolutionary path of socialist revolution involving the workers and peasants. In the context of a clear ideological shift during the 1920s, they succeeded in instilling a sense of involvement among the deprived sections despite the latter's secluded social background.[73] This does not appear to have changed in the years since: the majority of the leaders espousing the parliamentary left belonged to the educated middle class; unlike in Kerala and Tripura, the left leadership in Bengal continues to be dominated by the bhadralok comprising those with a definite upper-class lineage.[74] For the Naxalites, the legacy of the bhadralok class remained prominent within the rank and file of the movement, and its de facto prominence within the larger social context seems to have crippled this left-wing-extremist onslaught to a significant extent.[75] For the Maoists, this argument appears to hold because the composition of the politburo, the highest decision-making authority, also reveals the hegemonic importance of the relatively socio-economically better-off sections of society;[76] their support base is primarily among the tribals, and yet there is no tribal representation at the top level of decision-making. For encounters with the sources of state repression, the tribals are always placed in the front, but when it comes to the decision-making, they are the last and are hardly consulted even in situations where they are to put their lives at great danger, thus charges a surrendered Maoist leader.[77] This remains a constant source of irritation between the top leadership and the members of the People's Liberation Army who are just "fodders for both the security forces and also the Maoist political bosses."[78] Besides being dominated by non-tribals, the politburo is also charged with regional bias given the fact that the majority of its members hail from Andhra Pradesh. This is a source of bitter intra-organizational conflict. Recently the top leadership came under severe attack from a top Orissa Maoist leader, Sabyasachi Panda, who questioned the adoption of "the path of protracted people's war" since Indian masses were not ready for the revolution. Furthermore, he was not persuaded to accept the strategy of "intensification of war" in one or two Maoist stronghold areas (in Chhattisgarh, West Bengal, Bihar, and Jharkhand) given the military preparedness of the Indian state to crush the mass initiative.[79] By highlighting the composition of the Telegu-dominated politburo, Panda also charged the top leadership with a clear bias against other Maoists from different regions of the country. In his criticism, he heaped serious charges against the party leadership for being heavily tilted in favor of the "Andhra line" and disregarding the voices of non-Andhra Maoists—thereby consolidating harmful tendencies within the party to conceptualize the "future plan of action" in a very restricted manner. This is presumably the case because no other views receive importance given the preponderance of those belonging to Andhra Pradesh. Panda attributed the possible decline of Maoism in areas that were considered strongholds to "mindless violence, dictatorship, financial irregularity, tribal exploitation, sexual harassment, the hegemonic attitude of the Andhra Orissa Border Special Zonal Committee (AOBSZC) and discrimination against minorities."[80] He came out openly against the party bosses. In essence, Panda's diatribe against the leadership indicated that the reunification of Maoist forces, hailed as a milestone for the revolution, did not yield the results that were expected.[81] The difference that began with questioning "regional bias" of the top leadership finally led to a split when Sabyasachi Panda fell out with the CPI (Maoist) and formed a new Maoist outfit, called the Orissa Maovadi Party.[82] Instead of appreciating Panda's critique in the right spirit, the central committee not only dismissed "his rebellion as part of multi-pronged offensive launched by Indian security forces" but also reaffirmed its commitment to the path of the protracted people's war to build the movement to "finally seize political power all over the country by spreading from smaller areas to vaster [sic] areas, isolated areas to all over the country, and by developing from a small force to a mighty force."[83] Whether the split was due to ideological differences or personality clashes is difficult to say. What it showed however was the failure of the ultra leftists to evolve as a homogeneous unit with a common strategy or to fulfill a common ideological mission. Panda's critique of the protracted people's war "exposed the chinks in the movement's ideological armour."[84] His arguments and the rebuttal of the central leadership also confirmed that, given the well-entrenched societal pluralism and contextual variations in India, the same strategy for political mobilization may not always work. This is a real challenge to the Maoists if they would like to emerge as a vanguard of the people in the Leninist sense of the term.

Unlike the parliamentary left, which generally welcomed women (those of more or less identical social background) even in the highest decision-making body, like the politburo, the Maoist movement suffers on another count: while it aims to be transformative, it has not always been able to ensure equality in all respects to its "weaker" constituents: Dalits and women. It is more or less a well-established fact that Dalits, despite their critical role, are not adequately represented in the upper echelons of the Maoist organization. It has also been observed that those who get killed during conflict are mostly Dalits or persons belonging to the lower strata simply because they are the ones who are pushed into encounters, leaving behind the upper-caste Maoists. A similar criticism has been made regarding the position of women within the movement. Women who are a "strange mix of girly behaviour and warrior grit"[85] are not discriminated against and they are as welcome in *dalams*, the action squad, as their male counterparts. Nonetheless, like the Dalits, they are hardly well-represented in the leadership. The reason is located in the hegemonic influence of "patriarchy which permeates the functioning and ethos of the movement." The violent nature of the movement has, as has been further pointed out, "contributed to this, since patriarchy and violence have much in common and tend to reinforce each other."[86] Interestingly, one notices a pattern in this regard if one follows the trajectory of the Naxalite movement since it was conceptualized in the late 1960s. The role of women as fellow revolutionaries in the ultra-left-wing movement in the past was structured around patriarchy. A women participant in the Naxalbari movement in its earlier manifestation thus reminisced, "Never in the party has a woman received the same status and respect as a man, and women were never welcome in the highest levels of decision making. If women had an equal say in the decision making," she further exhorted, "perhaps the history of the Naxalbari movement would have been written differently then."[87] Ironically, there exists an eerie silence in the Maoist documents about the presence of the women activists despite their organic connection with the revolutionary activities at the grassroots. This failure to acknowledge the integral role of "the women comrades," argues an analyst, "carries an interconnected double meaning—it did not only erase from the official documents the physical presence of women in organizing and leading the movement, but equally important, it obfuscated the ideological possibility of redefining women's role and status in the larger social context."[88]

On the basis of the reminiscences of the surrendered women, it can fairly be argued that not only are the tribal women associated with Maoism being raped regularly by the security personnel, they are also subject to "sexual harassment by their male colleagues."[89] This was not an exception. Patriarchy seemed to have governed the Naxalite organization. Women activists do not appear to have been trusted in encounters with the security forces for reasons connected with a bias against their physical capability. Reflecting gender bias with devastating accuracy, a former Naxalite, Krishna Bandopadhyay, said,

> We, the women activists, underwent a nursing training in Medical College in Calcutta. Now, I wonder—the principal idea behind this training was that our male comrades will get wounded and we, the women, will nurse them back to battle condition! These ideas were harboured by the most progressive political party! . . . I was extremely bitter with this attitude of the party—was it any different from my parental aunt? And if there is no difference then why be there at all?[90]

In the southern Indian province of Kerala, a women cadre, Ajitha, also experienced gender bias when she, inspired by left-wing extremism, joined the Naxalbari movement. Although she was equally adept at handling firearms as her male colleagues, the leadership did not have as much confidence in her ability as in the male members. Reminiscing, she thus lamented,

Even while in the movement, I used to get upset by the denial of opportunities on the basis of gender. There were occasions when the attitude towards women in the revolutionary movement was condemnable. At one level the "men-comrades" had a protective attitude towards "women comrades" and at another level instead of being regarded as comrades, women were never involved in the decision making process and were looked at as sex objects.[91]

This was a perennial problem, confronted by the women revolutionaries whether in West Bengal, Kerala, or elsewhere. The gender bias is a "perpetuation of benevolent patriarchy in the sense that women are considered to be mute followers of male revolutionaries."[92] Reflective of a well-entrenched male bias, the attitude of the "men-comrades" toward their women counterparts was neither meaningfully challenged nor made subject to scrutiny even in the party congresses, presumably because of the male bias against "women's own version of the movement as well as discounting significant source of history"[93] that highlighted their creative intervention in left-wing extremism. In this sense, the Naxalites, despite their venom against feudalism, did not seem to have effectively challenged the deeply ingrained social values that they internalized, presumably because of their upbringing in a gender-biased social milieu. Reflective of the widely prevalent patriarchal sexual bias, the left-wing extremist response to sexual offenses against women is "neither straightforward nor consistent [but] is articulated within the discursive field of gender and class relations [where] some forms of sexual violence" seem inevitable.[94] Identifying clearly the gendered links between different forms of violence in the context of a radical movement articulating transformative politics, these women's narratives present "a structure of self-vulnerability and betrayal that was revealed by everyday life of the movement,"[95] demonstrating that the left-wing extremists, despite having imbibed the libertarian Maoist spirit, were not free from a patriarchal bias of gender discrimination. Although this history is being unearthed, it is illustrative of entrenched patriarchal forces even within the radical politics of the left. Besides portraying women participants in left-wing extremism as victims, the conventional studies are almost silent on gender bias, exposing a serious gap in our understanding of these radical anti-state counteroffensives, which are usually hailed as inclusive political movements. Instead of conceptualizing the role of women in binary opposites (either as victims or as agents), the available feminist accounts and their interpretations point toward the failure of the Maoists to address the gender issue in a creative manner. This has resulted in a conventional "bourgeois" approach.

VII

Indian communism is undoubtedly a creative experiment. Despite its "global" decline, the Marxist ideology continues to evoke support at the grassroots in both urban and rural areas. Organizationally strong and ideologically meaningful, communism—both the parliamentary and extra-parliamentary varieties—appears to have evolved an alternative model for political mobilization in democratic-socialist India. What is most unique in India's political trajectory is the rise and consolidation of the two clearly contradictory forms of communism along with other liberal democratic political forces. Given their diverse roots, it is difficult to develop a uniform conceptual framework to explain the phenomenon persuasively. The parliamentary left has developed organic roots in the three Indian states of Kerala, West Bengal, and Tripura, while the Maoist variety has been articulated in the large tracts of central India, which are inhabited primarily by the tribals. There are contextual reasons for this: in light of Congress malgovernance, the left parties seemed a panacea, given their commitment to honest and transparent governance; they played an unquestionably effective role in terms of organizing and leading militant mass struggles involving the industrial workers and peasantry, which contributed to the adoption of various ameliorative legislative steps for reforms in independent India. By bringing about radical policies that uphold the rights of the workers and the underprivileged agrarian masses, the parliamentary left showed beyond doubt that social democracy could be an effective means for significant socio-economic changes without indulging in violent overthrow of the state power. The mainstream left has also effected noticeable changes in rural governance by meaningfully articulating "the devolution of power at the local level through institutions of local governance such as panchayats in rural areas"[96] in the left-ruled states of West Bengal and Kerala and Tripura. A Gandhian prescription to the core, the idea of panchayati raj governance did not ever receive enthusiastic support from political parties other than the parliamentary left. It is also claimed that without the support of the elected panchayats in rural West Bengal and Kerala, "several provisions of the land reform laws could not have been implemented at the ground level."[97] Not only did these institutions act as the eyes and ears of the government at the grassroots, they, by engaging the local stakeholders in the policies for development and welfare, became the de facto center of decision-making in villages. Unlike the Kerala experiment of parliamentary communism that held state power intermittently, the Left Front stayed in power in West Bengal for more than three decades. It experienced decline in 2011 with its ignominious electoral defeat. After enjoying victory in successive assembly elections, the constituents of the Front, particularly its leading partner, CPI (M), became victims of their own arrogance. As a result, in West Bengal, in particular, the institutions that catapulted the masses to the center stage of governance through, for instance, panchayats, "eventually degenerated into instruments of party control over the affairs of the village, with the nexus between the party, local administration and the police establishing complete hegemony,"[98] leading to the creation of the overwhelming importance of a "party-society"[99] that always acted in a crude Stalinistic way to suppress the dissenting voices. After decades of "demonizing capitalism and capitalists,"[100] the Left Front that fought for *Operation Barga* in the 1970s provided land for rapid industrialization at the behest of private corporate houses. As is shown in chapter 4, through an abject surrender to an anti-people neoliberal economic design, not only has the parliamentary left in West Bengal failed to creatively combat the neoliberal onslaught, but it has also confirmed the obvious ideological limitations of social democracy, favoring the inherent capitalistic tendency of accumulation by dispossession.

Unlike the parliamentary left that is confined to a southern state of Kerala, an eastern state of West Bengal, and a northeastern state of Tripura, the Maoists have a larger support base in the red corridor of parts of Maharashtra and the entire tribal belt of Chhattisgarh, Andhra Pradesh, Orissa, Bihar, Jharkhand, and West Bengal. What catapulted the Maoists to the center stage of ultra-left-wing extremism was their success in giving the desperately poor tribal people a dream for a better life, free from hunger and indignity. Left-wing extremism is thus unlikely "to disappear because the root causes that feed it are unlikely to disappear for the next few decades."[101] There is no doubt that the journey of these hapless people back to "a semblance of human dignity is due in large part to the Maoist cadre who have lived, worked and fought by their side for decades."[102] Their continued association with the tribals in forests also supports the charge that "the Maoist party's militarized politics makes it almost impossible for it to function in places where there is no forest cover."[103] Nonetheless, unlike the previous Naxalite uprising, which was primarily an elite-driven, top-down ideological onslaught that mobilized the urban middle class and upheld the policy of individual annihilation of class enemies, the Maoist movement is more rural than urban and has a more substantial geographical spread over India's tribal heartland largely because of its success in linking endemic poverty of the rural masses with the failure of the state to provide even the basic necessities for human existence.[104] This appears to be a historical lacuna of the system[105] that hardly allows space for change; as a result, the fate of those at the lower rung seems to have been permanently sealed. Ethnographic studies[106] confirm the general argument attributing the increasing Maoist popularity among the poor, landless peasants, and Adivasis to their hapless existence, which they have accepted as "fated." On the basis of his field study, an analyst thus comments that by developing an emotional bond with the exploited, the Maoists not only become part of their daily struggle but also instilled in them an indomitable spirit to fight for their rights as citizens of the country. Maoists thus no longer remain "outsiders," because "the cadres used to sleep and eat in the mud houses of the villagers . . . and always fought for the issues [of] land and wages, as well as against social abuses, exploitation and sexual abuse of women."[107] The situation became far more complicated with the onset of neoliberal economic reforms. Maoism thus represents an effective ideological design "to keep the state away partly because [the local tribals] have experienced it as exploitative and oppressive, and partly because of the activities of the rural elite moving up in the class hierarchy [seeking] to colonize the [local] resources in connivance with the outsiders."[108] It is true that, like their parliamentary counterpart, the Maoists have so far not succeeded in providing a persuasive critique against the neoliberal offensive, except in mobilizing the dispossessed masses against the state-sponsored diktat supporting private investment for quick economic growth. A first-hand account reveals that, despite being vehemently opposed to "the onslaught of corporate mining, the Maoist policy (and practice) on mining remains pretty wooly," and there is also a persistent view that the Maoists are not averse to allowing mining and mining-related infrastructure projects to go ahead "as long as they are given protection money."[109] Nonetheless, given the immediate loss due to "forcible" land acquisition, the opposition to the mining acts as a "catalyst" in the context of well-entrenched mass socio-economic grievances. Here is an important clue as to why Maoism is a more attractive ideological input than its parliamentary counterpart.

Postscript

HELD IN 2014, the sixteenth parliamentary poll in India is a watershed in the country's recent political history for at least three significant reasons. First, breaking the trend of the last few decades in which no party was able to muster a majority in parliament, the Bharatiya Janata Party (BJP), with 282 of a total of 543 seats in the lower house, will no longer be dependent on the whims of its partners for survival. With the BJP winning a majority on its own, a remarkable shift is visible in the texture of India's parliamentary politics. The wave for the star campaigner, the former chief minister of Gujarat, Narendra Modi, which has caught the imagination of the large section of the voters, has given the BJP-led National Democratic Alliance (NDA) an unprecedented victory with 328 seats in the Lok Sabha. Not only has the principal partner of the NDA, the BJP, increased its tally in the sixteenth Lok Sabha poll, it has also significantly enhanced its vote share from the 2009 parliamentary poll. Second, voter turnout was unprecedented: in comparison with an all-time record 64 percent turnout in the 1984 election, which took place in the aftermath of the assassination of Indira Gandhi, the 2014 election witnessed an increase of more than 2 percent in the total number of voters who exercised their franchise. This is indicative of voters' confidence in democracy as a powerful mechanism for change even in adverse political circumstances. The BJP's landslide victory was also illustrative of a mass desire for effective governance in the light of the failure of the former Congress-led coalition government to meaningfully address the policy paralysis and a series of financial scandals that not only exposed its weaknesses against vested interests but also gave credibility to the allegation of the government complicity with those involved in corruption. Finally, the 2014 national poll stands out because the parliamentary left registered an ignominious defeat even in both West Bengal and Kerala, which were the left citadels in the recent past. The defeat of the left is attributed to the disenchantment of local voters with the left in these two Indian provinces where the parliamentary communists ruled for an extended period of time. In West Bengal, the left seems to have become irrelevant as it succeeded in winning only two of a total of forty-two Lok Sabha seats in comparison with its tally of sixteen seats in the last Lok Sabha; by winning eight of a total of twenty seats in Kerala, the parliamentary left has not only enhanced its share of the Lok Sabha seats from four in 2009, but it also sustained its vote share in midst of a national wave for the BJP.

As is evident, except in Tripura where the parliamentary left retained their earlier tally of two Lok Sabha seats, their counterparts in West Bengal and Kerala have failed to sustain their base. This is not a temporary setback because what was visible in the 2014 Lok Sabha poll seemed to have begun earlier: the decline was manifested in the 2009 Lok Sabha poll and 2011 state assembly election in West Bengal and in the 2009 Lok Sabha poll and 2013 state assembly election in Kerala. The left, which was considered invincible in the past due to the backing of a cadre-based organization, collapsed like a house of cards as soon as organized opposition emerged in these constituent states of India. It was possible for the parliamentary communists in Tripura, who unlike their counterparts elsewhere suffered less from internecine factional feuds, to maintain their hegemony over other contenders in the 2014 national poll largely because of a leadership that is organically linked with the grassroots despite being in power for more than a decade.

Like their parliamentary counterparts, the left-wing extremists seem to have lost their grip over the people in those areas that were, thus far, considered to be their strongholds. Despite their call for a boycott of the parliamentary poll in Chhattisgarh, Maharashtra, and Jharkhand, voters zealously participated in the poll, as evidence shows. The reports from Bastar (in Chhattisgarh), Gadchiroli (in Maharashtra), Palamu (in Jharkhand), and Malkangiri (in Orissa) confirm that the boycott call did not appear to have deterred the voters from exercising their democratic rights: in some villages, the voter turnout was as high as 60 percent. This also shows that India's democracy, despite being criticized as mere window dressing in the hierarchical social context, is definitely an empowering instrument for the masses, notwithstanding being frustrated with the prevalent socio-economic and political circumstances.

II

The rise of the right-wing BJP is proportionally linked with the decline of the left in India's parliamentary history. As is shown below in the table, the electoral defeat encountered by the parliamentary communists in 2014 was unprecedented.

The writing on the wall is very clear: the decline of the left that had begun in 2009 Lok Sabha poll is confirmed. In Kerala, the Community Party of India (Marxist; CPI [M]) of the Left Democratic Front won in five constituencies with only 21.6 percent of

Performance of the Parliamentary Left since 1971

Year	Number of Lok Sabha Seats, Won by the Parliamentary Left	Distribution of Seats in Provinces
1971	25	West Bengal: 20 Kerala: 2 Tripura: 2 Andhra Pradesh: 1
1977	22	West Bengal: 17 Maharashtra: 3 Orissa: 1 Punjab: 1
1980	37	West Bengal: 28 Kerala: 7 Tripura: 2
1984	22	West Bengal: 18 Tripura: 2 Andhra Pradesh: 1 Kerala: 1
1989	33	West Bengal: 27 Kerala: 2 Bihar: 1 Orissa: 1 Rajasthan: 1 Uttar Pradesh: 1
1991	35	West Bengal: 27 Kerala: 4 Assam: 1 Bihar: 1 Maharashtra: 1 Orissa: 1
1996	32	West Bengal: 23 Kerala: 5 Tripura: 2 Assam: 1 Andhra Pradesh: 1
1999	33	West Bengal: 21 Kerala: 8 Tripura: 2 Bihar: 1 Tamil Nadu: 1

Year	Number of Lok Sabha Seats, Won by the Parliamentary Left	Distribution of Seats in Provinces
2004	43	West Bengal: 26 Kerala: 12 Tripura: 2 Tamil Nadu: 2 Andhra Pradesh: 1
2009	16	West Bengal: 9 Kerala: 4 Tripura: 2 Tamil Nadu: 1
2014	09	Kerala: 5 West Bengal: 2 Tripura: 2

Source: The Hindu, 17 May 2014.

total votes; despite having 22.3 percent of total votes, CPI (M) in West Bengal registered victory only in two constituencies. One of the factors for this debacle is certainly the shifting of the minority, especially the Muslim votes. Modi's anti-Muslim rhetoric pushed the minorities, especially the Muslims, to the Congress-led United Democratic Front in Kerala while his virulent campaign against the Muslim infiltrators from Bangladesh in West Bengal drew them to the All India Trinamool Congress. This is a significant change in the perception of the minorities who always considered the left to be their natural savior in their day-to-day struggle for survival.

So, the parliamentary left has become rendered virtually irrelevant in the election to the sixteenth Lok Sabha, winning only nine seats in comparison with its tally of twenty-four in the last Lok Sabha. The total vote share of the constituents of the parliamentary left—CPI (M), Communist Party of India, Revolutionary Party of India, Forward Bloc—was drastically reduced from 7 percent in the 2009 parliamentary poll to a mere 4.5 percent in the 2014 election. The leading partner of the left, CPI (M), suffered most: its national vote share declined from 5.3 percent in 2009 to 3.2 percent in the 2014 poll.[1] The immediate outcome of the poor showing of the left results in CPI (M) losing its status as a national party, which left only the Congress and ruling BJP as national parties.[2]

The left stands decimated, and CPI (M), its main public face, recorded its worst electoral performance since its formation in 1964. In West Bengal, the state that it ruled for more than three decades, it failed to increase its tally beyond two seats—the same number of seats that its counterpart in Tripura won. The gradual decline of the parliamentary left, as it had happened elsewhere in the globe, confirms that "the spectre of its political irrelevance is staring at in India as well."[3] The poor result is the outcome of a combination of factors, including the failure of the leadership to address the genuine socio-economic grievances of the people at the grassroots; there are indications that its so-called committed cadres have not only been disenchanted with the leadership, but they are also reported to have worked for the All India Trinamool Congress candidates, exposing perhaps the failure of the party leadership to build a solid cadre-driven organization in the state. The left is thus not only faced with an existential crisis but is pitted against a new political rival in the state, namely the BJP, which has the potential to occupy the main opposition space because, as against the CPI (M)'s vote share of 22.3 percent, the BJP has 17 percent of the total popular votes. The scene in Kerala is not very different: like its Bengal counterpart, it is worse-hit by the indifference of the cadres who do not seem to be as enthusiastic as in the past. The impact was visible: despite having won five Lok Sabha seats, the 2014 national poll is also a break with the past because the well-established political trend of alternating between the CPI (M)-led Left Democratic Front and the Congress-centric United Democratic Front was broken this time. The Congress-led front walked away with the lion's share of seats, which is explained by reference to "the minority consolidation in favour of the Congress in the face of the Modi factor."[4] In view of the open and tacit internecine factional feuds among the leaders in Kerala and West Bengal, the party failed to address the rising resentments among the workers. Due to the constant tussle between the two top leaders of CPI (M), Pinarayi Vijayan and V. S. Achuthanandan, in Kerala, the organization could never mount a strong showing against the opposition. Similarly, the continuity of the Stalinistic leadership cost the party heavily in West Bengal. The leadership is "captured by a Kolkata-centric clique," which is incapable of understanding "the pulse of the people at the grassroots."[5] Thus, the rivalry at the top and the disconnect between the cadres and the central leadership was responsible for the declining importance of the parliamentary left in those states of India, which were the left bastion not so long ago.

III

The poor performance of the parliamentary left is, as mentioned above, illustrative of the gradual weakening of the organization that has consistently backed the left cause. The 2014 poll outcome also confirms that the left leadership did not seem to bother to address these weaknesses seriously even in the aftermath of the 2009 Lok Sabha poll when the left was trounced as well. Whether the 2014 poll debacle will wake them up cannot be answered now. It is clear however that the Indian voters cannot be taken for a ride, and it has again been established beyond doubt that mere ideological inclination of the voters will not always get translated into votes unless there is organizational back-up.

The parliamentary left seems to have lost its momentum. One of the major factors is certainly the appreciation of the Stalinistic version of Marxism even in the light of unforeseeable socio-economic changes in the domestic and global context. In view of the democratic upsurges across classes, it is now inconceivable that the iron-fist rule that Napoleon exerted in George Orwell's *Animal Farm* shall no longer be effective. The former supporters not only got frustrated with the indifferent leadership but were also terribly annoyed with "the strong-arm tactic of the left,"[6] which was indiscriminately utilized to quell the opposition voices within the party. The left leadership seems to have failed to read the writing on the wall in a correct perspective out of its arrogance or perhaps ignorance, which was visible in its failure to sustain its support base even in areas that were historically their strongholds. So, the parliamentary left is the victim of the highhandedness of the leadership that hardly endeavored to undertake any exercise beyond what was considered appropriate in the conventional understanding of Marxism. Locked into the textbook understanding of Marxism, the present leaders belong "to the genre of the past [and are] unable to understand the new language of politics and justice."[7] This is a serious symptom that needs to be addressed conclusively to stop the avalanche before it ruins the fulcrum of the parliamentary left in India.

The near decimation of the parliamentary left also shows how mature the Indian voters are: not only have they exercised their franchise judiciously for a conclusive verdict, but they have also endorsed their complete faith in democracy, which is not merely a structure of governance but also a mechanism of change. Even the left-wing extremists seem to have recognized the importance of participation in democratic elections. As reports from the Maoism-affected districts in Maharashtra, Chhattisgarh, and Andhra Pradesh show, the Maoists are reported to have asked the villagers not to support any candidate by pressing the none of the above (NOTA) button in the electronic voting machine. Given the wide use of NOTA in these districts, there are reasons to believe that the Maoists might have prompted the voters to go for this option. As per the figures given by the Election Commission of India, 24,488 voters exercised NOTA in Gadchiroli, the highest figure among forty-eight Lok Sabha constituencies in Maharashtra; Bastar in Chhattisgarh saw NOTA being used by 38,772 voters. In the Adilabad district of Andhra Pradesh, the number stood at 17,084. In proportional terms, the number of NOTA votes may not be very significant, but given the fact that the large chunk of NOTA data comes from those polling booths in those villages that belong to the so-called liberated Maoist zones where the Indian State is clearly peripheral, this is illustrative of an endeavor at utilizing conventional democratic means to articulate a voice. For the villagers, the NOTA is an empowering device to register their protests against those candidates "who had not done justice to them or even visited their hamlets ever."[8] It is true that the number of NOTA votes had hardly had any impact on the outcome of the poll in the first-past-the-post system of polling; nonetheless, it was indicative of a voice of frustration that was expressed through a well-established mechanism of liberal democracy that the Maoists loathe and are determined to destroy.

The nine-phase 2014 parliamentary poll—from 7 April to 12 May—was the second longest in India's democratic history after the 1951–1952 first Lok Sabha poll that continued for five months. This was an extraordinary election otherwise. With a vote share of 31 percent—or nearly every third vote cast in the country, the BJP obtained an absolute majority by winning 282 of 543 seats in the lower house of Indian parliament. The Congress share dwindled from 24 percent in 2009 to 19.3 percent in the 2014 Lok Sabha poll. Except for the right-wing BJP, none of the contending parties succeeded in retaining its earlier tally. The parliamentary left faced perhaps the most ignominious defeat ever in its journey as an alternative ideological discourse in democratic India. Despite not being participants in the democratic elections, the left-wing extremists were reported to have explored NOTA as an effective means to ventilate their grievances. This perhaps shows their willingness to engage with the Indian state that has opened a small window for further dialogues.

Examples can be multiplied to substantiate the point that, for the Indian voters, democratic election is a powerful mechanism to articulate their voice that the contenders for political power can afford to ignore only at their peril. The 2014 poll outcome has unambiguously established the point. Empowered by the constitutional guarantee to the citizens, the Indian voters chose the candidates in accordance with their priorities that cannot be so easily ignored. Challenging the conventional wisdom on democracy, as articulated by S. M. Lipset in his *Political Man: The Social Bases of Politics* or J. S. Mill in his *Considerations on Representative Government*, the Indian voters have proved beyond doubt that neither Lipset's notion of a nation's financial health[9] nor Mill's concern for social homogeneity[10] is enough to consolidate democracy. So, in the ultimate analysis, the 2014 poll may have sealed the fate of some of the contending parties, including the parliamentary left; nonetheless, it has confirmed once again that democracy in India is organic in character and spirit, and, in that sense, the 2014 epoch-making election celebrated Indian democracy in no uncertain terms.

PARTY CONSTITUTION OF THE COMMUNIST PARTY OF INDIA (MAOIST)[1]

The Joint CC meeting deeply studied these five draft documents, freely exchanged the rich experiences acquired through the revolutionary practice during the past three decades and more, and arrived at a common understanding on several vexed questions confronting the Indian revolution in the backdrop of the international developments.

The present document—**Party Constitution**—is the synthesis of all the positive points in the documents of the two erstwhile parties, as well as their experiences in the course of waging the people's war, fighting against revisionism and right and left opportunist trends in the Indian and international communist movement, and building a stable and consistent revolutionary movement in various parts of our country.

We are placing the present document before the entire rank and file of our new Unified Party for immediate guidance and implementation. At the same time, it should be borne in mind that this is a draft for the forthcoming Congress of the Unified Party. Hence, it has to be enriched further by the participation of all the Party members and suggesting amendments where necessary. Thus it should become an effective weapon in the hands of the Party for solving the fundamental problems of the Indian revolution and to advance it toward victory.

The Communist Party of India (Maoist)

21 September 2009

CHAPTER I: GENERAL PROGRAM

The Communist Party of India (Maoist) is the consolidated political vanguard of the Indian proletariat. Marxism–Leninism–Maoism is the ideological basis guiding its thinking in all the spheres of its activities. Immediate aim or program of the Communist Party is to carry on and complete the new democratic revolution in India as a part of the world proletarian revolution by overthrowing the semi-colonial, semi-feudal system under neo-colonial form of indirect rule, exploitation and control and the three targets of our revolution—imperialism, feudalism and comprador big bourgeoisie. The ultimate aim or maximum program of the party is the establishment of communist society. This New Democratic Revolution [NDR] will be carried out and completed through armed agrarian revolutionary war, i.e., the Protracted People's War with area wise seizure of power remaining as its central task. Encircling the cities from the countryside and thereby finally capturing them will carry out the Protracted People's War. Hence the countryside as well as the Protracted People's War will remain as the center of gravity of the party's work from the very beginning. During the whole process of this revolution the party, army and the united front will play the role of three magic weapons. In their interrelationship the party will play the primary role, whereas the army and the united front will be two important weapons in the hands of the party. Because the armed struggle will remain the highest and main form of struggle and army as the highest form of organization of this revolution, hence armed struggle will play a decisive role. Whereas the united front will be built in the course of advancing armed struggle and for armed struggle. Mass organizations and mass struggles are necessary and indispensable but their purpose is to serve the war. The immediate and most urgent task of the party is to establish full-fledged people's liberation army (PLA) and base areas by developing and transforming the guerrilla zones and guerrilla bases. Just after completing the NDR the party will advance toward establishing socialism without any delay or interception. Because the NDR will already lay the basis for socialism and hence there will be no pause. Thereafter, the party will continue to advance toward realizing communism by continuing the revolution under the dictatorship of the proletariat.

Socialist society covers a considerable long historical period. Throughout this historical period, there will be classes, class contradictions and class struggle. The struggle between socialist road and capitalist road will also continue to exist. Only depending on and carrying forward the theory of continuing the revolution under the dictatorship of the proletariat can correctly resolve all these contradictions. In this context the GPCR (Great Proletarian Cultural Revolution) initiated and led by Mao Tse-tung was a great political revolution carried out under the conditions of socialism by the proletariat against the bourgeoisie and all other exploiting classes to consolidate the dictatorship of the proletariat and there by fighting against the danger of capitalist restoration. Party will also continue to hold high the proletarian internationalism and will continue to firmly contribute more forcefully in uniting the genuine M-L-M forces at the international level. While uniting the M-L-M forces, it will also establish unity with oppressed people and nations of the whole world and continue its fight together with them in advancing toward completing the world proletarian revolution against imperialism and all reaction, thereby paving the way toward realizing communism on a world scale.

During the whole course the comrades throughout the party must cherish the revolutionary spirit of daring to go against the tide, must adhere to the principles of practicing Marxism and not revisionism, working for unity and not for splits, and being open and aboveboard and not engaging in intrigue and conspiracy, must be good at correctly distinguishing contradictions among the people from those between ourselves and the enemy and thereby correctly handling those, fighting left and right opportunism and nonproletariat trend must develop the style of integrating theory with practice, maintaining close ties with the masses and practicing criticism and self-criticism.

The future is certainly bright, though the road is tortuous. All the members of our party will wholeheartedly dedicate their lives in the lofty struggle for communism on a world scale must be resolute, fear no sacrifice and surmount every difficulty to win victory!

CHAPTER 2: THE PARTY, FLAGS, AND OBJECTIVES

Article 1: Name of the Party: The Communist Party of India (Maoist)

Article 2: Flag: Party Flag is red in color with hammer and sickle printed in the middle in white color. The hammer of the sickle will remain toward the side of the pole. The ratio of length and breadth of the flag is 3:2.

Article 3:

(a) The Communist Party of India (Maoist) is the consolidated vanguard of the Indian proletariat. It takes Marxism–Leninism–Maoism as its guiding ideology.

(b) The party will remain underground throughout the period of New Democratic Revolution.

Article 4: Aims and Objectives: The immediate aim of the party is to accomplish the New Democratic Revolution in India by overthrowing imperialism, feudalism and comprador bureaucratic capitalism only through the Protracted People's War and establishes the people's democratic dictatorship under the leadership of the proletariat. It will further fight for the establishment of socialism. The ultimate aim of the party is to bring about communism by continuing the revolution under the leadership of the proletariat and thus abolishing the system of exploitation of man by man from the face of earth.

The Communist Party of India (Maoist) dedicates itself at the service of the people and revolution, cherishes high affection and respect for the people, relies upon the people and will sincere in learning from them. The party stands vigilant against all reactionary conspiracies and revisionist maneuvers.

Article 5: The party will continue to hold high the banner of proletarian internationalism and will put its due share in achieving the unity of the Marxist–Leninist–Maoist forces at international level.

CHAPTER 3: MEMBERSHIP

Article 6: Any resident of India, who has reached the age of 16 years, who belongs to worker, peasant, toiling classes.

Article 7: Generally party members are admitted as individuals, through a primary party unit. Every applicant for membership must be recommended by two party members; they must have thorough knowledge about him/her and provide that necessary information to the party. And the applicant for party membership should submit an application.

Article 8: Concerned primary unit will investigate the applicant and it will be done secretly within party as well as among masses. Essentially the application must be recommended by concerned party cell/unit and finally by the next higher party committee. The applicant will then be admitted into the party as a candidate member. After candidate membership is given, he/she should be observed for a minimum period of six months for applicants from working class, landless-poor peasants and agricultural laborers; one year for middle peasants, petty bourgeoisie and urban middle class; and two years for those coming from other classes and other parties. From AC [Area Committee] to all other higher party committees will also have the right to give new membership, while following the same methods.

Article 9: Generally party members will be admitted from activist groups organized for party activity working under the guidance of party unit. They must be involved in party activities as decided by the concerned party unit at least for six months before admitting them as candidate member.

Article 10: By the end of the candidature period, the concerned party unit after reviewing can give full membership or his/her candidature can be extended for another six months, by explaining the reasons. This decision should be reported to the next higher committee. Higher committees may change or modify the decision taken by the lower committee. Zonal/Dist. Committee must approve the new membership. SAC/State Committee will finally approve.

Article 11: An Indian residing in a foreign country that has all the necessary qualifications for party membership may be given membership; a foreigner residing in India permanently can also be given membership.

If a member of other Marxist–Leninist groups wants to join our party, he/she may be admitted with the approval of the next higher committee. If his/her status is that of primary member in the original party, he/she shall be admitted as full-fledged member with the approval of the district/sub-zonal committee. If he/she is an AC member in the original party, he/she shall be admitted with the approval of the state/regional committee. If he/she was of the rank of district or regional level in the original party, he/she shall be admitted by the central committee.

If an ordinary member of a bourgeois or revisionist party wants to leave that party and join our party, his/her application shall be recommended by two party members, one of them a being a party member at least for two years. His/her candidate membership shall have to be accepted by the next higher committee. Similarly, if a member of a bourgeois or revisionist party bearing area level or above responsibilities wants to join our party, his/her application shall have to be recommended by two party members one of them being party member at least for five years. His/her membership shall have to be accepted by the state committee or by the central committees.

Article 12: Membership fees are Rs.10 per annum. Concerned unit after assessing the economic situation of the party member will fix monthly party levy.

Article 13: Proven renegades, enemy agents, careerists, individuals of bad character, degenerates and such alien class-elements will not be admitted into the party.

Article 14: No one from exploiting classes will be admitted into the party unless he/she hands over his property to the party and should deeply integrate with the masses.

CHAPTER 4: RIGHTS AND DUTIES OF PARTY MEMBERS
The Duties of the Party Members

Article 15: He/she shall study and apply Marxism–Leninism–Maoism lively. In the concrete condition of India, he/she must be creative, firm and capable in practice. He/she should try to develop his/her consciousness from the reach experiences of party's ideological, political and organizational line as well as style and method of work.

Article 16: He/she shall defend ideological and political basis of the party and shall consistently wage ideological and political struggle against various types of nonproletarian trends, revisionist policies, trends and style of work; "left" and right opportunism, economism, parliamentarianism, legalism, reformism, liberalism, sectarianism, empiricism, subjectivism, dogmatism and anarchist concepts and trends.

Article 17: He/she must study party organs, documents and magazines regularly and must take initiative in popularizing party's literature and collecting party fund.

Article 18: Party members must take part actively and regularly in the day-to-day work of those party units and organizations to which they are attached. They must follow party line, program, policies, principles, directives and decisions.

Article 19: Every member must be ready to participate and play a vanguard role in class struggle in the form of armed agrarian revolutionary war, i.e., Protracted People's War and other forms of revolutionary mass struggles. They must be prepared to take part in war and give leadership in Protracted People's War for seizure of political power.

Article 20: He/she must subordinate his/her personal interests to the interests of the party and the people. Party members must fight for the interests of the great masses of the people, must integrate with broad masses, learn from them, rely upon them and strengthen the party relations with the broad masses. He/she must be true servant of the people, sacrifice everything for them and must go to the people for taking the solution of their problems, i.e., keep to the principle of "from the masses to the masses." He/she must be concerned about the problems of the people, try for their solutions, intimate all those things to the party in time and explain the party line and policies to them.

Article 21: He/she should relentlessly fight with a proletarian class outlook against discrimination based on gender, caste, nationality, religion, region and tribe, and ruling class policies of divide and rule.

Article 22: With the aim of helping each other, he/she must develop the method of collective functioning by comradely criticism and self-criticism. He/she must have attitude to work even with those who raise criticism and hold different views and be able to unite with the great majority, including those who have wrongly opposed them but are sincerely correcting their mistakes.

Article 23: He/she must accept firmly in theory and practice of party unity, party committee functioning and party discipline.

He/she must safeguard the secrecy of the party. He/she must defend the party and hold its cause against the onslaught of the enemy. He/she must safeguard the unity of the party against factionalism. He/she must develop professional attitude toward his/her revolutionary work and must develop his/her level of skills, knowledge and proletarian outlook.

Article 24: The Rights of the Party Members:

(a) The right to elect and to be elected to party committees at the concerned levels.

(b) The right to get Party Magazines, documents, circulars, etc., and the right to freely discuss in the party meetings and party organs about the political and organizational line, policies and decisions of the party and about problems arising in implementing them.

(c) In case of any disagreement with the decision of the committee/unit, a member of the concerned committee/unit must remain loyal to carry out the decision, may retain his/her dissenting opinion and demand resettlement of the issue in any subsequent meeting or may even send his/her opinion to higher units for consideration through his/her respective party unit; when the respective committee fails to solve the problem within six months, he/she has the right to send his/her opinion directly also to higher units. It is, however, the discretion of the committee to decide whether to reopen the matter or not.

(d) Any member has the right to send criticism against any other party member not in his/her unit to the next higher committee. Any party member has right to send criticism and suggestions.

(e) The duties and rights of the candidate members and party members are identical but for one difference. The candidate members have no right to elect or to be elected or to vote.

(f) In case of punishment to any unit or party member, detailed explanation and discussion regarding the specific case must be conducted in his/her presence and information regarding decision must be sent to the higher committee in writing.

Article 25:

(a) The organizational principle of the party is democratic centralism. Party structure and internal life are based on this principle. Democratic centralism means centralism based on inner party democracy and inner party democracy under centralized leadership. While discussing open heartedly and being united in party work, such a political atmosphere has to be created where both centralism and democracy, discipline and freedom, unity of will and personal ease of mind and liveliness—all these will be present. Only in such an atmosphere the principle of democratic centralism can be implemented successfully.

(b) Most important principle of democratic centralism for organizational structure is that the leading committees at all levels shall be compulsorily elected on the basis of democratic discussion. Conferences, plenums and elected committee at all levels shall have approval from higher-level committees.

Essentially the whole party shall follow the principle that the individual is subordinate to the organization, the minority is subordinate to the majority, the lower level is subordinate to the higher level, and the entire party is subordinate to the Central Committee.

(c) Leading committees of the party shall present the organizational report in Congress/Conference or Plenum. These committees will listen to the opinions of people both inside and outside the party and will be answerable to them. Party members shall have the right to criticize and send their opinions/resolutions to the higher committee; even if any party member has a different point of view then he/she can send his views to the higher committee and even up to the central committee.

(d) Every member of the leading committees must bear the responsibility to give party leadership in a specified area and a front. They will take direct experience from it and knowledge acquired from this experience can help in guiding other committees, except special responsibility given by higher committees. The central committee can give responsibility to any member/members of all the leading committees including central committee.

(e) The leading committees must regularly send reports to their lower committees and must intimate their decisions promptly. All lower bodies shall likewise be responsible to make regular reports to higher committees about their respective activities.

(f) Except those who are given some special tasks, every party member shall be a member of any one of the party units.

(g) Before decisions are taken every party member may freely and fully discuss in the concerned party units. He/she may express his/her opinions on party policies and various problems and sometimes may abstain from expressing final opinion explaining the reason for it. But, after taking a decision, everybody must strictly abide by them. However, if a member still holds different opinion, he/she has the right to reserve it. It is not permissible to raise discussion on those issues immediately after they were discussed and decisions taken in Congress/conference.

Any member may raise discussion on new issues in the concerned committees. If he/she feels that the issues are concerned with the whole party then he/she may send his/her opinion up to the Central Committee through his/her committees or/and in special circumstances, directly. If one third of the Central Committee members opine so and also want to call plenum for its solution then it will be circulated at least up to the State Committees. In case the majority of the State Committees agree with this demand then the Central Committee will call the plenum. In such special circumstances also, the Central Committee will ensure that the democratic method of resolving issues is followed.

(h) Keeping in mind the difference between the tactics and method, every unit has the freedom to take initiative in developing new methods of implementation of the party general line and tasks given by higher committees.

(i) If a member is arrested, he/she shall be relieved of all responsibilities and the membership will be placed under observation. Depending on his/her behavior during the period of detention by enemy or in the jail or after coming out his/her membership shall be continued/cancelled. If continued he/she shall be admitted into the party committee to which he/she belonged prior to his/her arrest unless the party decides otherwise.

(j) The method of criticism and self-criticism shall be practiced in the party committee at all levels. There must be relentless struggle against bureaucratic, individualistic, liberal, ultra-democratic, multi-centered factionalist tendencies and trends in the functioning of the committees. The committees should function on the basis of collective leadership and individual responsibility.

(k) Comradely relations and mutual co-operation shall be extended in rectifying the mistakes of others. A party member's work has to be reviewed on the basis of his/her overall practice in party life and not on the basis of minor mistakes on some trifle matters.

(l) It is only the Central Committee that shall have the right to take decision on domestic and international issues. Decisions on various levels regarding local issues and problems shall be taken by the respective committees, which will be in accordance with the decisions taken by higher committees.

(m) When a party member is transferred to another region, she/he shall be recognized as party member of the same level of responsibility in that region. While transferring a member from one region to another all details about him/her shall be sent to the concerned unit in writing.

CHAPTER 6: PARTY DISCIPLINE

Article 26: Party Discipline is a must to defend unity of the party, to increase the fighting capacity and to implement the policy of democratic centralism. Without iron discipline no revolutionary party will be able to give capable leadership to the masses in the war and to fulfill the responsibility of revolution. Party discipline is same for all the party members including the leadership.

Article 27:

(a) To reject the aims and objective of the party, party program or organizational structure or to violate them will be tantamount to indiscipline and the member or unit involved in such activities will be liable to disciplinary action.

(b) When party members violate party discipline, the concerned party unit shall take appropriate disciplinary measures: warning, serious warning, suspending from party posts, removal from post, suspending or canceling the party membership, expelling from the party etc., subject to the approval of the higher committee. Cancellation and expulsion of party membership shall come into force only after the next higher committees approve them. Time limit shall be specified while suspending a member, which should not be more than one year. The next higher committee shall ratify suspension.

(c) When any Party unit violates the discipline, the higher committees shall take disciplinary measures such as reprimanding the unit to partially reconstituting the unit. For dissolving the unit, approval of the next higher committee is necessary.

(d) When a Central Committee member seriously violates party discipline (acts as enemy agent or indulges in open anti-party activities) the Central Committee shall have the right to remove him/her from his/her rank or to expel him/her from the party. But, such a measure will come into force only when two-thirds of Central Committee members give their approval.

(e) The party unit or the party member whom disciplinary measure is taken shall be submitted a charge sheet beforehand. If the unit or the member thinks that such a disciplinary measure was unjustified, then the unit or the member may raise objection, may request for reviewing the decision or may appeal to the higher committee. Such appeals shall be sent to the higher committees by the concerned lower committees without any delay. Every member shall have the right to defend himself/herself in person in his/her committee/unit or to submit his/her written explanation to the higher committee, which takes disciplinary action against him/her.

Article 28:

(a) Punishment should be given only if all other options of discussion and convincing to rectify a member or a party unit fails. Even after giving punishment, efforts must be made to rectify. Policy of saving the patient and curing disease should be followed. In special circumstances to defend party security and respect, punishment should be given as soon as possible.

(b) The lower committee cannot take any disciplinary action on any member of the higher committee. However, in case of dual membership they may send their allegations and suggestions about the members of the higher committees in writing to the concerned committees.

(c) In case of gross breach of Party discipline which may cause serious harm to the party, if he/she be allowed to continue his/her membership or post in the party, a member can be summarily suspended from party membership, removed from his/her party post by his/her committee or by higher committees pending framing charge sheet and getting his/her explanation. At the time of taking such disciplinary steps, the concerned committee should specify the period by which a final decision will be taken in the matter.

(d) If any party member or candidate member (or a member at any level) does not participate in party activities or does not implement party decisions for six months without showing proper reason, does not renew membership and does not pay membership fee and levy he/her shall be deemed to have voluntarily withdrawn from the party and his/her membership shall either be suspended or cancelled. Those members, who are corrupted in economic matters, degenerate politically, becomes characterless or betray the party-secrecy shall be liable to punishment.

(e) The harshest measures among all the disciplinary measures taken by the party are expulsion and cancellation from the party. Hence while taking such decision; concerned party unit shall observe utmost care. Such measures will be taken when all the efforts in rectifying the concerned member failed. The party members' appeal must be carefully examined by the concerned higher committee and the circumstances under which he/she committed the mistakes must be thxoroughly reviewed.

(f) If persons whose party membership has been cancelled or have resigned express their willingness again to join the party, the concerned committees should take a decision after thorough investigation. Membership should be given only after testing through practice for a minimum period of six months. Only the state or Central Committee may take members once expelled from the party barring betrayals. Lower committees may, however, forward recommendations in this regard.

CHAPTER 7: PARTY'S ORGANIZATIONAL STRUCTURE

Article 29:

(a) The party organization shall be formed according to geographical divisions or spheres of production.

(b) Party is constituted with two types of membership professionals and part-timers.

Article 30: The party structure at the various levels shall be as follows:

(a) The highest body of the party shall be the Central Committee. Below the Central Committee there will be Special Area Committee/Special Zonal Committee/State Committee; Regional Committee; Zonal Committee/District/Divisional Committee; Sub-Zonal/Sub-Divisional Committee; Area Committee; local level committees such as village/Basti/Factory/College party committee. The primary unit of the party will be cell. The Town and city committee will be formed and the concerned higher committee will decide the status of the committee.

(b) All committees will elect their secretaries. All committees may form secretariats according to the needs of the movement and the size of the committee. The secretaries of all committees and the secretariats are of the same level and will have same rights as the committee of which they are part. However they, secretaries and secretariats, will have special duties and responsibilities.

(c) All the leading committees from Area Committee onward will be constituted only with professional revolutionaries.

(d) The party congress is the supreme authority of the entire party. The Central Committee elected by the congress is the highest authority in between two congresses.

(e) Special Area Committee/Special Zonal Committee/State Committee elected by the SAC/SZC/SC conference is the highest authority at the SAC/SZC/State level.

(f) Regional committee elected by the regional conference is the highest authority at the region level. Regional committee can be formed by dividing the states or with parts of different states according to the requirements of the movement.

(g) Similarly, Zonal/District/Divisional and Sub-Zonal/Sub-Divisional Committees will be elected at their respective level conferences. Area Committees are elected at the Area level conference.

(h) Town/City Committee elected at the respective level conference.

(i) Party cell—it consists of three to five members in a village, or in two or three villages combined, or a factory, or educational institution, or a locality, or two or three localities combined. In mass organization units, cells will be formed.

(j) In the period between two conferences or congresses, the committees elected at the respective levels are the highest bodies.

(k) All committees elect their respective secretaries.

(l) Various sub-committees and commissions under the leadership at different levels may be formed to efficiently carry out the party's work in various spheres.

BASIC UNIT

Article 31:

(a) Party cell will be basic unit of the party. Party cell can be formed area wise or profession wise. Party cells are nucleus for day-to-day activities. The members in cells will be minimum 3 and maximum 5. Cell members will fulfill their responsibilities and duties as full-fledged party members and they will avail all the rights of party membership (except candidate members). The cell will elect its secretary.

(b) Candidate members will also work according to the decisions of the party cell. They shall participate in the discussions and follow the party directives but they will not have voting rights at the time of decision-making.

(c) While forming party cells area wise, efforts will be made to form party cells in factories and in mass organizations.

(d) If there are two or more cells in an area, a committee below that of AC can be formed.

(e) Party cell is a living link between broad masses of an area and the party. The cell will lead the revolutionary war of broad masses of people with full initiative. It shall make relentless efforts to bring the masses of factory, locality and peasant areas close to the political line and aims of the party. By involving militant activists and party followers in the revolutionary war against autocratic semi-colonial, semi-feudal state system, it will stress from the very beginning to educate the masses to function secretly, illegally and according to the strategy and tactics of the Protracted People's War. By selecting 3–5 party activists and organizing them in a group while educating them in party politics and organizing them as members the party cells discharge their responsibilities.

CHAPTER 8: PARTY CONGRESS

Article 32: Holding of the all India party congress shall be decided by the central committee. The party congress shall be held once in five years. Under special circumstances it may either be postponed or preponed though decision has to be taken by majority of the CC.

Article 33: The party congress elects a presidium to conduct the congress and discharges the following tasks:

(a) It undertakes the political and organizational review of the party since the preceding congress.

(b) It adopts the party program, party constitution, strategy and tactics besides being responsible for formulating policies in financial and other policy matters.

(c) Appraises the domestic and international situation and lays down the tasks.

(d) Decides the number of central committee members and elects the central committee members and alternate central committee members.

(e) It ratifies the financial statements.

Article 34:

(a) The central committee elects general secretary of the party. It also elects a politburo depending on the requirements of the movement, and will take political, organizational and military decisions according to the party-line and the decisions of the central committee in between the period of one central committee meeting to the next and will get its decisions ratified in the subsequent central committee meeting. It will also set up regional bureaus, CMC, and other sub-committees and departments. The general secretary also acts as the in charge of the Polit Bureau.

(b) To run its party organs, the central committee appoints editorial boards for each organ. The General Secretary will be the chief editor of the theoretical-ideological organ of the central committee.

Article 35: The central committee may convene central plenums to deal with special problems in the period between congress. These plenums can discuss and take decisions on problems relating to party line and policies in that period. Similarly election of new members into the central committee or removal of Central Committee members can also be taken up by the central plenums.

Whenever it is necessary, the central committee can co-opt members not exceeding one-fourth of its existing strength if two-thirds of its members agree.

Article 36: Special Area, state/regional, special zonal, zonal and/sub-zonal/district/ divisional plenums shall be held once in every three years.

Under special circumstances they may be held earlier or postponed. However area conferences/plenums should be held once every two years. These conferences take decisions after holding discussions on problems relating to their respective levels, send their opinions on the party line and policy to higher committees and elect the respective committees along with alternate members, if necessary.

Article 37: In the period between level conferences, if necessary, plenums may be convened, with the approval of the next higher committee. Decisions may be taken after discussion on problems in the areas under the jurisdiction of the various committees in their respective plenum where members may either be elected or removed. If plenums of any committee cannot be held due to special circumstances, the concerned committees may co-opt one-fourth of their respective strengths with the approval of the next higher committee.

Article 38:

(a) The number of delegates to the various conferences including the congress shall be decided by the respective committees according to membership strength as per the decisions of different levels of committees and party congress.

(b) The respective committees are empowered to specially invite up to ten percent of the strength of delegates attending the congress, and other different level conference. Observers and nonvoting delegates may also be invited to the conference of the respective committees.

Article 39: The Central Committee shall release relevant draft documents to be discussed in the party congress to all party members giving sufficient time as decided by the CC, before the process of the congress starts. All amendments to drafts submitted by the lower level conferences and by members should be sent to the Central Committee, which will place them before the party congress.

Delegates to the party congress shall enjoy the right to move amendments to the draft documents. After going through the draft documents, if any committee delegate/delegates want to move alternative document, he/she/they must immediately inform the Central Committee, and the Central Committee will decide about the time to be given to the concerned delegate/delegates committee for drafting the document. The concerned committee delegate/delegates have to draft the document within a scheduled time as decided by CC, and thus submit it to the Central Committee. The Central Committee deserves the right to circulate it with its own comment.

Article 40: The outgoing central committee shall propose to the congress a panel of members of the new central committee to be formed.

Any delegate shall have the right to object to any name in the panel, or can even propose a new panel, with the prior approval of the member whose name is proposed. If there is an agreement on the names, the change shall be accepted by a show of hands; in case of alternate proposal all committees including the Central Committee shall be elected by secret ballot.

Article 41: The number of delegates to the plenums at various levels along with the basis for the selection of delegates shall be decided by the respective committees.

CHAPTER 9: RIGHTS AND DUTIES OF CENTRAL COMMITTEE

Article 42: The Central Committee will be elected by the party congress. In between the two party congresses the Central Committee is the highest leading body of the party. The Central Committee represents the whole party and can take crucial decisions with full authority on behalf of the party. The Central Committee shall meet at least once in a year.

Article 43: Central Committee may form Politburo, Central Military Commission, regional bureaus and various sub-committees for smooth functioning of the party. The PB is of the same level and enjoys the same rights as the CC. However, it has special duties and responsibilities which it will fulfill on behalf of the CC in between two CC meetings.

Article 44: The Central Committee can take step and remove any Central Committee member for gross breach of discipline, serious anti party activities and heinous factional activities. The punished member has the right to appeal before the congress. Till the matter is not decided or settled, Central Committee's decision will remain standing. If two-thirds of the Central Committee members agree, they can take decision to oust any member of the Central Committee.

Article 45: The Central Committee can co-opt any member in the Central Committee if any post remains vacant or for the need of the movement. Whenever it is necessary the Central Committee can co-opt members not exceeding one fourth of its existing strength, if two-thirds of its members agree. But it is to be ratified in the next congress. Co-option should be made from among alternative members; if there are no alternate members, then CC can co-opt from others.

Article 46: The CCs will decide the date and time of the Central Committee meeting and will provide the agenda of the meeting beforehand. If one-third members of the Central Committee demand a meeting of the Central Committee the secretary will have to call the meeting.

Article 47: The Central Committee or Politburo holds the right to send any member or members to check up the work of any unit or any area. The Central Committee has the right to disband any committee and thereby form any organizing committee at any level.

Article 48: If necessary the Central Committee can convene special conferences and plenums in between two congresses. The Central Committee will decide the other members of the different committees who will attend this plenum other than the CCMs.

CHAPTER 10: INTERNAL DEBATES IN THE PARTY

Article 49: It is very essential to go through deep discussions to unify the whole party ideologically, politically and organizationally and to improve our methods. This is also the democratic right of party members. At different levels of party, we should strive to resolve the questions related with the tactics by openhearted and unbridled debates in respective committees. When needed, help and advice of higher committees shall be taken. In the name of democratic rights of party members, endless debates on a particular issue will only harm the party functioning. So, any type of controversial debate or discussion can be permissible only after the consent of the two-thirds members of the concerned committees.

Article 50: In case any member or committee has different views about the basic line of the party and it demands its circulation in the party, central committee has the right to take final decisions whether to accept or reject this demand.

Article 51: If any central committee member has different views in regard to all India or international questions and he/she demands to take this idea in the whole party, before he/she is allowed, the said views will be sent to state/regional committee or to any level according to the one-third members of the central committee. But state/regional committee member cannot send his/her different views to the lower level committees without the permission from the central committee.

Article 52: If any lower level committee or committee member has different views on the political and organizational line of the central committee, then they can send their views to the central committee. If needed, central committee can send these views along with its opinion in the whole party.

Article 53: All the democratic debates in the party under the control of central committee or under its direction shall be sent to special area, state/regional and zonal committees or to all the levels of party.

CHAPTER 11: PARTY FUNCTIONING IN THE PEOPLE'S ARMY

Article 54: The people's army is the chief instrument of the party. Hence the party will use this instrument in rousing, mobilizing, organizing and arming the people in carrying out the task of the revolution.

It will participate in social production also. Only through the Protracted People's War, with people's army as the highest weapon the Party will carry out the task of seizure of political power by overthrowing the present reactionary state power that represents the interests of imperialism, feudalism and comprador big bourgeois and thereby establishing a new democratic state. It will protect the country, defend the victory of NDR, with the goal of socialism. Party will educate the army with the weapon of MLM.

Article 55: The Party will exercise full control over the army from the very beginning. Because the party decides the overall political strategy and tactics of revolution hence it also decides the functioning and forms of party organizations in the army by keeping the level of development of the Protracted People's War before it. Central Military Commission constituted by the Central Committee will conduct the military affairs according to the military line of the party as well as the policies, directives and decisions of the Central Committee. In this light the Military Commissions and Commands will be constituted at various levels to conduct the military operations. Being the leader and organizer of the People's Army, the party ranks at various levels will play a leading and front-ranking role in all the affairs of the army.

Article 56: This People's Army will be constituted of three forces—that is the main force, the secondary force and the base force.

Article 57: In our guerrilla army all the formations from platoon, company and above level will have party committees. The party branch will be constituted with party members. Various squads will have party cells and party branches. Where needed, a party committee will be constituted at that level. Party members and ranks will also remain in the militia and play the leading and front-ranking role there.

Article 58: All members of military formations will function under the leadership of the respective party committees. The decisions of these party committees will be carried out and implemented by the respective military formations. Party members in PLGA will be invited to the party conference/plenums according to their respective level. In general, the party committees in the military formations at and above platoon level will be elected in conferences held at that level.

CHAPTER 12: PARTY FACTIONS

Article 59: The party factions shall be formed in the executive committees of mass organizations. Party factions will guide the executive committees of the mass organizations adopting suitable method in accordance with the correct concrete situation. Faction committees will function secretly. The opinions of party committee/member guiding the faction shall be considered as final opinion. If faction committee members have any difference of opinion, they will send their opinions in writing to the concerned party committee/higher committee. The concerned party committees shall guide faction committees of different mass organizations at their own level.

CHAPTER 13: PARTY FUNDS

Article 60: The party funds shall be obtained through the membership fees, levies, donations, taxes and penalties.

Article 61: The levy to be paid by party members shall be decided and collected in their respective state committees.

᷍‿

INTRODUCTION

1. George J. Kunnath, "Smouldering Dalit Fires in Bihar, India," *Dialect Anthropology* 33 (2009): 321.

2. Charles Tilly, "Processes and Mechanisms of Democratization," *Sociological Theory* 18 (March 2000): 8.

3. Ross Mallick, *Indian Communism: Opposition, Collaboration and Institutionalization* (Delhi: Oxford University Press, 1994), 10.

4. Mallick, *Indian Communism*, 1.

5. Jean Dreze and Amartya Sen, *An Uncertain Glory: India and Its Contradictions* (London: Allen Lane, 2013), 213.

6. Gunnar Myrdal, *Asian Drama: An Inquiry into the Poverty of Nations.* Vol. 2 (New York: Pantheon, 1968), 709–10.

7. Partha Chatterjee, "Development Planning and the Indian State," in *State and Politics in India*, ed. Partha Chatterjee (Delhi: Oxford University Press, 1997), 279.

8. Popularized by C. Rajagopalachari who also became the governor-general of independent India, this oft-quoted expression refers to the elaborate processes of regulations that the private operators had to negotiate to set up or run businesses in India between 1950 and the early years of the 1990s. The licence permit quota raj was a result of India's acceptance of the state-led development paradigm so that all aspects of the economy were controlled by the state and licenses for businesses were given to a select few. Due to the license permit quota raj, a deep distrust was reportedly born for big businesses in Indian minds.

9. Jagdish N. Bhagwati, "Indian Economic Policy and Performance: A Framework for a Progressive Society," in *Wealth and Poverty: Essays in Development Economics*. Vol. 1, *Wealth and Poverty*, by Jagdish N. Bhagwiti, ed. Gene M. Grossman (Cambridge, MA: MIT Press, 1985), 9.

10. Atul Kohli, *State-Directed Development: Global Power and Industrialization in the Global Periphery* (Cambridge, UK: Cambridge University Press, 2005), 258.

11. Pranab Bardhan provides a graphic illustration of the performance of the public sector in the first three decades of India's independence in his *The Political Economy of Development* (New Delhi: Oxford University Press, 2008; reprint), 63–4.

12. Kohli, *State-Directed Development*, 279.

13. Joseph Stiglitz, *Making Globalization Work: The Next Steps to Global Justice* (London: Allen Lane, 2006), 292. This argument was forcefully made by Margit Bussmann in his "When Globalization Discontent Turns Violent: Foreign Economic Liberalization and Internal War," *International Studies Quarterly* 51, no. 1 (March 2007): 79–97.

14. Amit Bhaduri and Deepak Nayyar, *The Intelligent Person's Guide to Liberalization* (New Delhi: Penguin, 1996), 159.

15. Ramchandra Guha, *India after Gandhi: The History of the World's Largest Democracy* (London: Picador, 2007), 710.

16. Aditya Nigam, "Rumour of Maoism," in *The Maoist Movement in India: Perspective and Counterperspectives*, ed. Santosh Paul (New Delhi: Routledge, 2013), 37.

17. V. S. Naipaul, *A Million Mutinies* (London: William Heinemann, 1991), 106. According to Naipaul, every protest movement strengthens the state, "defining it as the source of law and civility and reasonableness." The institutionalization of power in the form of a democratic state gives "people a second chance, calling them back from the excesses with which, in another century, or in other circumstances (as neighboring countries showed), they might have had to live: the destructive chauvinism of the Shiv Sena, the tyranny of many kinds of religious fundamentalism . . . the film-star corruption and the racial politics of the South, the pious Marxist idleness and nullity of Bengal."

18. Sudipta Kaviraj, "Modernity and Politics in India," *Daedalus* 129, no. 1 (Winter 2000): 156–7.

19. Satish Deshpande, *Contemporary India: A Sociological View* (New Delhi: Penguin, 2003), 103.

20. Javeed Alam, *Who Wants Democracy?* (New Delhi: Orient Longman, 2004), 22. According to Alam, "Democracy in India is an assertion of the urge for more self-respect and the ability to better oneself."

21. Christophe Jaffrelot pursues this argument in his *India's Silent Revolution: The Rise of the Low Castes in North Indian Politics* (New Delhi: Permanent Black, 2003).

22. Rajni Kothari, *Memoirs* (New Delhi: Rupa, 2002), 200.

23. Pratap Bhanu Mehta, *The Burden of Democracy* (New Delhi: Penguin, 2003), 129–30.

24. Anne Phillips, *The Politics of Presence* (Oxford: Clarendon Press, 1995).

25. For an analytical treatment of "the politics of inclusion" as an alter ego of "the politics of exclusion," see Zoya Hasan, *Politics of Inclusion: Castes, Minorities and Affirmative Action* (New Delhi: Oxford University Press, 2009).

26. Sanjay Sanghvi, "The New People's Movement in India," *Economic and Political Weekly,* 15 December 2007: 116.

27. Partha Chatterjee, "Democracy and Economic Transformation in India," *Economic and Political Weekly*, 19 April 2008: 54.

28. Rob Jenkins, "The Politics of India's Special Economic Zones," in *Understanding India's New Political Economy: A Great Transformation?*, ed. Sanjay Ruparelia, Sanjay Reddy, John Harriss, and Stuart Corbridge (London: Routledge, 2011), 50.

29. Jenkins, "The Politics of India's Special Economic Zones," 49.

30. Jenkins, "The Politics of India's Special Economic Zones," 56.

31. Statement of the Communist Party of India (Maoist), Central Committee, 16 March 2007 (obtained from a Maoist activist in Orissa).

32. Gautam Navlakha, *Days and Nights in the Heartland of Rebellion* (New Delhi: Penguin, 2012), 78.

33. Navlakha, *Days and Nights in the Heartland of Rebellion*, 202.

PART I

1. Edward Bernstein, *Evolutionary Socialism* (New York: Schocken Books, 1961), 166.

2. Bernstein, *Evolutionary Socialism*, 142.

3. Bernstein, *Evolutionary Socialism*, 218.

4. Bernstein, *Evolutionary Socialism*, xxvii.

5. Peter Gay pursues this argument in his *The Dilemma of Democratic-Socialism: Edward Bernstein's Challenge to Marx* (New York: Columbia University Press, 1952).

6. Jyoti Basu (1914–2010) was a member of the CPI (M) politburo since its inception in 1964 until 2008. He also served as the chief minister of the West Bengal Left Front government for twenty-three years (1977–2000), the longest-serving chief minister of an Indian state. During his student days in England, he joined the India League and London Majlis, two prominent organizations of overseas Indian students to pursue the cause of India's independence. It was in England that Basu was introduced to the Communist Party of Great Britain, especially its prominent ideologue, Rajani Palme Dutt. Directed by the Communist Party of India, Basu began working among the railway workers in 1944, and he soon became the secretary of the All India Railwaymen's Federation.

7. Sudhansuranjan Ghose, *Yukta Front–Ranga* (in Bengali) [United Front Drama] (Calcutta: Prafulla Granthagar, 1970), 16.

8. Ross Mallick, *Indian Communism: Opposition, Collaboration and Institutionalization* (Delhi: Oxford University Press, 1994), 29.

9. National Council, Communist Party of India, *Resolution on Splitters* (New Delhi: April 1964), 37, quoted in Mallick, *Indian Communism*, 40.

10. *Amrita Bazar Patrika*, 3 February 1963.

11. For details, see Ashok Majumdar, *Peasant Protest in Indian Politics: Tebhaga Movement in Bengal* (New Delhi: NIB Publishers, 1993).

12. Communist Party of India (Marxist), *New Situation and Party's Tasks* (Calcutta: Communist Party of India [Marxist], 1967), 37–8.

13. Zoya Hasan, *Congress after Indira: Policy, Power, Political Change (1984–2009)* (New Delhi: Oxford University Press, 2012), 215.

14. CPI (M), *Election Manifesto: 2013 State Assembly Election* (New Delhi: CPI [M], 2013), 5.

Chapter 1

1. In his well-researched article on the evolution of communism in Tripura, Harihar Bhattacharyya has shown how several splinter groups finally contributed to the institutionalization of the parliamentary left in Tripura: "Communalism, Nationalism and Tribal Question in Tripura," *Economic and Political Weekly*, 29 September 1990: 2209–14.

2. Subir Bhaumik, "Disaster in Tripura," *Seminar* 510 (2002): 5. Online: http://www.india-seminar.com/2002/510/510%20subir%20bhaumik.htm. Interview with Biren Dutta on 23 April 1987.

3. Bhaunik, "Disaster in Tripura," 2002.

4. Harihar Bhattacharyya in his *Communism in Tripura* (Delhi: Ajanta Publishers, 1999) narrates the story of the growth and consolidation of communism in Tripura.

5. Bhaumik, "Disaster in Tripura," 2002.

6. A printed pamphlet of Tripura Proja Mondal, September 1946, p. 1, quoted in Bhattacharyya, "Communalism, Nationalism and Tribal Question in Tripura," 2212.

7. The literature is abundant on the militancy in Tripura. I have drawn on the following texts: E. N. Rammohan, "The Insurgent Groups of Tripura," *Inter-State Conflict and Effects*, 24 July 2011; Praveen Kumar, "State of Politics in Tripura," *Institute of Peace and Conflict Studies* 989 (15 March 2003). Online: http://www.ipcs.org/article/terrorism-in-northeast/state-of-politics-in-tripura-989.html; Biswajit Ghosh, "Ethnicity and Insurgency in Tripura," *Sociological Bulletin* 52, no. 52 (September 2003): 221–43; Subir Bhaumik, *Tripura: Ethnic Conflict, Militancy and Counterinsurgency*, Policies and Practices 52 (Kolkata: Mahanirban Research Group, 2012), 8–19.

8. Bhaumik, "Disaster in Tripura," 10.

9. Ghosh, "Ethnicity and Insurgency in Tripura," 231.

10. Gayatri Bhattacharyya, *Refugee Rehabilitation and Its Impact on Tripura's Economy* (Guwahati: Omsons Publications, 1988), 57–8.

11. Subir Bhaumik, "Tripura's Gumti Dam Must Go," *Ecologist Asia*, 11, no. 1 (January–March 2003): 84.

12. Walter Fernandes and Gita Bharali, "Development-Induced Displacement, 1947–2000 in Meghalaya, Mizoram and Tripura: A Quantitative and Qualitative Database on Its Extent and Impact" (Mimeograph) (Guwahati: North-Eastern Social Research Centre, 2010), 11.

13. Bhaumik, *Tripura*, 11.

14. Government of Tripura, *Tripura Human Development Report 2007* (Agartala: Government of Tripura, 2007), 121.

15. Harihar Bhattacharyya and T. J. Nossiter, "Communism in a Micro-State: Tripura and the Nationalities Question," in *Marxist State Governments in India: Politics, Economics and Society*, ed. T. J. Nossiter (London: Pinter Publishers, 1988), 162.

16. The 1986 CPI (M) Report on the Nationality Question, quoted in Bhattacharyya and Nossiter, "Communism in a Micro-State," 167.

17. Government of Tripura, *Tripura Human Development Report 2007*, 122.

18. Government of Tripura, *Tripura Human Development Report 2007*, 122.

19. Government of Tripura, *Tripura Human Development Report 2007*, 119.

20. Government of Tripura, *Tripura Human Development Report 2007*, 121.

21. Out of a total of 5,733 elected representatives in 2004, 1,986 were women who were elected in Gram Panchayat, Panchayat Samity, and Zila Parishad. Directorate of Panchayat (Agartala: Government of Tripura, December 2004).

22. Sukhendu Debbarma and Mousami Debbarma, "Fifth Victory in a Row for CPI (M) in Tripura," *Economic and Political Weekly*, 26 September 2009: 173.

23. Suhrid Sankar Chattapadhyay, "The Tripura Election," *Frontline* 30, no. 5 (9–22 March 2013): 7.

24. Prakash Karat, "Towards a Seventh Left Front Government in Tripura," *People's Democracy*, 27 January 2013: 17.

25. Directorate of Economics and Statistics, Planning (Statistics) Department, Government of Tripura, *Economic Review of Tripura, 2010–11* (Agartala: Government of Tripura), 231. Online: http://www.destripura.nic.in/review2010_11.pdf.

26. Literacy rate in Indian states, 2011.

27. The United Nations Development Programme has set eight goals for 2015 which are (i) eradicate extreme poverty and hunger, (ii) achieve universal primary education, (iii) promote gender equality and empower women, (iv) reduce child mortality, (v) improve maternal health, (vi) combat HIV/AIDS, malaria, and other diseases, (vii) ensure environmental sustainability, and (viii) develop a global partnership for development.

28. As per the *Literacy Background and Progress Report of 9-Point Program* by the State Literacy Mission Authority (Agartala: Government of Tripura, September 2006), the specific objectives of the Nine Point Program are to achieve: (i) 100 percent enrollment of children in schools, (ii) 100 percent immunization of children up to 6 years old, (iii) total sanitation in educational institutions and homes, (iv) supply of safe drinking water to educational institutions, (v) adequate tree plantation in educational institutions, (vi) awareness of cleanliness in educational institutions, (vii) sports and cultural activities in schools, (viii) reduction in infant mortality and maternal mortality, and (ix) expansion of women's self-help groups.

29. B. L. Vohra, *Tripura's Bravehearts: A Police Success Story in Countering Insurgency* (Delhi: Konark, 2010), 14–15.

30. Debbarma and Debbarma, "Fifth Victory in a Row," 173.

31. Kerem Gabriel Oktem, "A Comparative Analysis of the Performance of the Parliamentary Left in the Indian States of Kerala, West Bengal and Tripura," *South Asia: Journal of South Asian Studies*, n. s, 35, no. 2 (June 2012): 325.

32. An interview with a Congress activist in Agartala, Tripura's capital, quoted in Chattapadhyay, "The Tripura Election," 3.

Chapter 2

1. I am thankful to Dr B. L. Biju for his contribution in the preparation of the first draft of this chapter.

2. E. M. S. Namboodiripad (1909–1998) was an Indian communist leader who was instrumental in establishing the first elected communist government in Kerala. A socialist–Marxist theorist, Namboodiripad initiated radical land reforms during his tenure as chief minister of the state. He was also credited with the idea of coalition government, which he constituted by involving various left groups and their sympathizers.

3. T. J. Nossiter, *Communism in Kerala: A Study of Political Adaptation* (Delhi: Oxford University Press, 1982), 1.

4. S. Gopal, *Jawaharlal Nehru: A Biography* (New Delhi: Oxford University Press, 1989), 345.

5. Jawaharlal Nehru's press conference in Delhi, 7 August 1959; *National Herald* (Delhi), 8 August 1959, quoted in Gopal, *Jawaharlal Nehru*, 355.

6. Jawaharlal Nehru's speech at the symposium on the prospects of democracy in Asian countries, Delhi, 12 December 1958; *The Hindu* (New Delhi), 13 December 1958.

7. Formed in 1934, the CSP merged with the CPI in Kerala in 1940. Manali Desai, "Party Formation, Political Power, and the Capacity for Reform: Comparing Left Parties in Kerala and West Bengal," *Social Forces* 80 (2001): 40.

8. The KMPP was founded by former Congress leaders of socialist and Gandhian orientation such as Acharya Kripalani, T. Prakasham in Andhra, and Kelappan in Kerala on the eve of the first general election. It was considered the second incarnation of the CSP. Later when Kelappan

and Prakasham rejoined the Congress, those who felt left out in the organization united with the rest of Socialist Party leaders to form the PSP, which is the third incarnation of the CSP. E. M. S. Namboodiripad, *The Communist Party in Kerala: Six Decades of Struggle and Advancement* (New Delhi: National Book Centre, 1994), 129.

9. Namboodiripad, *The Communist Party in Kerala*, 18.

10. Namboodiripad, *The Communist Party in Kerala*, 134.

11. Namboodiripad, *The Communist Party in Kerala*, 139–43.

12. Victor M. Fic, *Kerala: Yenan of India: Rise of Communist Power* (Bombay: Nachiketa Publications, 1970), 47–9.

13. Fic, *Kerala*, 70.

14. Fic, *Kerala*, 65–70.

15. Namboodiripad, *The Communist Party in Kerala*, 118–21.

16. Nossiter, *Communism in Kerala*, 107.

17. Fic, *Kerala*, 78–9.

18. This point is debatable. Nossiter points out that there was a big difference between the membership of SNDP, an Ezhava organization, and the party membership of the CPI. SNDP had a larger membership than that of the left parties. T. J. Nossiter, *Marxist State Governments in India: Politics, Economics and Society* (London: Pinter Publishers, 1988), 50.

19. N. E. Balaram (1919–1994) was one of the founding leaders of the communist movement in Kerala. A Marxist ideologue, scholar in Indian philosophy, and a well-known critic of Malayalam literature, he wrote perhaps the most authentic text on the communist movement in Kerala. He was elected to the first Kerala legislative assembly in 1957 and was reelected in 1960. When the Communist Party split in 1964, Balaram remained with the original communist party, the CPI.

20. N. E. Balaram, *A Short History of the Communist Party of India* (Thiruvananthaouram: Prabath Book House, 1967); Namboodiripad, *The Communist Party in Kerala*.

21. Fic, *Kerala*, 119–25; Nossiter, *Communism in Kerala*, 318–58.

22. By adopting such steps, the CPI-led left government seemed to have been inspired by its leader, E. M. S. Namboodiripad, who believed in "settling disputes through negotiations, arriving at agreements and making sincere and serious efforts to implement agreements." Namboodiriad, *The Communist Party of Kerala*, 79.

23. Patrick Heller, "Degrees of Democracy: Some Comparative Lessons from India," *World Politics* 52 (July 2000): 508.

24. Valarian Rodrigues, "The Communist Party in India," in *India's Political Parties*, ed. Peter Ronald deSouza and E Sridharan (New Delhi: Sage, 2006), 214.

25. While the Western scholars who studied this split in the CPI emphasized the Soviet Union versus China debate in international communism as the reason for the split within the Indian communists, writers like E. M. S. Namboodiripad and N. E. Balaram interpreted the division as an outcome of an ideological churning since the early 1950s when a selected group of Indian communists preferred a contextual assessment of India's socio-economic circumstances to the derivative classical Marxist–Leninist perspective as a theoretical aid to revolution. Balaram, *A Short History of the Communist Party of India*, 201–9.

26. Fic, *Kerala*, 164–5.

27. K. N. Govindan Nair expressed hope for a reunion since the ideological cause was identical. *Times of India* (New Delhi), 21 December 1964.

28. The press statement of E. M. S. Namboodiripad on 25 December 1964, in Calcutta. *Ananda Bazar Patrika* (Calcutta), 26 December 1964.

29. Nossiter, *Communism in Kerala*, 107.

30. Communist Party of India, *CPI Party Programme* (Trivandrum: CPI, 1951), 18.

31. Also known as the Naxalites, the CPI (Marxist–Leninist) believed in armed revolution based on the Maoist national-democratic line of thinking. The contemporary CPI (Maoist) that came into being in 2004 draws its ideological legacy from the CPI (Marxist–Leninist). Chapters 5, 6, and 7 deal with Maoist politics in India.

32. Despite not having a formal nomenclature, the social left includes those who always remained staunch critics of the established communist parties for not being adequately sensitive to the genuine socio-economic grievances of the marginalized. Several authors refer to the social left in their writings: Balaram, *A Short History of the Communist Party of India*; E. M. S. Namboodiripad, *Kerala Society and Politics: An Historical Survey* (New Delhi: National Book Centre, 1984); G. K. Lieten, *The First Communist Ministry in Kerala, 1957–9* (Calcutta: K. P. Bagchi, 1982); Nossiter, *Communism in Kerala*, 1982.

33. Fic, *Kerala*, 72–3.

34. The liberation struggle (1958–59) or *Vimochana Samaram* in local parlance was an anti-communist socio-political agitation against the first elected communist government in Kerala, which was led by E. M. S. Namboodiripad of the CPI as its chief minister. Peeved by the radical land reforms, reforms in education, the Catholic Church in Kerala, the NSS and the Indian Muslim League launched a movement to topple the government, which was successfully accomplished in 1959 when the Namboodiripad government was dismissed and presidential rule was promulgated in Kerala.

35. James Chiriyankandath, "Unity in Diversity? Coalition Politics in India (with Special Reference to Kerala)," *Democratization* 4, no. 4 (Winter 1997): 28.

36. Nossiter, *Communism in Kerala*, 206.

37. An allegation of corruption was raised against the first communist government in relation to importing rice from Andhra for supply during the Onam festival. There was basically a procedural mistake that was raised by the opposition, which the government immediately admitted to defuse the crisis.

38. Chiriyankandath, "Unity in Diversity?," 30–1.

39. *Malayala Manorama*, 11 October 1979.

40. Nossiter, *Communism in India*, 231.

41. Nossiter, *Communism in Kerala*, 241–58.

42. Nossiter, *Communism in India*, 358–61.

43. E. M. S. Namboodiripad, *Kerala, Yesterday, Today and Tomorrow*, 2d ed. (Calcutta: National Book Agency, 1968), 37.

44. Nossiter, *Marxist State Governments in India*, 175–6.

45. For details, see Nossiter, *Communism in India*; Nossiter, *Marxist State Governments in India*.

46. I have elaborated this argument in my *Indian Politics and Society since Independence: Events, Processes and Ideology* (London: Routledge, 2008), 153–69.

47. T. M. Thomas Isaac and Richard W. Franke, *Local Democracy and Development: The Kerala People's Campaign for Decentralized Planning* (Lanham, MD: Rowman and Littlefield, 2002), 5.

48. Government of Kerala, *Report of the Committee on Decentralization of Powers* (Thiruvananthapuram: Government of Kerala, 1999), preface, Part A, Vol. I, p. iv.

49. Patrick Heller, "Building Local Democracy: Lessons from Kerala," paper presented at the Workshop on Poverty and Democracy, Duke University, 17–18 February 2006, 6.

50. T. M. Thomas Isaac and Patrick Heller, "Democracy and Development: Decentralized Planning in Kerala," in *Deepening Democracy: Institutional Innovations in Empowered Participatory Democracy*, ed. A. Fung and E. O. Wright (London: Verso Press, 2003), 107–8.

51. Rashmi Sharma, "Kerala's Decentralization: Idea in Practice," *Economic and Political Weekly*, 6 September 2003: 3849.

52. Sharma, "Kerala's Decentralization," 3842.

53. Sharma, "Kerala's Decentralization," 3850.

54. K. M. Sajad Ibrahim, "Kerala: A Negative Verdict on LDF Government," *Economic and Political Weekly*, 26 September 2009: 120.

55. Ibrahim, "Kerala," 119.

56. Ibrahim, "Kerala," 120.

57. *The Mathrubhumi* (Kollam), 3 November 2010.

58. Rekha Raj, "Dalit Women as Political Agents: A Kerala Experience," *Economic and Political Weekly*, 4 May 2013: 56.

59. "Fourteenth Assembly Elections in Kerala," *Economic and Political Weekly*, 18 June 2011: 136.

60. Subin Dennis, "Kerala Elections: Nothing Mysterious," *Economic and Political Weekly*, 18 June 2011: 128.

61. T. M. Thomas Isaac, "The Left Position in Ponnani," 25 March 2009. Online: http://www.pragoti.in/node/3293.

62. Dennis, "Kerala Elections," 128.

63. "Fourteenth Assembly Elections in Kerala," 137.

64. Dennis, "Kerala Elections," 127.

65. Nossiter, *Communism in Kerala*, 77–82; Manali Desai, *State Formation and Radical Democracy in India* (London: Routledge, 2007), 75–9.

66. Chiriyankandath, "Unity in Diversity?," 24.

67. K. V. Varughese provides an excellent elaboration of the texture of the coalition in Kerala in his *United Front Government in Kerala (1967–69): A Study of the Marxist-led Coalition* (Bangalore: Christian Institute of Religion and Society, 1978).

68. E. M. S. Namboodiripad, "Castes, Classes and Parties in Modern Political Development with special reference to Kerala," *Social Scientist* 64 (November 1977): 3.

69. Chiriyankandath, "Unity in Diversity?," 33.

70. S. Ramachandran Pillai "E. M. S. Namboodiripad and the Communist Government of Kerala," *The Marxist* 25 (July–September 2009): 1.

71. Hutment dwellers (*kudikidappukars*) are the occupants of the small plot of land given to them for the erection of huts to live in. These households provided a cheap source of labor to the landlords through acting as attached laborers and sometimes sharecroppers.

72. T. A. Thomas dwelled on this issue in his *Tenure History Kerala and Land Reforms* (mimeograph). Online: http://shodhganga.inflibnet.ac.in/bitstream/10603/532/18/10_chapter3.pdf.

73. Namboodiripad, *The Communist Party in Kerala*, 111.

74. Ronald Herring, *Land to the Tiller: The Political Economy of Agrarian Reform in South Asia* (New Haven, CT: Yale University Press, 1983), 187–9.

75. Ronald Herring, *Land to the Tiller: The Political Economy of Agrarian Reform in South Asia* (New Haven, CT: Yale University Press, 1983), 211; M. A. Oommen, *Land Reforms and Socio-Economic Changes in Kerala* (Madras: Christian Literature Society, 1971), 120.

76. Communist Party of India (Marxist), *CPI (M): Party Programme* (Calcutta: CPI [M], 1964), 8–9.

77. Communist Party of India (Marxist), *CPI (M): New Situation and Party's Task* (Calcutta: CPI [M], 1967), 70.

78. Similar to its Kerala counterpart, the national level coalitions—National Democratic Alliance and United Progressive Alliance—have also developed a mechanism of coming together and their continuity through the formulation of Common Minimum Programs, which always remain a common reference point for all the constituents of these two major conglomerations of parties. For details, see Bidyut Chakrabarty, *Forging Power: Coalition Politics in India* (New Delhi: Oxford University Press, 2006), 206–9.

79. Chiriyankandath, "Unity in Diversity?," 33.

80. Heller, "Degrees of Democracy," 501.

81. Heller, "Degrees of Democracy," 510–11.

82. Heller, "Degrees of Democracy," 511.

83. As Dreze and Sen argue, "Public action should not be confused with state action only. Various social and political organizations have typically played a part in actions that go beyond atomistic individual initiatives, and the domain of public action does include many non-state activities." Jean Dreze and Amartya Sen, *Hunger and Public Action* (Delhi: Oxford University Press, 1999), 18–19.

84. Jean Dreze and Amartya Sen, *India: Economic Development and Social Opportunity* (Delhi: Oxford University Press, 1999), 89.

85. Dreze and Sen, *India*, 198.

86. Dreze and Sen, *India*, 200.

87. Dreze and Sen, *India*, 55.

88. Robin Jeffrey deals with this aspect of the evolution of Kerala in his *Politics, Women and Well-Being: How Kerala Became "a Model"* (Houndmills, UK: Macmillan Press, 1992).

Chapter 3

1. The figure is taken from Sumanta Banerjee, "Assembly Polls, 2006: Elections, *Jatra* Style, in West Bengal," *Economic and Political Weekly*, 11 March 2006: 864.

2. A. M., "Suffrage in West Bengal," *Economic and Political Weekly*, 27 May 2006: 2048.

3. Author's personal interaction with voters in the districts of Birbhum and Calcutta. This assertion is also corroborated by findings from other districts of West Bengal.

4. Ashok Mitra, "Take It as Red," *The Telegraph*, 13 May 2006.

5. That the names of genuine voters were deleted became a bone of contention, and the Election Commission was inundated with complaints from West Bengal voters. In a large number of booths in Calcutta and some of its adjoining districts that are CPI (M)'s strongholds, several genuine voters were denied entry simply because in the revised list their names did not figure.

6. The major Bengali newspapers, like *Anandabazar Patrika* and *Bartaman*, devoted a lot of space to the activities of these "central" observers and hailed their role "in restoring democracy" in West Bengal by ensuring a free and fair poll.

7. D. Bandyopadhyay, "Elections and Bureaucracy in West Bengal," *Economic and Political Weekly*, 15–21 April 2006: 1417.

8. I have drawn on A. M., "Suffrage in West Bengal," which elaborated these Election Commission guidelines (pp. 2048–9).

9. A. M., "Suffrage in West Bengal," 2049.

10. Yogendra Yadav, "The Opportunities and the Challenges," *The Hindu*, 16 May 2006.

11. TABLE 3.6

Seats and Share of Votes			
Name of Conglomeration	1996 (%)	2001 (%)	2006 (%)
Left Front	203 (46.7)	199 (48.9)	235 (50.5)
Trinamul-led Alliance		60 (38.9)	30 (28.5)

Note: Figures in the parentheses are the percentage of votes obtained by the Left Front constituents.

Source: Ananda Bazar Patrika, 12 May 2006; *The Telegraph*, 13 May 2006.

12. Marcus Dam, "Left Front's Support Base Widens," *The Hindu*, 13 May 2006.

13. The best though slightly dated account of the redistributive programs is articulated in Atul Kohli, *The State and Poverty in India: The Politics of Reform* (Cambridge, UK: Cambridge University Press, 1987).

14. While explaining the success of the Left Front in rural West Bengal as compared with its performance in urban areas, Dwaipayan Bhattacharyya adopts this line of argument—which is probably plausible given the performance of the Left Front in rural constituencies. See Dwaipayan Bhattacharyya, "Ominous Outcome for Left in West Bengal," *Economic and Political Weekly*, 20 November 1999: 3268–9.

15. For an in-depth study of this symbiotic network underling the agrarian changes in West Bengal in a comparative perspective, see Ben Rogaly, Barbara Harris-White, and Sugata Bose, eds., *Sonar Bangla: Agricultural Growth and Agrarian Change in West Bengal and Bangladesh* (New Delhi: Sage, 1999).

16. For a sympathetic account of the Left Front rule, see Atul Kohli, *Democracy and Discontent: India's Crisis of Governability* (Cambridge, UK: Cambridge University Press, 1991), 267–96.

17. Monobina Gupta, *Left Politics in Bengal: Time Travels among Bhadralok Marxists* (New Delhi: Orient Blackswan, 2010), 39.

18. T. J. Nossiter, *Marxist State Governments in India: Politics, Economics and Society* (London: Pinter Publishers, 1988), 139.

19. Sudhir Roy, *Marxist Politics of West Bengal in Opposition and in Governance, 1947–2001* (Kolkata: Progressive Publishers, 2007), 200.

20. Articulating the views of those who are critical of the West Bengal panchayats, Poromesh Acharya argues that, "no doubt, there emerged a new generation of leadership in rural West Bengal but the class and caste background of the new leadership" remain more or less unchanged. "There developed a new institutional structure, decentralized in form but still dominated by the middle and rich peasants. The agricultural labourers and poor peasants, though not in proportion, have their representatives in the new structure but their participation in the decision making process is still a far cry." See Poromesh Acharya, "Panchayats and Left Politics in West Bengal," *Economic and Political Weekly*, 29 May 1993: 1080.

21. Attributing the unparalleled success of the Left Front in every election in West Bengal since 1977 to an all-pervasive party organization, Partha Chatterjee thus argues that the consistent performance of the Left Front "has a great deal to do with elaborateness, intricacy and discipline of the CPI (M)'s organization in its campaign to mobilize votes." Apart from this, the CPI (M) also utilized a parallel structure consisting of units from its mass front organizations, more often the cultural front units. What sustains the party is its discipline, which is reinforced through the electoral process. Thus even from the perspective of the vote-getting machine, it is not as if campaign issues and political debate are irrelevant. They are "relevant because without them the machine cannot be fed with the political support which it can convert into votes." See Partha Chatterjee, *The Present History of West Bengal: Essays in Political Criticism* (Delhi: Oxford University Press, 1997), 141, 151, 157.

22. Gupta, *Left Politics in Bengal*, 39.

23. TABLE 3.7

Number Candidates Who Won Unopposed

Year	Number of Seats, Uncontested	Percentage of Total Seats
1978	338	0.73
1983	332	0.74
1988	4,200	8.00
1993	1,716	2.81
1998	600	1.35
2003	6,800	11.00

Source: D. Bandyopadhyay, "Caucus and Masses: West Bengal Panchayats," *Economic and Political Weekly*, 15–21 November 2003: 4826.

24. Bandyopadhyay, "Caucus and Masses," 4826.

25. Dwaipayan Bhattacharyya, "Limits to Legal Radicalism: Land Reform and the Left Front in West Bengal," *Calcutta Historical Journal* 16, no. 1 (January–June 1994): 86.

26. West Bengal CPI (M) State Committee Directives on Panchayats, CPI (M) State Committee, 31 January 1994 (unpublished), courtesy of the late B. T. Ranadeve.

27. West Bengal CPI (M) State Committee Directives on Panchayats.

28. Maitreesh Ghatak and Maitreya Ghatak, "Recent Reforms in the Panchayat System in West Bengal: Toward Greater Participatory Governance?," *Economic and Political Weekly*, 5–11 January 2002: 56.

29. A press statement by Maheshwar Murmu, the minister for tribal affairs, on 29 July 2005. *Dainik Statesman*, 30 July 2005.

30. Yogendra Yadav and Sanjay Kumar, "Why the Left Will Win Once Again," *The Hindu*, 16 April 2006.

31. The expression, Brand Buddha, highlighting the overwhelming importance of the West Bengal chief minister, Buddhadeb Bhattarcharjee, in winning the 2006 assembly election does not appear to hold much weight with the Left Front leadership because the 2006 historic victory was primarily an outcome of sustained pro-people activities by an organized party at the grassroots. The Left Front chairman, Biman Basu, made this point in the press statement. *Ananda Bazar Patrika* (Kolkata), 16 May 2006.

32. B. T. Randive, "The Sarkaria Commission Report: Empty Rhetoric," *The Marxist* 6 (January–March 1988): 19.

33. Suhrid Sankar Chattopadhyay, "Left Landslide," *Frontline*, 2 June 2006: 10.

34. The press conference, addressed by Buddhadeb Bhattacharjee on 12 May 2006. *Ananda Bazaar Patrika*, 13 May 2006.

35. This summary of the press conference of Bhattacharjee is drawn from Chattopadhyay, "Left Landslide," 10.

36. *Ananda Bazaar Patrika*, 13 May 2006.

37. Buddhadeb Bhattacharjee's press statement in *The Statesman*, 12 May 2006.

38. This is drawn on the press conference of Buddhadeb Bhattacharjee held on 15 May 2006. *Ananda Bazar Patrika* reproduced the views in its 16 May 2006 edition.

39. The figures are drawn from Yadav, "The Opportunities and the Challenges."

40. Thus it was not surprising that the strike over the hike of petrol price on 13 June 2006 was observed by resorting to only "five minute *chakka* jam" and street-corner meetings. This was inconceivable in the immediate past when CPI (M) cadres were instructed to paralyze civic life. The CPI (M) leadership announced that it would restrict the strike to a "token protest" because, as the chief minister stated, "it would give wrong signals to the investors." To highlight the changed perception of the Left Front, a newspaper thus reports, "While Left MPs in Delhi were busy courting arrest, Buddhadeb Bhattacharjee's cabinet colleagues and senior bureaucrats were working on details of the land acquisition plan for the state's FDI projects of Indonesia's Salem Group." *Indian Express*, 14 June 2006.

41. Paranjoy Guha Thakurta dwells on this question in his "When Left Is Right," *Times of India*, 17 May 2006.

42. Atul Kohli, *Democracy and Development in India: From Socialism to Pro-Business* (New Delhi: Oxford University Press, 2009), 367.

43. D. Bandyopadhyay, "West Bengal: Enduring the Status Quo," *Economic and Political Weekly*, 26 May 2001: 1011–3.

44. Kohli, *Democracy and Development in India*, 388.

45. Arlid Englesen Rudd, "Land and Power: The Marxist Conquest in Rural Bengal," *Modern Asian Studies* 28, no. 2 (1994): 369.

46. Rudd, "Land and Power," 370.

47. Rudd, "Land and Power," 379.

48. Dwaipayan Bhattacharya, "Politics of Middleness: The Changing Character of the Communist Party of India (Marxist) in Rural West Bengal (1977–90)," in *Sonar Bangla? Agricultural Growth and Agrarian Change in West Bengal and Bangladesh*, ed. Ben Rogaly, Barbara Harris White, and Sugata Bose (New Delhi: Sage, 1999), 293.

49. Prasenjit Maity, "Violence of Politics and Politics of Violence," *Seminar* 433 (2000): 38.

50. Bhattacharya, "Politics of Middleness," 296.

51. In terms of organizational network, the probable parallel is the Bahujan Samaj Party, which supports its electoral campaign with a well-entrenched election machinery. The Bahujan Samaj Party begins its electoral drill well in advance by choosing the candidates for most of the constituencies to develop better and more intimate interaction between them and the voters. Divided into twenty-five sectors (with ten polling booths in one sector), each constituency is being looked after by the High Command. Each booth, roughly with one thousand voters, is the responsibility of a nine-member committee comprising at least one woman to motivate and mobilize women voters.

52. Abhirup Sarkar, "Political Economy of West Bengal," *Economic and Political Weekly*, 28 January 2006.

53. Banerjee, "Assembly Polls, 2006," 865.

54. Yogendra Yadav, "How West Bengal Voted," *The Hindu*, 16 May 2006.

55. Bhaskar Ghose, "A Necessary Ritual," *The Telegraph*, 9 June 2004.

56. Mitra, "Take It as Red."

57. The height of the Congress factional fight was witnessed in Murshidabad where the district president who was a member of parliament, set up candidates in two constituencies in his district to contest the party's official nominees. Such was the state of affairs in the party that he could not be disciplined. He, in fact, shared the dais with the all-Indian party president, Sonia Gandhi, during the campaign, and nobody dared to even mildly reprimand him. *The Telegraph*, 12 May 2006.

58. Banerjee, "Assembly Polls, 2006," 866.

59. Mitra, "Take It as Red."

60. While explaining the objective of the coalition (when the CPI [M] itself could have formed the government in the state), *People's Democracy* hailed the coalition government under the CPI (M) stewardship as "the best example of unity" drawing upon more or less similar kinds of ideological belief. See *People's Democracy*, 11 November 1985. The continuity of the Left Front hegemony in West Bengal for more than two decades is no mean achievement in a period that saw radical changes in the political layout of the country. Its achievement in rural areas in particular— its land reform measures, the registration of sharecroppers (*operation barga*), and the panchayati system—has marked the state off from the rest of the country. Moreover, the CPI (M), in particular, has excellent organizational machinery at its disposal. With its long tradition of political mass mobilization and struggles in championing the cause of the working class, urban and rural workers, the poor peasants, and the middle-class employees, the Left Front has not only sustained but also gradually expanded its organizational network within the state.

61. This argument is followed in detail by Amrita Basu, "Parliamentary Communism as a Historical Phenomenon: The CPI (M) in West Bengal," in *Parties and Party Politics in India*, ed. Zoya Hasan (New Delhi: Oxford University Press, 2002), 341–2.

62. TABLE 3.8

Number of Seats Won, 1977–2006

Year	Left Front	CPI (M)
1977	231	178
1982	238	174
1987	251	187
1991	232	185
1996	203	150
2001	199	143
2006	235	176

Source: Ashok Mitra, "Take It as Red."

63. In the June 2005 election to the Kolkata Municipal Corporation, the Left Front regained its control by ousting the former coalition led by the Trinamul Congress. The poll reversal

suggests that it would not be correct to argue that the Left Front's support base is confined to the rural areas only; instead, this victory clearly placed the CPI (M)-led Left Front firmly in Calcutta as well. As the poll outcome shows, the Left Front obtained fourteen more seats than its tally in the earlier poll in 2000.

TABLE 3.9

Number of Seats, Won by Alliances in 2005 Kolkata Municipal Election

Parties	Number of Seats, 2005	Number of Seats, 2000
Left Front	75	61
Trinamul-led Coalition	45	61
Congress-led Coalition	19	15
Independent	2	4
Total	141	141

Source: Ananda Bazar Patrika, 22 June 2005.

64. CPI (M) press release, 26 May 2004, *Times of India* (New Delhi), 27 May 2004.

Chapter 4

1. An earlier version was published as "The Left Front's 2009 Lok Sabha Poll Debacle in West Bengal, India," *Asian Survey* 51, no. 2 (2011): 290–310; and as "The 2011 State Assembly Election in West Bengal: The Left Front Washed-Out!," *Journal of South Asian Development* 6, no. 2 (2011): 143–167.

2. Interview with a former CPI (M) member of village-level local committee in the district of Birbhum in West Bengal on 2 April 2009. He expressed his views on condition of anonymity.

3. For a sympathetic account of the Left Front rule, see Atul Kohli, *Democracy and Discontent: India's Crisis of Governability* (Cambridge, UK: Cambridge University Press, 1991), 267–96).

4. Articulating the views of those who are critical of the West Bengal panchayats, Poromesh Acharya argues that "no doubt, there emerged a new generation of leadership in rural West Bengal but the class and caste background of the new leadership" remain more or less unchanged. "There developed a new institutional structure, decentralized in form but still dominated by the middle and rich peasants. The agricultural labourers and poor peasants, though not in proportion, have their representatives in the new structure but their participation in the decision making process is still a far cry." See Poromesh Acharya, "Panchayats and Left Politics in West Bengal," *Economic and Political Weekly*, 29 May 1993: 1080.

5. Arild Engelsen Rudd, "Land and Power: The Marxist Conquest of Rural Bengal," *Modern Asian Studies* 28, no. 2 (1994): 369.

6. Jurgen Dige Pedersen elaborates this argument in his "India's Industrial Dilemmas in West Bengal," *Asian Survey* 41, no. 4 (2001); 600–3.

7. *The Times of India*, 17 May 2009.

8. Seeking to create an environment conducive for private business, the Left Front government pushed the SEZ Act in 2003, two years before it was adopted by the union government. SEZs are generally defined as specially demarcated zones that are exempt from various duties and tariffs by virtue of their treatment as a foreign territory for the purposes of trade operations. The scheme offers a vast range of economic activities including manufacturing, services, trading, reconditioning, labeling, repacking, and warehousing.

9. Author's interview with Haran Mondal, a Nandigram farmer, on 29 March 2007.

10. Press statement of Prakash Karat, CPI (M) general secretary, *The Times of India*, 24 March 2007.

11. Press statement of A. B. Bardhan, CPI general secretary, *The Times of India*, 23 March 2007.

12. Press interview of Abdur Rezzak Molla, the former CPI (M) land and land reforms minister, on 13 May 2011. *The Times of India*, 14 May 2011. While explaining the left debacle, Molla thus angrily stated, "Had they paid heed to my words earlier then we wouldn't have faced such a situation. I have heard that all big leaders of our party lost. He [Buddhadeb Bhattacharjee, the incumbent chief minister] cannot catch a benign snake and he went to catch a poisonous cobra. Industry is a poisonous snake and they did not listen to my words." Mollah retained his Canning (east) seat defeating his rival with a huge margin while his ministerial colleagues, including the chief minister, were soundly defeated.

13. Dipanjan Rai Chaudhuri and Satya Sivaraman, "Nandigram: Six Months Later," *Economic and Political Weekly*, 13 October 2007: 4103.

14. *Ananda Bazar Patrika*, 13 November 2007.

15. Sumanta Banerjee, "West Bengal's Next Quinquennium, and the Future of the Indian Left," *Economic and Political Weekly*, 4 June 2011: 16.

16. Comparative performance of the Left Front, the Congress, and the Trinamul Congress in Zila Parishad election. The total number of Zila Parishads in West Bengal is seventeen.

	2003	2008
Left Front	15	13
Congress	2	2
Trinamul Congress	–	2

Source: *The Telegraph*, 21 May 2008.

17. The poll outcome in four districts of West Bengal:

East Medinipur

	2003	2008
Left Front	50	17
Congress	–	–
Trinamul Congress	2	35
Socialist Unity Center	–	–

South 24 Parganas

	2003	2008
Left Front	61	31
Congress	–	3
Trinamul Congress	3	34
Socialist Unity Centre	2	5

North Dinajpur

Left Front	16	8
Congress	5	16
Trinamul Congress	–	–

Malda

Left Front	19	14
Congress	10	18
Trinamul Congress	–	–

Source: The Telegraph, 21 May 2008; The Statesman, 21 May 2008.

18. Sheikh Sukur's statements are quoted from *Tehelka*, 30 May 2009: 31.

19. Jamal's statement is quoted from *Tehelka*, 30 May 2009: 31.

20. Beneficiaries of Operation Barga (1978–1982) were little over 1.5 million households. Little over two million households received vested land on an average of one-half acres per household. Resurgence of agriculture and continued peace in rural areas following the implementation of Operation Barga made those with land Left Front friendly. As a result of radical land reforms, twenty-five to thirty million voters in rural Bengal could be counted as friendly to the incumbent Left Front government. D. Bandyopadhyay, "West Bengal: Enduring Status Quo," *Economic and Political Weekly*, 26 May 2001: 668–72.

21. Safiq Hussain's statement is quoted from *Tehelka*, 30 June 2009: 31.

22. Author's interview with a college teacher in Siuri in the district of Birbhum, 2 June 2009.

23. Aditya Nigam, "How the Sickle Slashed the Left," *Tehelka*, 30 May 2009: 45.

24. Abhijit Dasgupta, "On the Margins: Muslims in West Bengal," *Economic and Political Weekly*, 18 April 2009: 96.

25. Nigam, "How the Sickle Slashed the Left," 45.

26. Author's interview with a local school teacher in a village, close to Siuri, the district headquarters of the district of Birbhum.

27. The Todi family, which never endorsed Rizwanur Rahman's marriage with the daughter of the eldest Todi, was charged with murdering the groom. This resulted in a massive civil society campaign in Calcutta involving various sections of the city. The case is pending before the judiciary. The local media took up the issue and provoked an organized campaign that forced the state government to suspend the top city cops who were suspected to have had a role in concealing the alleged culprits.

28. The local vernacular media, especially *Bartaman* and *Ananda Bazar Patrika*, are full of such stories.

29. These inputs are drawn on Dipankar Basu, "The Left and the 15th Lok Sabha Election," *Economic and Political Weekly*, 30 May 2009: 10–15.

30. Rajarshi Dasgupta, "The CPI (M) Machine in West Bengal: Two Village Narratives from Kochbihar and Malda," *Economic and Political Weekly*, 22 February–9 March 2009: 71.

31. Monobina Gupta, *Left Politics in Bengal: Time Travels among Bhadralok Marxists* (New Delhi: Orient Blackswan, 2010), 141.

32. Gupta, *Left Politics in Bengal*, 141.

33. Interview of Shaoli Mitra, published in *The Times of India*, 7 May 2009.

34. Shuvaprasanna, "'Ozymandias' Certain Fall," *Tehelka*, 23 May 2009: 9.

35. A. M., "The State of the CPI (M) in West Bengal," *Economic and Political Weekly*, 25 July 2009: 8

36. Basu, "The Left and the 15th Lok Sabha Elections," 13.

37. Author's interview with Islam Ali, a sharecropper benefiting from the Operation Barga on 2 June 2009.

38. Press interview of Abdur Rezzak Molla, the CPI (M) land and land reforms minister in the West Bengal Left Front government on 28 May 2009, *Tehelka*, 6 June 2009.

39. Arild Engelsen Ruud, "Embedded Bengal? The Case for Politics," *Forum for Development Studies* 2 (1999): 238.

40. Atul Kohli, "From Elite Activism to Democratic Consolidation: The Rise of Reform Communism in West Bengal," in *Dominance and State Power in Modern India: Decline of a Social Order*, Vol. 2, ed. M. S. A. Rao and Francine Frankel (New Delhi: Oxford University Press, 1990), 380.

41. This argument has forcefully been made by Pranab Bardhan, Sandip Mitra, Dilip Mookherjee, and Abhirup Sarkar in "Local Democracy and Clientelism: Implications for Political Stability in West Bengal," *Economic and Political Weekly*, 28 February 2009: 46–58.

42. Banerjee, "West Bengal's Next Quinquennium and the Future of the Indian Left," 17.

43. For a perceptive analysis of the Amlashole starvation death, see Oliver Rubin, *Analyzing the Political Dynamics of Starvation Death in West Bengal* (Arbejdspapir: Institut for Statskundskab), 2008.

44. A press statement by Maheshwar Murmu, the minister for tribal affairs, on 29 July 2005. *Dainik Statesman*, 30 July 2005.

45. Rudd, "From Untouchable to Communist," 268.

46. Rudd, "From Untouchable to Communist," 268.

47. Partha Chatterjee, "The Coming Crisis in West Bengal," *Economic and Political Weekly*, 28 February 2009: 45.

48. CPI (M), Burdwan District Committee, *Samikshna Ashtam Lok Sabha Nirbachan* [Analysis of Eighth Lok Sabha Election] (Burdwan: CPI [M], 28 February 1985), 26–7, 31–2.

49. Dwaipayan Bhattacharya, "Of Control and Factions: The Changing Party: Society in Rural West Bengal," *Economic and Political Weekly*, 28 February 2009: 69.

50. Lalgarh, the relatively indiscreet hamlet in West Medinipur, hogged the limelight in June 2009 with the decision of the union government to send paramilitary troops to combat the ultra-left-wing extremists there. Lalgarh, reeling in severe poverty, remains a backward area since the government has hardly addressed the genuine socio-economic grievances of the local inhabitants

meaningfully. In the last thirty years, the Left Front has not built roads to connect far-flung villages, with virtually one bus running between the district headquarter of Jhargram and Bel-pahari daily. Also, the adjoining villages are Amlashole and Amjhora from where the first hunger deaths were reported in the state, pointing to the ruling Left Front government's oppression and dispossession. The National Rural Employment Guarantee Act has also failed to provide relief to the local tribal population who live mostly on forest resources. So, there is no respite for the rural poor who are increasingly being drawn to the ultra-left-wing Maoists to reclaim what is due to them. (This is drawn from *The Times of India*, 18–19 June 2008, and *The Hindu*, 18–19 June 2009.)

51. Sumanta Banerjee, "Assembly Polls: 2006 Election: *Jatra* Style in West Bengal," *Economic and Political Weekly*, 11 March 2006: 865.

52. Yogendra Yadav, "How West Bengal Voted," *The Hindu*, 16 May 2006.

53. Besides the Congress, the *mahajot* (grand alliance) includes the Socialist Unity Centre of India and the Party of Democratic Socialism.

54. M. J. Akbar, "In Bengal, the British PM Will Get Bang for Investment Buck," *Times of India* (New Delhi), 17 November 2013: 12.

55. Dwaipayan Bhattacharya and Kumar Rana, "West Bengal Panchayat Elections: What Does It Mean for the Left?" *Economic and Political Weekly*, 14 September 2013: 11.

56. Banerjee, "West Bengal's Next Quinquennium," 19.

57. Dwaipayan Bhattacharya, "Left in the Lurch: The Demise of the World's Longest Elected Regime?" *Economic and Political Weekly*, 16 January 2010: 52.

58. Buddhadeb Bhattacharjee's statement on the occasion of the forty-third anniversary of *Ganashakti* (the CPI [M] daily newspaper), 3 January 2009.

59. Gupta, *Left Politics in Bengal*, 129–30.

60. Dasgupta, "The CPI (M) Machinery in West Bengal," 81.

61. Ross Mallick, "Refugee Resettlement in Forest Reserves: West Bengal Policy Reversal and the Marichjhapi Massacre," *Journal of Asian Studies* 58, no. 1 (1999): 108.

62. Annu Jalais, "Dwelling on Marichjhanpi: When Tigers Became 'Citizens,' Refugees 'Tiger-Food,'" *Economic and Political Weekly*, 23 April 2005: 1760.

63. Atharobaki Biswas, "Why Dandyakaranya a Failure, Why Mass Exodus, Where Solution?," *The Oppressed Indian* 4, no. 4 (1982): 19.

64. The figures quoted from the National Sample Survey (sixty-first round) are drawn on Praful Bidwai, "Reading the Verdict," *Frontline*, 19 June 2009: 93.

65. Ashis Nandy, "The End of Arrogance," *Special Issue: Verdict, 2009, Tehleka*, 30 May 2009: 8.

66. Hindol Sengupta, "The Desai Verdict," *The Hindu*, 31 May 2009; an interview given by Meghnad Desai.

67. The CPI (M) Central Committee statement after the conclusion of the meeting on 12 June 2011 was reproduced in *The Hindu* (New Delhi), 13 June 2011; *The Economic Times* (New Delhi), 13 June 2011; and *The Telegraph* (Kolkata), 13 June 2011.

PART II

1. These details are drawn on *Times of India* (New Delhi), 29 May 2013.

2. *Hindustan Times* (New Delhi), 30 May 2013.

3. The editorial in *Economic and Political Weekly* (Mumbai), 8 June 2013: 8.

4. Police report is quoted in the *Times of India* (New Delhi), 31 May 2013.

5. Chapter 4 of the draft report of subgroup IV of Committee on State Agrarian Relations and Unfinished Task of Land Reforms, *Committee on State Agrarian Relations and Unfinished Task of Land Reforms: Draft Report* (New Delhi: Ministry of Rural Development, Government of India, 2013), 9.

6. Quoted from *Hindustan Times* (New Delhi), 2 June 2013.

7. Harinder Baweja, "The Dark Side of a Very Red Moon," *Hindustan Times* (New Delhi), 3 June 2013.

8. Interview with Ajit Buxla, conducted in his hideout in the district of Malkangiri, 9 December 2006.

9 . Nihar Nayak, "Maoists in Orissa Growing Tentacles and a Dormant State," South Asian Terrorist Portal. Online: http://www.satp.org/satporgtp/publication/faultlines/volume17/nihar.htm. Interview with Bidhu Bhusan Mishra, the Inspector General of Police, Government of Orissa.

10. Ministry of Home Affairs, Internal Security Division, *Status Paper on the Naxal Problem* (New Delhi: Ministry of Home Affairs, 2006), 1.

11. *Hindustan Times*, 21 January 2007.

12. Second Administrative Commission, *Eighth Report, Combating Terrorism* (New Delhi: Government of India, 2008), 8–9.

13. Gautam Navlakha, "Maoists in India," *Economic and Political Weekly*, 3 June 2006: 2187.

14. Minutes of the Twentieth Meeting of the Coordination Centre, Ministry of Home Affairs (IS Division), Government of India, 31 March 2006, quoted in Nandini Sundar, *Subalterns and Sovereigns: An Anthropological History of Bastar (1854–2006)* (New Delhi: Oxford University Press, 2008), 267.

15. Information drawn on interviews conducted in Malkangiri in December 2008.

16. Information available from the *Times of India*, 6 January 2009.

Chapter 5

1. Richard Mahapatra, *Unquiet Forests: A Comprehensive Look at How Forest Laws Are Triggering Conflicts in India with a Focus on Naxalite Movement* (New Delhi: Prem Bhatia Memorial Trust, 2004–2005), 4.

2. Ajit K. Doval, "Code Red, Naxals: The Biggest Threat," Sunday Hindustan *Times*, 26 March 2006. Doval is the former director of the Intelligence Bureau.

3. Interview with Ganapathy, General Secretary, CPI (Maoist). Text of the interview was released by Azad, spokesperson, CPI (Maoist), in April 2007.

4. In certain affected areas various Naxal groups have paralyzed the official mechanisms of governance. In these so-called liberated areas the Naxals are effectively running a parallel system of governance where they impose their dictates through their military units; they even collect tax (ransom), and in those areas they claim that they have established the Janata Sarkar.

5. These details are taken from Gautam Navlakha, *Days and Nights in the Heartland of Rebellion* (New Delhi: Penguin, 2012), 54.

6. Javeed Alam, "Communist Politics in Search of Hegemony," in *Wages of Freedom: Fifty Years of Indian Nation-State*, ed. Partha Chatterjee (New Delhi: Oxford University Press, 1998), 183.

7. Alam, "Communist Politics in Search of Hegemony," 184.

8. For details of these movements, see Sumanta Banerjee, *India's Simmering Revolution: The Naxalite Uprising* (New Delhi: Selection Service Syndicate, 1984), 18–28.

9. "Spring Thunder over India" (editorial), *Peking People's Daily*, 5 July 1967; reproduced in Samar Sen, Debabrata Panda, and Ashis Lahiri, eds., *Naxalbari and After: A Frontier Anthology*, Vol. 2 (Calcutta: Kathashilpa, 1978), 188.

10. Kanu Sanyal, "More about Naxalbari," April 1973, in Sen et al., *Naxalbari and After*, 330.

11. "Spring Thunder over India," 188.

12. Partha N. Mukherji, "Class and Ethnic Movements in India: In Search of a Pertinent Paradigm for Democracy and Nation Building in the Third World," in *When Democracy Makes Sense*, ed. Lars Rudebeck (Uppsala, Sweden: AKUT, 1992), 19.

13. Interview with Kanu Sanyal on 16 January 1991, quoted in Arun Prasad Mukherjee, *Maoist Spring Thunder: The Naxalite Movement (1967–1972)* (Calcutta: KP Bagchi, 2007), 3.

14. Kanu Sanyal, quoted in Sen et al., *Naxalbari and After*, 5.

15. Charu Majumdar, "Why Guerrilla War," in *Ghatana Prabaha* 2, no. 1, quoted in Sen et al., *Naxalbari and After*, 6.

16. Charu Majumdar, "On the Political-Organization Report," 13 September 1970, reproduced in Sen et al., *Naxalbari and After*, 293–4.

17. Ashim Chatterjee, "Hold High the Genuine Lessons of Naxalbari," in Sen et al., *Naxalbari and After*, 388–9.

18. Prabhat Jana, "Naxalbari and After: An Appraisal," 12–19 May 1973, in Sen et al., *Naxalbari and After*, 123.

19. Jana, "Naxalbari and After," 124.

20. Jana, "Naxalbari and After," 125.

21. This paragraph is based on the testimonial of Souren Bose, one of the top Naxal leaders who was sent to China during the heyday of the movement to ascertain the support of the Chinese Communist Party and the government. Bose's statements were recorded on 11, 20, and 24 April 1972 while he was in custody. These statements are quoted in Mukherjee, *Maoist Spring Thunder*, 232–5.

22. Praksh Louis, *People Power: The Naxalite Movement in Central Bihar* (Delhi: Wordsmiths, 2002), 277.

23. Partha Chatterjee, *The Present History of West Bengal: Essays in Political Criticism* (Delhi: Oxford University Press, 1997), 92–3.

24. *Thirty Years of Naxalbari*, an undated publication of CPI (ML) Liberation.

25. Bela Bhatia, "Naxalite Movement in Central Bihar," *Economic and Political Weekly*, 9 April 2005.

26. "History of Naxalism," *Hindustan Times*, 15 December 2005. Online: http://www.hindustantimes.com/news-feed/nm2/history-of-naxalism/article1-6545.aspx.

27. A party document of CPI (ML) Liberation titled *The General Programme*.

28. "30 Years of Naxalbari," *Vanguard* [n.d.], 30. Online: http://naxalresistance.wordpress.com/2007/09/17/30-years-of-naxalbari/. An undated Maoist literature; *Vanguard* was the organ of PWG.

29. "Path of People's War in India—Our Tasks!" is a comprehensive PWG party document highlighting its aims, objectives, and strategies. The document was adopted by All-India Party Congress in 1992. I obtained this document from one of the principal ideologues of the PWG.

30. Sharvan, the then-secretary of Bihar State Committee of CPI (ML) People's War, in an interview given to *People's March* 2, no. 3 (March 2001).

31. "Joint Declaration by Communist Party of India (ML) People's War and CPI (ML) (Party Unity)," August 1998; People's War literature.

32. "Joint Declaration by Communist Party of India (ML) People's War and CPI (ML)," 1998.

33. Interview of Muppalla Lakshmana Rao (alias Ganapathy), the then head of the Communist Party of India (ML) People's War. Online: http://www.rediff.com/news/1998/oct/07gana.htm.

34. *State Repression*, report on the special conference that was posted on a website (www.cpimlpwg/repression.html) that claimed itself as the unofficial website of PW. The website has since been withdrawn. During its existence the site claimed to be the unofficial website of PWG. But during my interaction with many PW rank and file, I found that it was no less than their official website.

35. *State Repression*.

36. In response to a government decision to launch a coordinated action against the Naxalites using police forces of the various Indian states affected by Naxal violence, the PWG formed the PGA, its military wing, in December 2000 by reorganizing its guerrilla force. The PGA functions under a single operational command, the Central Military Commission. In the Indian state where the PGA has a presence, there is a State Military Commission, and in special guerrilla zones there is a Zonal Military Commission. A Regional Military Commission supervises a group of State Military Commissions or Zonal Military Commissions. Each Regional Military Commission reports to the Central Military Commission. All armed cadre of the PWG are organized under the PGA. See "People's Guerrilla Army," South Asian Terrorist Portal. Online: http://www.satp.org/satporgtp/countries/india/terroristoutfits/peoples_guerrilla_arms_left_wing_extremists.htm.

37. "30 Years of Naxalbari," 36.

38. *Red Star, Special Issue*, 20, as quoted by Aloke Banerjee, *Inside MCC Country* (Calcutta: K. Das, 2003). *Red Star* was the English-language organ of the MCC. Also quoted in "MCC India Three Decades Leading Battalions of the Poor," published online by A World to Win. Online: http://www.awtw.org/back_issues/mcc_india.htm. Though it denies it, many treat this as the unofficial organ of the Revolutionary Internationalist Movement.

39. Ganapathy, in an interview given on the occasion of the formation of CPI (Maoist). *People's March* 5, no. 11–12 (November–December 2004).

40. "Maoist-Influenced Revolutionary Organizations in India," 25 November 2008. Online: http://www.massline.info/India/Indian_Groups.htm.

41. "Maoist-Influenced Revolutionary Organizations in India," 2008.

42. Ganapathy, in an interview given on the occasion of the formation of CPI (Maoist). *People's March* 5, no. 11–12 (November–December 2004).

43. Ganapathy, in an interview given on the occasion of the formation of CPI (Maoist). *People's March* 5, no. 11–12 (November–December 2004).

44. *State Repression*.

45. Political Resolution of the Communist Party of India (ML), 1969.

46. Banerjee, *India's Simmering Revolution*, 92.

47. George J. Kunnath, "Becoming a Naxalite in Rural Bihar: Class Struggle and Its Contradictions," *Journal of Peasant Studies* 33, no. 1 (January 2006): 92.

48. Mukherjee, *Maoist Spring Thunder*, 30.

49. Kanu Sanyal, "More about Naxalbari," April 1973, in Sen et al., *Naxalbari and After*, 347.

50. Partha N. Mukherji. "Naxalbari Movement and the Peasant Revolt in North Bengal," in *Social Movements in India*, ed. M. S. A. Rao (repr. New Delhi: Manohar, 2008), 75.

51. Mukherji, "Naxalbari Movement and the Peasant Revolt in North Bengal," 76.

Chapter 6

1. Excerpts of the letter of Satyanarayana Reddy (Kosa), printed in the *Hindustan Times*, 8 February 2009.

2. CPI (Maoist) Documents: Party Constitution. Online: http://www.satp.org/satporgtp/countries/india/maoist/documents/papers/partyconstitution.htm.

3. These sentences are literally lifted from Mao's 1938 report on the Chinese Communist Party, presented in sixth plenary session of the Sixth Central Committee. Mao Tse-tung, *Selected Works of Mao Tse-tung*, Vol. 2 (Peking: Foreign Language Press, 1975), 204.

4. Quoted from the CPI (Maoist) Constitution, reproduced in the appendix.

5. The definition of democratic centralism by Vinod Mishra, a Naxalite ideologue, is quoted by Arun Kumar in his "Violence and Political Culture: Politics of the Ultra Left in Bihar," *Economic and Political Weekly*, 22 November 2003: 4983.

6. Mao Tse-Tung, "The Role of the Chinese Communist Party in the National War," in Mao, *Selected Works*, 204; Speech delivered in October 1938.

7. The constitution is reproduced in the appendix.

8. Quoted from the constitution, which is reproduced in the appendix.

9. The following discussion is drawn from a report titled "Development and Internal Security in Chhattisgarh: Impact of Naxalite Movement," prepared by Rambhau Mhalgi Prabodhini, Mumbai, 18–20.

10. For details, see Mao, *Selected Works*, 201–5.

11. The inputs on the Maoist structure of the organization are drawn from *Tehelka* 6, no. 13 (April 2009): 12.

12. As the reports suggest, the number of farmers who have committed suicide in India between 1997 and 2007 now stands at a staggering 182,936. Close to two-third of these suicides have occurred in the five states of Maharashtra, Karnataka, Andhra Pradesh, Madhya Pradesh, and Chhattisgarh. Of these states, the Vidarbha region of Maharashtra, where Maoism seems to have struck an emotional chord with the local population, accounts for the largest number of suicides, with the largest number of suicides recorded in the district of Gadchiroli. P. Sainath, "The Largest Wave of Suicides in History," *Counterpunch*, 12 February 2009.

13. As the media report underlines, the north Gondia division under the Maharashtra State Committee of the CPI (Maoist) maintains two platoons (located around Korchi) and seven guerrilla squads; the north Gadchiroli division, under the Dandakaranya Special Zone Council, has one platoon and six guerrilla squads, and there are two platoons and two guerrilla squads in south Gadchiroli. *Hindustan Times*, 8 February 2009.

14. Drawn from the report of Presley Thomas of the *Hindustan Times*. The report was reproduced in the *Hindustan Times*, 8 February 2009.

15. The statement of the police officer (on conditions of anonymity) was quoted in the *Hindustan Times*, 8 February 2009.

16. The police report that was reproduced in the *Hindustan Times*, 8 February 2009, confirms this.

17. The statement of Ganapathy is quoted in a Maoist document entitled "Communist Party of India (Maoist)." Online: http://www.satp.org/satporgtp/countries/india/terroristoutfits/CPI_M.htm.

18. Interview by the Maoist spokesperson, Azad, April 2007. Online: http://satp.org/satporgtp/countreis/india/terroristoutfits/CPI_M.htm.

19. CPI (Maoist) Documents: Party Constitution: Online: http://www.satp.org/satporgtp/countries/india/maoist/documents/papers/partyconstitution.htm. The discussion on *Janathana Sarkar* is drawn on the CPI (Maoist) document titled "Policy Programme of Janathana Sarkar."

20. G. S. Ganapathy's interview with Jan Myrdal and Navlakha, January 2010, excerpted in Gautam Navlakha, *Days and Nights in the Heartland of Rebellion* (New Dehli: Penguin, 2012), 82–3.

21. The pamphlet is reproduced in Navlakha, *Days and Nights in the Heartland of Rebellion*, 2012, 86.

22. The pamphlet is reproduced in Navlakha, *Days and Nights in the Heartland of Rebellion*, 87.

23. The report of the special zonal committee of 28 April 2009, reproduced in Navlakha, *Days and Nights in the Heartland of Rebellion*, 78.

24. *Sunday Times* (New Delhi), 22 February 2009, *Tehelka* 6, no. 5 (7 February 2009); *Tehelka* 6, no. 13 (4 April 2009).

25. Report by Dan Morrison in the *Christian Science Monitor*, 9 September 2008.

26. The report of the social audit of the *Janathana Sarkar* in Chhattisgarh.

27. The statement of a tribal in Bastar, quoted in Navlakha, *Days and Nights in the Heartland of Rebellion*, 84.

28. Kundan Kumar, "Confronting Extractive Capital," *Economic and Political Weekly*, 5 April 2004: 66–73.

29. Planning Commission, Government of India, *Eleventh Five Year Plan, 2007–2012 (Inclusive Growth)*, Vol. 1 (New Delhi: Oxford University Press), 239.

30. Ministry of Tribal Affairs, *Annual Reports, 2006–07* (New Delhi: Government of India, 2007), 15.

31. Jonathan Kennedy and Lawrence King, "Advasis, Maoists and Insurgency in Central Indian Tribal Belt," *European Journal of Sociology* 54, no. 1 (April 2013): 22.

32. Kennedy and King, "Advasis, Maoists and Insurgency in Central Indian Tribal Belt," 21.

33. Planning Commission of India, *Development Challenges in Extremist Affected Areas: Report of the Expert Group* (New Delhi: Government of India, 2008), 60.

34. The detailed interview of Badrana was published in *The Hindu* on 14 April 2014.

35. Kennedy and King, "Advasis, Maoists and Insurgency in the Central Indian Tribal Belt," 22.

36. *The Hindu*, in its 27 March 2014 edition, reported such instances. If the workers were lucky and the contractors agreed to give the ransom money, the kidnapped workers came back home; otherwise, they simply became pray to the Maoists.

37. Sumantra Bose, *Transforming India: Challenges to the World's Largest Democracy* (New Delhi: Picador India, 2013), 217.

38. Jairus Banaji, "The Ironies of Indian Maoism," *International Socialism* 128 (14 October 2010): 145.

39. Azad, "Maoist in India: A Rejoinder," *Economic and Political Weekly*, 14 October 2006: 4182.

40. Information obtained from independent media sources.

41. Azad, the official spokesperson of CPI (Maoist), was killed in an encounter by the Andhra Police on 2 July 2010. Arguably the principal ideologue of CPI (Maoist), Azad hailed from Krishna district of Andhra Pradesh. He went underground in 1979. He was arrested in 1975 and 1978 and jumped bail. He carried a reward of Rs. 12 lakh on his head. He was entrusted with the task of reviving the Maoist movement in Andhra Pradesh. He was a member of the Urban Sub-Committee and was in charge of the South Western Regional Bureau of Maoists, which coordinates the movement in Kerala, Karnataka, Maharashtra, and Gujarat. Kishenji, considered to be the number-two man of the CPI (Maoist) was killed in a joint operation by security forces on 24 November 2011. Born in the Peddapalli town of Karimnagar district of Andhra Pradesh, Koteshwara Rao was one of the senior most Maoist leaders who belonged to the first generation of People's War group. In 1980s he became the secretary of the People's War Group in Andhra Pradesh and then shifted to Dandakaranya in 1985. In the early 1990s he was put in charge of Bihar, then a stronghold of the Maoist Communist Centre of India. He played a crucial role in the unification of the Maoist Communist Centre of India and PWG, resulting in the birth of CPI (Maoist). After the formation of CPI (Maoist), Kishenji moved into the tribal belt of West Bengal, where he successfully built an underground guerrilla network and a structure for the Maoist operations in the whole of eastern India. The Lalgarh movement, engineered by Kishenji, is seen as his biggest achievement.

42. South Asia Terrorism Portal, 29 July 2013, http://www.satp.org.

43. *The Hindu*, 10 April 2014.

44. *The Hindu*, (New Delhi), 21 January 2014.

45. P. V. Ramana, "A Critical Evaluation of the Union Government's Response to the Maoist Challenge," *Strategic Analysis* 33, no. 5 (2009): 749.

46. *The Hindu*, New Delhi, 5 March 2014.

47. CPI (Maoist) Central Committee, press statement, 5 July 2012; *People's March*, 11 July 2012.

48. *People's March*, 18 July 2012.

49. The Tritiya Prastuti Committee had broken away from the Maoist Communist Centre before the latter merged with the CPI (Marxist–Leninist) People's War to form the CPI (Maoist) in 2004. Originally led by one "Bharatji," a front-ranking Maoist Communist Centre leader in Jharkhand, the group is now said to be headed by Brajesh Kunju and is active in Gaya and Aurangabad in Bihar; Palamau, Latehar; and some other districts in Jharkhand. The People's Liberation Front of India, formed in 2007, is said to be another Maoist splinter group. Led by Dinesh Gope, it has been wreaking havoc in Jharkhand's Khunti, Ranchi, Gumla, and Simdega districts. The Jharkhand Jana Mukti Parishad, a break-away splinter group of CPI (Maoist), was formed on 4 February 2011.

50. Bose, *Transforming India*, 222.

51. Bose, *Transforming India*, 222.

52. Manmohan Singh, India's former premier, made this statement while inaugurating the Civil Services Day in New Delhi on 21 April 2010. *The Times of India*, 21 April 2010.

53. Manmohan Singh, "Speech of India's Prime Minister at the Chief Ministers' Meeting on Naxalism," 13 April 2006, http://pmindia.gov.in/speech-details.php?nodeid=302.

54. Robert Weil, "Is the Torch Passing: The Maoist Revolution in India," *Socialism and Democracy* 25, no. 3 (2011): 67.

55. Arundhati Roy, "The Trickledown Revolution," 11 September 2010, http://www.outlookindia.com/article.aspx?267040.

56. Arijit Mazumdar, "Left-Wing Extremism and Counterinsurgency in India: The Andhra Model," *Strategic Analysis* 37, no. 4 (2013): 452.

57. Weil, "Is the Torch Passing," 74.

58. K. Balagopal, "Physiognomy of Violence," *Economic and Political Weekly*, 3 June 2006: 2183–6.

59. Planning Commission, Government of India, *Eleventh Five Year Plan 2007–2012*, 239.

60. Mazumdar, "Left-Wing Extremism and Counterinsurgency in India," 453.

61. The 1950 Constitution of India has enacted special provisions for the Tribal areas, and the Fifth Schedule (along with Article 244) spells out the nature of administration and control of Scheduled Areas and Scheduled Tribes by guaranteeing the formation of the Tribal Advisory Council for these areas and segments of the population.

62. S. Sharma, "Law of the Jungle," *The Times of India*, New Delhi, 24 April 2011.

63. Aman Sharma, "Bihar Lags in Naxal Hub Development Scheme, *India Today*, 5 February 2012, http://indiatoday.intoday.in/story/bihar-lags-in-naxal-hub-development-scheme-iap-projects/1/172110.html. The details of India's developmental schemes are drawn from this website.

64. Weil, "Is the Torch Passing," 14.

65. Mazumdar, "Left-Wing Extremism and Counterinsurgency in India," 453.

66. *The Hindu*, 13 March 2014, provides a detailed account of these encounters, including the one that took place on 11 March 2014 in Chhattisgarh that killed so many security personnel.

67. Weil, "Is the Torch Passing," 74.

68. *The Hindu*, New Delhi, 13 April 2014.

69. Bose, *Transforming India*, 208–11.

70. Bose, *Transforming India*, 210.

71. "India's Naxalites: A Spectre Haunting India," *The Economist*, 17 August 2006. Online: http://www.economist.com/node/7799247.

72. Prakash Singh, "Terror Won't Work: Both Government and Naxalites Suffer from Delusions," *Times* of *India* (New Delhi), 6 July 2007.

73. "India's Naxalites."

Chapter 7

1. Some of the ideas in this chapter appeared in some of my earlier writings, including the book *Maosim in India: Reincarnation of Ultra-Left-Wing Extremism in the Twenty-First Century* (London: Routledge, 2010), which I wrote in collaboration with Rajat Kujur.

2. The report prepared by the People's Union of Democratic Rights is reproduced in Gautam Navlakha, "Savage War for Development," *Economic and Political Weekly*, 19 April 2008: 17.

3. Binayak Sen's public appeal is reproduced in *Economic and Political Weekly*, 25 October 2008: 4, 114; this appeal was first printed in *The Hindu*, 21 October 2008.

4. Ejaz Kaiser, Prasad Nichenametla, and Alok Tikku, "War of Complexities," *Hindustan Times* (New Delhi), 2 June 2013.

5. Government of India, *Government Challenges in Extremist Affected Areas: Report of an Expert Group to Planning Commission* (New Delhi: Government of India, 2008). Online: http://planningcommission.nic.in/reports/publications/rep_dce.pdf.

6. Government of India, *Government Challenges in Extremist Affected Areas*.

7. Sumanta Banerjee, "On the Naxalite Movement: A Report with a Difference," *Economic and Political Weekly*, 24 May 2008: 11.

8. Banerjee, "On the Naxalite Movement," 11.

9. For the Kalinganagar incident, see Ish Mishra, "Heat and Dust of Highway at Kalinganagar," *Economic and Political Weekly*, 10 March 2007: 822–5. For Singur, see Ranjit Sau, "A Ballad of Singur: Progress with Human Dignity," *Economic and Political Weekly*, 25 October 2008: 10–13; for the Nandigram episode, see Bidyut Chakrabarty, "Indian Marxists Throws Down the Gauntlet in Nandigram: Development at All Costs," *Opinion Asia*, 8 December 2007. There are, however, strong views supporting the decision of the Left Front government in West Bengal for imposing SEZ in Nandigram: Malini Bhattacharya, "Nandigram and the Question of Development," *Economic and Political Weekly*, 26 May 2007; Prabhat Patnaik, "In the Aftermath of Nandigram," *Economic and Political Weekly*, 26 May 2007; [A CPI (M) supporter], "Reflections in the Aftermath of Nandigram," *Economic and Political Weekly*, 26 May 2007.

10. The entire interview with Rangam was published in *Tehelka* (New Delhi) 6, no. 13 (April 2009).

11. Quoted in Sudeep Chakravarti, *Red Sun: Travels in Naxalite Country* (New Delhi: Penguin, 2008), 293.

12. *Times of India* (New Delhi), 15 May 2008.

13. *Times of India* (New Delhi), 15 May 2007.

14. *Times of India* (New Delhi), 15 May 2007.

15. Hindutva is an ideological endeavor to redefine and restructure India's plural sociopolitical identity in accordance with the exclusive claim of the majority Hindu community seeking to erase the historically evolved societal pluralism. I pursue a detailed discussion of Hindutva in my *Indian Politics and Society since Independence* (London: Routledge, 2008), 49–52.

16. The thirty-nine-year-old bespectacled Sabyasachi Panda, who hailed from the village of Mayurjholia in the district of Nayagarh, is the son of Ramesh Chandra. Panda's father, who belonged to CPI (Marxist), served three terms as a member of the Orissa Legislative Assembly, and in 1997 he joined the ruling Biju Janata Dal. Panda is also known as Sarat and Badal in the police records. He was the secretary of the Bansadhara division of the CPI (Maoist) Andhra Pradesh–Orissa Border Special Zonal Committee and is perhaps the most charismatic leader with a large number of followers along the Orissa–Andhra Pradesh border area who are fluent in Oriya, Telegu, and Hindi. *Times of India* (New Delhi), 20 February 2008.

17. The Kandhamal incident is attributed to "deep-rooted" social and ethnic antagonism among the local communities which were engineered by "the Hindutva brigade." This argument is pursued by Harish S. Wankhede in his "The Political Context of Religious Conversion in Orissa," *Economic and Political Weekly*, 11 April 2009: 36–8.

18. This discussion is drawn from Pralay Kanungo, "Hindutva's Fury against Christians in Orissa," *Economic and Political Weekly*, 13 October 2008: 16–19.

19. This report is reproduced in *Hindustan Times*, 30 April 2008. The police got ample proof, the report confirms, "of child soldiers being recruited by Maoists when two juvenile Naxalites surrendered to Dhenkanal Superintendent of Police, Sanjay K. Kaushal on 9 April 2008." The

surrendered children, Bijaye Hembram (fourteen years old) and Babuli Darel (twelve years old), admitted that they received firearm training in a reserve forest for fifteen days. Both of them had joined the Maoists in June 2006. They also admitted to having witnessed "the killing of three forest officials by their cadres in Kankadahada forests of Dhenkanal district of Orissa in February, 2007." These inputs are available in *Hindustan Times*, 30 April 2008.

20. Interview with S. N. Pradhan of the Jharkhand Police, 18 December 2008.

21. Chakravarti, *Red Sun*, 17.

22. Information obtained from a senior police officer (intelligence), Chhattisgarh, on condition of anonymity. The officer was interviewed by Rajat Kujur on 18 August 2008.

23. "Assessment: India," *South Asia Intelligence Review*, 4, no. 7 (29 August 2005). Online: http://www.satp.org/satporgtp/sair/Archives/4_7.htm; a weekly assessment and briefing.

24. Ajay Sahni, "Look Who Is Waving Red Flag Now?," *Indian Express* (New Delhi), 2 March 2006.

25. People's Union for Civil Liberties–Chhattisgarh and People's Union for Civil Liberties–Jharkhand, People's Union for Democratic Rights–Delhi, Association for Democratic Rights–West Bengal, and Indian Association for the Protection of Democratic Rights, "Fact-Finding Report on the Salwa Judum, Dantewara District," November 2005. Online: http://www.pucl.org/Topics/Human-rights/2005/salwa-judum-report.htm. The report was released to the press on 2 December 2005.

26. Human Rights Watch, *Being Neutral Is Our Biggest Crime* (New York: Human Rights Watch, 2008).

27. *Nandini Sundar and Others vs. State of Chhattisgarh*, Writ Petition (civil) no. 250 of 2007: Counter Affidavit on Behalf of the Respondents, 22 January 2008, 308–9, 312–3, reproduced in Human Rights Watch, *Being Neutral Is Our Biggest Crime*.

28. Ministry of Home Affairs, Government of India, Annual Report, 2005–2006. Online: http://www.mha.nic.in/sites/upload_files/mha/files/pdf/ar0506-Eng.pdf. Given the clear direction from the Government of India, it may not be a mere coincidence that the Salwa Judum campaign took off in Chhattisgarh in 2005.

29. Nandini Sundar, *Subalterns and Sovereigns: An Anthropological History of Bastar (1854–2006)* (New Delhi: Oxford University Press, 2008), 279.

30. Forum for Fact-Finding Documentation and Advocacy, "Salwa Judum and Society in Bastar." This report on the functioning of these relief camps was published in the now-defunct web journal of the Forum for Fact-Finding Documentation and Advocacy: Defending Human Rights in India.

31. Forum for Fact-Finding Documentation and Advocacy, "Salwa Judum and Society in Bastar."

32. Forum for Fact-Finding Documentation and Advocacy, "Salwa Judum and Society in Bastar."

33. Forum for Fact-Finding Documentation and Advocacy, "Salwa Judum and Society in Bastar."

34. Interview by Rangam, the Naxal Commander involved in an anti–Salwa Judum campaign in Chhattisgarh, *Tehelka* 6, no. 13 (April 2009).

35. Quoted from a report prepared by Ajit Sahi, which was published in *Tehalka* 6, no. 13 (2009): 12–13.

36. Sundar, *Subalterns and Sovereigns*, 287.

37. The Supreme Court Order was excerpted in *The Hindu*, 6 February 2009.

38. The Supreme Court Order was excerpted in *The Hindu*, 6 February 2009.

39. The judgment of the Supreme Court of India, 5 July 2011: 54.

40. Prabir Basu, "Lessons of Birbhum," in *Naxalbari and After: A Frontier Anthology*, Vol. 1, ed. Samar Sen, Debabrata Panda, and Ashis Lahiri (Calcutta: Kathashilpa, 1978), 128–9.

41. Drawn on a telephone conversation with Himanshu Lal, the Malkangiri subdivisional police officer, with Rajat Kujur in August 2008.

42. Chakravarti, *Red Sun*, 93–4.

43. Chakravarti, *Red Sun*, 94.

44. K. Srinivas Reddy, "Maoists to Improve Coordination," *The Hindu*, 29 September 2006.

45. *Our Financial Policy*, reproduced in Gautam Navlakha, *Days and Nights in the Heartland of Rebellion* (New Delhi: Penguin, 2012), 161–2.

46. *Our Financial Policy*, reproduced in Navlakha, *Days and Nights in the Heartland of Rebellion*, 161.

47. *Our Financial Policy*, reproduced in Navlakha, *Days and Nights in the Heartland of Rebellion*, 161.

48. Immediately after the Maoist ambush on the Congress leaders in Bastar on 25 May 2013, the media substantiated the claim by referring to the expensive foreign-made automatic weapons that the Maoist, carried during the operation. *Times of India* (New Delhi), 28 May 2013; *Hindustan Times* (New Delhi), 29 May 2013; *The Telegraph* (Kolkata), 27 May 2013.

49. The statement of Ashok Mallick is quoted in Nihar Nayak, "Maoists in Orissa Growing Tentacles and a Dormant State," *South Asia Intelligence Review* 17. Online: http://www.satp .org/satporgtp/publication/faultlines/volume17/nihar.htm.

50. While elaborating the sources of income for the Naxalites, we draw on Nihar Nayak, "Maoists in Orissa Growing Tentacles and a Dormant State."

51. Vineet Agarwal, *Romance of a Naxalite* (New Delhi: National Paperbacks, 2006), 33.

52. The statement of Ganapathy is quoted in Agarwal, *Romance of a Naxalite*, 55.

53. Randeep Ramesh, "Inside India's Hidden War: Mineral Rights Are behind Clashes between Leftwing Guerrillas and State-Backed Militias," *The Guardian*, 9 May 2006.

54. Ramesh, "Inside India's Hidden War."

55. The statement of Ganapathy is quoted in Agarwal, *Romance of a Naxalite*, 55.

56. Interview by Misir Besra, the incarcerated Naxal leader, to the press, *Hindustan Times*, 16 March 2008.

57. The address of the prime minister was reproduced in the *Times of India* (New Delhi), 14 April 2006.

58. Sumanta Banerjee, "Beyond Naxalbari," *Economic and Political Weekly*, 22 July 2006: 3159.

59. Press interview by Manish Kunjam, a former member of the Chhattisgarh Legislative Assembly, published in the *Times of India* (New Delhi), 18 March 2007.

60. Press interview by Manish Kunjam, *Times of India* (New Delhi), 18 March 2007.

61. Satya Prakash, "Civil War Situation in Three Chhattisgarh Villages," *Hindustan Times* (New Delhi), 5 January 2011.

62. A news report titled "Dantewada" stated that the police camp didn't even have a fence: cops were operating from a girls' hostel, *Sunday Times of India* (New Delhi), 18 March 2007.

63. Press interview of Ganapathy, general secretary, CPI (Maoist), April 2007; the text is reproduced in the *Times of India* (New Delhi), 15 May 2007.

64. The entire description of the people's government in Bastar (Chhattisgarh) is drawn from the news report titled "Area Liberated . . . No Salwa Judum Here," *Times of India*, 20 February 2009.

65. Ajay Dandekar and Chitrangada Choudhury, *PESA, Left-Wing Extremism and Governance: Concerns and Challenges in India's Tribal Districts* (Anand: Institute of Rural Management, [n.d.]), 1. Online: http://xa.yimg.com/kq/groups/13213061/2043902818/name/PESA+IRMA.pdf.

66. Navlakha, *Days and Nights in the Heartland of Rebellion*, 208.

67. Navlakha, *Days and Nights in the Heartland of Rebellion*, 207.

68. Ramchandra Guha, "Adivasis, Naxalites, and Democracy," in *Challenges to Democracy in India*, ed. Rajesh M. Basrur (New Delhi: Oxford University Press, 2009), 179.

Conclusion

1. In their commentary in *India since 1980* (Cambridge, UK: Cambridge University Press, 2011), Sumit Ganguly and Rahul Mukherjee make the argument by saying that what accounts for the Maoists' increasing popularity is their success in "the mobilization of extant grievances in India's more remote areas, which have not benefitted much from the country's surge of economic growth" (177).

2. Dwaipayan Bhattacharyya, "Party-Society, Its Consolidation and Crisis: Understanding Political Change in West Bengal," in *Theorizing the Present: Essays for Partha Chatterjee*, ed. Anjan Ghosh, Tapati Guha Thakurta, and Janaki Nair (New Delhi: Oxford University Press), 232.

3. Arild Englsen Ruud, "Land and Power: The Marxist Conquest of Rural Bengal," *Modern Asian Studies* 2, no. 2 (1994): 378.

4. Sumanta Banerjee, "Moral Betrayal of a Dream," *Economic and Political Weekly*, 7 April 2007: 1241.

5. Sobhanlal Datta Gupta, "Whither Indian Left?" *Frontier* 45, nos. 14–17 (14 October–10 November 2012): 2.

6. Verghese K. George, "Battle for Bengal: Comrade Mamata," *Hindustan Times*, 15 March 2011.

7. Atul Kohli, *Democracy and Development in India: From Socialism to Pro-Business* (New Delhi: Oxford University Press, 2009): 388.

8. Ross Mallick, *Indian Communism: Opposition, Collaboration and Institutionalization* (Delhi: Oxford University Press, 1994), 239.

9. Carl Schorske, *German Social Democracy, 1905–1917: The Development of a Great Schism* (New York: Wiley, 1955), 19.

10. Richard N. Hunt, *German Social Democracy, 1918–1933* (New Haven, CT: Yale University Press, 1964), 258.

11. Ramchandra Guha, *Patriots and Partisans* (New Delhi: Penguin, 2011), 94.

12. Atul Kohli, *The State and Poverty in India: The Politics of Reform* (Cambridge, UK: Cambridge University Press, 1987), 9.

13. Sanjeeb Mukherjee, "Questions of Democracy and Justice in India," *Economic and Political Weekly*, 7 August 2010: 33.

14. Rajnarayan Chandavarkar, "From Communism to 'Social Democracy': The Rise of Resilience of Communist Parties in India, 1920–1995," *Science & Society* 61, no. 1 (Spring 1997): 105.

15. Hunt, *German Social Democracy, 1918–1933*, 241.

16. Hunt, *German Social Democracy, 1918–1933*, 244.

17. CPI (M), Burdwan District Committee, *Samiksha: Ashtam Lok Sabha Nirbachan* [Analysis of Eighth Lok Sabha Election] (Burdwan: Burdwan District Committee, CPI [M], 28 February 1985), 31–2.

18. Mukherjee, "Questions of Democracy and Justice in India," 33.

19. Kohli, *The State and Poverty in India.*

20. Bhabani Sengupta, *Communism in Indian Politics* (New York: Columbia University Press, 1972).

21. Mallick, *Indian Communism,* 224.

22. Kohli, *The State and Poverty in India,* 113.

23. Department of Information and Cultural Affairs, *Left Front Government in West Bengal: Eight Years* (Calcutta: Government of West Bengal, 1985), i–ii.

24. Atul Kohli, *Poverty amid Plenty in the New India* (Cambridge, UK: Cambridge University Press, 2012), 209.

25. Kohli, *Democracy and Discontent,* 267.

26. T. J. Nossiter, *Marxist State Governments in India: Politics, Economics and Society* (London: Pinter Publishers, 1988).

27. Nossiter, *Marxist State Governments in India,* 174.

28. Prakash Chandra Upadhyaya refers to this point tangentially in his "Is There an Indian Form of Communism?" *Social Scientist* 17, nos. 1–2 (January–February 1989): 84–91.

29. Data are drawn from Nitin Sethi, "As Forests Feed Growth, Tribals Given Go-By," in *The Maoist Movement in India: Perspectives and Counter-Perspectives,* ed. Santosh Paul (New Delhi: Routledge, 2013), 131.

30. Sethi, "As Forests Feed Growth, Tribals Given Go-By," 131.

31. Author's personal interaction in Malkangiri (Orissa) on 11 April 2009 with a second-tier Maoist leader who would like to remain anonymous.

32. These details are from Gautam Navlakha, *Days and Nights in the Heartland of Rebellion* (New Delhi: Penguin, 2012), 233–4.

33. Arundhati Roy, *Walking with the Comrades* (New York: Penguin, 2011), 7.

34. Alpa Shah, *In the Shadow of the State: Indigenous Politics, Environmentalism and Insurgency in Jharkhand, India* (Durham, NC: Duke University Press, 2010), 183.

35. Amit Bhaduri, "Development or Developmental Terrorism?" *Economic and Political Weekly,* 17 February 2007: 552.

36. Navlakha, *Days and Nights in the Heartland of Rebellion,* 84.

37. P. C. Chidambaram's interview in *Tehelka,* 21 November 2009; Paul, *The Maoist Movement in India,* 209.

38. Arun Prosad Mukherjee, *Maoist Spring Thunder: The Naxalite Movement (1967–72)* (Kolkata: KP Bagchi, 2007), 5.

39. Union Home Minister P. C. Chidambaram's interview in *Tehelka,* 21 November 2009, in Paul, *The Maoist Movement in India,* 201.

40. Research and Policy Division, Ministry of Home Affairs. *Current Naxalite Activities in Tamil Nadu, Andhra Pradesh and Bihar* (New Delhi: Government of India, October 1980), 11–12.

41. Union Home Minister P. C. Chidambaram's interview in *Tehelka,* 21 November 2009, in Paul, *The Maoist Movement in India,* 200.

42. Government of India, *Development Challenges in Extremist Affected Areas, Report of an Expert Group to Planning Commission* (New Delhi: Government of India, April 2008), 59–60.

43. Government of India, *Development Challenges in Extremist Affected Areas*, 8.

44. Government of India, *Development Challenges in Extremist Affected Areas*, 22.

45. Government of India, *Development Challenges in Extremist Affected Areas*, 29.

46. The address of Manmohan Singh, the prime minister of India on 4 November 2009, at the conference on implementation of the Forest Rights Act of 2006, *Times of India*, 5 November 2009.

47. Navlakha, *Days and Nights in the Heartland of Rebellion*, 1.

48. Press interview of Jairam Ramesh, the rural development minister, Government of India, 2013, *Hindustan Times* (New Delhi), 10 June 2013.

49. Samarendra Das and Felix Padel, *Out of This Earth: East India Adivasis and the Aluminum Cartel* (New Delhi: Orient Blackswan, 2010), 131–3.

50. Arundhati Roy makes this point in her *Walking with the Comrades*, 211.

51. Ajay K. Mehra, "Maoism in a Globalizing India," in *The Dark Side of Globalization*, ed. Jorge Heine and Ramesh Thakur (Tokyo: United Nations Press, 2011), 111.

52. Nivedita Menon and Aditya Nigam, *Power and Contestation: India since 1989* (New Delhi: Orient Longman, 2008), 123.

53. Roy, *Walking with the Comrades*, 197.

54. Navlakha, *Days and Nights in the Heartland of Rebellion*, 218.

55. Tilak Gupta, "Maoism in India: Ideology, Programme and Armed Struggle," *Economic and Political Weekly*, 22 June 2006: 3173.

56. Judgment of the Supreme Court of India, Writ Petition (Civil) 250 of 2007, pronounced by Justice B. Sudarshan Reddy and Justice Surinder Singh Nijjar, 5 July 2011, 51.

57. This statement is made by a senior police officer during an interview that Rajat Kujur conducted in December 2008 in the district of Malkangiri.

58. Ramchandra Guha, "Advasis, Naxalites and Democracy," in *Challenges to Democracy in India*, ed. Rajesh M. Basrur (New Delhi: Oxford University Press, 2009), 183.

59. Judgment of the Supreme Court of India, Writ Petition (Civil) 250 of 2007, 37.

60. Not willing to treat Maoism as "a mere law and order problem," the Tribal Affairs Minister, V. Kishore Chandra Deo, of the United Progressive Alliance II government at the federal level described the plight of the hapless tribals in Chhattisgarh. *Times of India* (New Delhi), 31 May 2013.

61. Quote from Ramchandra Guha, "Advasis, Naxalites and Democracy," 186.

62. Nivedita Menon, "Radical Resistance and Political Violence Today," *Economic and Political Weekly*, 12 December 2009: 19.

63. Roy, *Walking with the Comrades*, 81.

64. Bela Bhatia, "On Armed Resistance," *Economic and Political Weekly*, 22 July 2006, 3181.

65. Menon, "Radical Resistance and Political Violence Today," 17.

66. Aditya Nigam pursues this argument in detail in his "Rumour of Maoism"; Paul, *The Maoist Movement in India*, 23–38.

67. An interview with Jairus Banaji: "The Maoist Insurgency in India: End of the Road for Indian Stalinism," *The Platypus Review* 26 (August 2010): 2.

68. Shah, *In the Shadows of the State*, 177–80. According to Shah, the fear of retaliation against those identified as "informers" is carried forward by "a highly centralized, hierarchical and organized" machinery, well-equipped with adequate fire-power. Furthermore, the myth that the radicals have their supporters everywhere in the government: Block officers, forest officers, and police have a double identity: beneath their uniform, they are actually Maoists.

69. Shah, *In the Shadows of the State*, 165.

70. Nandan Nilekani, *Imagining India: Ideas for the New Century* (New Delhi: Penguin, 2009), 175.

71. Kohli, *Democracy and Discontent*, 8.

72. Pranab Bardhan, "Dominant Proprietary Classes and India's Democracy," in *India's Democracy: An Analysis of State–Society Relations*, ed. Atul Kohli (New Delhi: Orient Longman, 1991), 214.

73. I have pursued this argument in my *Subhas Chandra Bose and Middle Class Radicalism: A Study in Indian Nationalism, 1928–1940* (Delhi: Oxford University Press, 1990), 16–20.

74. Guha, *Patriots and Partisans*, 81.

75. Rabindra Ray, *The Naxalites and Their Ideology* (Delhi: Oxford University Press, 1988), 208–10.

76. Available through informal interaction with a Maoist activist in a small village in Andhra Pradesh–Orissa border in the second week of April 2009.

77. The statement, made by Jagori Baske (supported by her husband, Rajaram Soren) after they surrendered on 17 November 2011. *Ananda Bazar Patrika* (Kolkata), 19 November 2011.

78. The press interview of Suchitra Mahato, the Maoist female squad leader and a former wife of another dreadful Maoist encounter specialist, Sasadhar Mahato, after she surrendered 8 May 2012 in *Ananda Bazar Patrika*, 9 May 2012.

79. Copy of the letter of Sabyasachi Panda was published in *The Hindu* (New Delhi), 13 September 2009.

80. The letter that Sabyasachi Panda wrote to the CPI (Maoist) general secretary, Ganapathy, on 1 June 2012 contains some serious charges, including a clear bias against the non-Andhra contingent of Maoism. The other charges that Panda hurled on the party bosses included: supporting and condoning unbridled use of violence, the policy of killing Naxalite cadres who leave to join the mainstream, domination of tribals by a section of leaders of the former CPI (ML) and People's War Group while denigrating the services of leaders belonging to Party Unity to which Panda belonged before it merged with CPI (Maoist).

81. K. Srinivas Reddy elaborates on this argument in his "A Question Not to Ask," *The Hindu* (New Delhi), 13 September 2013.

82. These details are taken from Rajat Kujur, "Contemporary Naxal Movement in India: New Trends, State Response and Recommendations," *IPCS Research Paper*, 27 May 2013: 6–7.

83. The 16 July 2012 response of the Maoist Central Committee. Online: http://www.bannedthought.net/India/CPI-Maoist-Docs/Statements-2012/120716-CC-ExpellingPanda_Eng.pdf.

84. Reddy, "A Question Not to Ask."

85. *Sunday Times of India*, 27 February 2009.

86. The Dalit and gender critique of Maoism is drawn from Bhatia, "On Armed Resistance," 3180.

87. Krishna Bandyopadhyay, "Naxalbari Politics: A Feminist Narrative," *Economic and Political Weekly*, 5 April 2008: 59.

88. Mallarika Sinha Roy, "Speaking Silence: Narrative of Gender in the Historiography of the Naxalbari Movement in West Bengal (1967–75)," *Journal of South Asian Development* 1, no. 920 (2006): 212.

89. Rajat Kujur, "Naxal Movement in India: A Feminist Critique," *Jadavpur Journal of International Relations* 15 (2011): 8.

90. Krishna Bandopadhyay, "Abirata Khoj [Relentless Struggle]," *Khonj Ekhon: Manabi Chetanar Patrika* new series, 1, no. 910 (1988): 88.

91. Ajitha, *Kerala's Naxalbari: Ajitha, Memoirs of a Young Revolutionary* (New Delhi: Srishti, 2008), 284–5; translated version of a memoir, originally written in Malayalam.

92. Roy, "Speaking Silence," 224.

93. Roy, "Speaking Silence," 224.

94. Srila Roy, "The Grey Zone: The Ordinary Violence of Extraordinary Times," *Journal of Royal Anthropological Institute* new series 14 (2008): 328.

95. Roy, "The Grey Zone," 329.

96. Menon and Nigam, *Power and Contestation*, 109.

97. Bhattacharyya, "Party-Society, Its Consolidation and Crisis," 241.

98. Menon and Nigam, *Power and Contestation*, 109.

99. Bhattacharyya, "Party-Society, Its Consolidation and Crisis," 227–31.

100. Guha, *Patriots and Partisans*, 83.

101. Sudeep Chakrabvarti, "Naxalism in India: Thriving or Surviving," *Hindustan Times* (New Delhi), 2 June 2013.

102. Roy, *Walking with Comrades*, 7.

103. Roy, *Walking with Comrades*, 196.

104. In his *Hell Baster: The Untold Story of India's Maoist Movement* (New Delhi: Tanquebar Press, 2011), Rahul Pandita provides a graphic description of how the appalling poverty in the large tracts of India's tribal areas created circumstances for Maoism to strike organic roots among the deprived.

105. Chitralekha provides evidence to this argument in her "Committed, Opportunists and Drifters: Revisiting the Naxalite Narrative in Jharkhand and Bihar," *Contributions to Indian Sociology* 44, no. 3 (2010): 299–329.

106. Bela Bhatia, "The Naxalite Movement in Central Bihar," *Economic and Political Weekly*, 9 April 2005: 1536–43; George Kunnath, "Becoming a Naxalite in Rural Bihar: Class Struggle and Its Contradictions," *Journal of Peasant Studies* 33, no. 1 (January 2006), 89–133; George Kunnath, "Smouldering Dalit Fire in Bihar," *Dialectical Anthropology* 33, nos. 3–4 (2009): 309–25; Alpa Shah, "Markets of Production: The Terrorist Maoist Movement and the State in Jharkhand, India," *Critique of Anthropology* 26, no. 3 (2006): 297–31.

107. Kunnath, "Becoming a Naxalite in Rural Bihar," 110.

108. Shah, *In the Shadow of the State*, 190.

109. Roy, *Walking with the Comrades*, 210.

Postscript

1. The total vote share of CPI is 1.4 percent while RSP and Forward Bloc only obtained 0.3 percent and 0.2 percent, respectively. *The Indian Express,* 17 May 2014.

2. As per the criteria set by the Election Commission of India, a party is eligible to be declared as a national party provided (a) it secures at least 6 percent of total votes, polled in four states, and wins four seats in the Lok Sabha, or (b) it wins at least 2 percent of total seats of 543 from no less than three provinces of federal India.

3. Akshya Mukul, "Red Star Fades Out, CPM Faces Total Eclipse," *The Times of India* (New Delhi), 17 May 2014.

4. *The Hindu* (New Delhi), 17 May 2014.

5. Quoting a member of the central committee of CPI (M), *The Times of India* (New Delhi), 19 May 2014, thus reports.

6. Puja Bhattacharjee, "Playing Left Out or Right Back," *Governance Now* 5, no. 8 (2014): 15.

7. Shiv Viswanathan, "An Election to Remember," *The Hindu* (New Delhi), 17 May 2014.

8. Soumitra S. Bose, "Did Naxals Push Voters to Press NOTA," *The Times of India* (New Delhi), 19 May 2014.

9. According the S. M. Lipset, "The more well-to-do a nation, the greater the chances that it will sustain democracy." S. M. Lipset, "Some Social Requisites of Democracy: Economic Development and Political Legitimacy," *American Political Science Review* 53, no. 1 (1959): 102.

10. According to J. S. Mill, "Free institutions are next to impossible in a country made up of different nationalities. . . . It is in general a necessary condition that the boundaries of government should coincide in the main with those of nationalities." J. S. Mill, *Considerations on Representative Government* (New York: Oxford University Press, 2008, repr.), 223.

APPENDIX

1. http://www.satp.org/satporgtp/countries/india/maoist/documents/papers/partyconstitution.htm.

BIBLIOGRAPHICAL NOTES WITH SELECT BIBLIOGRAPHY

The literature on communism in India is enormous. So the preparation of a reasonably balanced bibliography puts the author in a real difficulty. The task is made more difficult by the availability of the texts, produced by the parties or the activists, sympathetic to an ideological cause, which are invariably tilted toward a particular, if not partisan, point of view. Given their importance in understanding and also conceptualizing an ideological line of thinking, one can ignore them only at serious academic costs. These texts may not have academic rigor and finesse but are very useful to grasp the inner dynamics of movements that are drawn on the context-driven interpretation of an ideology. The problem is far less complicated with regard to the parliamentary left operating openly in the public domain to pursue social democracy in the name of Marxism–Leninism. At regular party plenums and core committee meetings, not only does the parliamentary left reveal the plan of action and core strategies, they also set in motion different kinds of ideology-driven political movements to create and consolidate their social base. Besides these texts that come out of these kinds of congregations, the parliamentary communists also produce tons of literature during the elections to seek to sway popular support in their favor. These act as important sources if one strives to understand the politico-ideological foundation of the system of governance in case the parliamentary left is elected to power.

It is rather easier to locate and get hold of pertinent textual materials for the parliamentary left; the task is terribly difficult once one strives to understand the left-wing extremism or Maoism in the Indian context for at least two major reasons. First, the effort to understand the phenomenon is marred by the lack of the availability of authentic texts relating to their activities for the fulfillment of the classical Marxist–Leninist ideological goal through the conventional Marxist–Leninist method of violent revolution. In the Internet era, the situation is slightly better because the apparently Web-friendly contemporary Maoists post their points of view to advance a specific ideological course of action favoring the marginalized. These are undoubtedly useful texts though their authenticity cannot be verified given the absence of comparable sources of information. Second, a difficulty emanates from the obvious constraints of drawing inputs out of a field survey. The available accounts, based on field visits, are very useful to prepare a general narrative, but they do not seem to be useful for obvious methodological reasons if one has specific questions. Furthermore, the field survey is not at all free from trouble. Not only are the outsiders considered suspects by the local people in the Maoist areas, they are also harassed by the security forces for being allegedly sympathetic to the left extremists. The ethnographic details that come out of field interaction are, on most occasions, likely to be doctored in the prevalent atmosphere of fear and suspicion. A serious methodological constraint also relates to the authenticity of the pamphlets and other printed texts since (i) their sources are mostly anonymous to avoid security risks and (ii) there are instances when both Maoists and the Indian intelligence spread concocted stories to score points against each other, thus putting the reliability of these sources in question.

Keeping in mind the obvious difficulties, the bibliography has three complementary components. First, like any other academic work, *Communism in India* draws on the derived wisdom through a careful scan of the available published literature. There is a fairly good amount of written texts, both books and articles, in English and other vernacular languages, on the left-wing extremism in India. However, given the space constraint, one has to be selective while preparing a bibliography on such a vast subject. Second, by including a specific section, called Webliography, the bibliography takes into account the party-produced texts that are posted on the Web for specific ideological purposes. Notwithstanding their utility in academic exercise, one has to be careful since these propagandistic texts do not usually project an authenticated line of thought as most of them are generally produced instantaneously to address ideology-driven concerns or challenges. Finally, the third component consists of national and local dailies, both in English and vernacular languages. Despite obvious methodological limitations, newspapers continue to remain critical in ethnographic research. Reflective of the public sentiments, the Fourth Estate cannot be ignored while assessing the parliamentary left and its bête noire, the extremist left-wing Maoist movement in India. There still remain the methodological problems that are likely to be less difficult to handle in view of the availability of contrasting points of view on the same phenomenon that allow an innovative and also independent reading of the materials.

This is not an unusual bibliography, but differently textured, seeking to highlight the probable methodological difficulties that one is likely to confront in ethnographic studies. By classifying the sources of inputs, the above bibliographical notes will surely be a useful aid for future researchers to take care of the difficulties while being engaged in unearthing the complexities of the organically evolved movements for specific ideological claims. There is thus an implicit assumption that a bibliography, as much as the text, is intellectually equally provocative to raise unique context-driven questions with potentials to initiate new debates or theoretical discourses. Despite not being exhaustive, the bibliography is thus not merely a list of relevant texts but also a pathfinder for different kind of creative exercises, based on new concerns and challenges.

SELECT BIBLIOGRAPHY

Agarwal, Vineet. *Romance of a Naxalite*, Delhi: National Paperbacks, 2006.

Ahmad, Muzaffar. *Myself and the Communist Party of India, 1920–9*. Calcutta: National Book Agency, 1970.

Ajitha. *Kerala's Naxalbari: Ajitha, Memoirs of a Young Revolutionary*. Translated by Sanju Ramachandran. New Delhi: Srishti, 2008.

Alam, Javeed. *India: Living with Modernity*. Delhi: Oxford University Press, 1999.

Alvares, Claude. *Science, Development and Violence: The Revolt against Modernity*. Delhi: Oxford University Press, 1992.

Arendt, Hannah. *Crisis of the Republic*. Harmondsworth, UK: Penguin, 1973.

Aron, Raymond. *History and the Dialectic of Violence*. Oxford: Basil Blackwell, 1975.

Bakunin, Michael. *Statism and Anarchy*. Translated and edited by M. S. Shastz. Cambridge: Cambridge University Press, 1990.

Balaram, N. E. *Communist Movement in Kerala*. Vol. 1. Trivandrum: Prabhat, 1973 (in Malayalam).

Banerjee, Sumanta. *In the Wake of Naxalbari: A History of the Naxalites Movement*. Calcutta: Subarnarekha, 1980.

Banerjee, Sumanta. *India's Simmering Revolution*. New Delhi: Select Book Syndicate, 1984.

Basrur, Rajesh M., ed. *Challenges to Democracy in India*. New Delhi: Oxford University Press, 2009.

Basu, Pradip, ed. *Discourses on Naxalite Movement, 1967–2009: Insights into Radical Left Politics*. Kolkata: Setu Prakashani, 2010.

Baviskar, B. S., and George Mathew, eds. *Inclusion and Exclusion in Local Governance: Field Studies from Rural India*. New Delhi: Sage, 2009.

Bergmann, Theodore. *Agrarian Reform in India*. New Delhi: Agricole Publishing Academy, 1984.

Bhaduri, Amit. *Development with Dignity: A Case for Full Employment*. New Delhi: National Book Trust, 2005.

Brinton, Crane. *The Anatomy of Revolution*. New York: Vintage Books, 1952.

Burton, J., and F. Dukes, eds. *Conflict: Readings in Management and Resolution*. New York: Macmillan, 1990.

Calman, Leslie J. *Protest in Democratic India: Authority's Response to Challenge*. Boulder, CO: Westview Press, 1985.

Campbell, D., and M. Dillon, eds. *The Political Subject of Violence*. Manchester, UK: Manchester University Press, 1993.

Chakrabarty, Bidyut. *Forging Power: Coalition Politics in India*. New Delhi: Oxford University Press, 2006.

Chakrabarty, Bidyut. *Indian Politics and Society since Independence: Events, Processes and Ideology*. London: Routledge, 2008.

Chakrabarty, Bidyut, and Rajat Kujur. *Maoism in India: Reincarnation of Left-Wing Extremism in the Twenty-First Century*. London: Routledge, 2010.

Chatterjee, Partha, ed. *Wages of Freedom: Fifty Years of the Indian Nation-State*. Delhi: Oxford University Press, 1998.

Chattopadhyay, Suchetana. *An Early Communist: Muzaffar Ahmad in Calcutta, 1913–1929*. Delhi: Tulika Books, 2012.

Crossley, Nick. *Making Sense of Social Movements*. Buckingham, UK: Open University Press, 2002.

Dagamar, Vasudha. *Role and Image of Law in India: The Tribal Experience*. New Delhi: Sage, 2006.

Damas, Marius. *Approaching Naxalbari*. Calcutta: Radical Impression, 1991.

Dasgupta, Biplab. *The Naxalite Movement*. Calcutta: Allied Publishers, 1974.

De Reuck, Anthony, ed. *Conflict and Society*. Boston: Little, Brown, 1966.

Desai, A. R. *Peasant Struggles in India*. Mumbai: Oxford University Press, 1969.

Desai, A. R., ed. *Agrarian Struggles in India after Independence*. Delhi: Oxford University Press, 1986.

Desai, Manali. *State Formation and Radical Politics in India*. New York: Routledge, 2007.

Domenach, Jean-Marie, ed. *Violence and Its Causes: Methodological and Theoretical Aspects of Recent Research on Violence*. Paris: UNESCO, 1981.

Downtown, James. *Rebel Leadership: Commitment and Charisma in the Revolutionary Process*. New York: Free Press, 1973.

Dube, S. C. *India Villages*. London: Oxford University Press, 1955.

Duyker, Edward. *Tribal Guerrillas: The Santals of West Bengal and the Naxalite Movement*. New Delhi: Oxford University Press, 1987.

Eyerman, R., and A. Jamison. *Social Movements: A Cognitive Approach*. Cambridge: Polity Press, 1991.

Fanon, Frantz. *The Wretched of the Earth*. Translated by C. Farington. Ringwood, VC: Penguin, 1980.

Fernandes, Leela. *India's New Middle Class: Democratic Polity in an Era of Economic Reforms*. New Delhi: Oxford University Press, 2006.

Fic, Victor M. *Kerala, Yenan of India: Rise of Communist Power (1937–1969)*. Bombay: Nachiketa Publications, 1970.

Franda, Marcus F. *Radical Politics in West Bengal*. Cambridge, MA: MIT Press, 1971.

Franke, Richard W., and Barbara H. Chasin. *Kerala Radical Reform as Development in an Indian State*. San Francisco: IFDP, 1989.

Ganguly, Sumit, Larry Diamond, and Marc F. Plattner, ed. *The State of India's Democracy*. New Delhi: Oxford University Press, 2009.

Ghosh, Amitav. *Two New Essays: Confessions of a Xenophile and Wild Fictions*. New Delhi: Outlook, 2008.

Ghosh, Sankar. *The Naxalite Movement: A Maoist Experiment*. Calcutta: Firmal K. L. Mukhopadhyay, 1974.

Ghosh, Suniti Kumar, ed. *The Historic Turning Point: A Liberation Anthology*. 2 vols. Calcutta: Pragnana, 1992.

Gibson, Nigel. *Frantz Fanon: The Postcolonial Imagination*. New York: Cambridge, 2003.

Guevara, Che. *Guerrilla Warfare*. Translated by J. P. Morray. New York: Vantage Books, 1961.

Guha, Ramchandra. *Patriots and Partisans*. New Delhi: Penguin, 2012.

Gupta, Monobina. *Left Politics in Bengal: Time Travels among Bhadralok Marxists*. New Delhi: Orient Blackswan, 2010.

Gupta, Ranjit Kumar. *The Crimson Agenda: Maoist Protest and Terror*. Delhi: Wordsmiths, 2004.

Gurr, Ted R. *Why Men Rebel*. Princeton, NJ: Princeton University Press, 1970.

Haralambos, M. *Sociology: Themes and Perspectives*. New Delhi: Oxford University Press, 1999.

Hasan, Zoya. *Politics of Inclusion: Caste, Minorities and Affirmative Action*. New Delhi: Oxford University Press, 2009.

Honderich, Ted. *Violence for Equality: Inquiries in Political Philosophy*. Harmondsworth, UK: Penguin, 1980.

Isaac, T. M. Thomas, and Richard Franke. *Local Democracy and Development*. New Delhi: Leftword Books, 2000.

Jawaid, Sohail. *The Naxalite Movement in India: Origin and Failure of Maoist Revolutionary Strategy in West Bengal*. New Delhi: Associate Publishing House, 1979.

Jeffrey, R. *The Decline of Nayar Dominance*. New York: Holmes & Meier Publications, 1976.

Jeffrey, R. *Politics, Women and Well-Being: How Kerala Became a "Model."* London: Macmillan, 1992.

Skolnick Jerome. *The Politics of Protest*. New York: Ballantine Books, 1969.

Johari, J. C. *Naxalite Politics in India*. Delhi: Institute of Constitutional & Parliamentary Studies/Research Publications, 1972.

Kishwar, Mudhu Purnima. *Deepening of Democracy: Challenges of Governance and Globalization in India*. New Delhi: Oxford University Press, 2005.

Kohli, Atul. *The State and Poverty of India*. Cambridge: Cambridge University Press, 1987.

Kohli, Atul. *Democracy and Discontent: India's Crisis of Governability*. Cambridge: Cambridge University Press, 1991.

Kohli, Atul. *State-Directed Development: Global Power and Industrialization in the Global Periphery*. Cambridge: Cambridge University Press, 2005.

Kohli, Atul. *Democracy and Development in India: From Socialism to Pro-Business*. New Delhi: Oxford University Press, 2009.

Kohli, Atul. *Poverty amid Plenty in the New India*. Cambridge: Cambridge University Press, 2012.

Lieten, G. K. *Continuity and Change in Rural West Bengal*. New Delhi: Sage, 1992.

Lieten, G. K. *Development, Devolution and Democracy: Village Discourse in West Bengal*. New Delhi: Sage, 1996.

Louis, Prakash. *People Power: The Naxalite Movement in Central Bihar*. Delhi: Wordsmiths, 2002.

Mallick, Ross. *Development Policy of a Communist Government: West Bengal since 1977*. Cambridge: Cambridge University Press, 1993.

Mallick, Ross. *Indian Communism: Opposition, Collaboration and Institutionalization*. Delhi: Oxford University Press, 1994.

Mao Tse-tung. *Selected Works of Mao Tse-Tung*, 4 vols. Peking: Foreign Language Press, 1975.

Menon, Nivedita, and Aditya Nigam. *Power and Contestation: India since 1989*. New Delhi: Orient Longman, 2007.

Menon, Dilip. *Caste, Nationalism and Communism in South India*. Cambridge: Cambridge University Press, 1994.

Mohanty, Manoranjan. *Revolutionary Violence: A Study of Maoist Movement in India*. New Delhi: Sterling Publishers, 1977.

Moore, Barrington. *Social Origins of Dictatorship and Democracy: Lord and Peasant in the Making of Modern World*. Harmondsworth, UK: Penguin, 1973.

Namboodiripad, E. M. S. *The Communist Party in Kerala: Six Decades of Struggle and Advancement*. New Delhi: National Book Centre, 1994.

Navlakha, Gautam. *Days and Nights in the Heartland of Rebellion*. New Delhi: Penguin, 2012.

Nigam, Aditya. *The Insurrection of Little Selves: The Crisis of Secular-Nationalism in India*. New Delhi: Oxford University Press, 2006.

Nilekani, Nandan. *Imagining India: Ideas for the New Century*. New Delhi: Penguin, 2008.

Nossiter, T. J. *Communism in Kerala: A Study of Political Adaptation*. Delhi: Oxford University Press, 1982.

Nossiter, T. J. *Marxist State Governments in India: Politics, Economics and Society*. London: Pinter Publishers, 1988.

Overstreet, Gene D., and Marshall Windmiller. *Communism in India*. Berkeley: University of California Press, 1959.

Rajgopal, P. R. *Social Change and Violence: The Indian Experience*. New Delhi: Uppal Publishing House, 1987.

Ram, Mohan. *Indian Communism: Split within a Split*. Delhi: Vikas Publications, 1969.

Ram, Mohan. *Maoism in India*. Delhi: Vikas Publications, 1971.

Rao, D. V. *Telangana Armed Struggle and the Path of Indian Revolution*. Calcutta: Proletarian Path, 1974.

Rogaly, Ben, B. Harris-White, and S. Bose, eds. *Sonar Bangla? Agricultural Agrarian Change in West Bengal and Bangladesh*. New Delhi: Sage, 1999.

Roy, Arundhati. *Walking with the Comrades*. New Delhi: Penguin, 2011.

Roy, Asish Kumar. *The Spring Thunder and After: A Survey of Maoist and Ultra-Leftist Movements in India (1962–75)*. Calcutta: Minerva Associates, 1975.

Rubin, Oliver. *Analyzing the Political Dynamics of Starvation Death in West Bengal*. Copenhagen: Institut for Statskundskab, University of Copenhagen.

Samaddar, Ranabir. *Passive Revolution in West Bengal, 1977–2011*. New Delhi: Sage, 2013.

Santosh, Paul. *The Maoist Movement in India: Perspectives and Counter Perspectives*. New Delhi: Routledge, 2013.

Sen, Sunil. *Agrarian Struggle in Bengal*. Bombay: People's Publishing House, 1972.

Shah, Alpa. *In the Shadows of the State: Indigenous Politics, Environmentalism and Insurgency in Jharkhand, India*. Durham, NC: Duke University Press, 2010.

Singh, Prakash. *The Naxal Movement in India*. New Delhi: Rupa, 1995.

Sudeep, Chakravarti. *Red Sun: Travels in Naxalite Country*. New Delhi: Penguin, 2008.

Sundar, Nandini. *Subaltern and Sovereign: An Anthropological History of Bastar (1854–2006)*. New Delhi: Oxford University Press, 2008.

Tornquist, Olle, and P. K. Michael Tharakan. *The Next Left: Democratization and Attempts to Renew the Radical Political Development Project: Case of Kerala*. Copenhagen: Nias Books, 1995.

Webster, Neil. *Panchayati Raj and Decentralization of Development Planning in West Bengal (A Case Study)*. Calcutta: K. P. Bagchi, 1992.

ARTICLES

Acharya, Poromesh. "Panchayats and Left Politics in West Bengal." *Economic and Political weekly*, 29 May 1993.

Alam, Javeed. "Debates and Engagements: A Look at Communist Intervention in India." In *Political Ideas in Modern India: Thematic Explorations*, edited by V. R. Mehta and Thomas Pantham. New Delhi: Sage, 2006.

Alam, Javeed. "Nation: Discourse and Intervention by the Communists in India." In *State and Nation in the Context of Social Change*, Vol. 1, edited by T. V. Sathyamurthy. Delhi: Oxford University Press, 1994.

A. M. "The State of the CPI (M) in West Bengal." *Economic and Political Weekly*, 25 July 2009.

Azad. "Maoists in India," *Economic and Political Weekly*, 14 October 2006.

Bajpai, Rochana. "Redefining Equality: Social Justice in the Mandal Debate, 1990." In *Political Ideas in Modern India: Thematic Explorations*, edited by V. R. Mehta and Thomas Pantham. New Delhi: Sage, 2006.

Balagopal, K. "Peasant Struggle and Repression in Pedapally." *Economic and Political Weekly*, 15 May 1982.

Balagopal, K. "Maoist Movement in Andhra Pradesh." *Economic and Political Weekly*, 22 July 2006.

Bandyopadhyay, D. "West Bengal: Enduring Status Quo." *Economic and Political Weekly*, 26 May 2001: 668–72.

Bandyopadhyay, D. "A Visit to Two 'Flaming Fields' of Bihar." *Economic and Political Weekly*, 30 December 2006.

Bandyopadhyay, D. "Land of the Overlords: A Field Trip to Katihar and Purnea." *Mainstream*, 12 March 2007.

Bandyopadhyay, Sekhar. "The Story of an Aborted Revolution: Communist Insurgency in Post-Independence West Bengal, 1948–50." *Journal of South Asian Development* 3, no. 1 (2008): 1–32.

Banerjee, Sumanta. "Naxalbari: Between Past and Present." *Economic and Political Weekly*, 1 June 2002.

Banerjee, Sumanta. "Naxalites: Time for Retrospection." *Economic and Political Weekly*, 1 November 2003.

Banerjee, Sumanta. "Assembly Polls: 2006 Election: *Jatra* Style in West Bengal." *Economic and Political Weekly*, 11 March 2006.

Banerjee, Sumanta. "Beyond Naxalbari." *Economic and Political Weekly*, 22 July 2006.

Banerjee, Sumanta Banerjee. "West Bengal's Next Quinquennium, and the Future of the Indian Left." *Economic and Political Weekly*, 4 June 2011.

Bardhan, Pranab. "Dominant Propertied Classes and India's Democracy." In *India's Democracy: An Analysis of Changing State–Society Relations*, edited by Atul Kohli. New Delhi: Orient Longman, 1991.

Bardhan, Pranab, Sandip Mitra, Dilip Mookherjee, and Abhirup Sarkar. "Local Democracy and Clientelism: Implications for Political Stability in West Bengal." *Economic and Political Weekly*, 28 February 2009.

Basu Dipankar. "The Left and the 15th Lok Sabha Election." *Economic and Political Weekly*, 30 May 2009: 10–15.

Bhaduri, Amit. "Development or Development of Terrorism." *Economic and Political Weekly*, 17 February 2007.

Bhatia, Bela. "On Armed Resistance." *Economic and Political Weekly*, 22 July 2006.

Bhatia, Bela. "Naxalite Movement in Central Bihar." *Economic and Political Weekly*, 9 April 2005.

Bhattacharya, Dwaipayan. "Of Control and Factions: The Changing Party—Society in Rural West Bengal." *Economic and Political Weekly*, 28 February 2009.

Bhattacharya, Dwaipayan. "Left in the Lurch: The Demise of the World's Longest Elected Regime?" *Economic and Political Weekly*, 16 January 2010.

Bhattacharyya, Sudipta. "Operation Barga, 'Efficiency' and (De)interlinkage in a Differentiated Structure of Tenancy in Rural West Bengal." *Journal of South Asian Development* 2, no. 2 (2007): 279–314.

Birinder, Pal Singh. "Violence: A Dominant Term of Discourse." *Studies in Humanities and Social Sciences* 2, no. 1 (1995): 85–96.

Biswas, Atharobaki. "Why Dandyakaranya a Failure, Why Mass Exodus, Where Solution?" *The Oppressed Indian* 4, no. 4 (1982).

Chatterjee, Partha. "The Coming Crisis in West Bengal." *Economic and Political Weekly*, 28 February 2009.

Chaudhuri, Dipanjan Rai, and Satya Sivaraman, "Nandigram: Six Months Later." *Economic and Political Weekly*, 13 October 2007.

Dasgupta, Abhijit. "On the Margins: Muslims in West Bengal." *Economic and Political Weekly*, 18 April 2009.

Dasgupta, Rajarshi. "The CPI (M) Machinery in West Bengal: Two Village Narratives from Kochbehar and Malda." *Economic and Political Weekly*, 28 February 2009.

Dash, Jatindra. "Mining Threatens Orissa's Environment." Indo-Asian News Service, 5 November 2004.

Dellaporta, Donatella. "Social Movements and Democracy at the Turn of the Millennium." *Social Movement and Democracy*, edited by P. Ibarra. New York: Palgrave MacMillan, 2003.

Fernandes, Walter. "Rehabilitation Policy for the Displaced." *Economic and Political Weekly*, 20 March 2004.

Fernandes, Walter. "Singur and the Displacement Scenario." *Economic and Political Weekly*, 20 Janaury 2007.

Gallantar, Marc. "The Aborted Restoration of Indigenous Law." In *Social Conflict*, edited by N. Jayaraman and Satish Saberwal. New Delhi: Oxford University Press, 1996.

Ganapathy. "Open Reply to Independent Citizens' Initiative on Dantewada." *Economic and Political Weekly*, 6 January 2007.

Goswami, Sandhya. "Assam: Mandate for Peace for Development," *Economic and Political Weekly*, 4 June 2010.

A Group of Citizens. "Open Letters to Government and Maoists." *Economic and Political Weekly*, 28 July 2006.

Gupta, Tilak. "Maoism in India: Ideology, Programme and Armed Struggle." *Economic and Political Weekly*, 22 July 2006.

Hardgrave, Robert L. "The Marxist Dilemma in Kerala: Administration and/or Struggle." *Asian Survey* 10, no. 11 (1970).

Hebbar, Ritambara. "Forest Bill of 2005 and Tribal Areas: Case of Jharkhand." *Economic and Political Weekly*, 2 December 2006.

Heller, Patrick. "From Class Struggle to Class Compromise: Redistribution and Growth in South Indian State." *Journal of Development Studies* 31, no. 5 (1995).

Heller, Patrick, and T. M. Thomas Isaac. "Democracy and Development: Decentralised Planning in Kerala." In *Deepening Democracy: Institutional Innovations in Empowered Participatory Democracy*, edited by Archan Fung and E. O. Wright. New York: Verso, 2003.

Jalais, Annu. "Dwelling on Marichjhanpi: When Tigers Became 'Citizens,' Refugees 'Tigerfood.'" *Economic and Political Weekly*, 23 April 2005.

Jeffrey, R. "Peasant Movements and the Communist Party in Kerala, 1937–1960." In *Peasants and Politics: Grass Roots Reaction to Change in Asia*, edited by D. B. Miller. New York: Edward Arnold, 1979.

Jena, Manipadma. "Orissa: Draft Resettlement and Rehabilitation Policy, 2006." *Economic and Political Weekly*, 4 February 2006.

Kannabiran, Kalpana, Vasanthi Kannabiran, and Volga. "Peace and Irresponsibility." *Economic and Political Weekly*, 26 March 2005.

Kanungo, Pralay. "Shift from Syncretism to Communalism. " *Economic and Political Weekly*, 5 April 2014: 48–55.

Khatua, Sanjay, and William Stanley. "Ecological Debt: A Case Study of Orissa, India: Integrated Rural Development of Weaker Sections in India." In *Ecological Debt: The People of the South Are the Creditors: Cases from Ecuador, Mozambique, Brazil and India*, edited by Athena K. Peralta. Geneva: World Council of Churches, 2006.

Kohli, Atul. "From Elite Activism to Democratic Consolidation: The Rise of Reform Communism in West Bengal." In *Dominance and State Power in Modern India: Decline of a Social Order*, Vol. 2, edited by M. S. A. Rao and Francine Frankel. New Delhi: Oxford University Press, 1990.

Kujur, Rajat Kumar. "Underdevelopment and Naxal Movement." *Economic and Political Weekly*, 18–24 February 2006.

Kujur, Rajat Kumar. "Naxalism in India." *Human Touch* 2, no. 6 (2005).

Kunnath, George J. "Smouldering Dalit Fires in Bihar, India." *Dialect Anthropology* 33 (2009).

Mallick, Ross. "Refugee Resettlement in Forest Reserves: West Bengal Policy Reversal and the Marichjhapi Masscre." *Journal of Asian Studies* 58, no. 1 (1999).

Kunnath, George J. "Becoming a Naxalite in Rural Bihar: Class Struggle and Its Contradictions." *Journal of Peasant Studies* 33, no. 1 (2006).

Kumar, Kundan. "Confronting Extractive Capital: Social and Environmental Movements in Odisha." *Economic and Political Weekly*, 5 April 2014: 66–73.

Manor, James. "Transformation of Opposition Politics in West Bengal: Congress (I), Trinamul and 1998 Lok Sabha Poll." *Economic and Political Weekly*, 15–22 April 1998.

Mehra, Ajay. "Naxalism and Militant Peasant Movement in India." In *Conflict and Violence in South Asia*, edited by K. M. de Silva. Kandy: Sri Lanka International Centre for Ethnic Studies, 2000.

Mishra, Banikanta, and Sagarika Mishra. "Mining and Industrialization: Dangerous Portents." *Economic and Political Weekly*, 5 April 2014: 56–65.

Mohanty, Biswaranjan. "Displacement and Rehabilitation of Tribals." *Economic and Political Weekly*, 26 March 2005.

Mohanty, Monoranjan. "Chinese Revolution and the Indian Communist Movement." *China Report* 27, no. 1 (1991).

Mohanty, Monoranjan. "Challenges of Revolutionary Violence: The Naxalite Movement in Perspective." *Economic and Political Weekly*, 22 July 2006.

Mohanty, Manoranjan. "Persisting Dominance: Crisis of Democracy in a Resource-Rich Region." *Economic and Political Weekly*, 5 April 2014: 39–47.

Mukherjee, Partha N. "Naxalbari Movement and the Peasant Revolt." In *Social Movements in India*, Vol. 1, edited by M. S. A. Rao. New Delhi: Manohar, 1979.

Nandy, Ashis. "The End of Arrogance." *Special Issue: Verdict. Tehleka*, 30 May 2009.

Narayanan, M. K. "Naxal Movement's Cruel Spring." *Asian Age*, 28 February 2000.

Nayak, Nihar. "Maoist Movement in Nepal and Its Tactical Digression: A Study of Strategic Revolutionary Phases and Future Implications." *Strategic Analysis* 31, no. 6 (November 2007): 915–942.

Nayak, Nihar. "Managing Naxalism in Tamil Nadu." *Tamil Nadu Police Journal* 2, no. 1 (January–March 2008).

Nayak, Nihar. "Maoists in Nepal and India: Tactical Alliances and Ideological Differences." *Strategic Analysis* 32, no. 3 (May 2008).

Nigam, Aditya. "Communist Politics Hegemonized." In *Wages of Freedom: Fifty Years of Indian Nation-State*, edited by Partha Chatterjee. Delhi: Oxford University Press, 1998.

Nigam, Aditya. "How the Sickle Slashed the Left." *Tehelka*, 30 May 2009.

Parthasarathy, G. "Land Reforms and the Changing Agrarian Structure in India." In *Agrarian Structure and Peasant Revolt in India*, edited by Anil Kumar Gupta. New Delhi: Criterion Publications, 1986.

Punwani, Jyoti. "Chhattisgarh: Traumas of Adivasi Women in Dantewada." *Economic and Political Weekly*, 27 January 2007.

Ram, Mohan. "The Communist Movement in India." In *Imperialism and Revolution in South Asia*, edited by Kathleen Gough and Hari P. Sharma. New York: Monthly Review Press, 1973.

Ramana, P. V. "Naxalism: Trends and Government Response." *Dialogue* 8, no. 2 (2006).

Rammohan, K. T. "Understanding Keralam: The Tragedy of Radical Scholarship." *Monthly Review* 43, no. 7 (1991): 18–31.

Rao, K. Ranga. "Peasant Movements in Telangana." In *Social Movements in India*, Vol. 1, edited by M. S. A. Rao. New Delhi: Manohar, 1979.

Rodrigues, Valarian. "The Communist Party of India." In *India's Political Parties*, edited by Peter Ronald de Souza and E Sridharan. New Delhi: Sage, 2006.

Rudd, Arild Engelsen. "Land and Power: The Marxist Conquest of Rural Bengal." *Modern Asian Studies* 28, no. 2 (1994): 357–80.

Rudd, Arild Engelsen. "Embedded Bengal? The Case for Politics." *Forum for Development Studies* 2 (1999): 235–59.

Sagar. "The Spring and Its Thunder." *Economic and Political Weekly*, 22 July 2006.

Sahu, Anadi. "Naxals in Orissa: Then and Now." *Shatabdi* (Oriya Monthly), 15 September 2001.

Sanyal, Kanu. "More about Naxalbari." *Proletarian Path*, May–August 1974.

Sarkar, Abhirup. "Political Economy of West Bengal." *Economic and Political Weekly*, 28 January 2006.

Shah, Alpa. "Markets of Protection: The 'Terrorist' Maoist Movement and the State in Jharkhand, India." *Critique of Anthropology* 36, no. 3 (2006): 297–314.

Sharma, Shailendra. "India in 2010: Robust Economics amid Political Stasis." *Asian Survey* 51, no. 1 (2011): 111–24.

Shuvaprasanna. "Ozymandias' Certain Fall." *Tehelka*, 23 May 2009.

Singh, Prakash. "Maoism Unmasked." *Dialogue* 6, no. 4 (2005).

Singh, Sekhar. "Displacement and Rehabilitation: A Comparison of Two Policy Drafts." *Economic and Political Weekly*, 30 December 2006.

Sinha, Santha. "Andhra Maoist Movement." In *State Government and Politics: Andhra Pradesh*, edited by G. Ram Reddy and B. A. V. Sharma. New Delhi: Sterling Publications, 1979.

Sundar, Nandini. "Bastar, Maoism and Salwa Judum." *Economic and Political Weekly*, 22 July 2006.

Sundaraya, P. "Telangana People's Struggle and Its Lessons." Calcutta: Communist Party of India (Marxist), 1972.

Tharakan, P. K. Michael. "Communal Influence in Politics: Historical Background Pertaining to Kerala." *Religion and Society* 34, no. 1 (1987): 3–9.

Thirumali, I. "*Dora* and *Gadi*: Manifestations of Landlord Domination in Telangana." *Economic and Political Weekly*, 19 February 1972.

Tornquist, Olle. "Movement Politics and Development: The Case of Kerala." *Social Scientist* 29, nos. 11–12 (2001): 57–87.

Wankhede, Harish S. "The Political Context of Religious Conversion in Orissa." *Economic and Political Weekly*, 11 April 2009.

Yechuri, Sitaram. "Learning from Experiences and Analysis: Contrasting Approaches of Maoists in Nepal and India." *Economic and Political Weekly*, 22 July 2006.

Zindabad, Inquilab. "The Red Sun Is Rising: Revolutionary Struggle in India." In *Imperialism and Revolution in South Asia*, edited by Kathleen Gough and Hari P. Sharma. New York: Monthly Review Press, 1973.

WEBLIOGRAPHY

Chandran, Suba, and Joseph Mallika. *India: The Naxalite Movement, Searching for Peace in Central and South Asia*. Global Partnership for the Prevention of Armed Conflict, 2002.

Collier, P. *Doing Well Out of War*. Paper presented at the Conference on Economic Agendas in Civil Wars, London 26–7 April 1999. http://www-wds.worldbank.org/external/default/WDSContentServer/WDSP/IB/2004/03/10/000265513_20040310163703/Rendered/PDF/28137.pdf.

Gupta, Kanchan. "Naxals, India's Enemy Within." http://in.rediff.com/news/2004/nov/25kanch.htm.

"History of Naxalism." *Hindustan Times*, 15 December 2005. http://www.hindustantimes.com/news-feed/nm2/history-of-naxalism/article1-6545.aspx.

Jha, Sanjay Kumar. "Left Wing Terror: The MCC in Bihar and Jharkhand." *South Asia Intelligence Review* 1, no. 40 (April 2003). http://www.satp.org.

Jha, Sanjay Kumar. "MCC and the Maoists: Expanding Naxal Violence in Bihar." Institute of Peace and Conflict Studies, 15 March 2003: art. no. 991. http://www.ipcs.org.

Jha, Sanjay Kumar. "Naxalite Consolidation in Orissa." *South Asia Intelligence Review* 2, no. 3 (August 2003). http://www.satp.org.

Kamboj, Anil. "Naxalism: India's Biggest Security Challenge." Institute of Peace and Conflict Studies, 20 April 2006: art. 1995. http://www.ipcs.org.

Kujur, Rajat Kumar. "Andhra Pradesh and Naxal Outfits: Again on Collision Course." Society for the Study of Peace and Conflict, 25 August 2005; art. no. 48. ww.sspconline.org.

Kujur, Rajat Kumar. "Human Rights in the Shadow of Red Terror." *Peace Journalism* 12 (10 October 2005): art. no. 6712. http://www.peacejournalism.com.

Kujur, Rajat Kumar. "Naxal War Zone in Chhatishgarh." Society for the Study of Peace and Conflict, 8 September 2005: art. no. 50. http://www.sspconline.org.

Kujur, Rajat Kumar. "Red Terror over Jharkhand." Institute of Peace and Conflict Studies, 3 November 2005: art. no. 1881. http://www.ipcs.org.

Kujur, Rajat Kumar. "Resurgent Naxal Movement in Bihar." Institute of Peace and Conflict Studies, 3 October 2005: art. no. 1852. http://www.ipcs.org.

Kujur, Rajat Kumar. "Naxal Warning in Maharashtra." Institute of Peace and Conflict Studies, 14 January 2006: art. no. 1925. http://www.ipcs.org.

Kujur, Rajat Kumar. "Andhra Pradesh: The Naxal Citadel." Institute of Peace and Conflict Studies, 14 March 2006: art. no. 162. http://www.ipcs.org.

Kujur, Rajat Kumar. "Train Hijacking: The New Face of Red Terror." Institute of Peace and Conflict Studies, 16 March 2006: art. no. 1967. http://www.ipcs.org.

Kujur, Rajat Kumar. *Left Extremism in India: Naxal Movement in Chhatisgarh and Orissa.* IPCS Special Report no. 25, Institute of Peace and Conflict Studies, June 2006. http://www.ipcs.org.

Kujur, Rajat Kumar. "Dantewada Jail Break: Strategic Accomplishment of Naxal Designs." Institute of Peace and Conflict Studies, 20 December 2007: art. no. 2446. http://www.ipcs.org.

Maoist-Influenced Revolutionary Organizations in India. http://www.massline.info/India/Indian_Groups.htm.

Nayak, K. "Maoists: Contagion in Orissa." *South Asia Intelligence Review* 3, no. 44 (16 May 2005). http://www.satp.org.

Nayak, K. "Maoist Consolidation Intensifies in Orissa." Society for the Study of Peace and Conflict, 16 May 2006: art. no. 70. http://www.sspconline.org.

Nayak, K. *Rourkela: A Historical Perspective.*

Nayak, K. "Nepal: Withering of Peace." Peace and Conflict Monitor (University of Peace, Costa Rica), 1 February 2006.

Pant, N. K. "Naxalite Violence and Internal Security." Institute of Peace and Conflict Studies, 13 July 2001: art. no. 523. http://www.ipcs.org.

Patwardhan, Amrita. *Dams and Tribal People in India.*

Project Ploughshares. *Armed Conflicts Report: India–Maoist Insurgency,* 2013. http://ploughshares.ca/pl_armedconflict/india-maoist-insurgency-1980-first-combat-deaths/.

Ramana, P. V. "Copy Cat: PWG and the Al-Qaeda Cell Model." Institute of Peace and Conflict Studies, 15 December 2002: art. no. 939. http://www.ipcs.org.

Ramana, P. V. "Unified Response Can Defeat PWG Paper Tigers." Institute of Peace and Conflict Studies, 5 August 2002: art. no. 819. http://www.ipcs.org.

Ramana, P. V. "Left Wing Extremism in India." Observer Research Foundation, 18 December 2003. http://orfonline.org/cms/sites/orfonline/modules/analysis/AnalysisDetail.html?cmaid=2543&mmacmaid=794.

Rao, Malleshwar. "Waves of Land Struggle in South Orissa." http://www.cpiml.org/liberation/year_2002/september/activities.htm.

Sahni, Ajay. "Bad Medicine for a Red Epidemic." *South Asia Intelligence Review* 3, no. 12 (October 2004). http://www.satp.org.

"Unification Is the Only Way to Advance the Cause of the Indian Revolution." http://www.rediff.com/news/1998/oct/07gana.htm. Interview of Muppalla Lakshmana Rao (*alias* Ganapathy), the then-head of the Communist Party of India Marxist–Leninist People's War.

NEWSPAPERS

The Times of India (English)
The Hindu (English)
The New Indian Express (English)
The Pioneer (English)
The Sambada (Oriya Daily)
The Prajatantra (Oriya Daily)
The Samaya (Oriya Daily)
The Dharitri (Oriya Daily)

Abject poverty and Maoism, 117
Abolishing zamindari system, 127
Abolition of the practice of forced labour, 184
Activities of Janashakti, 143
Adapting governmental ideology to the changed socio-economic environment, 83
Addressing a developmental challenge, 169
Addressing the superstitious belief in black magic, 161
Adivasis and extremism, 10
Aggressive CPI (M), 47
All India Coordination Committee of Communist Revolutionaries (AICCR), 1968 129
All India Muslim League, 41
All India Trade Union Congress, 39
All India Trinamul Congress (AITMC), 71
Alternative ideological discourse in democratic India, 238
Alternative to state-led development paradigm, 128
Ambush killing, 150
Amlasole hunger death, 80
Amnesty International, 182
Andhra leadership in opposition to Nizam, 127

Andhra Orissa Border Special Zonal Committee, 167
Animal Farm, 237–8
Annalu (shelter), 172
Anti-communal stance, 44
Anti-communist votes, 40
  in Kerala, 40
Anti-Naxal measures, 181
AOBSZC, 180, 189, 226
Appropriating panchayati institutions, 106–8
Archaic version of Marxism in West Bengal, 113
Armed civilians, 195
Armed rebellion in Telangana, 35
Armed struggle for seizure of power, 129
Asom Gana Parishad, 73
Assembly election in West Bengal, 2011, 210
Attacking pro-imperialist policies, 144
Attractive ideological inputs of Maoism, 231

Bal sanghams, 191
Bargadars (sharecroppers), 84
Basic spirit of democracy, 32
Battle between *paribartan* (change) and *pratyabartan* (return to power), 98
Battle of annihilation and debates, 130–2

Bengal Legislative Assembly, 14

Bengali backlash in Tripura, 23

Bengali-dominated communist movement in Tripura, 21

Bengalis as, 'outsiders' in Tripura, 22

Bernsteinian social democratic orientation, 3, 15

Bharatiya Janata Party, 194, 232

Bhumi Ucched Pratirodh Committee (Land Eviction Resistance Committee), 100

Biggest internal threat to India security, 220

Bipolar coalition, 50

Blueprint for industrial rejuvenation in West Bengal, 82

Bottom–up democracy, 224

Bourgeois political parties, 3

Brand Buddha in urban Bengal, 81–3

Breakdown of left social base, 97

Breaking the age-old domination of landlords, 78

Bridges between two conflicting ethnic groups in Tripura, 27

Cadre-driven election strategies, 60

Cadre-sponsored leadership in West Bengal, 84

Capitalistic-imperialist ideological design, 16

Cell as primary to the organization, 156

Central Military Commission, 186

Chaitanya Natya Manch, 191

Challenging feudal exploitation of a very primitive variety, 145

Challenging feudal land relations, 126

Challenging landlordism in Kerala, 68–9

Challenging patriarchy and feudalism, 164

Challenging state-sponsored industrialization, 176

Charges for squandering of central government funds, 80

Chashi Mulia Samiti, 189

Chief Ministers Conference, 118

Christian voters and election in Kerala, 55, 57

Class antagonism and egalitarian society, 3

Class-based political approach, 38

Class-divided social system, 15

Classical principles of Marxism–Leninism, 66

Class-sensitive principles of justice, 160

Clientelist equation and left, 107

Coalition government in Kerala, 40

Coalition of diverse social interests in Kerala, 61

Coalition partners without jeopardizing the government, 46

Coercive Indian state, 4

Collaborators of global-market capitalists, 8

Combative forces not adequately sensitized, 118

Combatting Naxal menace strategically, 119

Common struggle for egalitarian society, 38

Communist ministry in Kerala, 32

Communist Party in Kerala, 61

Communist Party of India, 1

Communist Party of Nepal (CPN (Maoist)), 179

Communist-based customary laws, 22

Community identity, 7

Compact Revolutionary Zone, 185, 202

Compatibility of interests between two fronts in Kerala, 62

Conceptual limitations of, 'one-size-fits-all' theory, 147

Conceptualizing left-wing-extremism, 218

Congress Socialist Party, 33

Congress–CPI alliance, 45, 47

Congress-led coalition government, 232

Considerations on Representative Government, 238

Consolidation of parliamentary left in Kerala, 66

Contextual roots of Indian communism, 11

Contextualization of Marxism in West Bengal, 81

Controversy over SEZ, 100

Conventional Maoist movement, 213

Coordination Committee of Government of India, 183

Coordination Committee of Maoist Parties in South Asia (CCOMPOSA), 2000, 197–9

Core supporters and CPI (M), 89

Corporate-led industrialization, 177

Corrupt-communal Congress leaders, 47

Countering political opponent and cultural dissent, 209

Counter-insurgency efforts with strong focus on rural development, 170

CPI (M), 208, 229

    alienation from Christians and Muslims, 57

    with its big brother attitude, 106

    as a catch-all party, 89

    as a ginger group in New Delhi, 90

    majority and Left Front, 89

    Party Program, 1964, 64

    State Committee's role, 79

CPI (ML) Liberation, 135–6
CPI as an appendage to the Congress Party, 42
CPN (Maoist), 185, 199
Creative blending of Marxism–Leninism and
    thought of Mao, 125
Crisis of governance in the affected districts, 171
Crisis of leadership in CPI (Maoist), 166–7
Critical role of voters in elections, 110
Criticism against the slogan –Chinese
    Chairman as our chairman, 132
Critique of the inefficacies of top–down
    model, 52
Critiquing the state-led development plans, 123
Crucial communities in Kerala, 35
CSP 49
Culling of birds reportedly affected by bird flu,
    104

Dakshin Desh, a radical outfit in south, 142
Dalam, 153–5
Dalit Christians, 190
    in Orissa, 120
Dalits in Kerala, 59
Dandakaranaya Special Zonal Committee
    (DSZC), 150
Decline of CPI (M) seats in Lok Sabha seats, 93
Decline of the opposition in Kolkata, 88
Decolonization of India, 34
Decrease of left vote proportionally-linked with
    the popularity of opposition in West Bengal,
    110
Deepening of democracy, 2, 7
Defence of India rules, 43
Degeneration of Naxalism as an ideology, 174
Demand for equal distribution of resources, 22
Democracy as a mechanism, 224
Democracy as an empowering instruments, 233
Democratic participation in West Bengal, 79
Democratic revolution in India, 205
Democratization of the development process,
    181
Dent in Maoist movement, 165
Departments of Janthana Sarkar (people's
    government), 159
Deployment of coercive forces in election in
    West Bengal, 74
Development Challenges in Extremist Affected
    Areas, 219
Development needs remaining unfulfilled,
    118

Developmental strategies, 202
Deviation from the classical articulation of
    Marxism, 19
Dexterous management of capitalism, 211
Dictatorial functioning of the party
    functionaries, 103
Disconnect between ideological belief and
    strategic calculations in West Bengal, 113
Displacement and dispossession of tribals,
    174
Dissension within Left Front, 101
Divergence between political and social left in
    Kerala, 64
Diverse nature of communism, 1
Domestic compulsion and left, 85
Domination of Andhra militants, 168
Downfall of left following Singur and
    Nandigram crises, 102–5
Draconian left in West Bengal, 112

Economic liberalization, 6, 8
Economic liberalization as bourgeois
    conspiracy, 82
Edward Bernstein, 33
Effective coordination between developmental
    initiative and stern police action, 29
Effective policies countering divisive
    sentiments, 30
Efforts at intensification of war, 225
Eight Congress of the Naxalities, 123
Electability of parliamentary left, 50
    in West Bengal, 71
Election cell in West Bengal, 86
Election Commission of India, 41, 72
    as a messiah, 75
Election Committees and election in West
    Bengal, 86
Elections in, 2006 72–4
Elite-driven top–down ideological onslaught,
    230
Emerging issues of globalization, 31
Emotional chord with indigenous population,
    173
EMS Namboodiripad, 32
Epoch making parliamentary poll, 2014 238
Ethnic groups in Tripura, 20
European social democracies, 33
European social-democratic path of
    development, 73
European social-democratic practices, 82

Expert Committee of the Planning
     Commission's Report, 2008, 118–9, 183
Exploiting India's mineral resources, 216
Exposing the obvious limitations of India's
     interventionist economic strategies, 148
Extra-parliamentary politics, 2

Failure of the implementation of National Rural
     Employment Guarantee Act, 104
Failure of the opposition to mobilize voters,
     87–8
Failure of the State to combat Naxalism, 125
Failure to redress genuine socio-economic
     grievances, 99
FDI in West Bengal, 72
Federal government-sponsored Public
     Distribution System, 28
Feudal labour arrangements losing importance
     in Kerala, 64
Feudal land relations, 176
Fifth column in Kerala, 44
Fifth Schedule Areas, 170
Fight for minimum wage, 184
Fight for nationality by the PWG, 139
Firing in Nandigram, 101
Forcible land acquisition, 3
Forest-dependent tribals, 173
Formulation of ideological agenda with rural
     bias, 158
Forty-Ninth Amendment Act, 1985, 23
Fragmented opposition in West Bengal, 87–9
Frog-in-the-well-strategy, 90
Fundamental ideological values of,
     Marxism–Leninism, 46

Ganapathy of CPI (Maoist), 141, 155, 167, 187,
     201
Gender bias in CPI (Maoist), 227–8
Global capitalism and neoliberal economic
     reforms, 10
Global decline of communism, 228
Globalization, –its impact at the grassroots, 208
Government machinery as appendage of the
     party, 103
Government strategies combatting the Maoists,
     168
Government's minimum wage policy, 163
Governmental pro-people agenda, 196
Governmentalization of rural localities, 77

Government-sponsored efforts for inclusive
     development, 27
Gradual decline of parliamentary left, 235
Gram Sabhas (village administration), 163
Gram Sadak Yojna (rural roadways), 119
Gramoday (self-sufficient village), 24–5
Greyhounds, 222
Growing consolidation of the ultra-radical
     extremist forces, 108
Growing disenchantment of the masses with
     the left, 99
Growing incidence of indebtedness among the
     tribes, 22
The Guardian, 202
Guerrilla zones, 154, 200

Health indices in West Bengal, 112
Hegemonic panchayat institutions, 107
Hegemony of the party in West Bengal, 80
Hindu–Muslims schism, 54
Holistic approach by the Expert Committee, 185
Honeymoon between CPI (Maoist) and
     Janashakti, 179
Humiliating Left Front defeat, 109

Ideological battle in rural Kerala, 55
Ideological goals of communists, 42
Ideological impact landed interests, 37
Ideological mission for tribal empowerment, 220
Ideological popularity of the left, 30
Ideology and mass mobilization, 60
Ignoring the commitment of tiller of the soild,
     101
Image of Mamata Banerjee as, 'a girl next door',
     98
Imitating Chinese model of revolution, 132
Imperialist war becoming people's war, 132
Implementation of government-sponsored
     developmental schemes in West Bengal, 97
Importance of area party committees, 156
Importance of landless agricultural labourers, 78
Importance of parliamentary institutions, 14
Importance of strategic alliance with non-left
     forces, 90
Improving access the tribal access to forest, 163
Inadequacy of administration leading left wing
     extremism, 118
Inclusive development in India, 121
Inclusive development in Kerala, 45

Inclusive growth, 185
Inclusive national movement, 65
Increasing numerical strength of middle class, 66–7
India, – a federation of all national people's republics, 139
India's abject poverty, 176
India's socio-economically imbalanced society, 219
Indian National League, 57
Indian People's Front, 135
Indianized version of Marxism–Leninism, 133
Indigenous innovations and left, 113
Indira Gandhi-led Congress, 48
Individual and socio-cultural environment, 62
Individual authority and parliamentary left, 37
Indo-China war, 42–3
Indo–US nuclear deal, 16–7
Inflicting irreparable damage to administration, 150
Infrastructure projects and development, 231
Initiating agro-business industries as a counter measure, 99
Institutionalized governance and tribals in Tripura, 25
Institutionalizing ideological priorities, 13
Insult to the entire Bengali jati, 74
Inter/intra organizational conflict in CPI (Maoist), 167
Internal squabbles in CPI (M), 60
Internecine factional feuds in CPI (Maoist), 173
Intra/inter-organizational feud among the extremists, 123
Invincible cadre-based organization, 110
Italian principality of Sani Marino, 32

Jal Jangle and Jameen, 203
Jan Adalat (people's court), 160, 164, 204
Jan militias, 191
Janathipathiya Samrakshana Samithy, 61
Janthana Sarkar (people's government), 158–9, 161
Juggernaut of the Left Front, 80, 87

Karshaka Thozhilali Party, 44
Kerala,
    electoral history, 51
    industrial potentials, 54
    parliamentary left, 43

past political history, 36
peculiar communal texture, 62
Kerala communism, 215
Kerala Land Reforms Act, 1969, 63
Kerala Pradesh Congress Committee, 39
Kerala Shastra Sahitiya Parishad, 52
Kisan Mazdoor Praja Party, 34
Kolkata-centric clique, 236
Konattumatam Chidrmbara Subrahmanaia, 53
Krishna's sermons in Bhagwad Gita, 120
Kudikidappukars (hutment dwellers) in Kerala, 63–4, 69
Kui Lalbanga Sangha, 189

Lack of an anti-left opposition in Tripura, 31
Land acquisition and private gain, 16
Land acquisition for agro-industries, 117
Land acquisition policy in West Bengal, 99–100
Land besides water, 20
LDF, 36, 50, 51, 53, 54–5, 59, 68, 72, 233
Leader-based factions in left, 93
Leadership of Chou-En-Lai, 132
Left as an ideology-driven political force in Kerala, 70
Left ascendancy in West Bengal, 78
Left bastion in West Bengal, 76
Left electoral supremacy in Tripura, 30
Left Front, 16
    reformist orientation, 77
Left hegemony in governance in Tripura, 30
Left ideology and displaced Bengalis, 20
Left wing extremis, 162
Left's conspiracy theory, 111
Left's conspirational motives of revenge and destruction, 111
Left-democratic Front in Tripura, 17
Left-wing-extremists and mass voters, 233
Leninist New Economic Program, 218
Leninist notion of democratic centralism, 120
Leninist organization in a Stalinist mould, 111
Leninist principle of democratic centralism, 151
Liaison committees in LDF and UDF 67
Liberal democracy of the Westminster type, 1
Liberal democratic discourses, 7
Liberated zones, 154
Licence-permit-quota-raj, 5
Liquidation of top Maoist leaders, 149
Local elections in Kerala, 2009, 60

local self-government institutions in Kerala, 52
Loosening of social strictures, 8

Ma, Mati O Manush (mother, motherland and people), 98, 106
Madrassas as, 'dens of terrorism' 104
Mahajat (grand coalition), 87, 109
Mahatma Gandhi National Rural Employment Guarantee Act (MNREGA), 170–1, 204
Majumdar,
    elitist leadership, 147
    quixotic misadventure, 146
Maladministration and corruption, 45
Malayalam speaking area, 36
Mao, 152
Maoism,
    attack on feudal land relations, 117
    an effective ideological alternative to state-led developmental plans, 171
    not a passing phase, 175
    and post-colonial state in India, 152
Maoist and Hindutva politics, 189
Maoist articulation of genuine socio-economic grievances, 221
Maoist attack in May, 2013, 115
Maoist blueprint for future, 149–75
Maoist blueprint for future India, 121
Maoist Communist Centre, 179
Maoist constitution, 153
Maoist courts exhibiting bias, 223
Maoist formula of unity with ruling class organizations, 157
Maoist idea of national democracy, 146
Maoist insurgency, – a fight for social justice, 164
Maoist vision of development, 216
Maoists in Bastar, 115
Marxism–Leninism, 4, 10, 11–4, 121, 149, 151, 160–1, 177, 198, 213, 215
    -driven social democracy, 33
    goal for a classless society, 1, 2
    not as sacrosanct, 147
Marxist revolutionary phraseology, 211
Marxist understanding of nationality question, 23
Marxist version of human salvation, 213
Mass resentment,
    against CPI (M), 94
    against left in Marichjhampi, 112

Massive force deployment to combat Naxalism, 188
MCC 140–1
Merger of CPI (ML) and PWG, 1993 138
Methodological alternative for understanding a transitional society, 12
Mindless mining for rapid industrialization, 221
Mindless opposition of AITMC 88
Mini front ministry, 45
Ministry of Home Affairs, Government of India, 169, 171, 194
Minority consolidation against the left, 236
MNCs, 9
Mobilizing masses against snatching of land for private gain, 187
Modernization of military, 181
Movement against forcible land acquisition, 231
Muslim Educational Society, 39
Muslim League alliance with other parties in Kerala, 40

Naga battalion, 193
Nagarik Suraksha Samitis (Civilian Protection Committee), 194
Nagaroday (self-sufficient towns), 25
Nagbhushan Patnaik, 189
Nair Service Society, 38
National Democratic Alliance, 90, 232
National Library in Kolkata, 74
National Rural Health Mission, 119
Naxal brand of politics, 191
Naxal free area, 201
Naxal Janata Sarkar, 125
Naxalbari Movement (1969–), 10, 129–34
    after Majumdar, 133–4
Naxalism in Bihar, 137, 190
Naxalite menace, 162
Near decimation of parliamentary left, 237
Nehruvian socialistic model of economic development, 218
Neoliberal economic reforms, 2, 230
    and classical Marxism–Leninism, 71
Neoliberal onslaught and Marxism–Leninism, 68
Neoliberal socio-economic goal, 221
New Democratic Revolution, 136, 157, 158
New democratic revolution-socialist revolution-ultimate communist revolution, 139
New version of ultra-left-wing extremism, 207

Nine-phase parliamentary poll, 237
Ninth Congress, 2007, 152, 187
Nizam-supported local feudal lords, 15
None of the above (NOTA), 237

Official assessment of Red corridor, 183–5
Operating illegal mines, sale of tendu leafs, 200
Operation Barga, 78, 84, 209
Operation Green Hunt, 172
Operation NGO Hunt, 169
Opium cultivation and Maoists, 200
Opposing destruction of school buildings, 166
Opposing neo-colonial form of indirect rule, 142
Opposing neoliberal development, 216
Opposing neo-liberal developmental packages,
    178
Opposing rent-seeking landlords, 146
Opposing SEZs, 147
Opposing the eviction of peasants from land,
    148
Opposition against individual terror among the
    Naxal activists, 131
Organization with wider network, 85–6
Organizational efforts and mobilization, 92
Organizational penetration by the center into
    the periphery, 107
Organizational politics within the Naxalite
    movement, 142
Orissa Maoists, 225
Orissa Maovadi Party (Maoist party in Orissa),
    168, 226
Orwellian animal farm and Snowball, 105
Our Financial Policy, 199–200
Oxfam, 182

Panchayati raj governance,
    in Tripura, 24
    in West Bengal, 212
Panchayats in rural development, 229
Parallel authority to establish people's power,
    202
Parallel defence administration, 222
Parallel institutions of power in rural areas, 204
Para-military forces, 109
Parliamentary communism, 221, 229
    in Tripura, 233
Parliamentary democracy, 42
Parliamentary democratic system, 64–5
Parliamentary left, 2

as both old and new, 84
and ideological bankruptcy, 12
in West Bengal, 214
Parliamentary mode of capturing power, 207
Parliamentary poll, 2014, 232
Parliamentary road to socialism, 32
Parties as instruments for distribution of public
    provisions, 92
Parties with bourgeois dispensation, 67
Party as a motivating ideological force, 151
Party as a parallel institution of governance in
    West Bengal, 85
Party as an effective organization, 26
Party-society interface, 229
Paschim Banga Khet Majoor Samiti
    (Organization of the Landless Laborers in
    West Bengal), 104
Patriarchy and Naxalite movement, 227
Pauperization of people, 6–7
Peasant struggle as the only form of struggle,
    130
People's Committee against Police Atrocities in
    Lalgarh, West Bengal, 108
People's democratic dictatorship and armed
    agrarian revolution, 136–7
People's Democratic Front, 46
People's Democratic Party, 54
People's Democratic Revolution, 136
People's Guerrilla Army, 119–20, 140, 158–9
People's Plan Campaign, 52–3
People's power, 203
People's tribunal, 101
People's Union for Democratic Rights, 177
People's War Group, 133
People-centric developmental policies, 172
Peoples' Plan, 24
Peripheral local tribals in Tripura, 20
PLA 225
Political activities at the grassroots, 206
Political baptization of the left, 49
Political centralization and organizational
    decentralization in CPI (Maoist), 155
Political immaturity and left, 96
Political Man: The Social bases of Politics, 238
Political right wingers, 50
Political strategy of the PW group, 140
Political vanguard of the Indian proletariat, 151
Politicization and democratization, 7
Politicization of administration, 107

Politico-organizational perspective of governance, 79
Politics of accommodation, 62
Politics of confrontation, 70
Poll debacle in, 2011, 94
Poll debacle of the opposition parties in West Bengal, 76
Popular disillusionment with the left, 102
Popular distrust and left decline, 108
Popular misery and government indifference, 154
POSCO 216
Praja Socialist Party, 33
Pre-election coalition, 35
Presence of committed cadres, 174
Presence of uniformed officers of the paramilitary forces, 195
Primacy of Marxist–Leninist goal, 63
Private capital for development, 83
Private investment for creation of jobs in West Bengal, 82
Private investment for industrial development, 71
Processes of governance, 2
Processing of aluminium, 220
Pro-people socio-economic and political agenda, 65
Protracted people's war, 141, 153
PUCL 203
Purba Bangla Communist Center, 198
PWG 136–40, 155, 189

Radical commitment of the left-leaning governments, 69
Radical ideology drawing on Maoist thinking, 116
Radical individualism, 49
Radical Students' Union and Rayatu Kuli Sangham, 140
Radicalism and well-entrenched organization, 175
Radicalization of rural poor, 219
Reclaiming Nandigram by force, 105
Red corridor, 9, 116, 164, 171, 173, 202
Red menace, 117
Red militants, 172
Red revolutionaries, 167
Red Star, the MCC weekly, 141

Refining left ideological priority in globalizing world, 102
Reforms and democratic change, 14
Reign of terror in rural areas, 102
Resource-based participatory planning, 25
Revolutionary agrarian and pro-worker reforms, 15
Revolutionary violence for social change, 13
Role of non-Tripuri scheduled tribes, 26
Role of private corporations, 6
Role of the party cadres, 41
Rubber cultivation in Tripura, 23
Ruling Congress Party, 217

SAARC (South Asian Association of Regional Cooperation), 198–9
Sachar Committee, 2005, 103
Sacrifice of Maoist cadres, 230
Salishis (arbitration hearings) in rural West Bengal, 104
Salwa Judum, 116, 169, 184, 189, 192–7, 203, 222
Samyukta Socialist Party, 44
Sangh parivar, 90
Sangham, 153–4
Sarkaria Commission, 1980 81
Sarva Siksha Abhiyan (universal education), 119
Scams and the Congress, 59
Scientific rigging, 75
Seeking to bring about radical agrarian changes, 145
Seeking to escape intolerable conditions of economic oppression and social humiliation, 128
Seeking to establish proletarian dictatorship, 131
Seeking to make maximum impact with minimum damage, 188
Seeking to redefine gender by the Maoists, 227
Selective application of disinvestment, 91
Semi-feudal authority in support of vested interests, 11
Settling long-standing agrarian issues, 130
Seventy-Third Amendment Act, 1992, 24, 53
SEZ (Special Economic Zone), 9, 93, 177, 184, 186, 188, 221
Shifting bases of class power, 107
Singur campaign, 100–1
Sixteenth Lok Sabha, 235

Skirmishes between Bengali migrants and indigenous communists, 26

Slash-burn cultivation (*jhum*) in Tripura, 23

Social and economic advancement of the adivasis, 205

Social base and organizational structure of Maoism, 215

Social base and socio-cultural diversity, 19

Social cleavage in Tripura, 26

Social democracy, 91, 206, 211

Social discontent and economic imbalances, 4

Social exclusion, 8

Social left in Kerala, 48–50
    divergence between social left and political left, 50
    importance of urban middle class and social left, 49

Socialist rhetoric, 5

Societal pluralism in Tripura, 19

Socio-economic issues for the downtrodden, 126

Socio-economic programs for rejuvenating the state's economy, 88

Solidarity with ultra-left movements elsewhere, 197

The sources of unfreedom, 69

Special Police force, 196

Splinter groups among the Naxals, 134

Split of CPI in, 1964, 128

Spring Thunder, 129, 145

Sree Narayana Dharma Paripalana Yogam, 39

Stakeholders,
    in policies for development, 229
    in political processes, 206

Stalinist feudal mindset, 105

Stalinist formula, 3, 94, 211

Stalinistic version of Marxism, 236

Stalling mining projects in Orissa, 177–8

State as a predator, 29

State being interventionist, 224

State enthusiasm for neoliberal economic reforms, 11

State-driven integrated action plan, 178

State-led counter-insurgency endeavor, 149

State-led planned economic development, 4–5

State-specific socio-economic realities, 17

State-sponsored market-centric neo-liberal policies, 8–9

Strategic failure of the anti-left political forces in West Bengal, 88

Strategies for combatting the Naxals, 180

Strategy of mixing coercion with persuasion, 111

Strong polarization in Kerala along class lines, 65

Strong-arm tactic of the left, 237

Successive electoral victories of Left Front, 209

Supreme Court verdict, 2009, 195

Tata's car factory, 209

Tebagha movement, 162

Telangana movement, 1946–51 127–8, 162

Telugu-dominated politburo, 225

Tendu leaf, – a source of income, 201

Thought of Mao-Tse-Tung, 121

Three-pronged approach of the Left Front, 28

Top–down mode of governance, 101

Total literacy campaign in Kerala, 52–3

Transfer of power, 1

Transitional collaboration with other parties, 37

Translating anti-left voices into votes, 109

Travancore Tamil Nadu Congress, 36

Tribal disenchantment with Maoism, 165

Tribal districts of India, 9

Tribal settlers in the Naxal-affected districts, 126

Tribals,
    becoming targets, 223
    as mere cannon fodders, 205
    in the Naxalite movement, 145
    veering toward ultra-left wing extremism, 117

Trinamul–Congress conglomeration, 210

Tripura as a less corrupt state, 29

Tripura National Volunteers and National Liberation Front, 21

Tripura Tribal Areas Autonomous District Council (TTAADC), 23–5, 27

Two completely different perspectives of development, 217

Two contradictory trends in the Naxalbari movement, 146–7

UDF 36, 50–1, 59, 68

UN Millennium Development Goals, 29

Unassailable popularity of Left Front in West Bengal, 83–4

Unbridgeable gulf between organization and leadership, 70

United Democratic Front, 17

United Front strategy, 35
United Progressive Allaince (UPA), 73, 109
Upajati Gana Mukti Parishad, 21
Upper caste Hindu organization, 38
Use of INSAS and AK series rifles, 182
Useful panchayati system of governance, 97

Varamdars (sharecroppers) in Kerala, 63
Verbonzung (bossification), 212
Verburgerlichung (bourgeoisification), 212
Verkalkung (ossification), 212
Vernacular scholars in Kerala, 48
Vidhan Sabha, 96, 113
Violence as endemic in a brutal state, 165
Vishwa Hindu Parishad, 190
Voters' choice and ideological preferences, 51
Voters' confidence in democracy, 232

Waging guerrilla war by poor and landless laborers, 130
Walking on two-legs strategy, 83–4, 168
War-like situation in Chhattisgarh, 196

Weakening of Muslims support base for the left, 103
Weakening of social base in West Bengal, 91
Weaknesses of the Congress in Tripura, 31
Weimer social democracy, 212
Well-grounded liberal democracy in India, 237
West Bengal College and University Teachers' Association, 86
West Bengal Government Teachers' Association, 86
Westminster path of democracy, 207
Working together against a common enemy, 157
Working towards bringing together left-wing extremist factions, 134
Writers' Buildings, 77

Youth Congress in Kerala, 48

Zigzag revolutionary path, 143
Zonal Military Commission, 182
Zone as a classic pyramid structure, 154